POPULAR MUSIC

Presenting a comprehensive A–Z glossary of the main terms and concepts used in the study of popular music, this fully updated second edition covers key new developments in the area, such as the impact of the Internet and reality TV.

Key definitions include:

- Important musical genres, from alt.country to techno
- Musical scenes, subcultures, and fandom, from goths to record collecting
- Methodologies, from biography to musicology
- Music industry terms, from indies to producers
- Musical phenomena, from girl groups to tribute bands

Roy Shuker is Programme Director in Media Studies at the School of English, Film, Theatre and Media Studies at Victoria University of Wellington, New Zealand. He is also the author of *Understanding Popular Music* (second edition, 2001).

YOU MAY ALSO BE INTERESTED IN THE
FOLLOWING ROUTLEDGE STUDENT
REFERENCE TITLES:

Blues: The Basics
Dick Weissman

World Music: The Basics
Richard Nidel

Musicology: The Key Concepts
David Beard and Kenneth Gloag

POPULAR MUSIC

The Key Concepts

Second Edition

Roy Shuker

Routledge
Taylor & Francis Group
LONDON AND NEW YORK

First published as Key Concepts in Popular Music, 1998
by Routledge

Second edition published 2005
by Routledge
2 Park Square, Milton Park, Abingdon, Oxon OX14 4RN

Simultaneously published in the USA and Canada
by Routledge
270 Madison Ave, New York, NY 10016

Routledge is an imprint of the Taylor & Francis Group

© 1998, 2005 Roy Shuker

Typeset in Bembo by Taylor & Francis Books
Printed and bound in Great Britain by TJ International Ltd, Padstow, Cornwall

British Library Cataloguing in Publication Data
A catalogue record for this book is available from the British Library

Library of Congress Cataloging in Publication Data
Shuker, Roy.
Popular music : the key concepts / Roy Shuker.– 2nd ed.
    p. cm.
"First published, as Key Concepts in Popular Music, 1998"–ECIP t.p. verso.
"This edition first published 2002"–ECIP t.p. verso.
Includes bibliographical references and index.
ISBN 0-415-28425-2 (pbk.) – ISBN 0-415-34770-X (hardback) 1. Popular music–
Encyclopedias. I. Title.
ML102.P66S58 2005
781.64'03–dc22

2004027956

ISBN 0-415-34770-X (hbk)
ISBN 0-415-34769-6 (pbk)

Taylor & Francis Group is the Academic Division of T&F Informa plc.

CONTENTS

LIST OF KEY CONCEPTS

a cappella
A&R
advertising
aesthetics
affect
aficionados
albums; album covers; concept
    albums/rock operas; tribute
    albums
alt.country
alternative music
ambient
Americana
appropriation; syncretism
art rock
audiences; consumers
auteur; auteurship
authenticity
avant-garde; experimental

back catalogue; reissues
beat music
bhangra
biography; autobiography
black music; African-American
    music
bluegrass
blues: country blues; classic
    blues; jump blues; Chicago
    (electric) blues; British
    R&B/blues rock

boogie-woogie
bootlegs
boxed set
boy bands
bricolage
British invasion
Britpop
broadcasting
bubblegum

canon
cassette audio tape; cassette
    tape players;
    cassette culture
CD (compact disc); CD-R
CD-ROMs
Celtic music
censorship
charts
Christian rock; CCM
class
classic rock
clubs; club culture
commercialism;
    commodification
communication
concerts
consumer sovereignty
consumption
copyright
counter-culture; underground

skinheads
songwriters; songwriting;
    singer–songwriters
soul
sound; sound production; sound
    recording; sound
    reproduction; sound
    systems
sounds
soundtracks
stars; stardom
structuralism; poststructuralism;
    semiotics
style
subculture
surf music
syncretism

taste; taste cultures
techno
technology
teenagers; teenyboppers; teen
    idols
television; reality television
Tex–Mex
text; textual analysis;
    intertextuality
Tin Pan Alley
tours; touring
tribute bands
trip–hop

voice

world music

ACKNOWLEDGEMENTS

As in the original edition of this book, I have relied on the insights of many critics and 'colleagues at a distance', who have written extensively on popular music studies. To name them all risks leaving out someone, and a check of the text references and bibliography provides a roll call of sorts; my thanks to you all. I have also benefited enormously from my membership of IASPM, the International Association for the Study of Popular Music, and its conferences, publications, e-mail lists. Several authors kindly provided information on, or copies of, forthcoming publications: Keith Beattie, Lee Marshall, and Shane Homan. Thanks also to Emma Shuker, for research assistance; Mary Jane for help with the bibliography; the patient editorial staff at Routledge: David Avital, Milon Nagi, Stephen Thompson, and Rosie Waters, and exemplary copy-editor Dominic Shryane.

INTRODUCTION

As I complete this volume, the American presidential election is coming to a frenetic conclusion. Dominating the front page of my local paper is a huge picture of Bruce Springsteen and Democratic candidate John Kerry at a rally in Madison, Wisconsin, arms around each other, beaming into the camera. The headline, 'Who Will Be the Boss', links the election outcome to the title Springsteen fans have long accorded the rock star (*Dominion Post*, 30 October 2004). Springsteen has just performed two songs, 'Promised Land' and 'No Surrender'. The latter is the Kerry campaign's unofficial theme song, and the singer refers to how 'Senator Kerry honors these ideals.' What clearer indication of the contemporary international visibility of popular music could there be?

As I delve further into the paper's weekend edition, I am bombarded with further items with a musical resonance. There is a review of the first instalment of Bob Dylan's eagerly anticipated autobiography, *Chronicles: Volume One*, praising the singer-songwriter as a key figure in the development of 'the rock canon'. The reviews section also includes the Wellington Jazz Festival's concluding concert; the movies *De Lovely*, the Cole Porter story, and *Coffee and Cigarettes*, with director Jim Jarmusch chatting with, among others, Tom Waits, Iggy Pop, and Meg and Jack White (the White Stripes). The reviews of new CD releases include Jan Garabeck's *In Praise of Dreams*, which is praised for 'breaking down musical barriers' and its 'crossover' into the mainstream music market. The 'Entertainment' pages include advertisements for concerts by Fleetwood Mac: The Experience (a tribute band); the musical *Saturday Night Fever*, with the claim that 'Travolta would APPROVE', reminding some of us of the original film's iconic status; the Chieftains, with their 'enduring Celtic music'; Brian Wilson presenting *Smile* ('the great lost album'); and the Sydney Dance Company season performance *Underground*, featuring music by Nick

Cave. Indicating the role of the Internet, the concert advertisements include the performers' websites, and, of course, you can book online. The 'Business' section of the paper includes stories on how music discounting by local retail chain the Warehouse is squeezing out traditional music retail outlets; the strength of the New Zealand rap scene and the associated merchandising possibilities being explored, especially through clothing lines; and concern from the local music industry about the impact of downloading and CD burning. The 'Television Guide' includes the regular chart shows on mainstream, free-to-air channels, including the internationally franchised British *Top of the Pops*, with local acts added; several music documentaries, and the Australian version of the reality show *Pop Idol*. And, of course, retail advertisements throughout the paper include those for various sound systems and recorded music in several formats.

This is the everyday discourse that surrounds popular music, and which provides much of the impetus for this book. Implicit within these stories, reviews, and advertisements are notions of musical authorship, canonical texts, history, authenticity, audiences, and music as a blend of entertainment, art, and commerce. Collectively, and alongside other such stories, they indicate the commercial and cultural significance of popular music. Its global and ubiquitous presence is undeniable: we are exposed to its various forms through 'muzak' in shopping malls; on the streets and in the parks with 'ghetto blasters' and Walkmen; on film and video game soundtracks; in popular musicals; through MTV and other television channels, especially as music video; on the radio at home and work; through the music press; and 'live' in a variety of settings, from the stadium concert to clubs. In cultural terms, popular music is clearly of enormous importance in people's daily lives, and for some it is central to their social identities. In economic terms, the products of the music industry outweigh those of any other cultural industry, with income including not just the sales of recorded music, but also copyright revenue, tour profits, sales of the music press, musical instruments and sound systems.

HOW ARE WE TO UNDERSTAND THE TERM 'POPULAR MUSIC'?

The term 'popular music' defies precise, straightforward definition. Culturally, all popular music consists of a hybrid of musical traditions, styles, and influences. At the same time, it is an economic product invested with ideological significance by many of its consumers. In one sense, popular music encompasses any style of music that has a following, and would accordingly include many genres and styles that are largely excluded from this volume, most notably the various forms of classical music and jazz. Obviously the criteria for what counts as popular, and their application to specific musical styles and genres, are open to considerable debate. Record sales, concert attendance, numbers of performers, radio and television air play, are all quantifiable indicators of popularity, but classical music clearly has sufficient following to be considered popular, while, conversely, some forms of popular music are quite exclusive (e.g. death metal). Many musical forms now cross over in the marketplace, with distinctions between 'high' and 'low' or popular culture increasingly blurred. For example, consider the highly commercial marketing of the Three Tenors, whose classical music topped the 'pop' charts in the 1990s.

For the purposes of this study, I have largely followed conventional academic practice, equating 'popular music' with the main commercially produced and marketed musical genres, primarily in a Western context. I am conscious that this emphasis is open to charges of ignoring many significant forms of popular music, located primarily in non-Western settings, but boundaries were necessary to make the project viable. Further, Western styles of popular music continue to dominate the international market place, at the same time appropriating local musical styles and being engaged with and absorbed by them. Accordingly, the emphasis is on traditional 'rock' and 'pop' forms, and their various derivative styles/genres, along with more recently prominent genres such as rap, 'world music', and the various styles of dance music. Styles such as jazz and blues are only dealt with here in so far as they have fed into contemporary mainstream popular music.

THE STATE OF POPULAR MUSIC STUDIES

In the first edition of this book, I observed that 'Popular music studies has become a growth area, and the field is now both extensive and highly active, with new emphases and agenda evident.' Both claims should now be heavily underlined. To begin with the first, the academic literature on popular music has simply exploded. The past six years have seen the publication of various edited books offering 'critical introductions', 'key terms', or 'companions' to the field (Clayton *et al.*, 2003; Dettmar and Richey, 1999; Frith *et al.*, 2001; Horner and Swiss, 1999; Swiss *et al.*, 1998). Alongside these is the monumental achievement of *The Continuum Encyclopedia of Popular Music*, with the 800-page *Volume One: Media, Industry and Society* (Shepherd *et al.*, eds, 2003) the first of five volumes. (Volume 2 is now also published.) In addition, there have been numerous in-depth studies of specific aspects of popular music, including: music, space, and place (Leyshon *et al.*, eds, 1998; Whiteley *et al.*, eds, 2004); music and technology (Lysloff and Gay, eds, 2003; Zak, 2001); the music industry and music policy (Hull, 2004; Homan, 2003); censorship and regulation (Cloonan and Garofalo, eds, 2003); and what can be termed 'popular musicology' (Covach and Boone, eds, 1997; Hawkins, 2002). In addition, there are new histories (Starr and Waterman, 2003; O'Brien, 2002); and profiles and reassessments of a range of genres, including punk (Sabin, 1999); rock (Beebe *et al.*, eds, 2002); electronic dance music (e.g. Reynolds, 1998); and progressive rock (Holm-Hudson, ed., 2002). Most visible of all is a plethora of writing on rap/hip-hop and its continued globalization (Mitchell, ed., 2001; Forman, 2002). We can add to these collected conference papers and numerous academic journal articles, with many of these drawing on impressive graduate theses; the music press and collected journalism (the Da Capo series; Hoskyns, ed., 2003).

Collectively, this work also demonstrates the second point above, as it reflects on-going shifts in the nature and influence of musical activity. The advent of the Internet, Napster, and downloading, and new technologies of sound recording and reproduction, especially digital sampling, has fundamentally changed the way that popular music is produced and consumed. Associated with this are issues of intellectual property rights, copyright, and the control of sound. The international music industry has changed radically. No longer so dominated by the traditional Anglo-American power centres, it is less concerned with the production and management of commodities, and more with the management of rights. The conventional distinction between the major record companies and the independents is now blurred. The significance of the national and questions of popular music and national cultural identity are subsumed under broader issues of the globalization of the culture industries and the tensions and communalities between the local and the global. Concern has shifted from a focus on production and textual issues to a concern with consumption. Subcultural theory, once the dominant approach to the study of audiences, has been displaced by the concepts of scene and locality. The traditional emphasis on rock, pop, and soul as the major constituent genres in popular music, situated around particular notions of musical value, has given way to a proliferation of musical styles, with hip-hop and electronic dance music to the fore. Audiences have splintered accordingly. The historical tension between musicological and sociological approaches to popular music remains, it continues to be rethought through the politics of musical production: 'what's at issue is not which analytical technique better gets at music's "meaning", but how to account for the different musical experiences involved in making and hearing music' (Frith, in Straw *et al.*, 1995: iii). Embracing all of the above is a continued concern with popular music as cultural politics. I have tried to incorporate these new emphases, and capture something of the present diversity and complexity of popular music studies, in this volume.

WHY THIS GUIDE?

The first edition of this book set out to provide a guide to the terminology and concepts common to popular music studies. This remains my ambition. The continued economic and cultural importance of popular music, and the amount of popular and academic discourse which now surrounds it, suggests that an update is timely. The majority of the entries in the first edition (1998) have been revised and reorganized, and a considerable number of new concepts added. As indicated above, there are a number of general studies which introduce students to many of the concepts used in the study of popular music; however, these 'definitions' are often embedded within the general text, and thus are not always easily accessible to students. Accordingly, this volume seeks to provide, in accessible form for relative newcomers to the field, a comprehensive guide to the key terms and concepts current in the broad body of writing within popular music studies.

This is, obviously, an extremely ambitious undertaking. The study of popular music embraces aesthetics and musicology, economics and sociology, and social psychology. It necessarily includes reference to the music industry, the creators of the music, its textual forms, the means whereby it is disseminated, and its reception and consumption. Further, these are active processes, which articulate and interact with one another. There is an obvious danger that 'dictionary'-style definitions will be simply encapsulations of particular aspects of this complexity, rather than a critical engagement with them. In too neatly labelling and packaging the field of popular music studies, there is the danger that students will treat concepts as tablets written in stone, rather than as a dynamic vocabulary which must be actively located within shifting contexts. Accordingly, the entries here must be regarded very much as introductions, signposts designed to lead into fuller engagement with the concepts and terms; to this end, I have placed considerable emphasis on the extensive provision of key further reading, listening, and viewing sources.

CONCEPTS AND TERMS

The term 'concept' is broadly interpreted here to mean a general analytical framing label; e.g. genre is a concept, exemplified with various degrees of cohesion by genres such as rap, heavy metal, and grunge. The latter constitute terms. Terms are usually more specific and more descriptive of particular musical practices: locality is a concept, while specific local musical scenes can be considered terms; e.g. the Liverpool Sound.

While the format of the book is alphabetical, there are identifiable 'sets' of related concepts. These have been written in a linked fashion, and need at times to be read as such. The broad groupings are:

(1) Theoretical paradigms and the methodological approaches associated with them, including major social/cultural theories (the various 'isms'; e.g. Marxism, feminism), along with aesthetics, cultural studies, ethnomusicology, history, and musicology. These are provided in very abbreviated fashion, as the main concern is with their application and utilization in popular music studies.

(2) Concepts and terminology associated with the operation of the music industry. Prominent entries here include the operation of recording companies (majors; independents); key 'cultural intermediaries' (e.g. A&R), market cycles, and the shifting status of formats. Topics such as the development of recording technology, sampling, and copyright, also fall within this group.

(3) Indicative of a new emphasis in popular music studies, derived from cultural geography, are locality, scenes, and sounds (a number of key examples of these are also included).

(4) A (new) group of historically oriented concepts: biography, canon, covers, discography, documentary, history, and tribute bands.

(5) Popular music genres: there are approximately sixty of these identified here, with more extensive coverage devoted to the metagenres of pop and rock, and the various styles linked to them; along with genres such rap/hip-hop, dance music, and heavy metal. The diversity of genres indicates the difficulties of defining

popular music in any succinct and broadly acceptable manner. Ultimately, genres defy static, academic definition independent of those *making* and *listening* to the music. The entry on each includes reference to the historical development and musical characteristics of the genre, its other stylistic attributes, and some of its main performers. Examples of key or illustrative recordings are provided (usually giving their American pressing; wherever possible, these are currently available in CD format). There is a marked tendency to situate genres simply by referring to exemplars, both artists and recordings. This device is both necessary and important, and I have used it here. However, a certain amount of caution is necessary given the circularity involved: genre X is illustrated by performer Y, who works within, and thereby defines, genre X. Where appropriate, major subgenres are also mentioned. Obviously, the treatment in this context can only be extremely cursory, serving to introduce each genre. Excluded here are more traditional forms of popular music which can now be considered largely obsolete, and primarily of historical importance, e.g. music hall, black-face minstrel, and vaudeville (though see Pearsall, 1976, 1975; Pickering and Green, eds, 1987). There are also a number of genres of 'world music', referred to under that meta-genre, which could have been accorded separate treatment had space been available (e.g. rai, bossa nova, juju); these can be found in *World Music: The Rough Guide* (Broughton *et al.*, eds, 1994) and its updates.

(6) Musicians and the process of creating music. This group includes the range of terms applied to performers, most notably stars and auteurs, and the concepts which underpin the value judgements frequently applied to musicians and their musics (e.g. authenticity).

(7) Modes of delivery: including formats, radio, the Internet (downloading, Napster, and MP3), and MTV.

(8) Consumption practices and audience-related concepts: fans, subcultures (along with major examples, such as punk); cultural capital; record collecting, and memorabilia.

What is consciously omitted? Specific individuals involved in the music industry, particularly musicians, are only mentioned as exemplars of concepts; for example, Elvis Presley is not an entry as such, but is used to illustrate aspects of stardom and fandom. There is some attention to basic musical terminology, but more specialized terms are excluded; they can be found in studies emphasizing a musicological approach. As already noted, most styles of 'world music' are excluded.

POPULAR MUSIC

The Key Concepts

A CAPPELLA

Group or choral singing without instrumental accompaniment. Religious orders, blues field hollers, and some traditional folk music all exemplify early forms of a cappella. Sometimes regarded as a 'purer' and more authentic musical form, since it is not mediated by technology, a view connected to the notion of the human voice as the instrument par excellence. In addition to a cappella groups as such, some contemporary popular songs and genres (e.g. **doo-wop**) include close vocal harmony sections without instrumental accompaniment, a form of a cappella. Interestingly, given their relative absence from many genres, women dominate membership of a cappella groups. This may be a reflection of a style not requiring technical resources (instruments), and able to be undertaken, initially at least, in domestic social settings. For example, Sweet Honey on the Rock are an all-woman African-American a cappella group, active since the mid-1970s; heavily gospel influenced, their work comments on contemporary political, social, and personal concerns.

See also: **doo-wop; voice**

Listening: Crosby, Stills, Nash and Young, *Déjà-vu* (Atlantic, 1970); 'All Around My Hat', on Steeleye Span, *Portfolio* (Chrysalis, 1988); Sweet Honey on the Rock, *Live at Carnegie Hall* (Flying Fish, 1988)

A&R

The artists and repertoire (A&R) department of a recording label is responsible for working with acts who are already under contract, and finding new talent; they are constantly seeking out new material and acts to sign, attempting to develop a roster of artists for the company. A&R staff are frequently involved in all aspects of an artist's relationship with the record company, including the initial negotiations and the signing of the contract, the rehearsal, arrangement, and recording of songs, and liaising with the marketing, video production, and promotion divisions of the recording company. It is a male-dominated sphere, a hierarchy divided according to seniority and experience, with successful A&R people among the highest paid employees in the music industry. The criteria A&R personnel generally use for judging potential artists are identified by Negus as 'the live, stage performance; the originality and quality of the songs or material; the recorded performance and voice; their appearance and image; their level of personal commitment, enthusiasm and motivation; and the achievements of the act so far' (1992: 53). A&R staff base their acquisition and development of artists on a mix of information about rapidly shifting styles and who are 'hot' new performers, acquired through extensive networks of contacts, and assessed largely through intuition and subjective response ('gut feeling').

See also: **music industry**

Further reading: Barrow and Newby (1996: ch. 7); Cusic (1996); Hull (2004); Negus (1992: ch. 3)

ADVERTISING

Popular music has historically used advertising to promote itself as a commodity form for leisure consumption, using posters, street advertising (through handbills, stickers, and posters), and the press (especially the music press). Popular music has also become a central part of advertising through the broadcast media (radio, television, cinema, and the Internet). It frequently provides a 'soundtrack' to product advertising, usually by associating products and brands with particular lifestyles and values (e.g. the use of classic rock songs by Levi's to promote its jeans as symbolic of youthful 'cool'). Such advertising has proven very effective, with some artists receiving huge sums to license their music to marketing campaigns (e.g. the Rolling Stones in 1995 for the use of 'Start Me Up' in Microsoft's Windows 95 promotional campaign). Artists can raise their public profile and achieve celebrity status with such associations; e.g. Madonna's 'Like a Prayer' and Pepsi-Cola in 1989, Fatboy Slim's 'Right Here Right Now' (1999) and Moby's 'Porcelain' (2002) to a range of products. These can be considered part of the incorporation of music into commerce, especially when the music involved has initially fallen under the 'alternative' rubric. Contemporary hip-hop has been closely associated with product placement and has abetted a shift from ghetto fashion to street fashion.

See also: **commercialism; commodification**

Further reading: Fowles (1996); Tagg and Clarida (2003)

AESTHETICS

In a general sense, aesthetics is the philosophical study of art, with particular emphasis on the evaluative criteria applied to particular styles/texts in order to distinguish the identifying characteristics of those of value. In its traditional form, aesthetics concentrates on the study of the work of art in and of itself (cf. an emphasis on the context of artistic production) and developed out of idealist philosophy. This approach included the notion that there existed universal and timeless criteria to determine beauty, 'good' taste, and (aesthetic) value in art works: 'transcendent values'. This has been challenged by more recent work, including Marxist and feminist aesthetics, and 'postmodern' aesthetics (for an overview, see O'Sullivan *et al.*, 1994).

An aesthetic approach can be seen in several aspects of popular music studies. First, in a negative fashion, it underpins the frequent criticism of popular culture forms, including popular music, as debased, commercialized, devalued, and lacking in artistic value; e.g. the high/mass culture critique, primarily associated with the **Frankfurt School**. Second, and more significantly, although in a rather amorphous and general sense, aesthetic criteria are routinely applied to various forms of popular music. This occurs in everyday discourse around music, amongst fans and musicians, and in the judgements of critics. The evaluative criteria employed are often unacknowledged, but are frequently underpinned by notions of **authenticity**, and perceptions about the relative value of musical genres associated with particular gender and ethnic groups (e.g. the denigration of dance pop and its female audience, compared with the validation of various styles of black music). Third, and more specifically, there is the aesthetic analysis of popular music through the application of **musicology**. This varies in the degree to which such analysis simply takes as a given the concepts/tools of traditional musicology, which is largely oriented toward classical music, or modifies these in relation to popular music. Indeed, there is argument as to whether popular music even merits such a 'serious' analysis.

All this raises the central questions, posed by Frith (1987: 134): 'how do we make musical value judgements? How do such value judgements articulate the listening experiences involved?' The second question raises the significance of differing listening competencies. Frith's own response to these attempts was to conflate 'the sociological approach to popular music', including a functional dimension drawn from ethnomusicology, and the aesthetic, through musicology.

The notion of a trash aesthetic is sometimes used in relation to popular media culture, including particular styles of music (Ross and Nightingale, 2003: 125). An example of this is the glorification of recordings regarded as the worst of all time (as in Guterman and O'Donnell, 1991), and Marsh's extended discussion of the 'primitive but compelling proto punk classic song "Louie, Louie"' (Marsh, 1993).

See also: **canon; taste**

Further reading: Chester (1990); Frith (1987), (1996); Gracyk (1996); Gendron (2002); Meyer (1995); Moore (1993)

AFFECT

A concept developed by the American cultural theorist, Lawrence Grossberg, who argues that the major aspect of popular music is that it brings its audience into an affective space: 'Affect is closely tied to what we often describe as the "feeling" of life. Such "feeling" is a socially constructed domain of cultural effects'. The same experience will change drastically as its affective investment or state changes: different affective contexts inflect meanings and pleasures in very different ways. 'Affect operates across all our senses and experiences, across all of the domains of effects which construct daily life' (1992a: 79–80). Affect is not purely emotional/physical, but also functions in a social sense, as a form of **cultural capital** contributing to the formation of **taste cultures**. Our response to music is one aspect of affect. It has been argued that the Internet has reconfigured the affective realm of popular music fans' engagement with music via mediation (Jones, 2002).

Further reading: Grossberg (1992a); Longhurst (1995)

AFICIONADOS *see* **fans**

ALBUMS; ALBUM COVERS; CONCEPT ALBUMS/ ROCK OPERAS; TRIBUTE ALBUMS

An album is a musical work of extended duration, a collection of recordings, usually at least thirty minutes in length. Albums have been released across a range of formats, but became largely associated with the twelve-inch, 33⅓ rpm disc, primarily between 1955 and 1985. The album became prominent as a format in the 1960s, but its vinyl form was largely displaced by CDs in the 1980s. As Keightley observes, the meaning of albums may be structured in opposition to the single: singles are expensive, transient, and commercial; albums, on the other hand, are artistic, have greater longevity, and cultural value. Albums 'foreground the authorial intentions of performers, thereby contributing to their legitimization as serious artists' (Keightley, 2003: 612). Most discussions of the popular music **canon** are based on albums.

Part of the appeal of albums was the development of their covers as an art form, with some creative packaging and the inclusion of supplementary material in releases during the 1960s (e.g. the Small Faces, *Ogden's Nut Gone Flake* (Sony, 1968); the Who, *Live at Leeds* (MCA, 1970)). The album covers of the Beatles recordings were especially notable: 'groundbreaking in their visual and aesthetic properties (and) their innovative and imaginative designs' (Inglis, 2001: 83). They forged a link with the expanding British graphic design industry and the art world, while making explicit the connections between art and pop in the 1960s. The prestigious Grammys began including an award for best album cover, won by the Beatles in 1966 for *Revolver* and again in 1967 for *Sgt. Pepper's Lonely Hearts Club Band*, undoubtedly the most celebrated album cover (on its genesis, and artist Peter Blake's work with the Beatles, see Miles, 1997).

Album covers perform several important functions: they are a form of advertising, alerting consumers to the artist(s) responsible, and thereby sustaining and drawing on an auteur/star image; and they make an artistic statement in relation to the style of music by association with particular iconography, e.g. the use of apocalyptic imagery in heavy metal (see Weinstein, 2000), and the fantasy imagery of progressive rock. Album cover liner notes function as a literary and advertising form, while the practice of printing song lyrics on covers often signals a 'serious' genre and artist.

Cover art has come to be considered an art form (as have concert posters), with the publication of collected volumes of the work of artists such as Roger Dean. Particular record companies are associated with a 'house' style of covers, e.g. the jazz label Blue Note from the mid-1950s employed a talented graphic artist, Reid Miles, to design most of its album sleeves (nearly 400 of these are reproduced in Marsh and Callingham, 2003).

Several special types of album can be identified: concept albums, including rock operas, and tribute albums. Concept albums and rock operas are unified by a theme, which can be instrumental, compositional, narrative, or lyrical. In this form, the album changed from a collection of heterogeneous songs into a narrative work with a single theme, in which individual songs segue into one another. Concept albums first emerged in the 1960s as **rock** music aspired to the status of art, and some were accordingly termed 'rock operas'. Pete Townshend of the Who is usually credited as pioneering the concept, with the double album *Tommy* (MCA, 1969), although Townshend was partly inspired by the Pretty Things' *P.F.Sorrow* (Edsel, 1968) which had appeared the previous year. Subsequent examples included Frank Zappa and the Mothers of Invention, *We're Only In It For the Money* (Verve, 1967); the Kinks' *Arthur, or Decline of the British Empire* (Reprise, 1969), initially planned as a TV musical, and one of several concept albums penned by Ray Davies, the leader of the group; the Who's *Quadrophenia* (MCA, 1973); and the Eagles' *Desperado* (Asylum, 1973), which equated rock'n'roll musicians with Old West outlaws. The Beatles' *Sgt. Pepper's Lonely Hearts Club Band* (1967) is often considered a concept album, for its musical cohesion rather than any thematic unity. These and similar efforts enjoyed various levels of success, and there is debate around the utility of the album format for such conceptual projects.

Tribute albums are compilations of covers of a performer's songs, put together ostensibly in celebration of or homage to the original work. The form has become increasingly popular, though there is some cynicism about the economic motives behind their release. Artistically well-received examples include albums on the music of Neil Young, the Carpenters, Gram Parsons, and Van Morrison. The critical and commercial status of tribute albums is indicated by their now being included as separate 'best of' lists in music guides. A related form are benefit albums, collections of songs by artists who have donated their performances/recording to a particular political or humanitarian cause. Examples include *Red Hot & Blue* (1989), supporting Aids awareness and research; and the New York *Concert for Tibet* (1995).

Further reading: Inglis (2001); Ochs (1996); Walker (1987)

ALT.COUNTRY *see* country

ALTERNATIVE MUSIC

A broad label, and (arguably) a loose genre/style, which has been used since the late 1960s for popular music seen as less commercial and mainstream, and more authentic and 'uncompromising'. At the historical heart of alternative music was an **aesthetic** rejecting the commercial music industry, and placing an emphasis on rock music as art or expression rather than as a product for sale for economic profit. Sonically, though hard to pin down, alternative music embraces 'a twisting of musical conventions, and so listening expectations' (Felder, 1993: 3).

The use of 'alternative' emerged in response to the co-option of **rock** music by the record industry in the late 1960s and through the 1970s; e.g. in the late 1960s the slogan 'The Revolution is on CBS' was used by the record company to market psychedelic rock. The term was originally used in the late 1960s to refer to UK and US underground or counter-culture performers. The broad genre was closely associated with independent record labels, and was accordingly sometimes referred to as **indie music**. Like rock, however, alternative soon became a marketing category: 'a corporate demographic and a new set of industry practices', as the indie labels effectively served as A&R wings for the majors (Weld, 2002: 212). By the 1990s, major record retail outlets usually featured an 'alternative' section.

Nonetheless, elements of the alternative constituency sought to maintain its original aesthetic of anti-commercialism (at least at a rhetorical level) and authenticity. **Punk** in the late 1970s was clearly alternative, and the subsequent styles identified as alternative (e.g. American **hardcore** and 1980s indie rock) built on punk. The alternative label has been applied to the **grunge** bands of the late 1980s and 1990s, and remnants of the underground/counter-culture. Such was its considerable commercial success during the 1990s, in part due to its association with the influential US college radio scene, that Kirschner refers to alternative as the new 'hip-mainstream'. Part of this process of mainstreaming had been the moves of leading performers from independent labels to major companies; e.g. U2, R.E.M., and Nirvana.

While there is a distinctive musical style here, it is an extremely broad constituency, embracing a number of strands. *Spin* writer Jim Greer noted that the alternative label 'encompasses college rock, rap, thrash, metal and industrial, and has as many variants as adherents, has slowly attracted a larger and larger audience, to the point where alternative *no* longer means anything. Alternative music is purely and simply the music kids are listening to today' (cited Kirschner, 1994: 73; Greer wrote in 1991). While such breadth makes alternative a ridiculously vague term, the rubric performs a useful function for the music industry, indicating an *attitude*. This is commonly accompanied by an attention to internal personal demons rather than public-sphere political concerns, addressed to youth very much in terms to which they can relate. Another common thread to the patchwork of alternative music was the appearance of many of the performers in the high-profile Lollapalooza tours of 1991 onward, and documentaries such as *Hype!* (Doug Pray, 1996).

Fairchild observes how the evolution of alternative music has been a process of constantly incorporating existing artistic elements into a new ensemble:

> It is impossible to adequately chart out the musical evolution of the alternative scene between 1980 and 1994 without tracing the developments and diaspora of a multitude of styles and genres. It is sufficient to note here that the broad contours of the musical development of the alternative music industry throughout the past 15 years have been consistently marked by detourment, negation, confrontation, localism, and a sometimes startling, often extreme stylistic experimentation (1995: 22–3).

See also: **authenticity; counter-culture; independents; scenes**

Further reading: Azerrad (2001); Fairchild (1995); Felder (1993); Heylin (1993); Kirschner (1994); Larkin, ed. (1995); Tucker (1992) (includes useful discographies)

Listening: Pere Ubu, *Terminal Tower: An Archival Collection* (Twin/Tone, 1985); X, *See How We Are* (Elektra, 1987); Pearl Jam, *Vs* (Epic/Sony, 1993); Hole, *Live Through This* (DGC, 1994); Pixies, *Surfa Rosa* (4AD, 1988)

AMBIENT

A broad musical metagenre, ambient and its variants (ambient dance; ambient house; ambient trance; hardtrance) developed out of, and alongside, techno/electronica. Broadly, ambient music is designed to lull your mind through more soothing rhythms, with the addition of samples in the case of ambient dance. Brian Eno's recordings of the early 1970s practically invented the form. Eno chose the term ambient to refer to a group of his instrumental pieces which favoured 'minimal musical syntactical content and presented in a slowly unfolding soundscape' (Zak, 2001: 208, footnote 42). Other central figures are Dr Alex Paterson, who formed the Orb; and Richard James, the

Aphex Twin. Ambient was also an element of new age music, and is part of the musical palette of musicians working in a range of styles, including goth, psychedelic, and Celtic.

See also: **new age; techno**

Further reading: Sicko (1999); Woodstra (2001)

Listening: Brian Eno, *Another Green World* (EG Records, 1975); U.F.Orb, *Big Life* (1992) ('a hypnotic series of trance inducing rhythms and interweaving synths' (Erlewine *et al.*, eds, 1995: 577)); Aphex Twin, *Selected Ambient Recordings 85–92* (R&S, 1993); Mazzy Star, *So Tonight That I Might See* (Capitol, 1993)

AMERICANA *see* country

APPROPRIATION; SYNCRETISM

Appropriation can be considered an umbrella term, a synonym for 'use', which includes related concepts such as transculturation, hybridization, indigenization, and syncretism. Collectively, these refer broadly to the process of borrowing, reworking, and combining from other sources to form new cultural forms and spaces, in a process that Lull (1995) terms 'cultural reterritorialization'. In relation to popular music, appropriation has been applied primarily to musical reworkings, including borrowings by individual performers of musical sounds, accents, and styles (adoptions, copies, reworking). The closely related term syncretism indicates a reconciliation, a blending or fusion of pre-existing elements. This involves the creation of a new style by combining rhythms, timbres, vocal styles, etc. from earlier forms; e.g. rock'n'roll in the 1950s was the result of blending R&B (itself derived from blues, boogie, and gospel), and southern country and bluegrass.

A major issue in discussions of appropriation has been its moral status, especially in regard to musical borrowings from marginalized genres and relatively disempowered social groups. The debate here is strongly present in discussions within United States popular music culture, primarily white appropriations of black music (e.g. George, 1989; Lipsitz, 1994).

Accordingly, the concept of appropriation is a contested one, with difficulties associated with determining when musical homage and acknowledged borrowings become musical 'rip-off'; e.g. the debate around Paul Simon's *Graceland* album (1986), and similar excursions into world music. Simon won a Grammy award for album of the year, but his critics accused him of exploiting the South African music and musicians featured on *Graceland* (see the discussion of the album and its reception in Keil and Feld, 1994: ch. 8). Appropriation is often seen as exploitative of weaker social and ethnic groups' music by more dominant cultures, but it is often part of a process of symbolic struggle, through which disenfranchised or marginal social groups reformulate dominant musical styles as a means of renegotiating their social situation. This is evident, for example, in the global adoption of rap by many immigrant communities and its re-articulation to the new context (see Bennett, 2000: ch. 6; Mitchell, 2001), and the adoption of US country music by Australian aboriginal performers.

Appropriation has also been applied to whole genres/works being based on earlier ones; e.g. 1990s **Britpop** bands using sixties bands such as the Beatles and the Kinks as reference points for much of their music. The creative adaptations of subcultural style can also be considered a form of appropriation (see **bricolage**). This can include adoption of preferred musical styles; e.g. white youth's appropriation of black musical styles (see Jones, 1988). This involves considerable contradictions, as with skinheads' adoption of ska, a musical genre popular among the West Indian immigrants targeted by the racist skins.

In a sense, all contemporary popular music is the result of syncretism, with the coexistence of various genres fuelling the emergence of new styles; e.g. the combination of pop, rock, and rap genres with various styles of world/beat music in the 1990s (for a positive view of appropriation, and some instructive examples of it, see Gracyk, 2001: ch. 5).

See also: **rap; world music**

Further reading: Born and Hesmondhalgh, eds (2000); Gracyk (2001); Hatch and Millward (1987); Keil and Feld (1994); Lull (1995: 145–64); Mitchell (2001)

Listening: Paul Simon, *Graceland* (WB, 1986)

ART ROCK *see* **progressive rock**

AUDIENCES; CONSUMERS

The study of media audiences is broadly concerned with the who, what, where, how, and why of the consumption by individuals and social groups. Historically we can identify a range of competing media studies approaches to the investigation of audiences. At the heart of theoretical debates has been the relative emphasis to be placed on the audience as an active determinant of cultural production and social meanings. Music is a form of communication, and popular music, as its very name suggests, always has an audience.

Social theorists critical of the emergence of mass society/culture in the later nineteenth and early twentieth centuries first used the term 'mass audience', alarmed at the attraction of new media for millions of people. Their fears were based on a conception of the audience as a passive, mindless mass, directly influenced by the images, messages, and values of the new media such as film and radio (and, later, TV). This view emphasized the audience as a manipulated market; in relation to popular music, it is best seen in the work of Adorno (1991). Later analyses placed progressively greater emphasis on the uses consumers (the term represents a significant change of focus) made of media: uses and gratifications, which emerged in the 1960s, largely within American media sociology; reception analysis, and subcultural analysis all stressed the active role of the audience. Most recently there has been an emphasis on the domestic sphere of much media consumption, and the interrelationship of the use of various media forms. The opposition between passive and active views of audiences must not be overstated. What needs highlighting is the tension between musical audiences as collective social groups and, at the same time, as individual consumers. (For an overview of the development of audience theory, see Ross and Nightingale, 2003.)

Studies of the audience(s) and consumer(s) of popular music reflect these broad shifts in the field of audience studies. Historically, such studies have drawn on the sociology of youth, the sociology of leisure and cultural consumption to explore the role of music in the lives of 'youth' as a general social category, and as a central component of the 'style' of youth subcultures and the social identity of **fans**. The previously neglected adult audience for popular music is also now being examined. The main methodologies used are: (i) empirical surveys of consumption patterns, relating these to sociological variables such as gender and class, and sometimes supplemented by more qualitative data from interviews and participant observation; and (ii) work primarily in a qualitative vein, especially studies of music and youth subcultures.

Two factors are seen to underpin the consumption of popular music: the role of popular music as a form of cultural capital, records as media products around which cultural capital can be displayed and shaped; and as a source of audience pleasure. To emphasize these is to privilege the personal and social uses people make of music in their lives, an emphasis which is within the now dominant paradigm of audience studies. This stresses the *active* nature of media audiences, while also recognizing that such consumption is, at the same time, shaped by social conditions.

The emerging information age is seeing a reorganization of everyday life: 'people are integrating both old and new technologies into their lives in more complex ways', and within an increasingly cluttered media environment, this means 'being an audience is even more complicated' (Ross and Nightingale, 2003: 1).

See also: **consumption; demography; Frankfurt School; high culture**

Further reading: Adorno (1991); Ang (1991); Ross and Nightingale (2003)

AUTEUR; AUTEURSHIP

Auteur theory attributes meaning in a cultural text to the intentions of an individual creative source. The auteur concept is historically linked to writing and literary studies, where it has been applied to 'significant' works deemed to have value, which accordingly are considered part of high culture. An ideological construct, it is underpinned by notions of creativity and aesthetic value. The concept of auteur has been especially important in relation to film, emerging as a core part of fresh critical studies in the 1950s, with the auteur usually regarded as the director (see Hayward, 1996). The concept has since been applied to other forms of popular culture and their texts, in part in an attempt to legitimize their study vis-à-vis 'literature' and 'art'.

Applying auteurship to popular music means distinguishing it from mass or popular culture, with their connotations of mass taste and escapist entertainment, and instead relating the field to notions of individual sensibility and enrichment. The concept underpins critical analyses of popular music which emphasize the intentions of the creator of the music (usually musicians) and attempts to provide authoritative meanings of texts, and has largely been reserved for the figures seen as outstanding creative talents. It is central to the work of musicologists, who identify popular music auteurs as producers of 'art', extending the cultural form and, in the process, challenging their listeners. Auteurship has been attributed primarily to the individual performer(s), particularly singer-songwriters, but has also been attributed to producers, music video directors, songwriters, and DJs.

In the late 1960s, rock criticism began to discuss musicians in auteurist terms. For example, John Cawelti claimed that 'one can see the differences between pop groups which simply perform without creating that personal statement which marks the auteur, and highly creative groups like the Beatles who make of their performance a complex work of art' (Cawelti, 1971: 267). American critic Jon Landau argued that 'the criterion of art in rock is the capacity of the musician to create a personal, almost private, universe and to express it fully' (cited in Frith, 1983: 53). By the early 1970s 'self-consciousness became the measure of a record's artistic status; frankness, musical wit, the use of irony and paradox were musicians' artistic insignia – it was such self commentary that revealed the auteur within the machine. The skilled listener was the one who could recognize the artist despite the commercial trappings' (ibid.). The discourse surrounding sixties rock established a paradigm **aesthetic** which has, until recently, dominated the application of the concept of authorship in popular music (see **ideology**).

At a common-sense level, auteurship would appear to be applicable to popular music, since while they are working within an industrial system, individual performer(s) are, at least primarily, responsible for their recorded product. There are 'artists' – the term itself is culturally significant – who, while working within the commercial medium and institutions of popular music, are seen to utilize the medium to express their own unique visions. Such figures are frequently accorded auteur status (and will frequently be stars as well). The concept of auteur stands at the pinnacle of a pantheon of performers and their work, an hierarchical approach used by fans, critics, and musicians to organize their view of the historical development of popular music and the contemporary status of its performers. Auteurs enjoy respect for their professional performance, especially their ability to transcend the traditional aesthetic forms in which they work.

Popular musicians accorded the status of auteur include the Beatles, the Rolling Stones, Bob Dylan, Aretha Franklin, James Brown, Jimi Hendrix, David Bowie, Prince, Michael Jackson, Bruce Springsteen, and Radiohead, who have all achieved commercial as well as critical recognition. (The absence of women from this list should be noted: see **gender**.) The status of several may have diminished, with later work largely being found wanting when placed against their earlier output, as with Bob Dylan and the Rolling Stones. However, such figures retain auteur status on the basis of their historical contribution, as do auteur figures whose careers were cut short, e.g. Jimi Hendrix, Janis Joplin, Kurt Cobain. There are also performers whose work has had only limited commercial impact but who are regarded as having a distinctive style and oeuvre which has taken popular music in new and innovative directions, such as Frank Zappa, Eno, Captain Beefheart. Among musicians, in the 1980s and 1990s it is singer-songwriters who are most likely to be considered auteurs; examples include Sting, Elvis Costello, Tracey Chapman, Alanis Morissette, and Steve Earle. The auteur status of some star performers has been a contested issue, especially with regard to Madonna (see Schwichtenberg, ed., 1993).

Since all music texts are social products, performers working within popular genres are under constant pressure to provide their audience with more of the music which attracted that same audience in the first place. This explains why shifts in musical direction often lose established audiences while, hopefully for the performer, creating new adherents. This is to emphasize the contradiction between being an 'artist' and responding to the pressures of the market, and to claim particular performers as auteurs despite their location within a profit-driven commercial industry (a similar process to that applied in film studies to Hollywood cinema's studio system in the 1950s). This leads to pantheons of musical value which are problematic, since all musical texts 'arrive on the turntable as the result of the same commercial processes' (Frith, 1983: 54). Furthermore, as in any area of 'creative' endeavour, there is a constant process of reworking the 'common stock' or traditions of generic popular forms, as continuity is self-consciously combined with change (see **appropriation**).

As in literary studies, auteurship in popular music is open to criticism: only some musicians are accorded such status, while achieving auteurship is regarded as possible in some musical genres but not others. Further, as with contemporary film-making, the creative process in popular music is a 'team game' with various contributions melding together, even if the particular artist is providing the overall vision (see **cultural intermediaries**). The concept of auteur represents a form of cultural hegemony, based on a Romantic conception of 'art', used to validate certain performers and styles of work.

See also: **stars**

Further reading: Cawelti (1971); Frith (1983); Gracyk (2001); McIntyre (2003). Studies of individual musicians use the concept of auteur, even if this is only implicitly; see e.g. the following biographies: Marsh (1983) on the Who; Miles (1999) on Paul McCartney; Murray (1989) on Hendrix; Norman (1981) on the Beatles. For biographical sketches of musicians considered auteurs, see Christgau (1998); Frith *et al.* (2001); Shuker (2001: ch. 7); Zak (2001)

AUTHENTICITY

A central concept in the discourses surrounding popular music, authenticity is imbued with considerable symbolic value. In its common-sense usage, authenticity assumes that the producers of music texts undertook the 'creative' work themselves; that there is an element of originality or creativity present, along with connotations of seriousness, sincerity, and uniqueness; and that while the input of others is recognized, it is the musicians' role which is regarded as pivotal. Important in identifying and situating authenticity are the commercial setting in which a recording is produced, with a tendency to dichotomize the music industry into (more authentic, less commercial) independent labels and the majors (more commercial, less authentic). Perceptions of authenticity (or non-authenticity) are also present in the degree to which performers and records are assimilated and legitimized by particular **subcultures** or communities. Authenticity is traditionally associated with live performance (Grossberg, 1992a: 208), a view undermined by the rise of disco and club cultures. Thornton (1995) suggests the existence of two distinct kinds of authenticity here, one involving issues of originality and aura, and another, natural to the community and organic to the subculture.

The use of authenticity as a central evaluative criterion is best seen in the discussions of the relative nature and merits of particular performers and genres within popular music culture; e.g. the vernacular community-based styles of folk, the blues, and roots music are frequently perceived as more authentic than their commercialized forms. In a similar fashion, commerce and artistic integrity are frequently utilized to demarcate rock from pop music. This romantic view has its origins in the 1960s, when leading American critics – Landau, Marsh, and Christagau – elaborated a view of rock music as correlated with authenticity, creativity, and a particular political moment: the sixties protest movement and the counter-culture. Closely associated with this leftist political ideology of a rock authenticity was *Rolling Stone* magazine, founded in 1967. This view saw authenticity as underpinned by a series of oppositions: mainstream versus independent; pop

versus rock; and commercialism versus creativity, or art versus commerce (Harron, 1988; Frith, 1987).

Inherent in this polarization is a cyclical theory of musical innovation as a form of street creativity versus business and market domination and the co-option of rock into the 'mainstream'. It assumes
commerce dilutes, frustrates, and negates artistic aspects of the music.
This uneasy alliance between art and commerce is frequently placed at
the heart of the history of popular music, and is widely alluded to by
musicians, fans, and critics. Counter to this is the view that popular
culture is never simply imposed from above, but reflects the complex
interrelationship of corporate interests, the intentions of those who
create the music, and the audience perceptions and use of musical texts.

Authenticity continues to serve an important ideological function,
helping to differentiate particular forms of musical cultural capital. It is
also central to debates around the use of studio musicians (see **bubblegum**), sampling and other innovative recording techniques (see
rap), and practices such as lip-synching, as in the Milli Vanilli affair
(Friedman, 1993).

Moore (2002) usefully moves the discussion of the concept beyond
simple polarities (authentic versus unauthentic), by postulating a tri-
partite typology dependent on asking who, rather then what, is being
authenticated. As he suggests, authenticity is most usefully conceived
of as 'a construction made in the act of listening' (Moore, 2002: 210).
This necessitates a broader focus on the strategies involved in constructing authenticity in diverse musical traditions (Butler, 2003: 14).

See also: **auteurship; sampling**

Further reading: Moore (2001); Negus (1996); Pickering (1986); Thornton
(1995)

AVANT-GARDE; EXPERIMENTAL

Terms applied to innovative new movements in art; usually associated
to breaks with established traditions, styles, and convention. The
recordings of a number of performers working within popular music
genres has been considered to be avant-garde, or experimental; although
their commercial success has usually been limited, they often have
something of a cult following. Performers working at the interface
between various musical genres are more likely to be labelled avant-garde,
with their work claimed as in some sense more authentic; e.g. John

Cale, Laurie Anderson, and classical musicians the Kronos Quartet, with several reworkings of Jimi Hendrix, most notably 'Purple Haze'.

In the late 1960s, musical experiment was part of the work of the Velvet Underground, associated with Andy Warhol and the New York avant-garde art scene; and Frank Zappa and the Mothers of Invention ('Help I'm a Rock' on their first album, *Freak Out* (1966)). In his ambitious volume *Lipstick Traces*, Greil Marcus argues for a clear connection between the avant-garde European Bauhaus movement and punk rock in the late 1970s. In the 1980s, alternative bands such as Sonic Youth and My Bloody Valentine experimented with unusual tuning systems, dissonant sounds, and song structures, and performers such as Mary Margaret O'Hara utilized unique vocal styles. Performers working within progressive and art rock also frequently experiment with sound and song structures.

See also: **progressive rock; art rock; voice**

Further reading: Bloomfield (1993); Gendron (2002); Gracyk (1996); Hesmondhalgh (1996b); Holmes (2002)

Listening: Sonic Youth, *Daydream Nation* (DGC, 1988); Eno, *Another Green World* (EG, 1975); Laurie Anderson, 'O Superman' (1981) on *Big Science* (WB, 1982); My Bloody Valentine, *Isn't Anything* (Creation/Sire, 1988)

BACK CATALOGUE; REISSUES

The back catalogue is the recordings available to record companies for reissue, which they still hold copyright on. These are often of commercial value given the introduction of new formats, especially the CD, and new technology enabling the remastering of originals, combined with the lack of development capital required since the recordings already exist. 'Greatest Hits' recordings can be considered part of the back catalogue, with a very significant market share (Hull, 2004; the recent success of such releases by the Beatles, Elvis Presley, and the Rolling Stones).

The **major** labels realized the sales potential of listeners, especially the affluent baby boomer generation, upgrading their vinyl collections by replacing them with CDs. There is also the appeal of adding bonus/rarity/alternative takes to the longer space available on the CD format, as for instance with the 1996–7 reissue of the Byrds' original 1960s albums. In some cases, the majors have licensed reissue rights, or created subsidiary labels for the purpose. The 1970s saw the first companies dedicated to reissues, producing 'thoughtful, intelligent compilations of vintage rock & roll' (Erlewine *et al.*, 1995); Sire in the USA (along with its contemporary artists), and Charlie in the UK, were joined in the 1980s by Ace, Demon/Edsel, and Rhino (US), the leading contemporary reissue company, with an extensive catalogue. Leading reggae and dub company, Trojan, is now a reissue label. These companies exploited the market niche created by the major labels' reluctance to release obscure, vintage material for small specialized audiences, and the collector market.

The back catalogue in general, and reissues in particular, represent a form of canonization, elevating performers, styles, and historical periods to 'classic' status. The remastering and other practices involved raise questions of what constitutes the definitive music text; see e.g. Ford's discussion (2002) of the various 'best of' James Brown recordings now available. Many such issues are targeting the affluent **record collecting** market.

Further reading: ICE magazine

BEAT MUSIC

A music style, and loose genre, characterized by a simple, strong beat. The term beat music was applied to the music of the Beatles and other English groups in the early 1960s: Gerry and the Pacemakers, the Dave Clark Five, the Searchers, the Hollies. Accordingly, the form is sometimes referred to as 'British Beat'. These performers had a repertoire grounded in rock'n'roll and rhythm & blues. Initially encouraged by the simplicity of skiffle, beat groups characteristically had a line-up of drums, lead guitar, bass and rhythm guitars, and a lead vocalist (sometimes, as with the Beatles, this would be one of the instrumentalists). Strong regional versions were present, with Liverpool (Merseybeat) the major focus. The beat bands were central to the **British invasion** of the American charts in the early 1960s.

See also: **British invasion; skiffle; Merseybeat**

Further reading: Clayson (1995); Houghton (1980); McAleer (1994)

Listening: The Searchers, *The Most of the Searchers* (EMI, 1994 CD); the Beatles, *Live at the BBC (1962–1965)* (Apple/Capitol, 1994)

BHANGRA

An Anglo-Indian musical genre, bhangra was based on traditional Punjabi folk dance music played on percussion instruments, combined with elements of Western pop styles by Asian musicians in the UK. Bhangra was developed in three waves in Britain: as dance pop music played on synthesizers, guitars, and drum kits in migrant Indian communities in the late 1970s; incorporating **house** and **dance music** and drum machines in the 1980s; and combining with **rap**, **sampling**, and Jamaican ragga or dancehall rhythms in the early 1990s to become bhangramuffin (Mitchell, 1996). The last was commercially successful throughout Asia, and in the UK with artists such as Sheila Chandra and Apache Indian. Bhangra has continued to be hybridized with emergent styles of electronic dance music (e.g. Cornershop).

Bhangra illustrates the role played by music in processes of relocation and cultural assimilation. For young Asians, bhangra is part of an assertion of cultural **identity** distinct from that of the establishment and their parents.

Further reading: Bennett (2000: ch. 5); Lipsitz (1994); Mitchell (1996); Oliver, ed. (1990); O'Brien, K. (1995) (profile of Sheila Chandra)

Listening: Sheila Chandra, *The Struggle* (Caroline Records/Indipop, 1995); Apache Indian, *Make Way for the Indian* (Island, 1995); East 2 West, *Bhangra for the Masses* (Music Collection International, 1993); Cornershop, *When I Was Born for the 7th Time* (Wiija Records, 1997)

BIOGRAPHY; AUTOBIOGRAPHY

A biography is a life history, usually a literary form, though it can also be visual (**documentary**). An autobiography is where such a history is written by the subject; often, in the case of popular culture figures, with the help of a professional journalist. Here, I use the term biography as shorthand for both types of work, which includes the lives of artists and groups, and key figures in the music industry. Label histories (e.g. Bowman, 1997, a history of Stax Records) can also be considered a form of institutional biography.

Popular music biography plays an important role in popular music. In relation to individuals they 'create, reinforce and also challenge the dominant representations of popular musicians' (Strachan, 2003: 13). The biography interpolates and reflects on fandom, stardom, marketing, and promotion. Writing in the early 1980s, Frith described biography as the 'dominant source of pop information'. In spite of the pro-liferation of general academic writing in the past twenty years, the journalistic biography remains a staple of the music press, and is essential to the construction and maintenance of fandom. A number of journalists are strongly identified with the biographical form; e.g. Dave Marsh, Victor Brockis, and Peter Guralnick, and biographical profiles/sketches are an integral part of edited collections of 'rock journalism' (e.g. Christgau, 1998; Hornby and Schaffer, 2003; Hoskyns, 2003).

Musical biographies cover a wide range of musical performers and genres, and vary widely in quality. There is a constant turnover of 'quickie' publications on the latest pop sensations. These remain interesting as they trace 'how star appeal has been defined at different historical moments' (Frith, 1983: 272). Then there are serious historical approaches that imbue particular performers, their musical styles, and their recordings with meaning and value, situating them as part of a critical tradition and the musical **canon** (e.g. Marcus, 1991b). In some instances, such biographies seek to undermine the general perception of star figures, highlighting the scandalous aspects of their lives; these are biographical exposés, as with Albert Goldman's studies of Elvis Presley and John Lennon.

A new style of biography emerged in the UK in the 1990s, the 'confessional memoir', in which **fans** describe their encounters with music, and, at times, their own unsuccessful attempt as musicians to 'break into' the music industry, with these often represented as 'celebrations of failure'; e.g. Giles Smith's *Lost in Music* (Strachan, 2003: 13).

As with literary biography, writers of popular music biographies grapple with issues of source materials and objectivity; the links between the subject's life and the social context within which it occurred; and questions of musical production, creativity, and authenticity. (For an insightful discussion of this process, see the Introduction to Guralnick, 2002.)

See also: **music press**

Further reading: Frith (1983); Guralnick (2002); Klosterman (2002); Strachan (2003)

BLACK MUSIC; AFRICAN-AMERICAN MUSIC

The concept of black music is sometimes equated with African-American music, or the two terms are used interchangeably. Both concepts are linked to emotive arguments over essentialism, authenticity, and the historical incorporation and marginalization of the music of black performers. The existence of black music is predicated on a notion of musical coherence and an identifiable constituency. According to George (1989: Introduction), 'black music is that which is recognized and accepted as such by its creators, performers and hearers ... encompassing the music of those who see themselves as black, and whose musics have unifying characteristics which justify their recognition as specific genres'. In such formulations, particular genres are considered 'black', most notably the **blues**, **soul**, and **rap**. This has led to questions and debate over how this 'blackness' can be musically identified, how 'black' performers can be defined/recognized, and how do we situate a song by a white composer being performed by a black artist?

In the development of popular music it has generally been agreed that the interaction between black and white styles, genres, and performers has been crucial. Early African-American music had three characteristics: a melodic line; a strong rhythmic accent; and songs which alternate improvised lines, shouts and cries, with repeated choruses. These were incorporated into **ragtime**, the **blues**, and **R&B**. These characteristics aside, it has been argued that it is difficult to identify common factors that characterize black music, rejecting the idea that there is an 'essence' to black music (Tagg, 1989; Gilroy, 1993).

Nonetheless, some writers consider black music to be a useful and important term. For example, Brackett (1995b) uses 'the presence or absence of musical elements that many writers have identified with African-American musical styles, elements derived in particular from gospel music and African-American preaching', to consider the relative success of a number of songs which crossed over from *Billboard*'s R&B to the Hot 100 charts in 1965 (see also Hatch and Millward, 1987). The concept of diaspora has been applied to the notion of black music to signal a community of musical expression transcending nationalism, but which avoids musical essentialism.

See also: **crossover; diaspora; history**

Further reading: Neal (1999)

BLUEGRASS

A style of American country music with regional origins in Kentucky in the mid-1940s, though with antecedents in 'hillbilly' music and minstrel styles. The style became recognizably formalized and widely popular through the work of Bill Monroe and his original Bluegrass Boys (who gave the music its name) during the years 1945–8. Prominent features are a melodic, three-finger style of banjo picking (Earl Scruggs), the mandolin as a lead instrument, often soloing against a rhythmic background, and close-harmony singing. Bluegrass influenced **rockabilly**; e.g. Elvis Presley's version of Monroe's 'Blue Moon of Kentucky' on his Sun debut. The style has been maintained and is evident in the work of 'mainstream' artists such as Emmylou Harris.

Bluegrass gained wider attention in the 1990s with the crossover success of Alison Krauss, and the soundtrack of the movie *O Brother, Where Art Thou?*, which showcased a range of traditional bluegrass songs covered by contemporary artists. The continued appeal of bluegrass can be partly attributed to its connotations of **authenticity**, as a form of **roots** music.

See also: **roots**

Further reading: Gammond, ed. (1991); Gillet (1983); Hardy and Laing, eds (1990: entries on Bill Monroe, Flatt and Scruggs); Larkin (1993); Clarke, ed (1990)

Listening: Best of Bill Monroe (MCA, 1975); Emmylou Harris, 'If I Could Only Win Your Love' (1975), a cover of the Louvin Brothers original bluegrass recording, which gave their music greater exposure; Alison Krauss & Union Station, *New Favorite* (Rounder, 2001); *O Brother, Where Art Thou?* Soundtrack (Mercury, 2000)

Viewing: *Lost Highway*, documentary series (2003), episode 2

BLUES: COUNTRY BLUES; CLASSIC BLUES; JUMP BLUES; CHICAGO (ELECTRIC) BLUES; BRITISH R&B/BLUES ROCK

A major musical genre, the blues have been hugely influential on the whole corpus of popular music. Initially a fundamental part of black secular music which emerged in the early 1900s, the blues includes a number of identifiable subgenres which can be historically and geographically located. These are dealt with only briefly here, primarily to indicate their influence on other genres of popular music.

Country blues

A two-bar, three-line format, played on acoustic guitar or piano, the country blues emerged in the still largely rural southern United States during the early 1900s, and became widely recorded during the 1920s. There were strong regional variants, with Texas and the Mississippi Delta (Delta blues) the most prominent. Leading performers included Skip James, Robert Johnson, Leroy Carr, Blind Lemon Jefferson, Charlie Patton, and Bukka White. Country blues was characterized by its strong social realism, with many songs/recordings which are both beautiful and tortured, with a sense of anguish and desperation in their vocals.

The country blues players developed the bottleneck or slide guitar technique, shaping the instrument's sound into another 'voice'. (A glass or metal tube is fitted over the guitarist's ring or little finger, stopping the strings of the guitar when it is slid up or down the fingerboard; the term comes from the use of the neck of a bottle that had been broken off and sanded down for the purpose.) Country blues fed into other forms of the blues, and strongly influenced later **rhythm & blues**, **rockabilly**, **rock'n'roll**, and **rock** performers (e.g. the Rolling Stones' version of Johnson's 'Love in Vain' on *Let It Bleed* (ABKCO, 1989)).

The early 1960s saw the 'discovery' of the blues by white middle-class youth. In the US and the UK (and then internationally), Delta blues legends such as Mississippi John Hurt and Skip James were recorded anew by such small folk-oriented labels as Vanguard, Prestige, and Piedmont. These performers were embraced by **folk music**, then enjoying a boom period, and appeared at the Newport Folk Festival in Rhode Island, and other **festivals**. Interest in the country blues continues: a **boxed set** of Robert Johnson's complete recordings was a somewhat unexpected huge commercial success in the 1990s; other reissues have also done well with the advent of the **CD**.

Further reading: Barlow (1989); Guralnick (1991); Ward (1992a)

Listening: *Slide Guitar – Bottles Knives & Steel, Vols. 1 & 2* (CBS); *Skip James Today!* (Vanguard, 1991); Robert Johnson, *The Complete Recordings* (Columbia, 1990); Blind Lemon Jefferson, *Milestone* (1974)

Classic blues

Classic blues evolved in the 1920s and was usually performed by a woman vocalist, with **jazz** group or piano backing, sometimes as part of a minstrel show; e.g. Bessie Smith, Ma Rainey, who gave her music the name 'blues'.

Further reading: Barlow (1989); Shaw, A. (1986)

Listening: Bessie Smith, *The Complete Recordings, Vols. 1 & 2* (Columbia/ Legacy, 1991) which includes her first major success, 'Downhearted Blues' (1923)

Jump blues

A hard-swinging transitional style of blues, which anticipated both R&B and rock'n'roll, jump blues is exemplified by Louis Jordan and the Tympany Five, who **crossed over** to enjoy success in both the black and pop charts in the late 1940s with dance-oriented and novelty numbers.

See also: **rhythm & blues**

Listening: *The Best of Louis Jordan* (MCA, 1975; 1989 (CD))

Chicago (electric) blues

Chicago or electric blues developed when blacks from the south moved to urban centres such as Chicago, Memphis, and New Orleans, looking for work and better lifestyle opportunities. Larger audiences necessitated the use of greater amplification, and saw the popularization of the electric guitar and the use of drums. Major performers included Muddy Waters, B.B. King, John Lee Hooker, and Willie Dixon, also a prolific and successful **songwriter**.

Further reading: Dixon (1989); Santelli (1993); Herzhaft (1992)

Listening: B.B. King, *Live at the Regal* (MCA, 1971); John Lee Hooker, *The Healer* (Chameleon, 1989)

British R&B/blues rock

English musicians popularized the electric blues in the early 1960s, producing a variant that is sometimes referred to as British R&B,

which developed into blues rock in the later 1960s. Alexis Korner's Blues Incorporated, the Rolling Stones, the Yardbirds, John Mayall's Bluesbreakers, Cream, Led Zeppelin, and the Pretty Things all mined the blues for inspiration and material, and brought the style to **rock** audiences, and the British and American charts, through the 1960s and early 1970s.

Further reading: Santelli (1993); *Record Collector*, 'Hoochie Coochie Men: The British R&B Explosion, 1962–1966', Issue 294, February 2004, 68–88 (includes full discographical references)

Listening: The Yardbirds, *Five Live Yardbirds* (1964; Rhino, 1988) (includes Howlin Wolf's 'Smokestack Lightning'); John Mayall with Eric Clapton, *Bluesbreakers* (London, 1965) (includes Freddie King's 'Hideaway' and Robert Johnson's 'Rambling on My Mind'); Cream, *Fresh Cream* (Polydor, 1966) (includes Skip James' 'I'm So Glad')

Viewing: *Dancing in the Street* (1995), episode 5: 'Crossroads'

Contemporary blues

Major black bluesmen still performing include B.B. King and Buddy Guy, while there is a new generation of black blues performers, such as Robert Cray. Prominent blues labels include Alligator. While there is still a debate about the **authenticity** of 'white blues', through the 1980s and 1990s, white artists have contributed much to the form; e.g. Stevie Ray Vaughan, Eric Clapton, John Hammond, and ZZ Top.

In the United States, 2003 was the Year of the Blues, with a range of documentaries, celebratory concerts, presentations, and even postage stamp issues.

See also: **black music; rhythm & blues; rock'n'roll**

Further reading: Santelli (1993); *Living Blues: The Magazine of the Afro-American Blues Tradition*

Listening: Eric Clapton, *From the Cradle* (Reprise, 1994); *The Blues, Vols. 1–6* (MCA 1986–9) (originally released by Chess in the mid-1960s as a sampler of the label's extensive blues catalogue); ZZ Top, *Deguello* (WB, 1979); Buddy Guy, *Damn Right I Got The Blues* (Silvertone, 1991); Robert Cray, *Strong Persuader* (Mercury, 1986)

Website: www.deltabluesmuseum.org (the Delta Blues Museum, Clarksdale, USA; see **history**)

BOOGIE-WOOGIE

A percussive, rhythmic style of black piano playing, boogie-woogie began in the mid- to late 1920s and flourished during the 1930s. Sometimes referred to as 'the left hand of God' because of the left hand playing repeated bass patterns, while the right hand plays short melodic figures (riffs). The style was based on the **blues** progression, but was freely improvised. Boogie is derived from bogey, meaning spirit, woogie was the name of pieces of wood tying railway tracks together; many of the black piano players associated with the style travelled on the railroad from town to town, playing for 'rent' parties (held by people to raise the rent money). Boogie-woogie strongly influenced the development of **rockabilly** and early **rock'n'roll** in the 1950s.

See also: **rockabilly; rock'n'roll**

Listening: *Blues Piano Orgy* (Delmark, 1972); Jerry Lee Lewis, 'Whole Lotta Shakin' Goin' On' (1957) on *18 Original Sun Greatest Hits* (Rhino, 1984); *My Blue Heaven: Best of Fats Domino* (EMI, 1990); *Little Richard, His Biggest Hits* (1959; Speciality, 1991)

BOOTLEGS

Bootlegs are illegally produced and distributed recordings which enjoy a rather ambivalent status. Frequently associated with a mystique and cultural cachet for avid consumers and completist fans, they are anathema to record companies, and criticized by many artists. There are several kinds: (1) unauthorized reissues, usually of rare or out-of-print material; (2) counterfeits, which simply duplicate official, authorized releases (see **piracy**); and (3) unreleased live performances. At times these are semi-condoned: ICE magazine refers to them as 'gray area, live recordings'; although containing a regular column on bootleg releases, the magazine notes that while bootlegs are readily available in Europe, they 'cannot definitely advise as to their legality in the US'. Bootleggers can claim to be fulfilling an important role of cultural preservation.

In some cases, bootlegs attain legendary status, occasionally prompting record companies to release an official/original recording, e.g. Prince's *Black Album* (WB, 1995), originally recorded in 1987 but not commercially released; Bob Dylan, *The Basement Tapes* (Columbia, 1995); and Bruce Springsteen, *Live 1975–1985* (Columbia, 1986), the last two a reaction against the flood of bootlegs of the artists' concert performances. In some instances, artists have condoned concert recordings – most notably the Grateful Dead (the deadheads). **Authenticity** is central to the nature and appeal of bootlegs: 'The measures of authenticity in unauthorized recordings are the same as within the legitimate music industry: an emphasis upon originality over imitation, feeling over reason' (Marshall, 2003: 69). The majority of bootlegs are of rock artists who are exemplars of authenticity, such as Dylan, the Rolling Stones, Springsteen, and Led Zeppelin.

Bootleg recordings have been prolific, and have warranted a substantial history (see Heylin, 1995); they have recently been the subject of a major study by Marshall (2003).

See also: **copyright; piracy**

Further reading: ICE. The CD News Authority: 'Going Underground' section; Marshall (2003)

BOXED SET

In its most extreme form, the exploitation of the **back catalogue** is represented by the boxed set: the extensive repackaging of a performer's work to present a career overview. Recent commercially and critically successful boxed sets include the Who, *Thirty Years of Maximum R&B* (MCA, 1994); Eric Clapton, *Crossroads* (Polydor, 1988); and *The Byrds* (Columbia, 1994). While sometimes criticized as exploiting consumers, such releases also preserve popular music history, making it more accessible, especially to younger listeners. A case in point is the phenomenal success of the Robert Johnson boxed set, *The Complete Recordings* (Columbia, 1990) bringing the blues legend to the attention of a new audience. Other types of boxed sets have been multi-album releases by a performer (e.g. George Harrison, *All Things Must Pass* (1970)), concert packages (e.g. *Woodstock* (1970)), and, a recent trend, collections of singles (e.g. the Smashing Pumpkins; Alanis Morissette). The last include creative repackaging of 1960s artists (the Who, the Rolling Stones), primarily for the collector market.

BOY BANDS

A term widely used in the 1990s for bands regarded as manufactured pop, in the sense of being deliberate industry constructions aimed primarily at teenage audiences, though there were significant examples from the 1960s onward (notably the Monkees in the 1960s: see Stahl, 2002) and 1970s British new pop (see Hill, 1986). Several boy bands enjoyed huge commercial success, while a few members went on to establish solo careers. Key examples are the Back Street Boys, Take That (Robbie Williams), N'Sync, and New Kids on the Block. One response was the creation and success of female equivalents of the boy bands (e.g. the Spice Girls), utilizing a similar marketing approach. The late 1990s phenomenon of using reality television shows to produce such groups has continued, although their membership may be more of a gender mix, e.g. S Club 7 (see **television**). The use of music video, the coverage in the music press, the album covers and posters, and distinctive performance styles (especially the highly choreo-graphed use of dance, the emphasis on vocals, the 'masking' of instru-mental accompaniment: see the N'Sync concert DVD) all contribute to the construction of a distinct image for boy bands: essentially they are teens marketed for teens, especially girls.

The discourse surrounding boy bands mirrors that of teen and chart-oriented pop more generally, especially their perceived lack of authenticity, seen as reflecting the power of the music industry to commodify such performers and their audiences. More complex analyses move past simple condemnation to consider the dynamics of the processes of creation and presentation of the boy bands and their music, and the nature of their appeal (e.g. Marshall, 1997).

See also: **commercialism; commodification; girl groups; pop**

Further reading: Marshall (1997) (ch. 6 includes a case study of New Kids on the Block)

Listening: Back Street Boys, *Backstreet's Back* (Zomba/Mushroom Records, 1997)

Viewing: N'Sync, *Pop Odyssey* (DVD, Zomba, 2002)

BRICOLAGE

The concept of bricolage was initially developed by anthropologist Lévi-Strauss, who observed that primitive people's modes of magic – superstition, sorcery, myth – while superficially bewildering, can be regarded as implicitly coherent, connecting things which enable their users to satisfactorily explain and make sense of their own world. Bricolage has been applied in popular music studies primarily in consideration of the nature and cultural significance of cultural style, especially in youth subcultures, and in relation to musical appropriations.

The Birmingham cultural studies writers, most notably Hebdige and the contributors to Hall and Jefferson, eds (1976) applied and developed the structured improvisations of bricolage to explain the spectacular youth subcultures which emerged in the UK in the 1950s and 1960s. These subcultures appropriated a range of goods from the dominant culture, assigning new meanings to them. Symbolic objects – music, language, dress, appearance – formed a unified signifying system in which borrowed materials reflected and expressed aspects of the subcultural group (see the essays in Hall and Jefferson, 1976). Punk best exemplified such stylistic bricolage.

'Normal' youth can also operate as bricoleurs. Clarke suggests that an examination of male working-class youth in the UK reveals that 'normal' dressing means using elements drawn from government surplus stores, sportswear, subcultural clothing appropriated from different historical eras via the second-hand clothing markets (in Hall and Jefferson, 1976). McRobbie (1988; 1991) demonstrates that this is not a process confined to boys, with fashion-conscious young girls also putting together ensembles. Mass-market fashion itself contains forms of recontextualized meaning, as with ski jumpers, tracksuits, and work overalls.

A number of studies have utilized bricolage in a more general sense to examine the social role of particular musical styles. Grossberg (in Gelder and Thornton, eds, 1997) argues that rock'n'roll is a particular capitalist and postmodernist form of bricolage:

> It functions in a constant play of incorporation and excorporation (both always occurring simultaneously), a contradictory cultural practice, in which youth celebrates the very conditions of its leisure – boredom, meaningless and dehumanization – through technology, commodity fetishism, repetition, fragmentation and superficiality (481).

In more precise terms, various musical styles have been credited with bringing a sense of play to the arts of bricolage, utilizing different musical sounds, conventions, and instrumentation. For example, Lipsitz documents how Los Angeles's Chicano rock'n'roll musicians drew upon street slang, car-customizing, clothing styles, and wall

murals for inspiration and ideas, in addition to more traditional cultural creations such as literature, plays, and poems: 'Their work is
intertextual, constantly in dialogue with other forms of cultural
expression, and most fully appreciated when located in context'
(Lipsitz, in Gelder and Thornton, 1997: 358).

All this is to see a process of semiotic guerrilla warfare at work in
and through popular music, operating in sites such as the home,
school, and the workplace.

Further reading: Hebdige (1979); Gelder and Thornton (1997)

BRITISH INVASION

A term used by the popular press, and subsequently by historians of
popular music, for the impact of British groups on the US popular
music scene and their dominance of the American charts from early
1960 to 1964–5. A strong British grassroots popular music scene
emerged in the late 1950s, encouraged by **skiffle**, and drawing on
American rock'n'roll and R&B for inspiration. The **beat** boom bands
inflected these sounds with their own styles and increasingly produced
their own material. The main centres were Liverpool (**Merseybeat**)
and London's R&B-based scene.

The Beatles were the crucial performers and their success opened
the way for the Dave Clark Five, Gerry and the Pacemakers, the
Rolling Stones, etc. Prior to this, few British recording artists had
found sustained popularity in America. Indeed, Capitol Records, the
US subsidiary of EMI, initially declined to release Beatles records in
the USA, licensing them to smaller labels; e.g. Vee Jay Records
released 'Please Please Me' in February 1963, and a modified version
of the group's first album (*Please Please Me*) as *Introducing the Beatles* in
July 1963. With little accompanying promotion, these releases failed to
do well on the charts, despite their UK success. This all changed with
the band's first US tour in 1964, and the accompanying Beatlemania
and chart domination (see Whitburn, 1988). The British invasion
withered in the mid-1960s, as the Beatles stopped touring in 1966,
and the United States produced a number of successful bands who
drew heavily on the British groups and their music (e.g. the Byrds).

Lester Bangs (1992a) is critical of much of the music as 'by and large
junk: perfect expressions of the pop aesthetic of a disposable culture'
and 'innocuous but raucous'. The British invasion was nonetheless
important in reshaping American popular music in the early 1960s,

while validating the emerging youth culture. Although it stifled the emergent black **R&B** and the **girl groups**, it prompted the emergence of **garage bands** and American **power pop**. The success of the Beatles, followed by the other British groups, created a standard **rock** group line-up, usually consisting of four, or possibly five players, with drum kit, lead, rhythm and bass guitars, plus vocals delivered by one (on lead) and all (chorus). The Beatles also established the importance of the singer-songwriter, and the cultural significance of groups performing their own material.

See also: **garage bands; girl groups; Merseybeat; power pop**

Further reading: Bangs (1992a); Clayson (1995); Ennis (1992); Friedlander (1996); Garofalo (1997)

Viewing: *Dancing in the Street* (1995), episode 3: 'So You Wanna Be a Rock'n'Roll Star?'

BRITPOP

The general label applied to the British guitar-based pop/rock bands of the 1990s, initially by the UK music press, with a distinctively British musical aesthetic. Britpop was a loose constituency of several distinct music styles. Performers looked for inspiration to 1960s British pop/rock bands such as the Beatles, the Who, and the Kinks, post-punk British rock of the 1980s (the Smiths, the Jam), elements of glam rock (T Rex was an acknowledged influence), and British 'new pop' of the 1980s (see **new romantics**). From an American perspective, Britpop has been described, not unfairly, as a 'defiantly nationalistic anti-grunge movement'. Whereas grunge had idealized an anti-star approach, Britpop was regarded as 'firmly cemented in snotty arrogance and aspirations to stardom' ('The Empire Gobs Back', *Rolling Stone, Yearbook 1995*: 32–4). Major Britpop bands included Blur, Suede, Pulp, and, above all, Oasis; with the label also applied to Ash, Echobelly, and Ride, among others. Along with electronic dance music, Britpop dominated the British charts through the 1990s, with Oasis's debut one of the biggest selling records in UK history. Oasis also succeeded in the American market, where *Morning Glory* sold 3.26 million copies during 1995–6, supported by extensive touring there, but otherwise Britpop had only limited impact in the US. Through its leader Tony Blair, the (then in) opposition New Labour Party cultivated connections to Britpop, which it invoked as symbolic of the need to reinvigorate British culture and the economy.

In a major study of Britpop, Harris (2004) argues that the groups who defined it ended up shifting British indie rock from its ideological and aesthetic traditions into the commercial mainstream of UK music. His account traces its rise, success, and dilution into a celebration of Britishness for its own sake, and a decline from artistic endeavour into drug-fuelled indulgence (notably in the case of Oasis). While several Britpop bands remain active (Blur, Oasis), Britpop as a generic label is now generally regarded as a historical curiosity.

See also: **indie**

Further reading: Harris (2004)

Listening: Blur, *Parklife* (Capitol, 1994); Oasis, *(What's the Story) Morning Glory?* (Creation, 1995); Suede's self-titled debut (Columbia, 1993)

Viewing: *Live Forever: The Rise and Fall of Britpop* (DVD, 2003)

BROADCASTING

Refers to the broadcast media: **radio**, **television**, and the **Internet**, which are vital to the dissemination of music, especially in recorded form. Discussion of this role has centred around questions of the various medium's relative historical importance, varying consumer access to them and their influence on modes of consumption, and the governmental regulation of broadcasting.

See also: **Internet; MTV; policy; radio; television**

BUBBLEGUM

A derogatory label initially applied to a genre of highly commercial and rather cynically manufactured **pop** of the late 1960s, usually aimed at pre-teenage listeners and reflecting their emerging purchasing power. The term came from the rock-based jingles that were produced for bubblegum adverts in the US. It was largely an American phenomenon, associated with the Buddah label and performers like the Lemon Pipers, the Archies (whose 'Sugar Sugar' single was the best-selling single of 1969), and the Ohio Express ('Yummy Yummy Yummy'). Bubblegum recordings often made extensive use of session musicians. Although frequently critically denigrated, bubblegum was at the core of commercially very successful performers such as the Monkees, Tommy Roe, and Tommy James and the Shondells: 'trash pop made in heaven' (DeCurtis, 1992: 360). Subsequently, bubblegum became the general term for popular music regarded as 'lightweight' and chart-oriented. Musically, it is associated with strong melodies and rhythms: insidious, catchy hooks that 'get inside your brain and don't leave'.

See also: **power pop**

Further reading: Bangs (1992b) (includes discography); Garofalo, 1997

Listening: *Very Best of the Ohio Express* (Buddah, 1970); Tommy James and the Shondells, *Anthology* (Rhino, 1980)

CANON

Issues related to the canon have long been at the centre of literary scholarship, and underpin several major public literary disagreements, most notably the 'Great Books' debate. The canon embraces value, exemplification, authority, and a sense of temporal continuity (time-lessness). Critics of the concept point to the general social relativism and value judgements embedded in it, and the often associated privileging of Western, white, male, and middle-class cultural work.

Notions of canon are frequently present in popular music discourse, implicitly in everyday conversations among fans, and more directly in critical discourse. Music critics and the music press are major contributors to the construction of a musical canon, with the use of ratings systems for reviews, annual 'best of' listings, and various 'guidebooks' (see **music press**).

The gendered nature of the musical canon has been strongly critiqued. Citron (1993) examines the question: 'Why is music composed by women so marginal to the standard "classical" repertoire?'. Her study looks at the practices and attitudes that have led to the exclusion of women composers from the received 'canon' of performed musical works. She explores important elements of canon formation: creativity, professionalism, music as gendered discourse, and reception. This historical absence of women has also been noted in popular music studies. For example, the marginalization of women in popular music histories (see O'Brien, 2002); the privileging of male performers and male-dominated or oriented musical styles/genres in discussions of authorship (Whiteley, 2000); and the consequent domination of popular music canons by male performers (see the 'best of' lists in Shuker, 2001: Appendix).

Further reading: Kerman (1984); Gabbard, ed. (1995)

CASSETTE AUDIO TAPE; CASSETTE TAPE PLAYERS; CASSETTE CULTURE

Compact cassette audio tape and cassette tape players, developed in the mid-1960s, appealed because of their small size and associated portability. Initially a low-fidelity medium, steady improvement of the sound, through modifications to magnetic tape and the introduction of the Dolby noise-reduction system, enhanced the appeal of cassettes. The transistor radio and the cassette had become associated technologies by the 1970s, with widely popular cheap radio-cassette players, and the cassette player incorporated into high-fidelity home stereos. The development of powerful portable stereo players (boom boxes), associated with inner-city African-American youth, created a new form of social identification and a new level of noise nuisance.

An efficient format for the expansion into remote markets, tape cassettes became the main sound carriers in 'developing' countries, and by the end of the 1980s cassettes were outselling other formats three to one. As a portable recording technology, the tape cassette has been used in the production, duplication, and dissemination of local musics and the creation of new musical styles, most notably punk and rap, thus tending to decentralize control over production and consumption. The term **cassette culture** has been applied to the 'do it yourself' ethic that underlies such practices, and the network of musicians and listeners it embraces.

Tape cassettes pose considerable problems of illegal copying and the violation of **copyright**. Fuelled by home taping, sales of blank cassette audio tapes peaked during the 1980s. Conversely, the advent of the **CD**, led to a sharp and on-going decline in the market share of pre-recorded audio cassettes, which dropped below 20 per cent in 2002 (Hull, 2004: 225). In Western countries, many music retailers no longer stock the format.

Further reading: Jones, Steve (1992); Millard (1995: ch. 15); Willis *et al.* (1990)

CD (COMPACT DISC); CD-R

Initially developed by Sony in Japan, and introduced in 1982, the compact disc is a 4.5 inch plastic, aluminium-looking disc, similar to the computer disk. In the 1980s the CD became established as the main medium for the recording and marketing of popular music, fuelled by ease of use, and (often debated) claims of a clearer, sharper sound along with greater durability and permanence, compared to vinyl. The shift to CDs was a major factor in the exploitation and availability of the **back catalogue**. Some regular CDs include **multimedia** material which can be accessed when the recording is played on an appropriate computer drive; e.g. the Rolling Stones, *Stripped* (1996).

The CD-R, a recordable CD, became more readily and cheaply available during 2000–1. Its rapid consumer take up has inverted the capitalist success story of the CD, which has in a sense created its own Frankenstein's monster: the market penetration of the CD prompting the development of a copying/dubbing technology analogous to earlier audio tape. As with **MP3s**, the CD-R shifts the balance of power between consumers and the record companies, with consequent music industry anxiety and attempts to police use of the new technology.

See also: **record formats; piracy**

CD-ROMS

CD-ROMs are 4.5 inch plastic, aluminium-looking discs, the same size as the musical CD, which can each hold up to 700 megabytes of data, in multimedia form. The music CD-ROM represented a new marketing niche and a new advertising avenue for the popular music industry, and were part of the explosion of new **multimedia** in the 1990s.

CD-ROMs became an important and influential part of the music industry, with an increasing number of popular music CD-ROM titles available through the 1990s. Most were artist-specific, but others let users compose, play guitar, and edit **music videos**. Due to the development costs involved, the format initially privileged established artists, but as the technology became cheaper and more available, CD-ROM was utilized by more performers. Best-selling titles included *XPLORA 1 Peter Gabriel's Secret World* (Interplay, 1993, various formats) and releases from Prince, Heart, and the Cranberries. These often extended the possibilities for listeners/viewers to interact with the musical performance. Music encyclopedias also became available in the format (e.g. *Music Central 96*).

A similar avenue for the marketing of popular music was through the exposure of artists and their products in multimedia magazines published on CD-ROM. The pioneer ROMagazine was *NautilusCD*, a monthly consumer/business journal of all things multimedia, which began in 1990 and became the model for others. 'ROMags' were a mix of text, graphics, sound bites, videos and music, all organized in roughly the same way as their paper equivalents.

The development of the **Internet**, with its ready access and the proliferation of music-related sites in the later 1990s, supplanted the CD-ROM and ROMags.

CELTIC MUSIC

Irish in origin but more widely influential, contemporary Celtic popular music is an example of a hybrid metagenre, variants of which have crossed over into the mainstream of popular music. Descriptions of it tend to be vague and lack specificity: 'The element that the music of the Celtic lands most commonly shares is a feeling or quality that evokes emotions of sadness or joy, sorrow or delight' (Sawyers, 2000: 5).

The influence of Celtic music is evident in the 'mainstream', commercially and critically successful music of Van Morrison, Clannad, the Chieftains, Enya (Celtic new age), and the Corrs. Celtic music frequently involves a blending of traditional and modern forms, e.g. the Celtic-punk of the Pogues; the ambient music of Enya and Canada's Coreena McKennitt; the Celtic-grunge of Cape Breton fiddle-player Ashley MacIsaac; the Celtic-rock of Rawlins Cross and Horslips. In much of this work, traditional Irish melodies are given a pop/rock dimension, with the lyrics sometimes in Gaelic.

The emergence of various hybrids of Celtic and popular music forms is part of a broader awakening of interest in Celtic traditional music and Gaelic culture and language. This appeal is attributed to the 'realness' and 'honesty' of the music, in other words, its authenticity as a music of the people.

See also: **diaspora; world music**

Further reading: Broughton *et al.* (1994); McLaughlin and McLoone (2000); Sawyers (2000)

Listening: Horslips, *Dance Hall Sweethearts* (RCA, 1974); Sarah McLachlan, *Solace* (Arista, 1991); the Pogues, *Rum, Sodomy & the Lash* (MCA, 1995); Enya, *Watermark* (Reprise, 1988)

CENSORSHIP

Censorship occurs whenever particular words, images, sounds, and ideas are suppressed or muted. This usually occurs through legislation at the national or local level, but can also take place through self-regulation and codes of practice within the media and communications industries. In a major study of the operation of popular music censorship in Britain, Cloonan (1996: 75) initially defines it as 'an attempt to interfere, either pre- or post-publication with the artistic expressions of popular music artists with a view to stifling, or significantly altering, that expression. This puts the emphasis on censorship as a *deliberate* act'.

Censorship operates at a number of levels in popular music. There is a long history of record companies refusing to distribute potentially controversial records or videos, of recordings subject to bans by radio, and recordings being subject to court action. Much of the associated debate is between supporters of the basic right of free speech, and those calling for the regulation of obscenity. A further dimension is a more covert one, where the market effectively acts as a censor. This includes record companies' decisions not to sign artists, or to fully support releases, because of their perceived lack of commercial potential; decisions by large retail outlets not to stock less commercial or controversial artists/genres; and decisions by radio stations not to play records which do not fit their general format. While these decisions are based on commercial rather than moral considerations, their net effect may be censorial. The licensing and regulation of live venues by local authorities also operates as a form of censorship (see **policy**).

In Britain and the United States, calls for stricter censorship of popular media culture have been strongly associated with the political activism and influence of the New Right, a loose amalgam of religious and conservative groups (see Grossberg, 1992a). Cloonan (1996) details a number of themes in the censorship of popular music in the UK: the ebb and flow of censorship in relation to contemporary events, with often high-profile crimes linked to violent media texts (e.g. the James Bulger case in 1993); the tendency of proponents of censorship to portray the popular music audience as passive dupes of the industry, accompanied by an aesthetic critique of pop; a concern for the welfare of children and adolescents; and xenophobia, as with the early British attacks on rock'n'roll which emphasized its American roots. Variants of these are present internationally, particularly in the views of the Parent's Music Resource Center (PMRC) in the US, formed in 1985.

The PMRC, headed by a group of 'Washington wives' (most were married to Senators or Congressmen, and were also 'born again' Christians) was dedicated to 'cleaning up' rock music, which they saw as potentially harmful to young people, terming it 'secondary child abuse'. The PMRC published a *Rock Music Report* condemning what they claimed to be the five major themes in the music: rebellion, substance abuse, sexual promiscuity and perversion, violence-nihilism, and the occult, and began a highly organized letter-writing campaign. They argued for the implementation of a ratings system for records. In response, some commercial record companies placed warning labels on records containing explicit lyrics. The PMRC also sent copies of lyrics of songs they saw as objectionable to programme directors at radio and television stations, to be screened for 'offensive material', and pressed record companies to reassess the contracts of artists who featured violence, substance abuse, or explicit sexuality in their recorded work or concerts.

All these measures were aimed at encouraging self-censorship in the **music industry**, and the group's tactics met with considerable success. The high point of their efforts was the 1985 US Senate Commerce Committee hearings on pornography in rock music (Denselow, 1990: ch. 10). No legislation came out of the hearings, but the Record Industry Association of America voluntarily responded by introducing a generic 'Parents Advisory – Explicit Lyrics' label to appear on albums deemed to warrant it. (A number of authors have addressed the episode and the cultural politics underpinning it; see in particular, Pratt, 1990; Denselow, 1990.) The PMRC remains active.

During the 1990s, **rap** music became the main target of pro-censorship forces internationally. The new genre had already been attacked from the political left for its sexism and homophobia, and was now criticized from the right for its profanity and obscenity. A judge in Florida declared the rap group 2 Live Crew's album *As Nasty as They Want to Be* to be obscene, the first such ruling for a recorded work in United States history. The anti-authority political attitudes and values in some rap music also attracted considerable criticism. The Los Angeles rap group NWA's (Niggers With Attitude) song 'Fuck the Police' (on their debut album, *Straight Outta Compton*, which was critically acclaimed for its depiction of black ghetto life), and Ice-T's song 'Cop Killer' both caused considerable controversy internationally and calls to ban their performers' concerts and records.

Such controversies continued to surface through the following decade, associated with new musical hybrids such as nu-metal, and rehearsing earlier arguments (see Garofalo and Cloonan, 2003).

Further reading: Denselow (1990); Garofalo and Cloonan (2003); Garofalo (1992b); Pratt (1990); *Index On Censorship*

CHARTS

The popular music chart is a numerical ranking of current releases based on sales and airplay, usually over a one-week period of time; the top-ranked album/single is number one and the rest are ranked correspondingly. The first UK chart appeared in 1928 (*Melody Maker*'s 'Honours List'); in the US, *Billboard*, the major trade paper, began a 'Network Song Census' in 1934. Such charts quickly became the basis for radio 'Hit Parade' programmes.

The precise nature of how contemporary charts are compiled, and their basis, varies between competing trade magazines, and national approaches also differ. In the United States, singles charts are based on airplay, while the album charts are based on sales. Current releases are generally defined for the singles charts as twenty-six weeks after the release. In the UK, the charts are produced by market research organizations sponsored by various branches of the media. In both countries, data collection is now substantially computerized and based on comprehensive sample data (Hull, 2004: 201–2). Airplay information is compiled from selected radio stations, sales information from wholesalers and retailers, assisted by bar coding. This represents a form of circular logic, in that the charts are based on a combination of radio play and sales, but airplay influences sales, and retail promotion and sales impacts on radio exposure.

Changes in the presentation of the charts can have important repercussions for the relative profile of particular genres/performers. The charts are broken down into genre categories; these can change over time, acting as a barometer of taste, as with the change of 'race' records to R&B. The decline of the single has influenced the way the charts are constructed: in the UK, in 1989 the **music industry** reduced the number of sales required to qualify for a platinum award (from one million to 600,000) to assist the promotional system, and ensure charts continued to fuel excitement and sales.

The popular music charts represent a level of industry and consumer obsession with sales figures almost unique to the record industry. The charts are part of the various trade magazines (e.g. *Billboard*, *Variety*, *Music Week*), providing a key reference point for those working in sales and promotion. The record charts play a major role: 'to the fan of popular music, the charts are not merely quantifications of commodities but rather a major reference point around which their music displays itself in distinction and in relation to other forms' (Parker, 1991: 205).

The charts both reflect and shape popular music, especially through their influence on radio playlists. Historically there has been frequent controversy over attempts to influence the charts (see **payola**), and debate still occurs over perceived attempts to manipulate them. Charts provide the music industry with valuable feedback and promotion, and help set the agenda for consumer choice. They have been an influential source of data for analyses of trends in the music industry (see **market cycles**), and the historical impact, commercially at least, of genres/performers. In addition to music magazines and the trade press, there is a market for chart listings (e.g. Whitburn, 1988). Only rarely, however, has the operation and significance of the charts received sustained academic attention.

See also: **discography; payola**

Further reading: Brackett (1995b); Cusic (1996); Hull (2004); Negus (1992); Parker (1991)

CHRISTIAN ROCK; CCM

A rather loose musical style/genre, applied initially to those artists associated with the emergence of a Christian music industry established by American evangelicals (in the 1970s) as an alternative to the mainstream 'secular' entertainment business. *Billboard* has a Top Contemporary Christian Music (CCM) category. A magazine, *Contemporary Christian Music* (later CCM), began in 1978. CCM has become a widely used term for artists whose work 'melds faith and culture. It is called Christian because of the messages in the lyrics, or at least because of the faith backgrounds of the artists' (Thompson, 2000: 11). While the beat and melody are indistinguishable from other mainstream music forms, differences are noted in the lyric content, where themes frequently used are personal salvation, the witnessing of one's faith, living by example, human frailties, rebellion, sin, forgiveness, God's love and mercy.

There is a debate over whether Christian music is primarily 'ministry' or 'entertainment' or whether particular artists' work is 'sacred' or 'secular'. The considerable commercial success of some artists, such as Amy Grant, have fuelled this debate. Christian themes are an element in the work of commercially successful performers who are located within general musical genres, including pop-metal (Stryper in the late 1980s), rock (Jars of Clay; POD), and pop (DC Talk, Sixpence None the Richer). Thompson's study of the 'birth, evolution, and growing popularity of Christian Rock Music' (2000: back jacket) shows a rich diversity of performers and musical styles.

The work of some 'mainstream' performers has, at times, been influenced by their Christian beliefs, usually in terms of a more mystic Christian spirituality: e.g. Bob Dylan, Van Morrison ('When Will I Learn to Live in God?' on *Avalon Sunset* (Polydor, 1989)), and U2 (*The Joshua Tree* (Island, 1987)).

See also: **gospel**

Further reading: Reid, J. (1993); Romanowski (1993); Thompson (2000)

Listening: Amy Grant, *Heart in Motion* (A&M, 1991); Bob Dylan, *Slow Train Coming* (Columbia, 1979); Jars of Clay's 'Flood' on the album *Frail* (Silvertone, 1995) draws on the imagery of baptism and Noah's Ark and is the most successful Christian **crossover** single ever; DC Talk, *Jesus Freak* (Virgin, 1995)

CLASS

Class is one of the fundamental types of social classification. The main theoretical tradition within sociology derives from the work of Marx and Weber, with an emphasis on defining classes primarily in economic terms. Subsequent theoretical debates have centred around the primacy of economic determinations of classes, compared with cultural indicators. Most contemporary classifications of class rely on employment categories, with class formation and identity variously related to educational attainment and life chances, and to patterns of cultural consumption. It is the last that has been a significant part of popular music studies.

The French social theorist Pierre Bourdieu observes that 'nothing more clearly affirms one's class, nothing more infallibly classifies, than tastes in music' (1984: 18). The class nature of popular music preferences is internationally evident, with class-linked taste cultures seemingly fairly fixed over time. It is now clear that patterns of music consumption, most notably genre preferences, follow discernible trends in terms of gender, age, ethnicity, and, in particular, class. In a pioneering study, Murdoch and Phelps established that English adolescents' popular music preferences were strongly differentiated by social class:

> The tastes of the majority of working class pupils were confined to the routine pop music of the Top Twenty and to the main Negro styles (Tamla Motown and Jamaican Reggae), whereas many middle class pupils largely rejected this 'mainstream' pop and preferred the various minority styles, generally lumped together under the umbrella heading of 'underground-progressive' rock music (Murdoch and Phelps, 1973: 8).

The internationally evident class nature of music preferences was documented consistently in studies through into the 1990s, with class-linked taste cultures seemingly fairly fixed over time (Shuker, 2001). The relative and sometimes greater influence of gender, ethnicity, age, and location as influences shaping musical tastes has also been acknowledged.

See also: **consumption; cultural capital; taste cultures**

Further reading: Hakanan and Wells (1993); Roe (1983); Shepherd (1986); Willis *et al.* (1990)

CLASSIC ROCK *see* **rock'n'roll**

CLUBS; CLUB CULTURE

Clubs emerged historically as venues where people met regularly to pursue shared interests, usually paying a membership fee. During the early 1900s, clubs became major venues for live music on a regular and continuing basis, often associated with particular genres (e.g. jazz, blues). They have continued to serve as training grounds for aspiring performers operating at the local level, and provide a 'bread and butter' living for more established artists, often through being part of an organized circuit of venues. They are also social spaces: 'At their best, clubs are places where the marginalized can feel at home, where we can experiment with new identities, new ways of being. They are places where cultures collide' (Garratt, 1998: 321).

The equation of live performance with musical authenticity and 'paying your dues' as a performer remains a widely held ideology among fans, musicians, and record company executives. Clubs have historically assumed mythic importance for breaking new acts, as with the Who at the Marquee in London in 1965. They can also establish and popularize trends, as in English punk at London's 100 Club and the Roxy in the late 1970s. A community network of clubs or pub venues can help create a local club scene, at times based around a particular sound; e.g. **Merseybeat**, associated with the Beatles, Gerry and the Pacemakers, and the Searchers in the early 1960s; and **Madchester** (the Happy Mondays, James, and the Stone Roses) of the early 1990s. While the cohesion of their 'common' musical signatures is frequently exaggerated, such localized developments provide marketing possibilities by providing a 'brand name' with which clubbers can identify.

Club venues remain important for establishing new trends and their associated groups, especially the various forms of **techno**. The UK music press in the mid-1990s documents the resurgence of the club and disco scene, partly through a new popularization of dance music. The cult of the **DJ** is a central part of the club scene, a star figure whose skill is to judge the mood on the dance floor, both reflecting and leading it, all the while blending tracks into a seamless whole.

Dance clubs have historically been important to growing up, especially in Britain, where young people have traditionally not been as mobile as their American counterparts. Club culture is 'the colloquial expression given to youth cultures for whom dance clubs and their eighties offshoots, raves, are the symbolic axis and working social hub. The sense of place afforded by these events is such that regular attendees take on the name of the spaces they frequent, becoming "clubbers" and "ravers"' (Thornton, 1996: 3). Club cultures are associated with specific locations which continually present and modify sounds and styles, 'regularly bearing witness to the apogees and excesses of youth subcultures. Club cultures are **taste cultures**. Club crowds generally congregate on the basis of their shared taste in music, their consumption of common media, and, most importantly, their preference for people with similar tastes to themselves. Crucially, club cultures embrace their own hierarchies of what is authentic and legitimate in popular culture' (ibid.).

The explosion of dance music in the 1990s saw a number of academic and popular studies of the new phenomenon and its associated club culture (Garrett, 1998; Malbon, 1999; Rietveld, 1998). These often drew on their authors' status as participants in such scenes, mixing ethnographic method and social theory.

See also: **DJ; dance music; house**

Further reading: Garrett (1998); Malbon (1999); MUZIK magazine; Rietveld (1998); Thornton (1996)

COMMERCIALISM; COMMODIFICATION

Commercialism is the general influence of business principles and practices upon social life, including leisure activities. A central part of the process of commercialization is the commodification of cultural commodities and symbolic goods; i.e. their production as material commodities for a market, consumer economy. The **Frankfurt School** theorists stressed the commodification of popular cultural forms under the conditions of capitalist production and the constant quest for profit.

While historically always present, both processes were given increased prominence with urbanization, industrialization, and the rise of consumer society in the nineteenth century, along with the creation of global markets. With increased and more differentiated consumer demand, individual social identity became more closely identified with the consumption (and display) of goods. Associated with these developments, was the rise of **advertising** as part of increasingly sophisticated marketing techniques and the significance of brand names (Fowles, 1996: ch. 1). These concepts have been at the heart of the on-going debate over the nature and influence of **mass culture**.

There are aspects of popular music as a commodity form which distinguish it from other cultural texts, notably its reproducibility, its ubiquity of formats, and its multiple modes of dissemination. While creating and promoting new music (the industry term is 'product') is usually expensive, actually reproducing it is not. Popular music has been increasingly commodified, recorded, and reproduced in various formats – vinyl, audio tape, CD, DAT, and video – and variations within these: the dance mix, the cassette single, the limited collector's edition, and so on. These are disseminated in a variety of ways – through radio airplay, discos and dance clubs, television music video shows and

MTV-style channels, and live performances. In addition there is the memorabilia available to the fan, especially the posters and the T-shirts; the use of popular music within film soundtracks and television advertising; and the ubiquity of 'muzak'. The range of these commodities enables a multimedia approach to the marketing of the music, and a maximization of sales potential, as exposure in each of the various forms strengthens the appeal of the others.

Given that the capitalist music industry is central to the process of making and marketing recorded music, there is a spectrum of aesthetic experience that ranges across the artistic to the commercial in all musical genres, including the classical. Early practices such as the eighteenth-century patronage of composers, the commissioning of work, and the advent of public (but paying) concerts, show that popular music was hardly immune from commercial influences and constraints (Cowen, 1998). In the nineteenth century, the sale of home pianos, sheet music, and the phonograph further demonstrated the considerable commercial potential of popular music. Commodification was accelerated with the advent of recorded sound in the late nineteenth century, and the subsequent rise of record companies, licensing and copyright legislation, and the establishment of associations of composers and musicians (Chanan, 1995; Millard, 1995).

An instructive historical example of how the means of sound reproduction are a significant part of the commodification of music is provided in Gerry Farrell's account of the early days of the gramophone in India. The gramophone arrived in India only a few years after its invention in the West, and recorded sound brought many forms of classical Indian music out of the obscurity of performance settings such as the courtesan's quarter and on to the mass market. Indian musicians now entered the world of Western media, as photography and recorded sound turned 'native' musics into saleable commodities. Economics underpinned the move of GLT (Gramophone and Typewriter Ltd) into the Indian subcontinent. As John Watson Hawf, their agent in Calcutta, put it: 'The native music is to me worse than Turkish but as long as it suits them and sells well what do we care?' (Farrell, 1998: 58). For the emergent Indian middle class, the gramophone was both a technological novelty and a status symbol.

Commodification has been used in recent popular music studies to critically analyse the relationship between the music industry, the market, and music-making. The term became largely used in a negative sense, in critiques of the aggressive and calculated marketing of popular music trends, as with the British 'new pop' performers of the early 1980s, associated with the rise of music video and MTV

(Frith, 1988a; Harron, 1988; Rimmer, 1985). New musical genres are frequently seen to begin with Romantic overtones (essentially valuing creative over commercial considerations), but are soon commodified. There is a familiar historical litany here, moving through rock'n'roll in the 1950s, soul in the 1960s, reggae and punk in the 1970s, rap in the 1980s, and alternative in the 1990s, with a considerable discourse around the extent and cultural significance of episodes (see **political economy**).

Further reading: Eliot (1989); Frith (1988a); Harron (1988); Hesmondhalgh (2002); Hill (1986); Negus (1996)

COMMUNICATION

Communication is: (i) the conveying of information from A to B, with effect (Lasswell's classic flow model); and (ii) the negotiation and exchange of meaning (for a discussion of these, see O'Sullivan *et al.*, 1994). Music is a fundamental form of human communication; along with many other animal species, humans use organized sound to communicate. We are musically 'wired' at birth; infants respond to intonation and at six months of age are able to recognize musical structures and identify 'wrong' notes. There has been a good deal of experimental, laboratory research on the manner in which the brain handles such processes.

'Music is a passionate sequencing of thoughts and feelings that expresses meaning in a manner that has no parallel in human life' (Lull, ed., 1992: 1). That music produces 'sense' and conveys meanings is clear and unquestionable. What needs to be considered are 'the attributes of the processes governing *musical* meaning' (Middleton, 1990: 172), and how these operate in particular contexts. This requires an examination of: (1) the communicative role of musicians, who communicate – 'speak' – directly to individual listeners and to particular audience constituencies, often through particular genres. (2) The communicative role of the music; e.g. the conveying of implicit political messages ('protest song') and, often at a more implicit level, ideologies of romance, personal and social identity, and so forth. (3) The communicative role of the means by which the music is transferred to its audiences, and the influence of these 'communicative vehicles' (Negus, 1996: 169), which are far from neutral (see **technology**). (4) The ways in which music is received, listened to, interpreted, and used by listeners in a wide variety of contexts.

This last dimension has been the subject of considerable analytical discussion. People and groups interact with popular music in a physical way (e.g. singing along, clapping, foot tapping, dancing, 'air guitar'); emotionally (e.g. romanticizing, letting the music 'wash over you', becoming 'lost in music'); and cognitively (e.g. stimulating thought, framing perceptions, processing information). These different modes of engagement can be in a very personal manner, through individual listening to relax or escape or distance oneself from other commitments and people, but it is the social experience of music which is more frequent. Music provides a soundtrack for daily experience; e.g. studying, doing domestic chores, shopping (see **muzak**); and the stimulus to physical activities, notably dancing, but also aerobics, driving, and sex. Music can operate as a companion, something to 'unwind' and relax with; its use contributes to the context and meaning of many other activities, e.g. as film soundtrack, weddings, and sporting events.

Music as organized sound is traditionally defined in terms of beat, harmony, and melody, and, in much popular music, song lyrics. Particular popular music texts shape audience consciousness through sheer thematic repetition (hooks), and by repeated exposure via radio and music video channel playlists.

See also: **listening; musicology**

Further reading: Middleton (1990: ch. 6); Lull, ed. (1992)

Viewing: *Music and the Mind* (TV documentary series, BBC, 1996)

CONCERTS

Popular music concerts are complex social phenomena, involving a mix of music and economics, ritual and pleasure, for both performers and audiences. Concerts assert and celebrate the values of the music, endorse performers, and provide solidarity in a community of companionship. There is a tension between concerts as exemplifying a sense of community, albeit a transient one, and their economic and promotional importance (Weinstein, 1991a: 199–200).

The backstage area is a highly complex work site, with a range of specialized workers. The number of personnel reflects the size of the tour and the economic 'importance' of the performers, but can include technicians in charge of the instruments and equipment (amplifiers, etc.); stage hands, who often double as roadies, people to work the sound and lighting boards, security guards, and the concert tour manager. The successful operation of the backstage area at concerts involves the integration of these workers into a stable and impersonal time schedule, where each person does his job as and when required.

Concerts are a ritual for both performers and their audience. Symphony orchestra concerts celebrate 'the power holding class in our society' (Small, 1987); popular music concerts frequently celebrate youth, not purely as a demographic group, but the *idea of* youth. The behaviour of concert goers depends on the performer(s) and their associated musical style(s); e.g. audiences at rock and heavy metal concerts are considerably more outgoing and demonstrative, consistent with the essential physicality of the music.

Part of the ritual of attending concerts is getting 'pumped up' for the occasion, a process which includes spending hours in queues to ensure tickets (many concerts by top acts sell out in a matter of hours), listening once again to the performer's albums, talking with friends about the coming event (especially where expectations have been generated by previous concerts by the performer), travelling, often over long distances, to the concert venue, possible pre-concert drug use, and 'dressing up' for the concert. These all become part of the celebratory experience.

The performers themselves conform to ritual forms of behaviour in performance, with particular performance styles and images associated with specific genres. For example, the model of the rock band, at least at the level of image, is anti-hierarchical: 'on stage the players come close to one another, even lean on one another, and circulate to interact with different members of the band' (Weinstein, 1991a: 99). This public image often conceals the personal animosities present within the group, which are frequently concealed or played down in the common interest of maintaining the group's career. The typical rock stage performance is heavily theatrical and physically energetic, especially in the case of the lead singer and lead guitarist.

See also: **festivals; live performance; tours**

Further reading: Eliot (1989); Fink (1989); Garofalo (1992a); Walser (1993); Weinstein (1991a: ch. 6)

CONSUMER SOVEREIGNTY

The view that consumers/audiences exercise of their 'free' choice in the marketplace is a major determinant of the nature and availability of particular cultural and (economic) commodities. Consumer sovereignty emphasizes the operation of human agency. While the elements of romance and imagination that have informed individual personal histories and the history of popular musical genres are frequently marginalized in the commodification process, they remain essential to the narratives people construct to help create a sense of identity. In some contemporary forms of cultural studies, consumer sovereignty has been tied to the notion of the active audience, to produce a debated view of semiotic democracy (see Fiske, 1989).

An emphasis on consumer sovereignty as the primary factor whereby social meaning is created in the music, is in contradistinction to the view that the process of **consumption** is constrained by the processes of production: production determines consumption (see **political economy**). Yet production and consumption are not to be regarded as fixed immutable processes, but must be regarded as engaged in a dialectic. While economic power does have a residual base in institutional structures and practices (in this case, the record companies and their drive for market stability, predictability and profit), this power is never absolute. Recent writing in popular music studies has emphasized a 'middle way' approach to the issues here, utilizing the concepts of articulation and mediation (see Negus, 1996).

See also: **audiences; fans**

CONSUMPTION

The study of the consumption of economic and cultural goods has paid particular attention to the patterns of such consumption and the processes whereby it occurs. Popular music consumption embraces a wide variety of social practices (the more significant are treated separately); these include the purchase of recorded music, attending live performances, clubbing, watching music videos, listening to the radio, making tape compilations (home taping), and downloading from the Internet. The discussion here covers patterns and processes evident in the consumption of popular music (for a general discussion of the concept of consumers, and its relationship to audience studies, see **audiences**).

Patterns of consumption

Historically, the main consumers of contemporary (post-1950) popular music, especially rock music, have been young people between twelve and twenty-five. At the same time, as the charts have frequently indicated, adult tastes are significant; indeed, they have become increasingly so, with the ageing of rock's original audience (see **demography**). As a general social category, one factor youth have in common internationally is an interest in popular music, and cultural surveys in North America, the UK, and New Zealand all indicate the high levels of popular music consumption by youths. The profiles of this consumption show a clear pattern of age- and gender-based genre preferences. Younger adolescents, particularly girls, prefer commercial pop; older adolescents express greater interest in more progressive forms and artists. High school students tend to be more interested in alternative/indie genre tastes, and less interested in the more commercial expressions of popular music. As consumers get older, their tastes in music often become more open to exploring new genres and less commercial forms. This trend is particularly evident amongst tertiary students, reflecting the dominant forms of musical cultural capital within their peer groups. There is some evidence of an association between commitment to school, 'antisocial' attitudes and behaviours, and preferences in popular music (see **education**). In studies of music consumption in ethnically mixed or diverse populations, black adolescents are demonstrably more likely (than their white or Asian counterparts) to favour black music genres, most notably soul, R&B, blues, reggae, and rap. Such genres are carriers of ideology, creating symbols for listeners to identify with. Rap has emerged as a major genre preference among black youth internationally.

Adult music tastes generally remain fixed at the commercial level, even when they may largely abandon more direct interest – through record purchases, concert going etc. – in popular music. However, there is a substantial older audience for genres and styles such as country, 'easy listening', jazz, blues, and world music.

Modes of consumption

Studies of the process and nature of music consumption have used qualitative methodologies to examine individual record buyers, concert goers, radio listeners, and music video viewers. These reveal a complex set of influences upon the construction of individual popular music consumption. Even younger adolescent consumers, who are often seen as relatively undiscriminating and easily swayed by the influence of market forces (see **teenyboppers**), see their preferences as far from straightforward, with the views of their friends paramount.

Young people's musical activities, whatever their cultural background or social position, rest on a substantial and sophisticated body of knowledge about popular music. Most young people have a clear understanding of its different genres, and an ability to hear and place sounds in terms of their histories, influences, and sources. Young musicians and audiences have no hesitation about making and justi-fying judgements of meaning and value (see Willis *et al.*, 1990).

Patterns of consumption are complex, involving record buying, video viewing, radio listening, and home taping; along with the var-ious secondary levels of involvement: the music press, dance, clubbing, and concert going.

Making copies of recordings is a significant aspect of people's engagement with popular music. During the 1970s and 1980s this was primarily through audio tape. Aside from the convenience of ensuring access to preferred texts, selected (particularly with albums) to avoid any 'dross' or material not liked sufficiently to warrant inclusion, there is an economic aspect to such home taping: 'Home taping of music is, in one sense, a strategy directly tailored to recession conditions. The tape cassette has proved to be a practical, flexible and cheap way of consuming and distributing music' (Willis *et al.*, 1990: 62). Home taping was primarily from the radio, but 'Young people frequently rely on friends, with larger record collections to make tapes for them. There is something of an informal hierarchy of taste operating here' (ibid.: 63). Home taping was significant as an aspect of consumption largely beyond the ability of the music industry to influence tastes. The modern form of home taping is downloading from the **Internet**.

Buying recorded music in its various formats is central, and involves gathering information from peers, older siblings, and retrospectives in the music press; and systematically searching for items out of the back catalogue. This search is primarily through second-hand record shops, which are currently thriving because of the limited purchasing power of unemployed youth and the high prices of new CDs and albums. It can also be seen in the bargain bins and at record sales.

Radio remains the major source for most people's engagement with popular music, with surveys indicating that young people in particular frequently 'listen to the radio' (and watch less television). Although this is generally listening at an unfocused level, with the radio acting as a companion and as background to other activities, at times listening to the radio is deliberately undertaken in order to hear and tape new music. This is frequently done in relation to particular specialist shows or DJs. Preferences for particular radio stations/formats are related to factors such as age and ethnicity.

Further reading: Hakanen and Wells (1993); Koizumi (2002); Negus (1996); Willis *et al.* (1990)

COPYRIGHT

Copyright is central to the music industry. The basic principle of copyright law is the exclusive right to copy and publish one's own work. That is, the copyright owner has the right to duplicate or authorize the duplication of his property, and to distribute it. The full legal nature of copyright is beyond our scope here (see Fink, 1989: 36–47; Hull, 2004: ch. 3); its significance lies in its cultural importance. The development of new technologies of sound recording and reproduction raise issues of intellectual property rights, particularly copyright and the control of sounds.

In addition to deriving income from unit sales of records, record companies, performers, songwriters, and music publishers derive income from the sale of rights. Ownership of rights are determined by copyright in the master tape, the original tape embodying the recorded performance from which subsequent records are manufactured. The global music industry is now less concerned than previously with the production and management of commodities, with the management of rights providing an increasingly important share of its revenues.

This rights income includes: (i) mechanical income: payable by the record company (to the owner of the copyright) for permission to reproduce a song on record; this is a fixed percentage of the recommended retail price; (ii) performance income: a licence fee paid by venues, TV and radio stations for the right to publicly perform or broadcast songs; and (iii) miscellaneous income: payment for the use of songs in films, adverts, etc.

The first US copyright statute was enacted in 1909, and protected the owners of musical compositions from unauthorized copying (**piracy**), while making a song into a commodity product that could be brought and sold in the marketplace. With copyright protection, sheet-music writer-publishers could afford to spend a great deal of money promoting a new song because other printers could not pirate the valuable properties thus created. Their activity fostered musical innovation, most notably in ragtime and jazz (Peterson, 1990: 99). Similar legislation was enacted in Britain in 1911. The development of recording raised the question of whether the publishers of recorded and sheet music could claim the same rights as literary publishers.

British and American legislation differed on this, with the former being more restrictive in its approach.

Copyright laws provided no mechanism for collecting the royalties from the public performance of music. In 1914, the American Society of Composers, Authors and Publishers (ASCAP) was formed, to issue licences and to collect all royalties due from three sources: the performance of songs, with recording artists receiving income based on the revenue made from the sale of their records; the sale of original music to publishers, and subsequent performance royalties; and money paid to the publishers for their share of the sales and performances, usually split 50–50 between composers and publishers. ASCAP's role was confirmed by a Supreme Court decision in 1917 validating the organization's right to issue membership licences and collect performance royalties. However, broadcasters resisted all ASCAP's attempts to collect royalties for music played on the radio, and went so far as to create their own organization to break what they claimed were ASCAP's monopolistic tactics, establishing Broadcast Music Inc. (BMI) in 1939.

The Rome Convention and the Berne Convention are the major international agreements on copyright. The IFPI, the International Federation of the Phonographic Industries, globally regulates the application and enforcement of copyright (not always successfully; see **piracy**). Rights income is collected by various local and regional agencies, such as AMCOS, the Australasian Mechanical Copyright Owners Society; and APRA, the Australasian Performing Rights Association.

Attempts to ensure international uniformity in copyright laws have met only with partial success; even within the European Union conventions and practices vary considerably. Attitudes towards copyright diverge depending on whose interests are involved. The 1990s saw an emerging hostility towards copyright among many music consumers and even some musicians, due to its regulatory use by international corporations to protect their interests. On the other hand, the companies themselves are actively seeking to harmonize arrangements and curb piracy, while the record industry associations (especially the IFPI), which are almost exclusively concerned with copyright issues, largely support the industry line. Ultimately, it is market control which is at stake. There is a basic tension between protecting the rights and income of the original artists, and the restriction of musical output.

Canada, the United States, Australia, Japan, and Ghana all demonstrate different responses to the development of copyright, depending on the nature of interest groups that make up the local performing rights societies, and national concerns about the potential exploitation of local music, the outflow of funds to overseas copyright holders, and the stifling of local performers' ability to utilize international material (see Frith, ed., 1993). To take one example: through a detailed exposition of the regulatory structures and networks in the Australian recorded music industry, and the 1990 public inquiry into copyright, Breen (1999) shows how in Australian copyright law has largely helped protect the interests of the major music companies.

As early case studies of the legal and moral arguments surrounding the **sampling** used in records by the JAMS, M/A/R/R/S, De La Soul, and others (see Beadle, 1993) showed the issues involved were extremely complex. They centred around the questions of what is actually 'copyrightable' in music. Who has the right to control the use of a song, a record, or a sound? And what is the nature of the public domain?

Frith (ed., 1993) observed that the advent of new technologies of sound recording and reproduction have coincided with the globalization of culture, and the desire of media/entertainment conglomerates to maximize their revenues from 'rights' as well as maintaining income from the actual sale of records. What counts as 'music' is changing from a fixed, authored 'thing' which existed as property, to something more difficult to identify. As Théberge concludes:

> The introduction of digital technologies in music production during the past decade has resulted in the development of new kinds of creative activity that have, on the one hand, exacerbated already existing problems in the conceptualization of music as a form of artistic expression and, on the other, demanded that even further distinctions be made in copyright legislation (in Frith, ed., 1993: 53).

The music industry's historical concern with threats to copyright has been exacerbated in the past decade, notably in the debate surrounding sampling and practices such as Internet downloading. Accordingly, Hull (2004), in his recent study of the music industry, devotes three chapters to copyright, while articles and exchanges have proliferated around the impact of new technologies and the Internet upon the nature and operation of copyright (e.g. Garofalo, 2003).

See also: **bootlegs; MP3; piracy; sampling**

Further reading: Frith, ed. (1993); Hull (2004); Jones, Steve (1992); Marshall, 2004; Negus (1992)

COUNTER-CULTURE; UNDERGROUND

Indicating a loose, expressive social movement, the term counter-culture was initially applied to groups such as the beats in the 1950s, and subsequently to the largely middle-class subcultures of the mid- to late 1960s. The sixties counter-culture was most evident in North American communal and anti-conformist lifestyles, but it quickly became an international phenomenon. It was strongly present in the UK, where it was more commonly referred to as the underground. Both terms continue to be applied to various groups/subcultures outside of, and at times in opposition to, the social and economic mainstream (see **scenes**).

The counter-culture had its origins in the beats (or beatniks) of the 1950s. The beats developed in post-war Paris, in the student area of the Left Bank, influenced by the French bohemian artistic intelligentsia. Strongly centred around existentialist values, the futility of action and a nihilism about social change, the beats also took on board Eastern mysticism, jazz, poetry, drugs (primarily marijuana), and literature. Popularized by writers such as Kerouac and Ginsberg, the movement spread across America in the early 1960s, centred initially on Greenwich Village in New York. The beats had a romantic, anarchic vision, with individualism a major theme, and were highly antagonistic to middle-class lifestyles and careers. They were influential on the values of the later counter-culture and Generation X, and helped bring jazz, especially its more modern forms such as bebop, to wider attention

In the 1960s, the term counter-culture was used by social theorists, such as Roszak and Marcuse, as an integrative label for the various groups and ideologies present in the American movement. The counter-culture was seen as a generational unit, the 'youth culture' challenging traditional concepts of career, education, and morality, and seeking an identity outside of occupational role or family. The 1960s counter-culture/underground embraced a range of groups and lifestyles, who broadly shared values of drug use, freedom, and a broadly anti-middle class stance. In the US elements of the counter-culture were sympathetic to New Left politics (Students for a Democratic Society), and embraced some political concerns, especially community activism in relation to health, education, and the environment. While this led some observers to see youth as a generationally political progressive group, at heart the movement represented a form of symbolic, cultural politics (exemplified by the hippies). The counter-culture embodied a series of contradictions; e.g. it developed at a time of relative economic prosperity, enabling the economy to carry substantial numbers of voluntarily unemployed people living on subsistence incomes, who were antagonistic to the 'mainstream' economy and society.

A significant part of the counter-culture were the hippies; initially centred on San Francisco's Haight Ashbury district, they came into international attention during 1966–7. 'Soft' drug use (cannabis, LSD), long hair, communes, peace, love-ins/free love, flowers and psyche-delic/acid rock were all aspects picked up on by the press. Hippies represented a form of cultural politics, ostensibly rejecting 'main-stream' society and values, but with clear contradictions present. They were generally from comfortable middle-class backgrounds, but the material affluence of the Western economies during the 1960s made their opting out possible; they were anti-technology but often pos-sessed impressive sound systems; and their espoused 'freedom' at times sat uneasily alongside sexism and gender stereotyping.

Musically, the counter-culture was linked to the genres of pro-gressive and psychedelic rock. The hippies' preference for psychedelic rock was consistent with the other values of the subculture, especially its 'laid back' orientation and drug use (see Willis, 1978; Pichaske, 1989). Counter-culture 'radical' youth, mainly students, were part of the US civil rights movement, with its use of political folk songs and negro spirituals, and supported the Campaign for Nuclear Disarma-ment in the UK, which drew on similar sources, along with trad jazz, during its marches in the late 1950s. All of these musics were soon subject to **commodification**, with sincerity becoming highly mar-ketable during the mid-1960s.

The counter-culture persisted into the 1980s and onward, though arguably more in terms of the encapsulation of its values in the private lives of the baby boomer generation. The underground is evident in various **alternative scenes** and **subcultures**.

See also: **jazz; progressive rock; psychedelic music**

Further reading: Brake (1985); Garofalo (1997: ch. 6); Nuttal (1968); Reich (1972); Whiteley (1992)

COUNTRY; C&W/COUNTRY & WESTERN; COUNTRY ROCK; ALT.COUNTRY; AMERICANA

Country music is an American genre now internationally popular; it has been variously known in the past as folk music, old-time music, hillbilly, C&W/country & western. According to Bill Malone (1985: 1) 'it defies precise definition, and no term (not even "country") has ever successfully encapsulated its essence'. As an identifiable genre C&W can be traced back to the American rural south in the 1920s; Okey issued the first country catalogue in 1924. It has evolved into primarily an American form with two general strands: traditional country and a more commercial mainstream of pop country. Within these are various identifiable sub-genres and related styles: 'progressive country', country rock, bluegrass, rockabilly, Western Swing, new country, Tex–Mex, Cajun, Zydeco, and Conjunto. Leading traditional country performers included Johnny Cash, the Carter Family, Hank Williams, Willie Nelson, and Dolly Parton.

Country emerged in the US as a major market force in popular music in the 1990s, and classic stereotypes associated with the genre (especially its maudlin themes and limited appeal) no longer hold up. *Billboard* placed Garth Brooks as Top Country Album Artist *and* Top Pop Album Artist for the years 1990, 1991, and 1993. In 1993, all six of his albums were included among the 100 most popular albums of the year, with two – *No Fences* and *Ropin' the Wind* – having sold about 10 million copies each. In performance, Brooks adopted an arena rock aesthetic, using theatre smoke, fireworks, and sophisticated lighting shows (Garofalo, 1997: 457). His crossover success opened the way on the pop charts for other country artists, with Billy Ray Cyrus, Dwight Yoakum, Mary Chapin Carpenter, and Reba McIntyre among the best-selling artists of the early to mid-1990s. Along with Brooks and others, these artists are often referred to as 'new country'. At the same time, country radio became the second most listened to music format in the United States, second only to adult contemporary, and video channel CMT gained a significant market share. The recent crossover success of the Dixie Chicks and Shania Twain reflected this aggressive resurgence of country music.

Further reading: Ennis (1992); Endres (1993); Lewis, G., ed. (1993); Malone (1985); Wolff (2000)

Listening: *Hank Williams* (Polydor series, released in 1986, covering his 1946–52 releases); Garth Brooks, *No Fences* (Capitol/EMI, 1989); Rosanna Cash, *Retrospective 1979–1989* (CBS, 1989); Dixie Chicks, *Wide Open Spaces* (Monument, 1998); Shania Twain, *Come On Over* (Mercury, 1999)

Country rock

Representing an amalgam of country and rock styles, the term **country rock** was first applied in the mid-1960s to American rock performers who looked to country music for inspiration, including the Byrds (see Scoppa, 1992), the Flying Burrito Brothers, and Gram Parsons (a short, but influential career; see Fong-Torres, 1991). Country rock was carried into the 1970s with the Eagles, Poco, Ozark Mountain Daredevils, and the Amazing Rhythm Aces, all of whom mixed country with other rock genres, and enjoyed commercial success. Country rock combined traditional country harmonies and phrasing with a rock beat, adding instruments such as the pedal steel guitar, the dobro, and mandolin to the electric guitar and bass of rock music.

In the 1980s and 1990s country has been drawn on by various artists as part of a hybridization of musical styles; e.g. Jason and the Scorchers, the Blasters. While primarily a male-dominated genre, some women performers enjoyed critical and commercial success with 'soft' country rock; e.g. Emmylou Harris. In the 1990s, country rock became indistinguishable from much contemporary country music. The audience for country rock is under researched, but appears to be a mix of those favouring either, or both, of the parent genres. Urban listeners were arguably drawn to country rock's rural aesthetic and associated authenticity.

Further reading: Doggett (2000); Einarson (2001); Garofalo (1997)

Listening: Gram Parsons, *GP/Grievous Angel* (Reprise, 1990) (rerelease, both albums on single CD); the Byrds, *Sweetheart of the Rodeo* (Edsel, 1997); Bob Dylan, *Nashville Skyline* (Columbia, 1969); Emmylou Harris, *Luxury Liner* (WB, 1977)

Americana and alt.country

Along with 'No Depression' and 'Roots Rock', **Americana** and **alt.country** began being used in the 1990s for performers who positioned themselves as producing 'something heartfelt and worthwhile outside the foul and cancerous dreck which typifies country music in the last 15 years' (Tom Russell, UNCUT, May 2004: 98). Russell's comment typifies the discourse surrounding alt.country, with **authenticity** a central referent. The music evokes 'traditional', often threatened, American cultures and peoples, and rural landscapes. The loose style was picked up and marketed by record labels such as Hightown, and championed and popularized by the magazine *No Depression* (which took its name from the Carter Family song, later covered by Uncle Tupelo). Other music magazines began devoting considerable coverage to alt.country, notably UNCUT in the UK, helping to internationalize interest in the style and its performers.

Although their music frequently hybridizes rock and other styles, artists linked to alt.country/Americana include Whiskey Town, Ryan Adams, Lucinda Williams, Gillian Welch, and Wilco.

Further Reading: *No Depression*; UNCUT, especially the September 1998 issue: 'Sounds of the New West' (cover story with accompanying twenty-track CD of alt.country)

See also: **roots**

Listening: Tom Russell, *Indians Cowboys Horses Dogs* (Hightown, 2004); *No Depression: What it Sounds Like, Vol. 1* (Dualtone, 2004) (compilation by the editors of *No Depression*); Lucinda Williams, *Car Wheels on a Gravel Road* (Mercury, 1998)

COVERS

Cover versions are performances/recordings by musicians not responsible for the original recording. Historically, these were often 'standards' which were the staples of singers for most of the 1940s and 1950s. Record companies would release their artists' cover versions of hits from their competitors. In the 1950s, white singers covered the original rock'n'roll recordings by black artists (e.g. Pat Boone's cover of Little Richard's 'Tutti Frutti'), in an effort by record companies to capitalize on the ethnic divide in American radio. Criticism of this frequently exploitative practice led to covers being equated with a lack of originality, and regarded as not as creative, or authentic, as the original recording. This view was reinforced by the **aesthetics** and ideology of sixties rock culture, valuing individual creativity and the use of one's own compositions.

At times, however, covers have been perceived as creative in their own right; e.g. Elvis Presley's cover of 'That's Alright Mama' (Sun, 1955), originally recorded by R&B singer Arthur 'Big Boy' Crudup, and his version of the **bluegrass** classic 'Blue Moon of Kentucky' contributed to the formation of rockabilly and rock'n'roll in the 1950s.

Some covers have replicated the popularity of the original; e.g. Joan Jett's version of 'Crimson and Clover', originally a number one hit for Tommy James and the Shondells in 1967; others have been successful renditions of relatively ignored originals; e.g. Tommy James and the

Shondells' 'Hanky Panky' (1966, a US number 1). Cover songs are a proven product that an audience can often identify with. While some reinterpret the original song in a fresh and distinctive way, the majority are regarded as simply 'retreads'. Covers have featured strongly in the **charts** throughout the late 1980s and since. There is a fresh generation of listeners and a new market for a recycled song, as reissue/compilation albums and film soundtracks also demonstrate. Playing and recording covers is a way for artists to authenticate themselves with their audience, by identifying with respected original artists (see Weinstein, 1998).

A particular form of covers are represented by 'song families', a term developed primarily by Hatch and Millward (1987) to describe particular songs which are revived and reworked. Constructed out of existing lyrics, melodies and rhythmic structures, they are adapted to new musical developments by successive generations of musicians, reshaping generic conventions in the process. Willie Dixon's 'Spoonful', recorded by a number of artists, illustrates this process, both musically and in terms of the social meanings ascribed to various renditions of the song (Shuker, 2001: 144–5).

See also: **authenticity**

Further reading: Hatch and Millward (1987); Moore (2001); Weinstein (1998)

Listening: Cowboy Junkies, 'Me and the Devil' (original: Robert Johnson) and 'Sweet Jane' (original: Lou Reed; Velvet Underground), on *2,000 More Miles: Live Performances 1985–1994* (BMG Canada, 1995); Joan Jett, *The Hit List* (Epic, 1990) (an album of cover versions); the Chimes, 'I Still Haven't Found What I'm Looking For' (CBS, 1990), first recorded by U2

CROSSOVER

The move of a record/performer from success in one genre/chart area to another, usually with a more mainstream audience. The term is usually associated with black music achieving more mainstream chart success. Less commonly, crossover has also been applied to the early 1990s success of 'new country', and to gay musicians 'coming out'. With the exception of a brief period (November 1963–January 1965), *Billboard* had a separate R&B chart, with some R&B records 'crossing over' to the pop chart, e.g. the Four Tops, 'I Can't Help Myself' (Motown, 1965). Music classified as R&B was neither promoted as heavily as 'pop' nor did R&B recordings have access to the extensive distribution network of pop records, though Gordy at Motown in the 1960s successfully pursued a policy of making black music attractive to a white audience (e.g. the Supremes, the Four Tops). In the 1980s, with the success of performers such as Michael Jackson and Prince, *Billboard* inaugurated a Hot Crossover 30 chart (1987–), codifying the pacesetting nature of black music.

Crossover is predicated on the existence of discrete boundaries, and a hierarchy of racially distinct genres and audiences. At times it sits awkwardly with the bi-racial composition of those working within particular genres; e.g. 1950s rock'n'roll. Brackett (1995b) provides an interesting case study of five R&B songs that achieved varying degrees of crossover success in 1965. He demonstrates clear connections between their musical style and the degree to which they crossed over, and argues that the country and R&B charts served as 'testing grounds' to identify potential crossover records to the mainstream pop chart.

Crossover music has been criticized by some (notably Nelson George) as a sellout of the tougher styles of black music, and as a threat to the livelihoods of independent black entrepreneurs. There are black nationalist underpinnings to such views, linked to the notion of compromising the authenticity of black music. Other commentators (notably Perry, 1988) view crossover as a metaphor for integration and the upward social mobility of the black community. Crossover is not such an issue in music markets outside the United States. In the UK the term is rarely used, and then usually to refer to successful dance and indie music doing well in the main pop charts (see *Music Week*).

The popularization of American indie music via grunge in the early 1990s; Britpop's moving UK indie into the mainstream; and 'country' Shania Twain's success in the pop charts, provide recent examples of crossover.

See also: **rhythm & blues; soul**

Further reading: Perry (1988); Brackett (1995b); Garofalo (1993); George (1989)

Listening: James Brown, 'Papa's Got A Brand New Bag' (King, 1965), *20 All Time Greatest Hits* (Polydor 1991); Marvin Gaye, 'I Heard It Through the Grapevine', *Anthology* (Motown, 1982) (originally released in 1968); Michael Jackson, *Thriller* (Epic, 1982)

CULTURAL CAPITAL

Originating in the work of Pierre Bourdieu, cultural capital 'describes the unequal distribution of cultural practices, values and competencies characteristic of capitalist societies', with classes defined not only by their economic capital, but also by their differential access to cultural capital and symbolic power (O'Sullivan *et al.*, 1994: 73). In simple concrete **consumption** terms, in relation to the media, this means the preference of individuals and social groups for particular **texts** – e.g. European movies or Hollywood action movies – and the role such tastes play as both means of self-identification and as social indicators to others.

The designation of popular music is as much sociological as musical, a view reinforced by the varied reception of specific music texts. Bourdieu (1984) showed how 'taste' is both conceived and maintained in social groups' efforts to differentiate and distance themselves from others, and underpinning varying social status positions. Music has traditionally been a crucial dimension of this process. The musical tastes and styles followed or adopted by particular groups of consumers are affected by a number of social factors, including class, gender, ethnicity, and age. Consumption is not simply a matter of 'personal' preference, but is, in part, socially constructed. Linked to this process, is the manner in which musical tastes serve as a form of symbolic or cultural capital.

Musical cultural capital is demonstrated through a process whereby the individual, in acquiring a taste for particular artists, both discovers the 'history' and assimilates a selective tradition. He or she is then able to knowledgeably discuss artists, records, styles, trends, recording companies, literature, etc. This process occurs with music which is popular among the individual's peer group or subculture. In both cases, it serves a similar function, distancing its adherents from other musical styles. In the case of allegiance to non-mainstream genres/ performers, cultural capital serves to assert an oppositional stance; this is the pattern with many youth subcultures, which appropriate and innovate musical styles and forms a basis (subcultural capital) for their identity.

There is a historical tendency to dichotomize cultural capital in popular music by distinguishing between listeners oriented toward a commercial mainstream and a marginalized minority preferring more independent or alternative music. For example, in 1950 Reisman distinguished between two teenage audiences for popular music in the US. First, a majority group with 'an undiscriminating taste in popular music, (who) seldom express articulate preferences', and for whom the functions of music were predominantly social. This group consumed 'mainstream', commercial music, following the stars and the hit parade. Secondly, Reisman identified a minority group of 'the more active listeners', who had a more rebellious attitude towards popular music, indicated by 'an insistence on rigorous standards of judgement and taste in a relativist culture; a preference for the uncommercialized, unadvertized small bands rather than name bands; the development of a private language ... (and) a profound resentment of the commercialization of radio and musicians' (Reisman, 1950: 412; also in Frith and Goodwin, eds, 1990). Later studies documented similar patterns (e.g. Trondman, 1990).

See also: **class; subcultures; taste**

Further reading: Willis (1990)

CULTURAL IMPERIALISM

Cultural imperialism developed as a concept analogous to the historical political and economic subjugation of the Third World by the colonizing powers in the nineteenth century, with consequent deleterious effects for the societies of the colonized. This gave rise to global relations of dominance, subordination, and dependency between the affluence and power of the advanced capitalist nations, most notably the United States and Western Europe, and the relatively powerless underdeveloped countries. This economic and political imperialism was seen to have a cultural aspect:

> namely the ways in which the transmission of certain products, fashions and styles *from* the dominant nations *to* the dependent markets leads to the creation of particular patterns of demand and consumption which are underpinned by and endorse the cultural values, ideals and practices of their dominant origin. In this manner the local cultures of developing nations become dominated and in varying degrees invaded, displaced and challenged by foreign, often western, cultures (O'Sullivan *et al.*, 1994: 74).

Evidence of cultural imperialism was provided by the predominantly one-way international media flow, from a few international dominant sources of media production, notably the USA, to media systems in other national cultural contexts. This involved the market penetration and dominance of Anglo-American popular culture, and, more importantly, established certain forms as the accepted ones, scarcely recognizing that there are alternatives. The international dominance of the media conglomerates and the associated major record companies, suggested that the cultural imperialism was applicable to popular music. The extent to which this situation can be seen in terms of cultural invasion and the subjugation of local cultural identity has been debated.

The cultural imperialism thesis gained general currency in debates in the 1960s and 1970s about the significance of imported popular culture. Such debates were evident not only in the Third World, but in 'developed' countries such as France, Canada, Australia, and New Zealand, which were also subject to high market penetration by American popular culture. Adherents of the thesis tended to dichotomize local culture and its imported counterpart, regarding local culture as somehow more authentic, traditional, and supportive of a conception of a distinctive national cultural identity. Set against this identity, and threatening its continual existence and vitality, was the influx of large quantities of commercial media products, mainly from the United States. Upholders of the cultural imperialism view generally saw the solution to this situation as some combination of restrictions upon media imports and the deliberate fostering of the local culture industries, including music.

Although the existence of cultural imperialism became widely accepted at both a 'common-sense' level and in left academia, its validity at both a descriptive level and as an explanatory analytical concept came under increasing critical scrutiny into the 1980s. In a sustained critique of the concept, Tomlinson argued that it concealed a number of conceptual weaknesses and problematic assumptions about national culture and the nature of cultural homogenization and consumerism. In the 1980s, the active audience paradigm in media and **cultural studies**, with its emphases on resistance and polysemy, challenged the value of cultural imperialism.

The cultural imperialism thesis is predicated on accepting the national as a given, with distinctive national musical identities its logical corollary. However, the validity of a local/authentic versus imported/commercial dichotomy is difficult to sustain with reference to specific examples, while media effects are assumed in a too one-dimensional fashion, conflating economic power and cultural effects. This is to underestimate the mediated nature of audience reception and use of media products. Anglo–American popular culture has become since the 1950s established as the international preferred culture of the young. Locally produced texts cannot be straightforwardly equated with local national cultural identity, and imported product is not to be necessarily equated with the alien. Indeed local music is frequently qualitatively indistinct from its overseas counterpart, though this in itself is frequently a target for criticism. While specific national case studies demonstrate the immense influence of the transnational music industry on musical production and distribution everywhere, they 'just as clearly indicate that world musical homogenization is not occurring' (Robinson, 1991: 4). A complex relationship, often more symbiotic than exploitative, exists between the majors and local record companies in marginalized national contexts such as Canada and New Zealand (Shuker, 2001: ch. 4). Local musicians are immersed in overlapping and frequently reciprocal contexts of production, with a cross-fertilization of local and international sounds. Attempts at the national level to foster local popular music production are primarily interventions at the level of the distribution and reception of the music. They attempt to secure greater access to the market, particularly for local products in the face of overseas music, notably from England and the United States.

The **globalization** of Western capitalism, particularly evident in its media conglomerates, and the increasing *inter*national nature of Western popular music undermined the applicability of cultural imperialism, at least in any straightforward fashion. However, it remains a useful concept in popular music studies, providing that it refers to 'the processes and struggles through which dominant power is exerted' (Negus, 1996), rather than simply its effects or impact on the culture.

See also: **identity; globalization; majors**

Further reading: Garofalo (1993); Hesmondhalgh (2002: ch. 6); Laing (1986); Negus (1996); Roach (1997); Robinson *et al*. (1991); Shuker (2001: ch. 4); Tomlinson (1991); Wallis and Malm (1984)

CULTURAL INTERMEDIARIES

Bourdieu's notion of cultural intermediaries has been used to examine the role of personnel in the music industry in terms of their active role in the production of particular artists and styles of music, and the promotion of these: 'Although often invisible behind star names and audience styles, recording industry personnel work at a point where the tensions between artists, consumers and entertainment corporations meet and result in a range of working practices, ideological divisions and conflicts' (Negus, 1992). These personnel include **A&R** (artists and repertoire) staff responsible for finding new artists and maintaining the company's roster of performers; the record producers and sound engineers, who play a key role in the recording studio; video directors; marketing directors and the associated record pluggers; press officers; record retailers; radio programmers and disc jockeys; concert and club promoters.

While there is an anarchic aspect to many of these industry practices, the result of the essential uncertainty endemic to the music business, the industry has come to privilege particular styles of music and working practices, and quite specific ways of acquiring, marketing, and promoting performers. Such established modes of operating work against new artists, styles outside of the historically legitimized white **rock** mainstream, and the employment of women. The concept of cultural intermediaries is more useful than the related concept of **gatekeepers**, primarily because of its greater flexibility.

See also: **A&R; marketing; producers; retail**

Further reading: Bourdieu (1984); Hull (2004); Negus (1992); Toynbee (2000)

CULTURAL STUDIES

The term cultural studies became current in the late 1960s and early 1970s, and was initially associated with its institutional base at the Centre for Contemporary Cultural Studies (BCCCS) in England's Birmingham University. Cultural studies represented a reaction against the high culture tradition's strongly negative view of popular culture. Stuart Hall initially mapped the field according to a distinction between the paradigms of culturalism and structuralism, a neo-Gramscian synthesis of '**hegemony** theory' and a series of post-structural variants. Cultural studies expanded and become more diverse, with developing international interest, especially in North America, and the establishment of further institutional bases. There in no sense exists a cultural studies orthodoxy, although there is a general recognition that cultural studies focuses on the relations between social being and cultural meanings. This embraces the analysis of institutions, texts, discourses, readings, and audiences, with these understood in their social, economic, and political context. (For overviews of the development and scope of cultural studies, see Brantlinger, 1990; Turner, 1994; for a helpful summary, see Stevenson, 2002.)

Several key figures working within British cultural studies have been primarily concerned with the question of how the media actually undertake the production of 'consent' for social, economic, and political structures which favour the maintenance of dominant interests. Their approach was markedly influenced by Gramsci's concept of ideological or cultural hegemony. This vein of cultural studies has exerted the greatest influence on popular music studies, primarily through the 1970s work on music and youth **subcultures** associated with the BCCCS (Willis, 1978; Hebdige, 1979; Hall and Jefferson, 1976), and critics who attempted to place popular music, especially **rock**, at the centre of oppositional ideology (Chambers, 1985; Grossberg, 1992a; Middleton, 1990). These writers emphasize the place of the individual in the determination of cultural meaning; e.g. Chambers' theme is the constant interplay between commercial factors and lived experience: 'For after the commercial power of the record companies has been recognized, after the persuasive sirens of the radio acknowledged, after the recommendations of the music press noted, it is finally those who buy the records, dance to the rhythm and live to the beat who demonstrate, despite the determined conditions of its production, the wider potential of pop' (Chambers 1985: xii). Middleton similarly places popular music in the space of contradiction and contestation lying between 'imposed' and 'authentic', and also emphasizes the relative autonomy of cultural practices.

See also: **subcultures**

Further reading: Chambers (1985); Grossberg (1992a); Middleton (1990)

CULTURE; MASS CULTURE/SOCIETY; POPULAR CULTURE

The meaning and utility of 'culture', and the words used to qualify culture, namely 'popular' and 'mass', have been the subject of considerable discussion and debate. The difficulties surrounding these linked concepts is evident in their application to popular music.

Culture is one of the most difficult words in the English language. It is used in a variety of discourses, including fashion, the arts, nationalism, and cultural studies, with each discursive context signalling a particular usage. Cultural and media studies, which have underpinned this volume, maintain a sociological rather than an aesthetic sense of culture, with a focus on popular culture rather than artistic pursuits associated with particular values and standards: elite or mass culture. In this approach, evident throughout popular music studies, culture is a sphere in which social inequalities are reproduced; a site of struggle over meanings. An aspect of this is the way in which music studies in education have historically largely stressed the classical musical tradition, seeing popular music as inferior and paying it little attention.

Mass culture/society refers to the manufacture of culture as a commodity on a massive scale to mass markets, composed of undiscriminating consumers, for large-scale profit; as such, it clearly includes popular music. The notion of mass culture/society is closely allied to two broad sociological traditions: the **high culture** tradition of a narrowly defined high or elite culture; and the **Frankfurt School**. Both critique popular music for its commodification and negative social influence.

Popular culture was historically a term applied during the nineteenth century to the separate culture of the subordinate classes of the urban and industrial centres (see Storey, 1993). This culture had two main sources: a commercially oriented culture, and a culture of and for the people (often associated with political agitation). While some subsequent usages of popular culture reserve it for the second of these, the term became more generally associated with the commercial mass media: print, aural, and visual communication on a large scale, including the press, publishing, radio and television, film and video, telecommunications, and the recording industry.

Used as an adjective here, 'popular' indicated that something – a person, a product, a practice, or a belief – is commonly liked or approved by a large audience or the general public, with this popularity indicated by ratings, sales, etc. To a degree, this definition of popularity reifies popular cultural texts, reducing them to the status of objects to be bought and sold in the marketplace, and the social nature of their consumption must always be kept in mind. In considerations of popular music as a form of popular culture, the emphasis has been on texts and audiences, and the relationship between them – the way individuals and social groups use popular music within their lives.

Further reading: Hesmondhalgh (2002: ch. 1); Williams (1983)

CULTURE INDUSTRIES; ENTERTAINMENT INDUSTRIES

A term first coined and developed by Adorno, the culture industries are those economic institutions 'which employ the characteristic modes of production and organization of industrial corporations to produce and disseminate symbols in the form of cultural goods and services, generally, though not exclusively, as commodities' (Garnham, 1987: 25). In analyses situated in business economics, they are referred to as the entertainment industries. Such industries are characterized by a constant drive to expand their market share and to create new products, so that the cultural commodity resists homogenization. In the case of the record industry, while creating and promoting a new product is usually expensive, actually reproducing it is not. Once the master copy is pressed, further copies are relatively cheap as economies of scale come into operation; similarly, a music video can be enormously expensive to make, but its capacity to be reproduced and played is then virtually limitless.

The culture industries are engaged in competition for limited pools of disposable income, which will fluctuate according to the economic times. With its historical association with youthful purchasers — though their value as a consumer group is not as significant as it once was — the music industry is particularly vulnerable to shifts in the relative size of the younger age cohort and their loss of spending power in the recent period of high youth unemployment worldwide (see **demography**). The culture industries are also engaged in competition for advertising revenue, **consumption** time, and skilled labour. **Radio** especially is heavily dependent on advertising revenue. Not only are consumers allocating their expenditure, they are also dividing their time amongst the varying cultural consumption opportunities available to them. With the expanded range of leisure opportunities in recent years, at least to those able to afford them, the competition amongst the cultural, recreational, and entertainment industries for consumer attention has increased.

The **music industry** demonstrates most of the features identified by Vogel (1994) as characteristic of the entertainment industries: (1) Profits from a very few highly popular products are generally required to offset losses from many mediocrities; overproduction is a feature of recorded music, with only a small proportion of releases achieving chart listings and commercial success, and a few mega sellers propping up the music industry in otherwise lean periods (e.g. Michael Jackson's *Thriller* (1982), with sales of some 20 million copies through the

1980s). (2) **Marketing** expenditures per unit are proportionally large; this applies in the music industry to those artists and their releases with a proven track record. (3) Ancillary or secondary markets provide disproportionately large returns; in popular music through licensing and revenue from copyright (e.g. for film soundtracks). (4) Capital costs are relatively high, and oligopolistic tendencies are prevalent; in the music industry this is evident in the dominance of the **majors**, in part due to the greater development and promotional capital they have available. (5) On-going technological development makes it ever easier and less expensive to manufacture, distribute, and receive entertainment products and services. This is evident in the development of recording technology. (7) Entertainment products and services have universal appeal; this is evident in the international appeal of many popular music genres and performers, enhanced by the general accessibility of music as a medium, no matter what language a song may be sung in.

In addition to these characteristics, it is noteworthy that the music majors and their associated media conglomerates reveal different patterns of ownership in relation to the levels of production, distribution, and retail (see the case studies in Barnett and Cavanagh, 1994).

See also: **music industry**

Further reading: Adorno (1991); Garnham (1987); Hesmondhalgh (2002); Hull (2004); Vogel (1994)

DANCE; DANCING

As a social practice dance has a long history, closely associated with music, ritual, courtship, and everyday pleasure. Historically, organized social dancing dates back at least to the sixteenth century and the private balls of the aristocracy, with ballroom dancing popularized in the early nineteenth century (the waltz). 'The demands of the dancer tended to shape the course of ragtime and jazz rather than the obverse . . . and this status has continued into the rock age' (Gammond, ed., 1991: 144). Dance is associated with the pleasures of physical expression rather than the intellectual, the body rather than the mind. At times, the closeness and implied sexual display of dance has aroused anxiety and led to attempts to regulate dance, or at least control who is dancing with whom.

Forms of dance subject to considerable social criticism include the Charleston, jitterbugging, **rock'n'roll** in the 1950s, the twist in the 1960s, and **disco** dancing in the 1970s. Adorno saw jitterbugging, a popular and flamboyant form of dance in the 1940s, as a 'stylized' dance style whose performers had 'convulsive aspects reminiscent of St. Vitus's dance or the reflexes of mutilated animals' (1991: 46). As Negus (1996) observes, such responses reflected a distaste for overt expressions of sexuality, a racist fear of 'civilized' behaviour being undermined by 'primitive rhythms', and a concern that young people are being manipulated and effected by forms of mass crowd psychology (see **effects**).

Dance is central to the general experience and leisure lives of young people, and many adults, through their attendance at, and participation in, school dances, parties, discos, dance classes, and **raves**. The participants in the dance break free of their bodies in a combination of 'socialised pleasures and individualised desires', with dancing operating 'as a metaphor for an external reality which is unconstrained by the limits and expectations of gender identity and which successfully and relatively painlessly transports its subjects from a passive to a more active psychic position' (McRobbie, 1991: 194, 192, 201). Dance also acts as a marker of significant points in the daily routine, punctuating it with what Chambers (1985) labels the freedom of Saturday night. These various facets of dance are well represented in feature films such as *Flashdance* (1983) and *Strictly Ballroom* (1995).

Dance is associated with some popular musical genres to a greater extent than others, most obviously disco, rap, and rock'n'roll. Chambers (1985) documented the clubs and dance halls of English post-war urban youth culture, referring to 'the rich tension of dance' in its various forms, including the shake, the jerk, the Northern soul style of athletic, acrobatic dance, and the breakdancing and body-popping of black youth. There are forms of dance which are genre- and subculture-specific, such as line dancing in country, slam-dancing and the pogo in punk, breakdancing in some forms of rap, and headbanging and moshing at concerts by heavy metal and grunge and alternative performers.

These represent new forms of dance, less formally constrained than traditional dance forms. For example, while the audience does not 'dance' at **heavy metal** concerts, as the subculture stresses male bonding rather then male–female pairing, it is 'nonetheless engaged in continuous kinesthetic activity' (Weinstein, 1991b: 216), moving the body in time with the beat. This includes 'headbanging', which involves keeping the beat by making up-and-down motions of the head, and 'moshing', a form of circle dance: 'a hard skipping, more or less in time to the music, in a circular, counterclockwise pattern. Elbows are often extended and used as bumpers, along with the shoulders' (Weinstein, 1991a: 228). There is a moshing circle, the 'pit', located close to centre stage, and visible to both performers and the audience.

Similar dance styles are linked to identifiable subcultures in the **alternative** scene. Slam-dancing mirrors an 'apolitical punk ideology of rebellion' in the breakdown of symbolic order which seems to occur in the pit, with its 'assertions of individual presence and autonomy'. At the same time, it creates and reinforces unity through concern with the welfare of others, with practices such as the picking up of fallen dancers (Tsitsos, 1999: 407). Moshing, in contrast, lacks the elements, such as circular motion, which promote unity in the pit, and is identified with a 'straight edge ideology of rebellion' (ibid.: 410). Through their participation in (and rejection of) these dances, 'members of the scene pledge allegiance to the rules which govern their rebellion' (ibid.: 413). There is a process of gender discrimination at work in the maintenance of such male-dominated dance practices, which stress male bonding rather than male–female pairing.

There are three pillars of contemporary dance music: the venues, the DJs, and the music. A detailed history of American dance music from 1970 to 1979 traces the development of 'a new mode of DJ'ing and dancing that went on to become the most distinctive cultural ritual of the decade' (Lawrence, 2003: Preface). Drawing in part on interviews with the key figures involved, Lawrence provides a narrative web of clandestine house parties and discotheques, traced back to legendary pre-disco New York dance clubs the Loft and the Sanctuary. Similar dance scenes are present around subsequent locales and musical genres.

The close link between dance and contemporary popular music is indicated in the title of a major documentary series on popular music, *Dancing in the Street* (1995), which shows changing dance styles and their associated musical genres.

Further reading: Chambers (1985); Lawrence (2003); McRobbie (1991); Straw (2001); Thomas (1995)

Viewing: *Dancing in the Street* (1995)

DANCE MUSIC

Dance bands and dance music came into general use as phrases from around 1910 onwards, with radio playing a major role in the popularization of dance. Dance bands, notably 'Big Bands', were a feature of many hotels and clubs during the interwar period and into the early 1950s. Dance music came to be used in a general sense for those popular music genres capable of being danced *to*. Accordingly, it includes music from a range of styles and genres, most prominently pop and many of its variants (e.g. disco, teen pop, Motown), as well as various styles of rock, metal, rap/hip-hop, and techno/electronica. In most cases, certain styles of dance, and venues or locations, are associated with particular styles of dance music, such as Northern soul, thrash metal, and disco.

In the late 1980s and through the 1990s 'dance music' become associated with dance club scenes, rave culture in the UK, and various styles of 'dance-able' musics. As a metagenre, (primarily) electronic dance music has become a prominent part of the global music scene, with substantial sales and its own charts. In Britain, Europe, and the United States dance is now an essential part of mainstream popular music, embraced by the music industry as an antidote to the declining sales in the highly fragmented rock/pop market. Dance music has also become hugely popular in Asia and is making inroads in Australia and New Zealand.

In the 1980s **techno**, which had become identified *as* contemporary dance music, mutated into a number of different musical styles, with associated scenes and loose subcultures. These were broadly characterized by their extensive use of state-of-the-art technology and samples, musical eclecticism, and links to dance/club scenes. As music press reviews and articles and marketing hype indicate, there is considerable overlap between the various forms, with shifting and unclear boundaries present, and subgenres splintering off. As Straw observes, 'the growth and fragmentation of dance club music culture has meant that almost all of these [its styles] now continue to develop, each with its specialized clubs and record labels, and each allotted a different review section in the dozens of magazines which have merged to catalogue and evaluate new dance records' (Straw, 2001: 172). Their increased prominence warrants separate treatment: see **house; drum'n'bass; techno**

Further reading: Reynolds (1998); Straw (2001); Thornton (1996)

DEMOGRAPHY

Demography is the study of human populations, primarily with respect to their size, their structure, and their development. It includes aspects of the age structure and its relationship to social, economic, and cultural structures. In popular music studies, research drawing on demography has been primarily concerned with examining the relationship between age structure and consumption, and the relevance of this to explaining the historical advent of particular genres and radio formats, and their shifting popularity/market share.

A major example of such an approach is the explanation for the emergence of **rock'n'roll** in the mid-1950s in terms of a combination of age group demographics and individual musical creativity. The post-war baby boom was 'a crucial condition of the rearticulation of the formations of popular culture after the Second World War and the Korean War'; there were 77 million babies born between 1946 and 1964, and by 1964, 40 per cent of the population of the United States was under twenty (Grossberg, 1992a: 172). The baby boom and the emergence of a youth market made the young a desirable target audience for the culture industries: 'post-1945 American teenagers enjoyed an unprecedented level of affluence. Their taste in film, music, literature and entertainment was backed up by enormous purchasing power which record producers and film-makers were quick to satisfy' (Welsh, 1990: 3). One aspect of this search was the development of a young white audience for rhythm & blues.

American suburbia, where the baby boomers were concentrated, neither represented nor catered for the desires of American youth. As Grossberg (1992a: 179) puts it: 'Rock emerged as a way of mapping the specific structures of youth's affective alienation on the geographies of everyday life.' This is to emphasize the point that the social category of youth 'is an affective identity stitched onto a generational history' (ibid.: 183); the particular configuration of circumstances in the 1950s forged an alliance of 'youth' and rock music as synonymous with that particular age cohort of young people. For Grossberg,

> Rock's special place (with and for youth) was enabled by its articulation to an ideology of authenticity, an ideology which involved providing youth with cultural spaces where they could find some sense of identification and belonging, where they could invest and empower themselves in specific ways (ibid.: 204–5).

Authenticity, in Grossberg's sense of the term, is equated here with the ability of rock to resonate with youth's common desires, feelings, and experiences in a shared public language.

The baby boom elevated youth to a new level of social, political, and economic visibility, and clearly the emergence and vitality of any cultural form is dependent on the existence of an audience for it. However, we must not overprivilege this 'audience explanation' for the emergence of rock in the 1950s. Audiences are selecting their cultural/leisure texts from what is available to them, and the nature of the market is determined by much more than the constitutive qualities of its potential audience (see **history**).

Demographic analysis shows the changing **audience** for popular music over time. Goodwin observed at the end of the 1980s: '"older" music has become contemporary for audiences of *all* ages' (Frith and Goodwin, eds, 1990: 259). The absolute numbers of young people entering the labour market in the UK and Europe had declined during the 1980s, and continued to fall in the 1990s. Similar demographic trends have been observed in most other Western countries. Through the 1990s 'nostalgia rock' was prominent in popular music, with the release of 'new' Beatles material (*Live at the BBC*); the launch of MOJO magazine, placing rock history firmly at its core and with 35 per cent of its readers aged over 35; and successful tours by the Rolling Stones, Pink Floyd, and the Eagles, among other ageing performers. This high level of interest in popular music's past was evident amongst both greying consumers and young people. Youth were constructed by the popular and academic media, and the advertising industry, as 'Generation X': a very media self-conscious group of youth, primarily associated with **grunge** as a style.

This repackaging and marketing of our collective musical memories is hardly new, but the scale is different, and it raises questions about the vitality of popular music in the early twenty-first century. As an age cohort, seen usually as around 13 to 24 years of age, youth have historically been among popular music's major consumers, and young people continue to have considerable discretionary income for the leisure industries to tap. The straightforward association of popular music with youth, however, now needs qualifying. By the late 1980s, Frith could accurately observe that 'In material terms, the traditional rock consumer – the "rebellious" teenager – is no longer the central market figure' (Frith, 1988c: 127).

The market for popular music has extended to those who grew up with the music in the 1950s and 1960s, and who have continued to follow it. Research by the Demos thinktank in 2004, found that people in their forties and fifties are maintaining their interest in popular music; they represent a more profitable market then their teenage children because they have more disposable income and a greater desire for luxury goods (press report, July 2004). Ageing along with their favoured surviving performers of the sixties, these older listeners largely account for the present predominance of 'golden oldies' radio formats and occupy an increasing market share of record sales, especially **back catalogue** releases (see Hull, 2004). These trends illustrate how demography continues to play a significant role in reshaping the cultural market place.

See also: **audiences**

Further reading: Grossberg (1992a); Welsh (1990)

DIASPORA

Originally used to refer to the dispersal of the Jews in the Greco-Roman period, diaspora has become applied to modern, often forced migrations of people. Diaspora is now commonly used in relation to contexts where cultural assimilation is incomplete and the culture of the originally displaced group, often ethnically identifiable, survives and is actively maintained in the new geographical locale (see Slobin, 2003).

Gilroy has been prominent in theorizing (and, via the impact of his work, popularizing) diaspora, primarily as a central concept to examine how dispersed black people are both unified and differentiated from each other ('the Black Atlantic'). Music provides a significant example of this process, through what Gilroy terms 'diasporic conversations'; as in 'the mutation of jazz and African-American cultural styles in the townships of South Africa and the syncretised evolution of Caribbean and British reggae music and Rastafari culture in Zimbabwe' (Gilroy, 1993: 199). Lipsitz extended diaspora to the global music industry, seeing dispersed peoples acting as 'cross cultural interpreters and analysts' (1994: 7), especially through their use of music.

There has been considerable discussion of the nature of contemporary diasporic 'ethnic' identities and the musical styles associated with them. While such accounts can be celebratory of the resultant hybridized musical styles, they also seek to avoid the fetishization of marginality and the erosion of the frequent distinctions present within such communities. Negus, however, recognizes a common problem that theorists of diaspora have encountered: 'once in circulation, music and other cultural forms cannot remain "bounded" in any one group and interpreted simply as an expression that speaks to or reflects the lives of that exclusive group of people' (1996: 121; on this point, see **black music**).

See also: **globalization**

Further reading: Gilroy (1993); Lipsitz (1994); Mitchell (2001); Slobin (2003); Whiteley *et al.* (2004)

DISCO

A term derived from French 'discothèque' – record library – referring to a club where you dance to records, disco became the label of a style of dance music in the period 1977–83. Internationally, disco was a pervasive and commercially highly successful genre, with prominent variants such as Eurodisco (see Sicko, 1999: 44–8, and the discography included). In the US the genre had a strong initial association with gay bars, and remained a cult there until the huge hit of the film and soundtrack *Saturday Night Fever* (1977).

As a musical form, disco is frequently denigrated. Clarke describes it as a 'Dance fad of the '70s, with profound and unfortunate influence on popular music' ... 'because the main thing was the thump-thump beat, other values could be ignored; producers used drum machines, synthesisers and other gimmicks at the expense of musical values' (Clarke, ed., 1990: 344). Other commentators celebrated the form's vitality and emphasis on dance: 'Superficial, liberating, innovative, reactionary, sensuous, lifeless, disco emerged out of a subculture at the beginning of the 70s, dominated pop music for a few years at the end, and then shrank back ... But during its brief dominance, it restored the dance groove as pop imperative' (Smucker, 1992: 562).

While most disco hit-makers were virtually anonymous, with **producers** to the fore (e.g. Giorgio Moroder), there were a few stars: Labelle, Hot Chocolate, Donna Summer, K.C. & the Sunshine Band, and the Bee Gees. Although disco had faded by the early 1980s, its influence remained an integral part of chart pop, with performers such as the Pet Shop Boys celebrating the disco tradition and their place in it (Butler, 2003). Disco enjoyed something of a mid-1990s revival, helped by a renewed interest in Abba, whose music featured on several hit film soundtracks, such as *Muriel's Wedding* (P.J. Hogan, 1994). In the UK, impetus for the Abba revival also came from various covers and tributes to their songs, such as Erasure's version of 'Take a Chance on Me' (on *Pop! The First 20 Hits* (Sire/Reprise, 1992)) and the success of the **covers** band Bjorn Again. Disco has also been an element in the eclectic make-up of the hybrid metagenre of contemporary **dance music**.

See also: **dance music**

Further reading: Charlton (1994); Dyer (1990); Jones and Kantonen (1999); Smucker (1992)

Listening: Abba, *Abba Gold: Greatest Hits* (Polydor, 1992); Grace Jones, *Warm Leatherette* (Island, 1980); K.C. & the Sunshine Band, *Greatest Hits* (Rhino, 1990); Donna Summer, *Endless Summer: Donna Summer's Greatest Hits* (Polygram, 1994)

DISCOGRAPHY

A discography is a systematic listing of sound recordings, usually in the form of a catalogue. Discographies vary widely in their comprehensiveness and level of detail, depending on the compiler's intent in producing the listing, the information available to him, and the intended readership. Accordingly, they can include (or exclude): details of the recording artist; names of the recording personnel; composer credits; the date and place of the recording (along with the recording studio); the title of the musical work; issue details (the original release, issues for other markets, and reissues); sales data, chart success, and the market value of the recording. Specialist discographies are usually of individual artists, musical genres/styles, or record labels.

The early recording companies were frequently very unsystematic in their cataloguing practices. There was a general lack of catalogues of released recordings, especially from the smaller companies, along with a failure to keep thorough records of releases. There was also the ephemeral nature of such material. This lack of systematic and accessible information on releases made **record collecting** a challenge, and fostered the growth of discography, especially among jazz enthusiasts and record collectors, who popularized the term in the 1930s. In 1934, the French critic Charles Delaunay was the first to publish a comprehensive discography, a word he coined (his *Hot Discography* was published in English in 1936). In 1935 the first such British compilation was published: *Rhythm on Record*, by Hilton Schelman, assisted by Stanley Dance. These two books were a basis for and inspiration to similar later works. Through the later 1920s and through the 1930s, hundreds of discographies of early jazz and jazz-related recordings were produced by collector enthusiasts, often in home-produced magazines, sometimes in the pages of *Melody Maker*,

Hot News, and *Swing Music*. At times, heated arguments raged over attribution and provenance of particular artists and recordings, and the intricacies of various labels' notation/cataloguing practices. This vernacular scholarship provided an essential resource for later major compilations, including those by Brian Rusk in the UK.

Painstaking discographical research and publication was also central to the initial collecting of blues and other 'race' music (Oliver, 2001), and to popular dance music of the 78 rpm era. Jazz and blues discography informed and was extended into rock'n'roll, rock music, and various other genres from the 1960s onward. Examples of contemporary 'rock' discography include the series of volumes by Strong, and the chart tables and listings produced by Whitburn. There are different emphases present in these, compared with their jazz and blues counterparts, with rock and pop discographies more concerned with the life history of the recorded artefact.

Popular music magazines frequently include extensively researched artist, label, or genre retrospectives with accompanying discographies. This is especially so with those aimed at collectors: e.g. the US-based *Goldmine* (1974–) and *Discoveries* (1986–), and the UK-published *Record Collector* (c. 1978–). There is also now a plethora of record collecting guidebooks, often 'doubling' as discographies. Selective discographies, such as the MOJO collection edited by Irvin (2000), contribute to **canon** formation: the identification of which artists/recordings/genres are 'worthy' of being collected, and the relative status of these.

See also: **record collecting; music press**

Further reading: Irvin, ed. (2000); Strong (1998); Whitburn (1988). The US-based monthly ICE lists all current CD releases, and includes recording/selection details on a selection of these, especially retrospective compilations.

DISCOURSE ANALYSIS

At a popular level, discourse refers to a body of meaning associated with a particular topic or field, regardless of the form of its transmission, e.g. medical discourse. Discourse is the domain of language use, especially the common ways of talking and thinking about social issues. Discourse analysis is a method of analysing such patterns of language use, and their social function. While discourse is often manifest in language, it is embedded in organizational and institutional practices. Accordingly, discursive practices are real or material, as well as being embodied in language and function as a form of ideology. They help constitute our personal, individual identity, our subjectivity.

In social science, discourse analysis seeks to tease out the underlying assumptions and belief systems, and their associated meanings, embedded within a particular discourse. This is undertaken through an analysis of various forms of **text,** including documents such as policy statements, novels, and interview transcripts. In post-structuralist social theory, discourse refers to a historically, socially, and institutionally specific structure of meaning(s); statements, terms, categories, concepts, about the nature of individuals and the world they inhabit. While there are dominant discourses, what Foucault terms 'truth generating discourses', discourses are multiple; they offer competing and frequently contradictory ways whereby we give meaning to the world and our social existence within it.

As with other forms of discourse, popular music contains meanings that both reflect and help constitute wider social systems and structures of meaning. There are discourses around many of the terms used to describe the field and its constituent genres (see the discussion under **popular music**). More specifically, discourse analysis has been utilized, at times implicitly rather than directly, to examine popular music: song **lyrics** as performed language; discourses around musical styles and stars, especially in relation to sexuality (e.g. Walser, 1993, on heavy metal as a masculine/male form); DJ talk (see Brand and Scannell, 1991 on the UK *Tony Blackburn Show* in the UK; also Montgomery, 1986; Gill, 1996); and music video (Goodwin, 1993; Vernallis, 2004). There is also a debate about whether music itself can be analysed as a discourse (Shepherd and Wicke, 1999: 144–9).

To take one example of the value of such an approach, Gill used discourse analysis to provide 'a thorough and principled approach to analysing *talk*' (1996: 210); in this case, the responses of male DJs and programme controllers from two commercial radio stations in the UK, to a question about the lack of female DJs, a pertinent issue given male DJs' domination of the airwaves. She observes that a traditional approach to this issue would use attitude surveys, questionnaires, or structured interviews with those responsible for appointment decisions, trying to pinpoint a single answer to why there are so few female DJs. 'Discourse analysis, in contrast takes variability seriously, as something interesting in its own right' (ibid.: 213). This is facilitated by the use of informal interviews, and an analytical approach which sought to tease out the practical ideologies through which the employment of women DJs are understood and legitimized. The interviewees used a range of reasons to account for the lack of women DJs, including women not applying to become DJs; listeners' preference for male presenters; women's lack of the necessary skills; and the unsuitability of womens' voices. 'It is important to note that these were not alternative accounts ... each was drawn on by all or most of the broadcasters at different points in the interviews'. Utilizing discourse analysis, Gill sought not simply to identify the different accounts selectively drawn upon, but 'to examine how they were constructed and made persuasive' (ibid.). Her analysis shows how the broadcasters constructed the problem as lying in women themselves or in the particular wants of the audience. Both of these discursive practices, describing the way the broadcasters' accounts were organized, enabled the broadcasters to present themselves as non-sexist: 'The role of the radio station was made invisible, and discussions of employment practices and institutionalized sexism were conspicuous by their absence' (1996: 217).

Further reading: Potter and Wetherell (1987)

DJ

The disc jockey (DJ) is the person responsible for presenting and playing the music which is a part of radio and music video programming, and central to many clubs, dances, discos, etc. Popular music studies have concentrated on the role of the DJ in the history of radio, especially the emergence of personality radio and the elevation of DJs to **star** status in the 1950s and DJs as central figures in contemporary **club culture**. In each case, the notions of **gatekeeper** and **cultural intermediary** have been used to examine the influence of DJs.

DJs and the history of radio

Initially, music radio announcers were primarily responsible for cueing records and ensuring smooth continuity, and had little input into the determination of radio playlists. The reshaping of radio in the 1950s was a key influence in the advent of **rock'n'roll**, while radio airplay became central to a performer's commercial success. As Barnes observes, hit radio was 'one of America's great cultural inventions', revitalizing a medium threatened by **television** (Barnes, 1988: 9). The DJ emerged as a star figure, led by figures such as Bob 'Wolfman Jack' Smith, Dick Clark, and Alan Freed. Freed's *Morning Show* on WJW in Cleveland in the early 1950s, and his subsequent New York radio programmes and associated live shows, popularized the very term rock'n'roll and helped introduce black **R&B** music to a white audience. The considerable influence wielded by DJs on music radio playlists, and the associated pay-to-play practices, led to official investigations of **payola**. Personality radio and the cult of the **DJ** was very much part of **pirate radio** in the 1960s. The role and status of contemporary radio DJs depends very much on the type and format of the **radio** station.

Further reading: Barnes (1988); Brand and Scannell (1991); Ennis (1992: ch. 5: 'The DJ Takes Over, 1946–1956')

DJs and club culture

When DJs became mixers, they entered the world of musicianship. For example, DJs played a major role in the emergence of the twelve-inch single as a standard industry product amongst United States, then British, record companies in the 1970s. American DJs began mixing seven-inch copies of the same record for prolonged play, then recording their own mixes, firstly on tape then on vinyl, to play in clubs. The practice became sufficiently widespread to make it worthwhile for record companies to cater for this new market. Initially produced for public performance only, twelve-inch singles became retail products from 1978 on, and by the early 1990s represented some 45 per cent of the singles sold (Thornton, 1995). In the process of mixing, DJs created new music, becoming 'turntable musicians'.

The role of the DJ is vital to dance **club culture**. The club atmosphere, mood, or 'vibe' is created in the interaction between the DJ, the crowd, and the physical space which they share. The DJ's choice and sequencing of records, in a dialectic with the mood of the clubbers, is central to this interaction. **House** DJs in the late 1970s took 'the first tentative steps of a development which would eventually transform the DJs role from one of "human jukebox" to a position as the central creative focus of dance music culture' (Kempster, 1996: 11; see also Straw, 2001).

See also: **dance music; radio; payola**

Further reading: Kempster (1996); Reynolds (1998); Straw (2001)

DOCUMENTARIES

'Constructed as a genre within the field of nonfictional representation, documentary has, since its inception, been composed of multiple, frequently linked representational strands' (Beattie, 2004: 2). Popular music documentaries include concert, tour and festival films; profiles of performers, and scenes; and ambitious historical overviews. Such documentaries can be produced for either film or television (as both 'one-offs' and series). The various forms of popular music documentary have served a number of economic and ideological functions. As a form of programming, they create income for their producers and those who screen them, via rights and royalties. They validate and confirm particular musical styles and historical moments in the **history** of popular music as somehow worthy of more 'serious' attention. While celebrating 'youth' and the mythic status of stars, they also confirm their status as 'the other' for critics of these sounds and their performers.

Concert/tour/festival/scene documentaries demonstrate a close link between the documentation of musical performance and observational modes of documentary film making. Referred to in the United States as 'direct cinema', and evident from the early 1960s, these documentaries have a well-established tradition, exemplified in the work of director D.A. Pennebaker (*Don't Look Back* (1966); *Monterey Pop* (1968); and *Down From the Mountain* (2002)). Direct cinema has recently mutated into 'docusoap' and other variants of reality **television**, as in MTV's *The Real World* series (which frequently featured participants who were seeking musical careers), and *Meet the Osbournes*, a fly-on-the-wall depiction of the family life of ageing heavy metal rocker Ozzy Osbourne.

Films of music festivals have consolidated the mythic status of events such as *Monterey Pop* (1968) and, especially, *Woodstock* (1969), with the 1970 film a major box office success. A number of other concert and concert tour films have had a similar but more limited commercial and ideological impact. See e.g. *The Last Waltz* (Martin Scorcese, 1978), a record of the Band's final concert; *Hail, Hail Rock and Roll* (Taylor Hackford, 1987), featuring Chuck Berry and other seminal rock'n'roll performers; *Stop Making Sense* (Jonathon Demme 1984), featuring Talking Heads; Prince's *Sign O' The Times* (Prince, 1987); and Neil Young and Crazy Horse in *Year of the Horse* (1998), directed by Jim Jarmusch. Such films capture particular moments in 'rock history', while at the same time validating particular musical styles and performers. *Stop Making Sense* won the 1984 Best Documentary Award from the US National Society of Film Critics. A record of **new wave** band Talking Heads in concert, the film used material from three Hollywood shows in December 1983. The documentary is shot in a cool, almost classical style, with the unobtrusive camera subservient to the performances. Instead of stage histrionics and overpowering light shows, Demme used minimalist staging, lighting, and presentation. The film helped bring a moderately successful 'cult' band to a broader audience. The problem for film-makers with such projects is that there are only so many things you can do with concert performances, given their restricted ambit, and many of the conventions they rely on have become cinematic cliché, as in *Rattle and Hum* (Phil Joanou, 1988), the film of U2's 1987 *Joshua Tree* tour.

Other documentaries consolidate particular historical moments like the Beatles' first tour of America (*What's Happening! The Beatles in the USA* (2004), directed by Albert and David Maysles); the Rolling Stones' Altamont concert of 1969 (*Gimme Shelter*, 1970) (released on DVD by Criterion in 2000); and Julien Temple's examination of the Sex Pistols phenomenon, including the television interview that sparked off controversy (*The Filth and the Fury* (2000)). Documentaries have also been important in exposing particular scenes, sounds, and performers to a wider audience, as in *The Decline of Western Civiliza-tion, Part One* (1981) on the Los Angeles **punk/hardcore** scene circa 1981, featuring Black Flag, the Circle Jerks, X, and the Germs; its 'sequel', *The Decline of Western Civilization, Part Two: The Metal Years* (1988), featuring Aerosmith, Alice Cooper, Ozzy Osbourne, Kiss, Metallica, and Motörhead; and *Hype* (1996) on the Seattle grunge scene. The success of *Buena Vista Social Club* (1999) introduced Cuban jazz to an international audience, and led to massive sales of the accompanying soundtrack album (which had initially gone largely ignored following its first release in 1996). *Genghis Blues* (2000) consolidated the appeal of **world music**, and *Down From the Mountain* (D.A. Pennebaker, 2002) did the same for contemporary **bluegrass**. Documentaries have reminded us of the role of largely forgotten session musicians and 'house bands', e.g. the Funk Brothers in *Standing in the Shadows of Motown* (Paul Justman, 2002). Other popular music documentaries have celebrated major performers, for instance, the Who in *The Kids Are Alright* (Jeff Stein, 1979; released as a special DVD edition, 2004). As with any genre, the ultimate accolade is parody, best represented by *This is Spinal Tap* (Rob Reiner, 1984).

Documentary series on the history of popular music, made for television, include the BBC and US co-production *Dancing in the Street* (1995); *Walk on By* (2003), a history of songwriting; Ken Burns'

Jazz (2000); and the Australian series *Long Way to the Top* (ABC, 2001). In addition to the income from their initial screenings and international licensing, such series have produced accompanying books (Palmer, 1995), soundtracks, and 'sell through' video/DVD **boxed sets**. Though their selection of material depends heavily on the nature and quality of what is available, such series visually construct particular historical narratives, reframing the past. For example, in the case of *Dancing in the Street* (1995), the emphasis is on 'authentic artists' rather than commercial performers: on the episode 'Hang on to Yourself', Kiss get barely a minute, while 'punk icon' Iggy Pop features throughout. In sum, music documentary history is situated primarily around key performers and styles, a form of **canonization**.

Further reading: Beattie (2004); Corner (2002)

DOO-WOP

Doo-wop is derived from two of the many nonsense syllables sung by back-up vocalists. As a **genre**, doo-wop is primarily equated with the mainly black vocal harmony music of the 1950s, although its origins were in the late 1930s and the ballad style of the Ink Spots. Doo-wop evolved out of the gospel tradition, and was characterized by close (four-part ballad) harmonies. As essentially an **a cappella** style, doo-wop was developed by New York groups, often originally singing on street corners, in the period 1945–55. The songs were relatively simple and extremely formulaic, with a sentimentalized romance as the dominant theme. Pioneer performers included the Ravens, and the Orieles, with their single 'Crying in the Chapel' (1953), the first doo-wop release to gain acceptance with white listeners. Doo-wop spread to other US cities, reaching its zenith in the late 1950s with the Platters, the Clovers, the Coasters, and Dion and the Belmonts.

Gribin and Schiff argue that doo-wop deserves greater recognition for its contribution to **rock** music's development during the 1950s. Groups such as the Drifters and the Coasters added a stronger beat and more pronounced gospel elements, providing a bridge to what became known as **soul** music. The genre did not survive the **British invasion** of the early to mid 1960s, although it remained evident in the work of artists such as the Four Seasons, who enjoyed considerable chart success, 1962–7. The genre enjoyed a brief nostalgic revival in the 1970s with the popularity of groups such as Manhattan Transfer and Sha-Na-Na, whose name is taken from the background harmony of the Silhouettes' earlier doo-wop classic 'Get a Job' (1958). In the 1990s, the influence of doo-wop was evident in the work of performers such as Boyz II Men (sometimes referred to as 'hip-hop doo-wop') and in several of the **boy bands**.

Further reading: Gillet (1983); Gribin and Schiff (1992); Hansen (1992a) (includes a useful discography)

Listening: The Four Seasons, *Anthology* (Rhino, 1988); *The Best of Doo Wop Up Tempo* (Rhino, 1989); Boyz II Men, *Cooleyhighharmony* (Motown, 1991)

DRUM'N'BASS

A variant of **dance music**, which achieved a high profile in the UK music press in the mid-1990s. Originally, the style was called 'jungle', but the racist connotations led to the term's displacement. An eclectic style, 'brought on by the advances and prevalence of digital sampling technology' (Sicko, 1999), drum'n'bass represented the increasing eclecticism and hybridity of contemporary dance music. It drew variously on funk, techno, jazz fusion, house, reggae, and hip-hop. With its high beats per minute (175–85), drum'n'bass was an accelerated form of hip-hop, and regarded as a 'harder' descendant of house and techno music (Sicko, 1999). Leading practitioners included Goldie and Roni Size, while the style was associated with specialist record labels Moving Shadow, Prototype, and, especially significant, Metalheadz.

Further reading: Reynolds (1998); Sicko (1999); Woodstra and Bogdanov, eds (2001) (especially the 'music map', p. 637)

Listening: Breakbeat Science Vol. 1 (Volume/Vital, 1996); Roni Size/Reprazent, *New Forms* (Talkin Loud, 1998); Goldie, *Timeless* (FFRR, 1995)

DUB *see* **reggae**

DUNEDIN SOUND

New Zealand South Island city Dunedin was home to an arguably distinctive **alternative** music sound which developed during the

1980s, associated with the **independent** label Flying Nun, founded in 1981, and later Xpressway, founded in 1988. Leading bands included the Chills, the Verlaines, the Clean, and Toy Love.

The Dunedin sound was generated through a cultural geography of living on the margin, producing a 'mythology of a group of musicians working in cold isolation, playing music purely for the pleasure of it' (McLeay, 1994: 39). As with similar local sounds, there has been debate over the constituent elements, distinctiveness, and coherence of the Dunedin Sound. 'Pure pop melody' and 'guitar jangle' were frequently used descriptors, although in themselves these are hardly geographically distinctive. There was also a tendency, initially at least, towards low-tech production values, and a shared aesthetic which emphasized the primary importance of the song, and valorized the 'roughness' of the music.

For many, especially overseas followers of alternative music, Dunedin and Flying Nun became a metonym for New Zealand music as a whole, although the Flying Nun label embraced a range of performers and styles (see Mitchell, 1996). Flying Nun rarely achieved local commercial success, but built up a considerable reputation in the international indie/alternative scene. The notion of the Dunedin Sound continues to be present in discussions of New Zealand music, although the Flying Nun label has relocated (to Auckland and London), and many of the bands associated with it are not based on 'guitar jangle'.

See also: **locality**

Further reading: McLeay (1994); Mitchell (1996)

Listening: Tuatara, *A Flying Nun Compilation* (Flying Nun, 1985); the Chills, *Solid Gold Hits* (Flying Nun, 1995); the Clean, *Compilation* (Flying Nun/ Homestead, 1986)

EDUCATION

There has been a good deal of discussion of educational issues in popular music studies: the validity and place of popular music within the school and post-school curriculum; how the study of popular music can best be approached, especially the role of 'theory'; and the professional training of musicians and music industry personnel, notably the continuum between formal and informal learning. The relationship between student attitudes towards school and their music preferences is also considered here.

The curriculum status of popular music studies

Popular music can be a subject in its own right, but is more commonly found as a component of other courses. For example, in the school systems of Canada, the UK, the USA, and Australia popular music may be studied within music, social studies, and media studies. In the tertiary sector, it is usually found within departments of music, media/communication studies and cultural studies. Such courses usually emphasize Anglo-American pop/rock music and its associated genres, representing a form of musical hegemony.

At all levels, the subject has usually had to struggle to be accepted as a legitimate educational study. Writing in 1982, Vulliamy and Lee argued that the majority of young people faced a clear opposition between music which is acceptable to the school, usually based in the classical tradition, set against their own (usually popular) musical preferences, which by inference they were led to see as of little value or significance. This situation exacerbated the conflict between the cultural values transmitted through schools and the cultural values of young people. Vulliamy and Lee argued that forms of musical analysis through notation are inappropriate to popular music, which can be legitimized in school by establishing different evaluative criteria (from traditional **musicology**). This is in line with the view that all music is bounded by particular styles and traditions and occurs within a socio-cultural context, as cogently argued by Shepherd *et al.*, (1977). These views have continued to be debated (see the journal *Music Education*, published by Cambridge University Press; Green, 2001).

At tertiary level, popular music has only recently been accorded much recognition within cultural and media studies. The attainment of a certain level of academic credibility for the field is indicated the appointment of professors of popular music studies; the creation and growth of specialist research centres and research archives (e.g. the Institute of Popular Music at Liverpool University); the proliferating tertiary-level courses, both industry-oriented and of a more general media and cultural studies nature; the existence of a number of now well-established academic journals on popular music, considerable cultural journalism in the commercial music press and in fanzines, and an explosion of the critical literature; and the existence, since 1981, of the International Association for the Study of Popular Music.

Pedagogy

Attempts to teach popular music are seen to confront a number of difficulties, both theoretical and practical in nature. There is a tendency to either overtheorize, or not to theorize: 'Theoretical abstractions and rote memorization tends to take students further away from the music itself, while musical transcriptions and technical analyses are scarcely more effective at getting the energy that made the music so exciting to begin with' (Gass, 1991: 731). Accordingly, many commentators consider it necessary to begin with students' own consumption, the context within which it occurs, and the meanings they attach to it. However, to neglect theoretical concerns and terminology is to risk the danger of turning popular music studies into a nostalgic form of populism, largely focused on the products of the record industry and viewing their history as one of shifts in genre popularity and the relative status of musicians. While it is necessary to engage with theory, constantly seeking to demonstrate its links with students' own lives and experiences, this creates its own problems, especially the difficulty of opening popular music up for critical discussion (see Grossberg, 1986). This 1980s discussion has been an ongoing one (see Richards, 1995), and is often evident at popular music studies conferences. A further issue is the balance in tertiary courses, especially those with a vocational aspiration (industry training), between 'academic' knowledge and 'practical' work. This is related to the continuum which exists between formal and informal learning, and the manner in which musicians are socialized into their practices (Green, 2001). An example of this is the development of their skills by songwriters (McIntyre, 2003).

Current 'textbooks' offer various approaches to the study of popular music, emphasizing musicology, usually in a modified form (Brown, 1994; Charlton, 1994); cultural studies/sociology (Shuker, 2001; Negus, 1996; Longhurst, 1995); and an historical/sociological approach (Garofalo, 1997; Friedlander, 1995; Ennis, 1992).

Further reading: Gass (1991); Green (2001); Grossberg (2002); Richards (1995); Tagg (1990)

School commitment and music preferences

During the 1980s, a number of studies established an association between commitment to school and preferences in popular music. For example, Tanner (1981) found that students with a low commitment to school (a Likert-type attitudinal scale of six items was used to judge this) were more likely to favour 'heavy' rock than those with a high school commitment, were correspondingly less committed to 'top forty' rock, and were, as a group, predominantly working class; they also were more likely to be associated with delinquent activity. This relationship between delinquent activities, social class, and school commitment, on the one hand, and the predilection for 'heavy rock' on the other, was 'the clearest association' uncovered by Tanner's study. He plausibly suggested that **heavy metal** provided 'a symbolic rejection of the prevailing values and assumptions of the schooling process', and indicated 'a correspondence between "heavy metal" and a subcultural solution rooted in action physicality and collective solidarity' (Tanner, 1981). In his study of Scandinavian adolescents, Roe (1983) similarly concluded that music functions to symbolically express 'alienation from school', and that low school achievement and a greater preference for 'socially disapproved music' were strongly linked. Subsequent studies have largely confirmed these findings, especially in relation to heavy metal (Arnett, 1996).

Further reading: Christenson and Roberts (1998)

EFFECTS

A major tradition in American media research seeks to identify the specific effects of the media on behaviour, attitudes, and values. This approach is most evident in studies of television, but is also seen in many of the claims made for the negative influence of popular music. Groups such as the Parents Music Resource Center in the United States (see **censorship**) have used 'effects' research to support their arguments.

The effects tradition is based on behaviourism: a major school of psychology, based on stimulus–response theory and the work of B.F. Skinner, behaviourism was developed in the 1920s in the US. Although remaining influential, it has been strongly criticized for its lack of attention to the importance of the complex social situation in which media consumption occurs, the absence of any satisfactory theory of personality, and the neglect of the particular self of the individual consumer. The behaviourist approach reduces the interaction between medium and recipient to a simple model of communication flow, and accordingly fails to offer a satisfactory explanation for the operation of the popular media (Ross and Nightingale, 2003: ch. 3, provides a useful historical overview and informed discussion of effects research).

An example of the use of 'effects research', and the assumptions underpinning it, is the debates surrounding the relationship between popular music and adolescent suicide. During the 1980s, there were several celebrated court cases in the United States in which unsuccessful attempts were made to hold popular music responsible for teenage 'rock suicides'. The main targets were **heavy metal** performers Ozzy Osbourne (especially his song 'Suicide Solution' on *Blizzard of Ozz* (Jet, 1981)), and Judas Priest (and their album *Stained Glass* (Columbia, 1978)). Similar arguments resurfaced following a spate of teenage suicides in the New York and New Jersey areas, and 'copycat' suicides after Kurt Cobain's suicide in 1994. These featured prominently in the popular press, where objective reasons for such tragedies were ignored in favour of more sensational accounts. Heavy metal and **gothic rock** were the main genres held accountable by critics. While they did not always reach the courts, similar claims and arguments about a connection between adolescent suicide and genres such as heavy metal have been evident in other countries.

The relationship between popular music and behaviour in such cases, and the public/press response to them, have been the subject of a number of academic studies (on the US cases, see Gaines, 1991; Walser, 1993; Weinstein, 1991a; Shuker, 2001 gives an account of the New Zealand experience). These consider how the press coverage of 'rock suicides' has treated them as a form of **moral panic**, and critically examine the claims of causality, perceived subliminal messages in the music, and the preferred readings of songs such as Osbourne's 'Suicide Solution' present in such cases. These studies largely conclude, along with more balanced press accounts, that popular music could hardly be held accountable (at least solely) for such suicides. Teenagers attempt suicide for complex and frequently interrelated reasons: growing unemployment, family breakdown, lack of communication in families, peer pressure, sexuality, and low self-esteem. In the case of the suicides reported by the press, it is possible that the music may have acted as a final catalyst, contributing to depression. More likely, however, is that the youth involved were already depressed or psychotic.

Effects research has also been prominent in the study of 'television violence', including the analyses of **music video**. Aikat (2004) surveys this body of work, to situate his investigation of the incidence and extent of violent content in music videos on four leading music television websites (BET.com; country.com; MTV.com; and VH1.com). He found that 'audiences for hip-hop/rap and hard-rock videos are the most likely to be exposed to violence, while audiences for adult-contemporary, country, and R&B music videos are least likely to see violence when viewing online music videos' (2004: 235). This was a finding 'of particular concern when considering that music videos generally are targeted toward younger audiences' and music video content may be capable of guiding adolescent behaviour (234). However, the qualified nature of his conclusions illustrates the limitations of studies drawing primarily on content analysis: 'The results here suggest that *at least some* young audience members who are frequently exposed to music videos *could be* adversely affected by their exposure, as previous effects research has concluded' (ibid.; my emphases).

See also: **audiences; gothic rock; heavy metal**

Further reading: Critcher (2003); Ross and Nightingale (2004)

EPS *see* **singles**

ETHNICITY; RACE

While the term 'race' is still used in popular discourse, and in some academic work, it has been superseded by the more correct term, 'ethnicity'. 'Race' has historically often been considered a biological concept, whereby humans can be classified according to a number of physical criteria. This is an untenable and ideologically motivated view, associated with *racism*. 'Ethnicity' is defined on the basis of shared cultural characteristics for a group of people, based in part on cultural self-identification, but can also be an overlay of cultural criteria on to perceived racial characteristics. There is considerable debate around both terms, which should be considered *social* categories.

Ethnicity has been an important consideration in virtually all aspects of popular music studies, particularly in regard to **black music** in the US. For the sake of brevity and focus, I have concentrated on the American debates, but popular music is involved in the social processes of 'racialization' internationally, and can both cross and reinforce ethnic/racist boundaries. (The following topics are covered separately and only summary reference is made to them here – see the related entries.)

(1) The lack of black ownership of record companies (with a few exceptions, notably Berry Gordy and **Motown**), or representation in management, has been critiqued and debated, along with the **marketing** of black music, and the use of racist practices; e.g. the use of the term 'race music' to describe **R&B** (see Garofalo, 1994; George, 1989).

(2) The **appropriation** of black music is a contentious issue, as is the status of **crossover**. A considerable body of writing, much of it historical, has examined these issues in the history of American popular music, for instance, Neal, 1999 and Shaw, 1986.

(3) The use of the term **black music**, and the associated notion of an identifiable 'black voice' in vocal styles, is sharply contested (Tagg, 1989).

(4) Studies of the **consumption** of popular music in ethnically mixed or diverse populations and communities show that blacks are more likely (then their white or Asian counterparts) to favour 'black' music genres, most notably **soul**, **R&B**, **blues**, **reggae**, and **rap**. These genres have become virtually synonymous with 'black music' and black culture, notably among black adolescents and young adults. However, as the mainstreaming of **reggae**, **rap**, and hip-hop demonstrates, their following is hardly confined to black populations alone.

Further reading: Gracyk (2001); Hebdige (1990); Jones (1988); Oliver, ed. (1990); Rose (1994)

ETHNOGRAPHY

A research method initially developed in social anthropology, ethnography has been utilized in a variety of disciplines. In the anthropological sense, ethnography refers to the description and analysis of a way of life, or **culture**, and is based on direct observation of behaviour in particular social settings. In contemporary usage, ethnography has become a broad term, associated with a range of methods, including case study, participant observation, life history, and symbolic interactionism. There is considerable debate over the status of ethnography as a form of knowledge and the various approaches to 'field work'. In the traditional, anthropological sense, ethnography involves extensive and intimate involvement in community studies, but much contemporary 'ethnography' is limited to forms of participant observation. Ethnography was increasingly utilized in the **cultural studies** 'turn' towards the study of the 'active' audience in the 1980s.

Cohen (1993) has argued that popular music studies (at least in Western contexts) lack ethnographic data and micro-sociological detail, especially in relation to the grassroots of the industry, 'the countless, as yet unknown bands struggling for success at a local level', and the actual process of music-making. The following decade has seen a variety of studies along such lines, drawing on various forms of ethnography: community studies, such as Cohen's work in Liverpool (1991) and Finnegan's examination of music-making in Milton Keynes (1989); studies of the geographic popularization of specific genres, along with their local music scenes, as in Guilbault on Caribbean zouk (1993); investigations of popular music and youth cultures and **subcultures** (e.g. Fornas *et al.*, 1995 on rock music and Swedish youth; Takasugi, 2003 on Honolulu's underground scene); and studies of the process of music-making and becoming a musician, notably the classic studies by Becker on **jazz** musicians (1997) and Bennett on the musical socialization of **rock** musicians (1990).

Accounts of music-making in non-Western settings are more numerous, and there is a rich tradition of ethnography within **ethnomusicology**.

Recent interest in ethnographic approaches, and qualitative approaches, marks the continued shift within cultural and media studies, from the global to the local, and to an emphasis on the study of consumption and audiences.

See also: **ethnomusicology; youth subcultures**

Further reading: Cohen (1991, 1993); Finnegan (1989); Guilbault (1993); Keil and Field (1994); Kruse (1993); O'Connor (2002)

ETHNOMUSICOLOGY

A division of musicology which emphasizes the study of music in its cultural context: the anthropology of music. The term ethnomusicology gained currency in the mid-1950s, replacing the traditional 'comparative musicology'. 'Ethnomusicology includes the study of folk music, Eastern art music and contemporary music in oral tradition as well as conceptual issues such as the origins of music, musical change, music as symbol, universals in music, the function of music in society, the comparison of musical systems and the biological basis of music and dance' (Myers, 1992). This broad scope aside, the main areas of study in ethnomusicology have been music in oral tradition and living musical systems, usually in non-Western settings or in relation to indigenous people in Western societies, e.g. the American Indians, Australian Aboriginals, and the New Zealand Maori, with particular interest in the relationship of cultural context and musical style. Fieldwork has been the main research method, using various forms of **ethnography**, and with considerable use of recordings and written notation. While historically the field was split between **musicology** and anthropology, the two strands fused in the 1980s, as 'interest shifted from pieces of music to processes of musical creation and performance – composition and improvisation – and the focus shifted from collection of repertory to examination of these processes' (Myers, 1992). Recently, Lysloff and Gay (eds, 2003: ch. 1) have argued for a more contemporary oriented 'ethnomusicology of technology, an ethnographic study with emphasis placed on techno-logical impact and change'.

A fascinating example of ethnomusicology is Neuenfeldt's edited collection (1997), tracing the changing place of the didgeridoo in Australian Aboriginal culture from a range of musical, cultural, and sociological standpoints.

See also: **ethnography; folk culture**

Further reading: *Ethnomusicology* (journal); Lysloff and Gay, eds (2003); Myers (1992); *The Yearbook for Traditional Music*; Neuenfeldt (1997); Steingress (2003)

EXPERIMENTAL *see* **avant-garde**

FANS; FANDOM; AFICIONADOS

Popular music fans are people who avidly follow the music, and lives, of particular performers/musical genres, with various degrees of enthusiasm and commitment. Fandom is the collective term for the phenomenon of fans and their behaviour: concert-going, record collecting, putting together scrapbooks, filling bedroom walls with posters, and discussing the star with other fans. Music industry practices help create and support fandom; record labels and the artists them-selves have frequently supported official fan clubs and appreciation societies. Many fan clubs (especially those associated with the Beatles and Elvis Presley) conduct international conventions, even well after the performers celebrated are dead, or groups have disbanded

Writing in 1991, Lewis correctly observed that while fans are the most visible and identifiable of **audiences**, they 'have been overlooked or not taken seriously as research subjects by critics and scholars' and 'maligned and sensationalized by the popular press, mistrusted by the public' (Lewis, 1992: 1). Although there has been considerable study of fandom since Lewis wrote, and academic discussions emphasize a less stereotyped image, the popular view of fans has arguably not changed much. This situation reflects the traditional view of fandom, which situates it in terms of pathology and deviance, and reserves the label 'fans' for teenagers who are generally presented as avidly and uncritically following the latest pop sensation. (An early example of such fans were the 'bobby soxers', Frank Sinatra's adolescent female fans in the 1940s.) These fans are often denigrated in popular music literature and, indeed, by many followers of popular music. Their behaviour is often described as a form of pathology, and the terms applied to it have clear connotations of condemnation and undesirability: 'Beatlemania', 'teenyboppers', and 'groupies'. The last can be considered an extreme form of such fan, moving beyond vicarious identification and using their sexuality to get close to the **stars** – even if the encounter is usually a fleeting one.

Fandom is now best regarded as an active process: a complex phenomenon, related to the formation of social identities, especially sexuality. Fandom offers its participants membership of a community not defined in traditional terms of status. Fiske sees it as the register of a subordinate system of cultural **taste**, typically associated with cultural forms that the dominant value system denigrates, including popular music. Grossberg defines fandom as a distinct 'sensibility', in which the pleasure of consumption is superseded by an investment in difference: 'A sensibility is a particular form of engagement or mode of operation. It identifies the specific sorts of effects that the elements within a context can produce; it defines the possible relations between texts and audiences located within the spaces' (Grossberg, 1992b: 54). Fandom is located within a sensibility in which the fan's relation to cultural texts 'operates in the domain of affect or mood' (ibid.: 56; and see **affect**). Pleasure and difference are central to fandom.

Hills distinguishes 'cult fandom' as a form of cultural identity, partially distinct from that of the 'fan' in general, related to the duration of the fandom concerned, especially in the absence of new or 'official' material in the originating medium or persona (Hills, 2002: x).

Pop fans' commitment may last only as long as an often brief career, as with the Spice Girls, whereas the fans of performers such as Bruce Springsteen (Cavicchi, 1998) maintain their fandom over time, as do the Deadheads (see below).

A distinction can also be made between fans and aficionados, with the latter more focused on the music, and with different affective investments present. Aficionados are those who see themselves as 'serious' devotees of particular musical styles or performers. They are fans in terms of the word's origins in 'fanatic', but their emotional and physical investments are different from mainstream 'fans', as are the social consumption situations in which they operate. Aficionados' intense interest is usually at more of an intellectual level and focused on the music per se rather than the persona(e) of the performer(s). Aficionados prefer to describe themselves as 'into' particular performers and genres, and often display impressive knowledge of these. They are characterized by what can be termed 'secondary involvement' in music: the seeking out of rare releases, such as the picture discs and bootlegs; the reading of fanzines in addition to commercial music magazines; regular concert-going; and an interest in record labels and producers as well as performers. Aficionados frequently become record collectors on a large scale, supporting an infrastructure of specialist and second-hand record shops. At times, their **record collecting** can become a fixation bordering on addiction. They may also be involved in music-oriented **subcultures**.

Fans, in the more widely accepted pejorative sense of the term, will collect the records put out by their favoured stars, but these are only one aspect of an interest which focuses rather on the image and persona of the star. For example, studies of the post-punk British 'new pop' performers of the 1980s (Culture Club, Duran Duran, Wham!, Spandau Ballet, Nick Kershaw, and Howard Jones), showed how they drew upon a fanatical female following. As such, fans' consumption becomes a significant part of the star system. These fans represent a merchandising dream, buying up practically anything associated with the group, with their support in extreme cases bordering on the pathological. At the same time, such 'Pop fans aren't stupid. They know what they want. And ultimately, all the media manipulation in the world isn't going to sell them something they haven't got any use for' (Rimmer, 1985: 108). This is to argue that whatever the press of 'context' – the intentions of the industry, the pop press, and musicians themselves – meaning in the music is ultimately created by the consumers. Fans are often fiercely partisan. Such strong identification with the star becomes a source of pleasure and empowerment. The discomfort or even pain involved is an important part of this, since it is its resolution – or, at least, the possibility of resolution – which provides the pleasure.

For many fans, their idols function almost as religious touchstones, helping them to get through their lives and providing emotional and even physical comfort. Elvis scholars have debated whether Elvis fandom is best understood as a secular form of religion, with Elvis acting as a religious icon (Doss, 1999; Duffett, 2003). Duffett sees this as too simplistic, arguing that such an emphasis means 'we miss the complexity, the diversity of investments, and the rich array of informal institutions that support fans' interests' (Duffett, 2003: 520).

In fandom 'moods and feelings become organized and particular objects or personas take on significance. By participating in fandom, fans construct coherent identities for themselves. In the process, they enter a domain of cultural activity of their own making which is, potentially, a source of empowerment in struggles against oppressive ideologies and the unsatisfactory circumstance of everyday life' (Lewis, 1992: 3). Most fans see themselves as part of a wider community, even if their own fan practices are 'private', individual activities undertaken alone.

Examples of such empowerment are as diverse as heavy metallers, and fans of the Bay City Rollers, the Grateful Dead (deadheads), and Bruce Springsteen. There is an assertion of female solidarity evident in the activities of girl fans, e.g. those of the Spice Girls (see **dance pop**). Similar cultural self-assertion is present in the knowledge of the associated music in many adherents of youth subcultures.

The deadheads, fans of the American band the Grateful Dead, provide an example of long-term fandom. The band were leading figures in San Francisco's psychedelic scene since the early 1960s, and continued to tour and record extensively until the death of band leader Jerry Garcia in 1996. Deadheads attended large numbers of the band's concerts, often making extensive tape compilations of the various performances, or purchasing **bootlegs** of such performances, with the band unofficially condoning such practices. The Grateful Dead's **concerts** functioned as secular rituals for the band's hardcore followers, who were also frequently identified with the broadly counter-culture values and style of the band. This last point led some municipalities to ban Dead concerts, because of the 'undesirable elements' attending (Sardiello, 1994).

Beyond possible empowerment, popular music fandom as a form of cultural activity has a number of pleasurable dimensions common to both fans and aficionados: dance and its associated rituals of display and restraint; the anticipatory pleasure of attending a concert or playing a new purchase; the sheer physical pleasure of handling records/tapes/CDs; the pleasure of finding that rare item in a second-hand store bin; and the intellectual and emotional pleasures associated with 'knowing' about particular artists and genres valued by one's peers and associates. Fans actively interact with **texts** 'to actively assert their mastery over the mass-produced texts which provide the raw materials for their own cultural productions and the basis for their social interactions', becoming 'active participants in the construction and circulation of textual meanings' (Jenkins, 1997: 508). This active engagement with texts has been termed 'textual poaching' (drawing on the work of de Certeau, who applied the term 'poaching' to such practices by readers).

The rise of interactive media (e-mail, listservs, and the Internet) have added a new dimension to fandom, aiding in the formation and maintenance of fan bases for performers and musical styles. Fandom is a central theme in some popular music fictional narratives, and in many films, e.g. *Almost Famous* (2002).

See also: **cultural capital**

Further reading: Hills (2002); Lewis (1992); Ross and Nightingale (2003: ch. 6). Arguably the best accounts of fandom are those which document the perspective of the fans themselves: Aizlewood (1994); Cavicchi (1998); Cline (1992); Klosterman (2002); Smith (1995); Vermorel and Vermorel (1985)

FANZINES

Fanzines are a form of publication, but they are considered separately from the bulk of the **music press** because of their largely non-commercial nature. Fanzines are part of alternative publishing, which is characterized by the centrality of amateurs, readers as writers; non-mainstream channels of distribution; a non-profit orientation; and a network based on non-professional expertise from a wide base of enthusiasts (Atton, 2001).

Produced by one person, or a group of friends, working from their homes, popular music fanzines are usually concentrated totally on a particular artist or group, and are characterized by a fervour bordering on the religious: 'Fanzines accumulate rock facts and gossip not for a mass readership but for a small coterie of cultists, and they are belligerent about their music' (Frith, 1983: 177). This stance can be a reactionary one, preserving the memory of particular artists/styles, but is more usually progressive. As Savage acutely observes, fanzines were historically tied to the English radical tradition of pamphleteering. Many of the original **punk** fanzines were characterized by a broadly leftist cultural politics, challenging their readers to take issue with the views presented by bastions of the status quo and reasserting the revolutionary potential of rock. Fanzines like *Crawdaddy* in the 1960s and *Sniffin' Glue* in the 1970s had tremendous energy, reflecting the vitality of live performances and emergent scenes.

The initial impact of punk rock was aided by a network of fanzines and their enthusiastic supporters. Savage argues that in the early days of punk in the UK, nobody was defining 'punk' from within: 'the established writers were inevitably compromised by age and the minimal demands of objectivity required by their papers. The established media could propagandize and comment, but they could not dramatize the new movement in a way that fired people's imagination' (Savage, 1991: 200). With photocopying cheap and accessible for the first time, the fanzines were a new medium tailor made for the values of punk, with its do-it-yourself ethic and associations of street credibility, and there was an explosion of the new form. These fanzines provided a training ground for a number of music journalists (e.g. Paul Morley, Jon Savage, and Lester Bangs), and in some cases useful media expertise for those who, taking to heart their own rhetoric of 'here's three chords, now form a band', subsequently did just that. Fanzine producers/writers did not have to worry about deadlines, censorship, or subediting, and 'even the idea of authorship was at issue, as fanzines were produced anonymously or pseudonymously by people trying to avoid discovery by the dole or employers' (Savage, 1991: 279). Fanzine readers tend to actively engage with the publication: they debate via the 'letters to the editor', contribute reviews of recordings and concerts, provide discographies, and even interviews with performers.

A number of studies have demonstrated the value of fanzines to producing and maintaining particular musical styles and scenes. The growth of the audience for **heavy metal** in the 1980s was accompanied by a proliferation of metal fanzines, which played an important commercial role in the absence of radio airplay for metal and the hostility of the mainstream press toward it. These metal fanzines create an information network connecting fans and bands globally. As with fanzines in other youth subcultures, they were 'characterized by a passionate, almost proselytizing, tone. Fanzine editors adhere *fanatically* to the metal conventions, standards, and practices' (Weinstein, 1991a: 178). Fanzines have been integral to the development and popularization of alternative **scenes**, as with Seattle in the early 1990s. In the case of progressive rock, fanzines maintain interest long after the genre had been discarded by the mainstream (Atton, 2000). There was a mushrooming of UK club fanzines in the early 1990s, linking a network stretching from Manchester to London (Thornton, 1995).

Despite their essentially non-commercial and often ephemeral nature, fanzines remain a significant part of the popular music scene. They represent a cultural space for the creation of a community of interest. The **Internet** has provided a new medium for the international dissemination of fanzines; through their 'printing' of contemporary concert reviews and tour information, such 'e-zines' have an immediacy that provides a form of virtual socialization for fans.

See also: **music press; punk**

Further reading: Atton (2001); Gorman, 2001; Savage (1991); Weinstein (2000). For reviews of current fanzines, see *Record Collector* magazine (UK)

FASHION

Fashion is central to popular music. Music preferences and the status of genres are subject to fluctuation in critical and commercial popularity, with changing fashions related to shifts in the constitution of the genre, its audience, the music industry, and social trends. The music aside, genres can be in part based around fashions and style. Their performers and their fans present, adopt, and popularize particular clothing and hair fashions; as did the British new romantics of the 1980s. This process is clearly evident in the styles of youth **subcultures**. While fashion and style are indicative of individual and group subjectivities, and serve to demarcate them from other styles and the 'mainstream', they are subject to commodification; e.g. the **'grunge** look' was the subject of major spreads in the fashion press in 1992–3. Particular historical moments and locations can be closely identified with fashion, as in 'Swinging London' in the 1960s, centred around a scene including rock stars (notably the Beatles and the Rolling Stones), film directors, fashion designers (Mary Quant), and photographers (David Bailey).

Further reading: Ash and Wilson (1992); Levy (2003); McRobbie (1988); the contemporary music press and lifestyle magazines, e.g. *The Face* (before its demise in April 2004), *i-D*, *Sleazenation*, etc.

FEMINISM

Feminism can best be considered as a body of social theory, with a number of distinct strands, or 'schools', each associated with different theoretical assumptions and political agendas: liberal, Marxist, radical, psychoanalytic, socialist, existentialist, postmodern, etc. (for a useful overview, see Tong, 1989). Feminism has most notably informed media and cultural studies through considerations of representation, the proportion and role of women in the media industries, and gender as a crucial aspect of audience subjectivities.

Studies of the following aspects evident in popular music studies have taken a feminist perspective, or drawn on it in their analysis (these are only alluded to here; see the entries mentioned):

(1) The analysis of **stars**; e.g. Madonna has been the focus of a range of feminist readings.

(2) The relationship of girls (and women) to **fandom, teeny-bopper** culture, and **MTV**.

(3) The representation of women in **music video**, and the nature of the gaze (usually constructed as male) of the viewer of such texts.

(4) General studies of women in the **music industry**, especially the experiences of female **musicians** who have struggled against the patriarchal and masculinist structures and assumptions which feminist writers see as dominating much popular music.

(5) The treatment of women within the **history** of popular music, especially the marginalization of female performers, and their stereotypical representation.

(6) The relationship between gender, sexuality, and particular genres, most notably **rock**, **country**, and **disco**. One aspect of this is the emergence of a 'queer musicology'.

See also: **gender**

Further reading: Carson *et al.* (2004); Gracyk (2000); O'Brien (2002); Reynolds and Press (1995); Schwichtenberg, ed. (1993); Wald (2002)

FESTIVALS

A festival is a concert, usually outdoors, often held over several days. There is an established historical tradition of popular music festivals, with regular events such as the Newport Folk and Jazz Festival and the New Orleans Mardi Gras in the US, and the UK's Cambridge Folk Festival. Festivals play a central role in popular music mythology. They keep traditions alive, maintaining and expanding their audience base, legitimizing particular forms of that tradition, and giving its performers and fans a sense of shared, communal identity.

A number of festivals at the end of the 1960s and in the early 1970s helped create the notion of a youth-oriented rock **counter-culture** while confirming its commercial potential: Monterey, 1967; Woodstock, 1969; the Isle of Wight, 1970. The other side of the 1960s rock ideology was revealed in the violence at the Rolling Stones free concert at Altamont, near San Francisco, at the end of their 1969 tour of the United States. The 1980s saw the reassertion of the music festival, with the success – both financially and as ideological touchstones – of the politically motivated 'conscience concerts': Live Aid, 1985, and the various Amnesty International concerts. The Knebworth and WOMAD (the World of Music, Arts and Dance, begun in 1982) concerts have become an established feature of the UK popular music scene, with WOMAD being exported to Australia, New Zealand, Denmark, Spain, and Italy. WOMAD has helped **world music** gain mainstream exposure, although in a commodified manner: 'a kind of commercial aural travel-consumption, where the festival, with its collections of "representative" musicians, assembled from "remote" corners of the world, is a (very) late-twentieth-century version of the Great Exhibitions of the nineteenth century' (Hutnyk, 1997: 108).

A summer festival season is now a feature of the UK, Europe, and North American music calendar. The festivals usually include a range of performers, often spread across several days on multiple stages. In the UK during June–July 2004, for instance, there were the Carling Weekends in Leeds and Reading, headlined by Green Day, the Darkness, and the White Stripes; Guildfest, with Blondie, Simple Minds, and UB40; and Finsbury Park, London, featuring Bob Dylan. In the face of such a range of choices facing fans, festivals often place an emphasis on a particular musical style; a grouping of artists aimed at attracting a particular fan constituency. Festivals are big business: Bonnaroo in Tennessee, in June 2003, featured sixty-eight acts, and attracted 80,000 fans (*Rolling Stone*, 24 July 2003: 21). Internationally, local communities are using (usually smaller-scale) music festivals as a form of cultural tourism.

Surprisingly, given their scale and significance, festivals have received only limited attention within popular music studies. In addition to their economic importance, music festivals, as a form of extended **concert**, reinforce popular music personae, creating icons and myths in the process. The performers are made 'accessible' to those attending the concert, and, increasingly with large-scale festivals via satellite television, as with Woodstock 94, to a national and even a worldwide audience. At the same time as it forms a temporary community, joined in celebration and homage to the performers/the genre, the festival audience is being created as a commodity. If it attracts the projected audience, the festival is a major commercial enterprise, with on-site sales of food and souvenirs, the income from the associated television broadcasts via satellite to a global audience/market, and the subsequent 'live' recordings, e.g. Knebworth and Rock in Rio.

See also: **concerts; documentaries**

Further reading: Hutnyk (1997); Morthland (1992c); Schowalter (2000); Taylor (1985)

FICTION

Popular music offers to musicians and listeners a form of fictional narrative, presented through songs. This tradition is most fully present in the folk, country, pop, and blues genres. For example, in pop, a major form of song narrative is love – celebrated; thwarted; unrequited; lost and found; found, lost, and found again. Working within generic forms, the work of singer-songwriters is located primarily as a form of storytelling. Part of the appeal of such song narratives is the sense of identification and associated pleasure they create for listeners.

Popular music has also provided a source of inspiration and theme for prose fiction; sometimes based (loosely) on the author's own experience in music, the music press, or associated lifestyles. A major theme is the role of popular music in adolescent rites of passage and subcultures. Examples of this are Colin McInnes, *Absolute Beginners* (1959) (jazz and rock'n'roll); Irvine Welsh, *Trainspotting* (1993), and Jim Carroll, *The Basketball Diaries* (1978) (punk/alternative); Jack Kerouac, *On the Road* (1957) (the beats and jazz). The 'rock lifestyle' and the pressures of touring and fame are the focus in Bruce Thomas' *The Big Wheel* (1991); Nik Cohn's *I am Still the Greatest says Johnny Angelo* (1967), and Ray Connolly's *Stardust* (1974). **Fandom** is central to Nick Hornby's *High Fidelity* (1996), Linda Jarvin's *Rock n Roll Babes from Outer Space* (1996), and Jenny Fabian and Johnny Byrne's *Groupie* (1969). In the late 1980s, the 'ecstasy novel', linked to the **dance music** scene, became fashionable (e.g. *Disco Biscuits* (1987), a collection of short stories edited by Sarah Campion; Alan Warner, *Morvern Callar* (1987)). Most recently, there is what reviewers have termed the 'sex and hip-hopping novel', exemplified by Erica Kennedy's *Bling* (2004).

Such work has in turn frequently been the basis for feature **films**, such as *Absolute Beginners* (Julien Temple, 1986) and *High Fidelity* (Stephen Frears, 2000). This media cross-fertilization has been significant in exposing particular texts to a wider audience, albeit in different forms and contexts. Despite their arguable status as a literary subgenre, these and similar novels have been largely neglected in popular music studies.

FILM

Film has had an important relationship to popular music. Early silent films often had a live musical accompaniment (usually piano), and with the 'talkies' musicals became a major film genre in the 1930s and continued to be important into the 1960s. Composers and musicians, primarily those who were **stars**, provided a source of material for these films, as did Broadway musicals. The various genres of popular music, its fans and performers have acted as a rich vein of colourful, tragic, and salutary stories for film-makers. A new form of musical, the 'rock musical', played an important part in establishing **rock'n'roll** in the mid-1950s. Allied with such musicals were youth movies, with a range of subgenres, and various types of music **documentaries**. Over the past thirty years or so, considerable synergy has been created between the music and film industries, with film **soundtracks** representing another stream of revenue for recordings, including the **back catalogue**, and helping to promote contemporary releases.

The discussion here deals with mainstream feature film and popular music, the classic Hollywood musicals, and the popular/rock musicals that followed. (Popular music documentaries and soundtracks warrant separate treatment.) In each case, the historical development of the form or genre is sketched, and an attempt made to establish its central themes and conventions, and how these create meaning for the viewing/listening audience. Given the vast scope of the topic, the exploration can be only preliminary.

The classic Hollywood musical

The musical is a hybrid film genre, descended from European operetta and American vaudeville and the music hall. While *The Jazz Singer* (Alan Crosland, 1927) was the first feature film with sound, the first 'all-talking, all-singing, all dancing' musical was *The Broadway Melody* (Harry Beaumont, 1929), which was important also for establishing the tradition of the backstage musical. The musical soon became regarded as a quintessentially American or Hollywood genre, associated primarily with the Warner and MGM studios, and RKO's pairing of Fred Astaire and Ginger Rogers. A major source of Hollywood's musicals was New York's Broadway (see **musicals**).

Early 'classic' musicals had simple even naive plots, promoting 'a gospel of happiness' (Hayward, 1996: 235), and were mainly perceived as vehicles for song and **dance**. The routines and performance of these became increasingly complex, culminating in the highly stylized films of Busby Berkeley. *The Wizard of Oz* (Victor Fleming, 1939) introduced a new musical formula, combining youth and music. Other new forms of the musical were introduced during the 1940s, including composer biographies, and biographical musicals of 'showbiz' stars. The vitality and audience appeal of the musical continued into the 1950s, with contemporary urban musicals such as *An American in Paris* (Vincent Minnelli, 1951), which portrayed the vitality of the Paris music scene, with a cast including musical stars Frank Sinatra and Bing Crosby.

'The period 1930–1960, despite some severe dips, marked the great era of the Hollywood musical' (Hayward, 1996: 239). Although the 1960s did see several blockbuster musicals, notably *The Sound of Music* (Robert Wise, 1965), the heyday of the classic musical had passed, with fewer Broadway hits now making it to the screen. The 1960s saw a move towards greater realism in the musical, exemplified by *West Side Story* (Robert Wise, Jerome Robbins, 1961), an updated version of *Romeo and Juliet*. In the late 1960s and through the 1970s, the classic Hollywood musical was primarily kept alive by the films of Barbra Streisand (e.g. *Funny Girl* (William Wyler, 1968)). Subgenres such as the performer biography still appeared (e.g. *Lady Sings the Blues* (Sydney Furie, 1972)), along with the occasional backstage musical (*Fame* (Alan Parker, 1980)). The classical musical's place was taken by a plethora of new forms associated with the popular musical genres spawned by the advent of **rock'n'roll**.

The classic musicals were a narcissistic and exhibitionist genre, extremely self-referential: 'the general strategy of the genre is to provide the spectator with a utopia through the form of entertainment. The entertainment is the utopia' (Haywood: 241), which is constituted and characterized by energy, abundance, intensity, community, and transparency. Pleasure, especially the visual enjoyment of the dance, is derived from both female and male forms. Ideologically, the genre is selling marriage, gender fixity, communal stability, and the merits of capitalism. Classic musicals are situated around a series of binary oppositions, most notably the duality of male and female, which it ultimately resolves, and work versus entertainment. These codes and conventions were questioned by the popular musicals of the 1950s and beyond as discussed in the next section.

Popular/rock musicals

Films dealing in some way with popular music, or drawing on it for their soundtrack, are frequently treated as a generic group. Szatz calls them 'popular musicals', although this term could apply equally to their historical predecessors, and they are also accorded the more appropriate label 'rock film'. There is now a substantial body of such films, including a number of identifiable subgenres, with a considerable literature on them (see the extensive bibliography in Cooper, 1992; also the filmography in Romney and Wootton, 1995) and the discussion here is highly selective.

During the 1950s the decline of the Hollywood studio system and a dwindling cinema audience led to the need to more systematically target particular audience **demographics**. Hollywood linked up with the record industry to target youth with a spate of teenage musicals. Many of these starred Elvis Presley, who 'sold sex' through his song and dance routines in films such as *Jail House Rock* (Richard Thorpe, 1957). *Blackboard Jungle* (Richard Brooks, 1954) used the new genre of **rock'n'roll** to symbolize adolescent rebellion against the authority of the school. Most early popular musicals had basic plots involving the career of a young rock performer: *Rock Around the Clock* (Fred Sears, 1955), *Don't Knock the Rock* (Fred Sears, 1956), and *The Girl Can't Help It* (Frank Tashlin, 1957). These were frequently combined with the other stock form, films serving purely as contrived vehicles for their real-life stars. Most of Elvis Presley's movies, from *Love Me Tender* (Robert Webb, 1956) onward, were of this order, while British examples include Cliff Richard in *The Young Ones* (Sydney Furie, 1961), and Tommy Steele in *The Tommy Steele Story* (Gerard Bryant, 1957).

Any interest such films retain is largely due to their participants' music rather than their acting talents, though they did function as star vehicles for figures like Presley. In helping establish an identity for rock'n'roll, the teenage musicals placed youth in opposition to adult authority, and for conservatives confirmed the 'folk devil' image of fans of the new genre, associating them with juvenile delinquency, a major concern internationally through the 1950s. Thematically, however, the popular musicals actually stressed reconciliation between generations and classes, with this acting as a point of narrative closure at the film's ending. Such musicals also helped create an audience and a market for the new musical form, particularly in countries distant from the initial developments. These related roles continued to be in evidence in the subsequent development of the popular/rock musical.

British **beat music** and the **British invasion** of the early 1960s were served up in a number of films. Gerry and the Pacemakers brought a taste of the moment to a broader audience with *Ferry Across the Mersey* (J. Summers, 1964). This stuck to what had already become a standard formula – struggling young band makes good after initial setbacks – which was only shaken when the Beatles enlisted director Richard Lester to produce the innovative and pseudo-biographical *A Hard Day's Night* (1964). Along with Lester's *Help* (1965), this consolidated the group's market dominance, and extended the rock film genre into new and more interesting anarchic forms. In the mid- to late 1960s, with the emergence of the **counter-culture**, popular music was a necessary backdrop and a cachet of cultural authenticity for films such as *Easy Rider* (Dennis Hopper, 1969) and *The Graduate* (Mike Nichols, 1967). Both fused effective rock soundtracks with thematic youth preoccupations of the day: the search for a personal and cultural identity in contemporary America.

During the 1970s and 1980s there was a profusion of popular musicals: the realist Jamaican film *The Harder they Come* (Perry Henzel, 1972); the flower power and religious fantasy of *Godspell* (David Greene, 1973) and *Hair* (Milos Forman, 1979); the disco-dance musicals of *Saturday Night Fever* (John Badham, 1977), *Grease* (Radnal Kleister, 1978); and the dance fantasies of *Flashdance* (Adrian Lyne, 1983) and *Dirty Dancing* (Emile Ardolino, 1987). The 'rock lifestyle' was the focus of *That'll be the Day* (1973) and Ken Russell's version of *Tommy* (1975). Nostalgia was at the core of *Amercian Graffiti* (George Lucas, 1973), *The Blues Brothers* (John Landis, 1978), *Quadrophenia* (Franc Rodham, 1979), and *The Buddy Holly Story* (Steve Rash, 1978). Grossberg (1992a) claims that the success of these popular musicals prepared the ground for the success of **MTV**, launched in 1981, by redefining the political economy of rock, moving the emphasis from sound to images.

Since the 1980s, popular musical films have continued to mine a range of themes: youth subcultures (*River's Edge* (Tim Hunter, 1987)); adolescent and young adult sexuality and gender relations (*Singles* (Cameron Crowe, 1992)); class and generational conflict; nostalgia; stardom and the rock lifestyle (*Backbeat* (Iain Softley, 1994; 1995), *The Doors* (Oliver Stone, 1990), *Sid and Nancy* (Alex Cox, 1986), *Rock Star* (Stephen Herek, 2001), and *Purple Rain* (Albert Magnoli, 1984)); dance fantasies such as *Strictly Ballroom* (Baz Luhrmann, 1992); and fandom and the joy of making music (*School of Rock* (Richard Link-later, 2004)). *The Rocky Horror Picture Show* (Jim Sharman, 1975) created a new subgenre: the cult musical, with the audience becoming an integral part of the cinematic experience, an indulgence in fantasy and catharsis. The film went on to became the king of the 'midnight movies' – cult films shown at midnight for week after week, usually on Friday and Saturday nights (see Shuker, 2001).

The storylines of these musicals involve popular music to varying extents, ranging from its centrality to the narrative theme, to its use as soundtrack. These films articulate the hopes and dreams, and fantasy lives, which popular music brings to people. When an actual artist is drawn on, or featured, such films help the process of mythologizing them, as with Elvis Presley. Dominant themes include youth/adolescence as a rite of passage, frequently characterized by storm and stress, and using subcultural versus 'mainstream' affiliations to explore this; reconciliation, between generations, competing subcultures, and genders, frequently expressed through the emergence of couples; and the search for independence and an established sense of **identity**. Given such themes are ones identified in the literature as central adolescent 'tasks' and preoccupations, they clearly appeal to youthful cinema audiences, and to film-makers looking for box office appeal.

See also: **documentaries; soundtracks**

Further reading: Grant (1986); Hayward (1996) (an excellent overview); Mundy (1999); Romanowski and Denisoff (1987); Romney and Wootton (1995)

FOLK CULTURE; FOLK MUSIC; FOLK ROCK

The term folk culture is applied to forms of culture which are tightly linked to particular social groups and which are not subject to mass distribution, even if electronically produced (Longhurst, 1995: 145). The concept is sometimes conflated with the notion of **roots** music. Often rooted in specific localities, early forms of many popular music genres can be regarded as folk culture, including the pre-ska forms of Jamaican reggae, and the hillbilly styles which contributed to country & western and rockabilly. In particular, folk culture has been used in considerations of the musical characteristics and social dynamics of folk music.

While in a sense it can be argued that all popular music is a form of folk music, more specifically, and historically, the term is reserved for music passed from person to person or generation to generation without being written down. Folk is regarded as simple, direct, acoustic-based music, drawing upon the experiences, concerns, and customs (folklore) of 'common people' and their communities. Folk music includes ethnic music, such as the social and religious cere-monial music of Africans or American Indians, Negro spirituals and blues, work songs (e.g. sea shanties), political and protest songs (broadsides), and love songs. Its forms and variants exist in every country and are often regionally based (e.g. the Appalachians in the United States). Considerable mixing and mingling of different tradi-tions, song structures, and instrumentation is evident. There are important folk music archival collections, associated magazines, and record companies (e.g. Folkways). Festivals, such as Newport in the US and Cambridge in the UK, have been central to the continued vitality of the music, while helping to maintain what counts as 'folk music'.

Folk music has taken differing paths in the UK and the US, and in other national contexts, as a shifting signifier which continuously mutates in meaning. The genre's history is one of debates around **authenticity** (on this point, see Moore, 2002), and its role in the enculturation of folk culture. The genre experienced a strong revival in the US and the UK in the late 1950s through to the early 1960s. In the US, leading performers included Bob Dylan, Joan Baez, and Phil Ochs, who built on the radical activist, popular traditions developed by Woody Guthrie and Pete Seeger in the 1930s. There were influ-ential local scenes in Greenwich Village in New York, and Cam-bridge, Boston. The British folk scene of the 1960s was oriented more towards a folk club circuit, and regular major festivals. Leading per-formers included John Renbourne, Davy Graham, and Bert Jansch. Many of these performers went on to be influential in the develop-ment of British folk rock styles.

Folk music continues to be an active genre in its own right, while many 'mainstream' musicians have come out of folk, particularly

singer-songwriters. The study of folk music has long been academically regarded as a more valid, or 'respectable' form of popular music
studies, reflecting its *perceived* roots in people's common experience, its
general lack of mass commercialization, and the associated connotations of authenticity.

Further reading: Ennis (1992); Frith (1983); Gammond (1991); Pratt (1990: ch.
5); Redhead and Street (1989)

Listening: Joan Baez, *Joan Baez* (Vanguard, 1960); Bob Dylan, *Columbia*
(1962); Woody Guthrie, *The Legendary Performer* (RCA, 1977); Tanita
Tikaram, *Ancient Heart* (Reprise, 1988)

Folk rock

Folk music provided the basis for **folk rock** in the mid-1960s, a genre
built around folk song structures and topical themes, adapting
instruments and techniques associated with folk styles while using
amplified instrumentation and rock conventions. Folk rock also had
links with country rock and psychedelic rock (the early Grateful Dead,
Jefferson Airplane, and Country Joe and the Fish). The new genre
arguably first came to wider attention with Bob Dylan's famous double
set (half acoustic, half electric) at the Newport Festival in 1965, and
subsequent 'electric' tour. As Dylan's hostile reception indicated, such
innovations were not always welcomed by folk purists. Leading
exponents of folk rock included the Byrds, the Flying Burrito
Brothers, and the Loving Spoonful in the US; and Lindisfarne,
Steeleye Span, Pentangle, Donovon, and Fairport Convention in
the UK. The Byrds' 'Mr Tambourine Man' (1966) is regarded as the
archetypal folk rock record. The genre has lived on in the guitar-based
sound of much mainstream rock music since the 1980s, often blended
with country rock (e.g. the Long Ryders), and in alternative bands
such as R.E.M.

Further reading: Garofalo (1997); Nelson (1992); Unterberger (2002) (includes
a discography); Vassal (1976)

Viewing: *Dancing in the Street* (1995), episode 3

Listening: The Loving Spoonful, 'Do You Believe in Magic?' (1965); Bob
Dylan, 'Like A Rolling Stone' (1965); the Byrds, 'Turn! Turn! Turn!' (1965)

on *Turn! Turn! Turn!* (CBS, 1966); *Portfolio – Steeleye Span* (Chrysalis, 1988); R.E.M., *Murmur* (RS, 1983); Richard and Linda Thompson, *I Want to See the Bright Lights Tonight* (Island, 2004) (CD reissue)

FRANKFURT SCHOOL

A group of German intellectuals, the Frankfurt School developed a revolutionary philosophical variant of Western Marxism, which became know as 'critical theory'. Initially based at the Institute of Social Research in Frankfurt, the school moved to the USA during the 1930s. Its principal figures included Adorno, Marcuse, Horkheimer, Fromm, and Benjamin.

The Frankfurt theorists criticized mass culture in general, arguing that under the capitalist system of production culture had become simply another object, the 'culture industry', devoid of critical thought and any oppositional political possibilities. This general view was applied more specifically to popular music by Adorno, especially in his attacks on Tin Pan Alley and jazz. When Adorno published his initial critique 'On Popular Music' in 1941, the music of the big bands filled the airwaves and charts, operating within the Tin Pan Alley system of songwriting that had been dominant since the early 1900s, with the majority of songs composed in the thirty-two-bar AABA format.

Adorno' s writings on popular music were only a minor part of his attempt to develop a general **aesthetics** of music (see Paddison, 1993, for a systematic outline and discussion of this intellectual project). Adorno was not opposed to popular music as such, but rather to its ruthless exploitation by the **culture/music industries.** His examination of the development of music utilized the concepts of diachronic, the analysis of change, and, synchronic, the analysis of static states. At the heart of his critique of popular music was the standardization associated with the capitalist system of commodity production:

> A clear judgement concerning the relation of serious to popular music can be arrived at only by strict attention to the fundamental characteristic of popular music: standardization. The whole structure of popular music is standardized even where the attempt is made to circumvent standardization (Adorno, 1941: 17).

In this essay and his subsequent writings on popular music, Adorno continued to equate the form with Tin Pan Alley and jazz–oriented variations of it, ignoring the rise of rock'n'roll in the early 1950s. This undermined his critique and resulted in his views generally being strongly rejected by more contemporary rock analysts (see e.g. Frith, 1983: 43–8). Gendron forcefully recapitulates the failings of Adorno's theory, particularly his exaggeration of the presence of industrial standardization in popular music, but also suggests that 'Adorno's analysis of popular music is not altogether implausible', and merits reconsideration (Gendron, 1986). To support this argument, Gendron examines the standardization of the vocal group style **doo–wop**, rooted in the black gospel quartet tradition, which had a major **chart** impact between 1955 and 1959.

Adorno's views on popular music remain widely utilized and debated. Paddison argues that Adorno's defence of the musical **avant-garde** can be applied to the work of composers and performers of popular music such as Frank Zappa and Henry Cow.

See also: **culture industries**

Further reading: Adorno (1941, 1991); Gendron (1986); Paddison (1993); Stevenson (2002)

FUNK

The term funk was originally used in the 1950s to describe a form of modern jazz concentrating on 'swing' and 'soul' – the latter synonymous with authenticity and sincerity. Funk was also used in a more negative sense to refer to music considered low-down, earthy, or crude. Subsequently, funk was applied to the 'anarchic and polyrhythmic' late 1960s and 1970s derivatives of soul: 'High energy, mind-expanding black rock & roll, a soulful psychedelic reaction' (DeCurtis, 1992: 268). Major performers included James Brown, George Clinton (Parliament, Funkedelic), Kool & the Gang, and Earth, Wind and Fire. Funk was an element in subsequent black-oriented genres, such as hip-hop and techno-funk, and the eclectic work of artists like Prince and Living Colour. It also made a major contribution to disco (the Ohio Players), rap, and hip-hop. Indeed, funk encompasses such a variety of associated musical styles that it can be considered a meta-genre (see Vincent, 1996, who comprehensively identifies a succession of 'Funk Dynasties', extending from the late 1960s to the 1990s).

Musically, funk tends to have little melodic variation, and rhythm is everything ('the groove'). 'The funk style requires a particular rhythmic ensemble – percussion and bass line – and either sustained chords or rhythmic interpolations by other instruments. Funk is an attitude, which when expressed musically transforms the listener into a particular mood, usually described as laid-back or mellow' (Brown, 1992: 211).

Further reading: McEwen (1992) (includes discography); Chip Stern, interview with George Clinton, in T. Scherman, ed. (1994); Vincent (1996)

Listening: James Brown, *Cold Sweat* (King, 1967); Funkadelic, *One Nation Under a Groove* (WB, 1978); Parliament, *Mothership Connection* (Casablanca, 1976); Michael Jackson, 'Billy Jean' on *Thriller* (Epic, 1982); Prince, *1999* (WB, 1984)

GARAGE BANDS; GARAGE ROCK

The garage bands of the late 1960s, so called as exponents made the music in the garage or basement, were especially prominent in the USA, where they responded to the **British invasion** of the American market. Playing basic rock music with lots of enthusiasm, these performers produced some classic one-hit wonders. Some bands were more enduring, including the Standells, the Electric Prunes, and the Count Five. Frequently covered standards were 'Gloria' (originally a single B-side for Them in the UK in 1966), 'Hey Joe' (the Leaves), and 'Louie, Louie' (Kingsmen). In the UK, garage was best represented by the proto-punk of the commercially successful Troggs ('Wild Thing' (1966)).

In 1972 a compilation of garage band releases, *Nuggets*, by Lenny Kaye, created new interest in their work, spawning a whole series of reissues (*Nuggets*, vols. 1–12 (Rhino); and *Pebbles*, vols. 1–10 (AIP)). In his liner notes, Kaye termed the genre 'punk rock', a prescient acknowledgement of garage rock's subsequent influence: the advent of **punk rock** in the late 1970s and 1980s saw a revival of interest in the garage bands, whose sound is not dissimilar.

Garage rock's musical characteristics were 'a premium on sheer outrageousness, over-the-top vocal screams and sneers, loud guitars that almost always had a fuzztone' (Erlewine *et al.*, eds, 1995). The genre was the province largely of white teenage suburbanites. It first emerged around 1965, predominantly on tiny, local record labels, linked to strong regional scenes (especially Texas, California), each with a distinctive style. The genre declined through 1967–8 with the impact of the Vietnam War draft/college attendance on band members, and the performers' general lack of commercial success. The surviving garage bands moved towards more progressive, **psychedelic** sounds; e.g. the Electric Prunes, the Blues Magoos, and the Chocolate Watchband.

The genre and its sixties performers are strangely neglected in otherwise comprehensive American **rock** histories (Garofalo, 1997; Friedlander, 1996), but have retained a cult following, including fanzines and websites.

In 2000–3 there was an international revival of the style, identified with bands such as the White Stripes and the Strokes in the US, the Hives (Sweden), the Vines (Australia), and the Datsuns (New Zealand). The music press gave this 'new garage rock revolution' (NME, 8 March 2003: 38) considerable coverage, according a stylistic coherence that is difficult to validate. The new garage rock bands displayed similar characteristics to their 1960s predecessors: a preference for 'stripped back' rock'n'roll, but with a range of inflections; an emphasis on energetic live performance, and personal styles (hair, clothes) aligned with those of their fans. These cohered around a conception of 'rock authenticity', appealing to traditional fans of that style who were disenchanted with commercialized and MTV-oriented nu-metal and hip-hop, and electronic dance music.

Further reading: Bangs (1992b) (includes discography); Heylin (1992); Hicks (1999: ch. 3); MOJO, June 2003 (with accompanying 'Instant Garage' CD compilation)

Listening: *Nuggets Volume One: The Hits* (Rhino, 1984); *The Best of the Troggs* (Polygram, 1988); *The Best of the Chocolate Watch Band* (Rhino, 1983); The Strokes, *Is This It* (RCA, 2001); the Vines, *Highly Evolved* (Capitol Records, 2002); the White Stripes, *Elephant* (XL Records, 2003)

GATEKEEPERS

A media studies term initially applied to how telegraph wire editors selected items for inclusion in local papers, gatekeepers became an established approach to analysing the way in which media workers select, reject, and reformulate material for broadcast or publication. Based on a filter-flow model of information flow, gatekeepers 'open the gate' for some texts and information, and close it for others.

The **music industry** has a number of gatekeepers, making the initial decision about who to record and promote, and filtering material at each step of the process involving the recording and marketing of a song. Studies of **radio** have been the main users of the concept; e.g. Rothenbuhler (1985) examined one US radio station in depth to determine how, within a given airplay format, the programmer decides which songs to play. The main gatekeepers were the station's programme director and music director, or outside consultant. Subsequent studies of radio have confirmed this finding in various national settings (e.g. Brennan, 1996). Decisions on which releases, artists, and genres to accord airplay or screentime help shape consumption preferences, and can consolidate new genres; e.g. US college radio and alternative rock, and MTV and heavy metal, in the late 1980s.

Organizations involved in industry regulation (e.g. the various performing rights collecting bodies), and government regulatory agencies act as gatekeepers. The editors of music trade publications, and the popular music press, can also be considered a form of gatekeeper, since reviews, artist profiles, chart lists, and publicity information help shape radio programmers' choices.

The concept became critiqued for being too mechanistic, and it has been claimed that 'the gatekeeper concept is now generally regarded as oversimplified and of little utility' (O'Sullivan *et al.*, 1994: 126–7; see also Negus, 1992). Nevertheless, it remains useful if used in conjunction with considerations of how musical forms 'arrive' at a 'gate', and how they are subsequently modified.

See also: **radio; censorship; music industry; music press; A&R**

Further reading: Brennan (1996); Burnett (1996); Hull (2004); Negus (1992); Cusic (1996); Barrow and Newby (1996)

GENDER

Gender is the cultural differentiation of females from males, a signifying distinction; compared with sexual differentiation, which is a biological/physical difference. There is considerable debate over the extent to which particular gender differences can be attributed to culture and socialization. It has been forcefully argued that the dominant ideologies and discourses throughout popular music generally privilege males, while at the same time constructing a normative masculinity. There is rather less literature on male gender issues (cf. female) in popular music. The dominance of male-gender binaries in popular music's analysis of gender has been challenged by studies of 'queer music', a term appropriated by gays and lesbians.

The significance of gender is evident in a number of areas of popular music studies, which can only be briefly alluded to here:

(1) The **history** of popular music is largely constructed around male performers and male-dominated genres. Such histories are underpinned by a 'rockist' ideology, privileging the various rock styles. While there is a recognition of women's contribution to gospel, the blues, and soul, there is a tendency to marginalize their place in the development of rock and pop styles. Even when they are credited, their contributions are seen in stereotypical terms: divas, rock chicks (e.g. Suzi Quatro, Janis Joplin), men-pleasing angels (Doris Day), victims (Billie Holiday), or problem personalities (Judy Garland). Linked to this, both traditional **musicology** and the popular **music press** have constructed a male-dominated musical **canon**, with this challenged by feminist scholars and music critics (Citron, 1993).

(2) The perceived masculine or feminine nature of particular **genres**/styles has been identified and debated. For example, pop is generally seen as 'a girls' genre', while hard rock and heavy metal are regarded as primarily male-oriented genres: encoded as signifying masculinity (McClary, 1991; cf. Gracyk, 2001: ch. 10). Women performers predominate in a cappella and gospel music, and are prominent in folk and country, and among singer-songwriters. These are socially constructed patterns, reflecting differential expectations and resources, including access to musical knowledge and equipment (see Whiteley, ed., 1997).

(3) In relation to **audiences**, girl fans and their musical tastes are often denigrated (e.g. teenyboppers), while male fans are validated (especially in legitimizing non-mainstream musical styles). **Record collecting** presents itself as a highly gendered practice.

(4) There is a lack of women in the male-dominated **music industry**; traditionally they are largely in stereotypically 'female' roles, e.g. press and office personnel. There are few women working in A&R, or as producers, managers, and sound mixers, all spheres that are male-dominated, a situation partly related to technologies being perceived as masculinist.

(5) Youth **subcultures** as largely a male preserve, with girls generally absent, 'invisible', or socially insignificant.

(6) The treatment of gender and **sexuality** in song lyrics, with some genres having a clear misogynist strain; e.g. hard rock, light metal.

(7) Stereotyped gender representations in **music video** (see Lewis, 1990).

As even this cursory list indicates, much of the work around gender issues in popular music has focused on girls and women. The term 'women in rock' emerged as a media concept in the early 1970s, and has persisted despite being criticized as a 'generic mushy lump' (O'Brien, 1995: 3), unrelated to the wide variation among female performers, even those within the rock genre. There are two dimensions here, women as performers and women in the music industry, with women being marginalized/stereotyped in both. For example, Cohen found that, in the Liverpool rock music scene she studied, women were not simply absent, but were actively excluded. All-male bands tended to preserve the music as their domain, keeping the involvement of wives and girlfriends at a distance. This situation reflects the more restricted social position of women, with greater domestic commitments and less physical freedom; the lack of encouragement given to girls to learn rock instruments; and rock sexuality as predominantly masculine. Consequently, there are few women bands in rock, or women instrumentalists, and most women rock performers are 'packaged as traditional, stereotyped, male images of women' (Cohen, 1991: 203). In the early 1990s this soundscape was challenged by the **riot grrrl** movement.

Further reading: Bayton (1990); Cohen (1991); Frith and McRobbie (1990); Gaar (1992); McClary (1991); O'Brien (2002) (includes discography); Reynolds and Press (1995); Steward and Garratt (1984); Wald (2002); Whiteley (1997)

GENRE; METAGENRES; SUBGENRES

Genre can be basically defined as a category or type. A key component of **textual analysis**, genre is widely used to analyse popular culture texts, most notably in their filmic and popular literary forms (e.g. thrillers, science fiction, and horror). The various encyclopedias, the standard histories, and critical analyses of popular music (see below), all use genre as a central organizing element. Some accounts tend to use style and genre as overlapping terms, or prefer style to genre (e.g. Moore, 1993). The arrangement in retail outlets also suggests that there are clearly identifiable genres of popular music, which are understood as such by consumers. Indeed, **fans** will frequently identify themselves with particular genres, often demonstrating considerable knowledge of the complexities of their preferences (subgenres). Similarly, musicians will frequently situate their work by reference to genres and musical styles.

The usual approach to defining musical genres is 'to follow the distinctions made by the music industry which, in turn, reflect both musical history and marketing categories' (Frith, 1987). Another approach, suggested by Frith, is to 'classify them according to their ideological effects, the way they sell themselves as art, community or emotion'. He gives the example of a form of **rock** termed 'authentic', exemplified by Bruce Springsteen: 'The whole point of this genre is to develop musical conventions which are, in themselves, measures of "truth". As listeners we are drawn into a certain form of reality: this is what it is like to live in America, this is what it is like to love or hurt. The resulting work is the pop equivalent of film theorists' "classic realist text"' (p. 147). Against and in interplay with authentic genres can be placed a tradition of artifice, as in **glam rock**.

Critical analysis of popular music genres has concentrated on the tension between their emphasis on standardized codes that 'allow no margin for distraction' (Fabbri, 1999), and their fluidity as these codes are elaborated on and challenged and displaced by new codes. Chambers in the mid-1980s correctly observed that there were by then quite rigid boundaries between genres, as exemplified by art rock. Currently, while musical genres continue to function as marketing categories and reference points for musicians, critics and fans, particular examples clearly demonstrate that genre divisions must be regarded as highly fluid. No style is totally independent of those that have preceded it, and musicians borrow elements from existing styles and incorporate them into new forms. Performers have always absorbed influences across genre (and colour) lines. In the 1920s, country pioneer Jimmie Rogers drew extensively from the blues and popular music traditions just as, in the 1980s, Prince reworked the imagery and sounds of white sixties rock. Further, many performers can fit under more than one classification, or shift between and across genres during their careers. There is also considerable genre bending: subverting or playing with the conventions of existing musical genres, or adopting an ironic distance from those same conventions. This process is strongly present in hybrid genres, where different styles inform and engage with each other, as with **jazz rock**). Moreover, 'while the surface styles and fashions of popular music change rapidly, the underlying structures move far more slowly' (Hardy and Laing, eds, 1990: Introduction).

It is useful to distinguish between metagenres, which are rather loose amalgams of various styles (e.g. alternative rock, world music), and genres, which arguably exist in a purer, more easily understood and specified form (e.g. disco). It is also important to acknowledge the significance of subgenres, which are particularly evident in well-established and developed styles/genres, and qualify any simplistic depiction of a genre; the blues, heavy metal and techno provide good examples of strongly differentiated genres. 'Mainstream' musical genres are operating within a commercial system of record companies, contracts, marketing, publicity, management, support staff and so on; within this context performers tour and perform, make recordings, and create an image. As Breen (1991: 193) observed, moving into the 1990s 'every genre and sub-genre of popular music shares a location on the totalized map of popular music culture, where the bridges that form the industrial crossovers from one domain of the popular music industry to the next are increasingly interconnected'.

In the light of the above, several distinguishing characteristics of popular music genres can be identified. First, there are the stylistic traits present in the music: their musical characteristics, 'a code of sonic requirements ... a certain sound, which is produced according to conventions of composition, instrumentation and performance' (Weinstein, 1991a: 6). These may vary in terms of their coherence and sustainability, as examples such as **Christian rock** and **glam rock** clearly demonstrate, particularly in metagenres. Along with other aspects of genre, particular musical characteristics can be situated within the general historical evolution of popular music. Of particular significance here is the role of **technology**, which establishes both constraints and possibilities in relation to the nature of performance, and the recording, distribution, and reception of the music. Second, there are other, essentially non-musical, stylistic attributes, most notably image and its associated visual style. This includes standard iconography and record cover format; the locale and structure of performances, especially in concert, and the dress, make-up, and hairstyles adopted by both the performers and their listeners and fans. Musical and visual stylistic aspects combine in terms of how they operate to produce particular ideological effects, a set of associations which situate the genre within the broader musical constituency.

Third, there is the primary **audience** for particular styles. The relationship between fans and their genre preferences is a form of transaction, mediated by the forms of delivery, creating specific cultural forms with sets of expectations. Genres are accorded specific places in a musical hierarchy by both critics and fans, and by many performers. This hierarchy is loosely based around the notions of authenticity, sincerity, and commercialism. The critical denigration of certain genres, including disco, dance pop, and the elevation of others, such as alt.country, reflects this, and mirrors the broader, still widely accepted, high/low culture split. We must acknowledge the ultimately subjective nature of these concepts, and the shifting status and constituency of genres. This point becomes clear when we check the genres listed here against those included in the major encyclopedias, compendiums, and histories of popular music. Furthermore, genres are historically located; some endure, others spring briefly to prominence then fade.

In terms of the identification and delineation of various genres, it is instructive to see which have, or have not, been accorded separate treatment in some of the major overviews of popular music. For example, Gammond (ed., 1991) excludes, among others, art rock, Christian rock, folk rock, and glam rock; Clarke (ed., 1990) concentrates on performers, and 'major' genres: blues, country, folk, heavy metal, jazz, reggae, rock, and soul, with considerably briefer entries on several other genres (e.g. doo-wop; bubblegum); DeCurtis (1992) has no separate contributions for country, the blues, and jazz, though these are necessarily alluded to where they have influenced and fused with rock'n'roll. Further, this major history relies on the concept of scenes and sounds, and the role of key performers, as much as genre. Hardy and Laing (1990) include a fairly inclusive glossary of styles and genres, with the brief entries supplemented by the discussions of associated artists. This device works quite well, and is illustrative of how genres defy static/academic definition independent of those *making* the music. Of course, all this raises the whole thorny question of the definition of **popular music**, an issue considered in the entry for that concept.

See also: genre entries

Further reading: Charlton (1994); Fabbri (1999)

GIRL GROUPS

While often the studio creations of producers such as Phil Spector, girl groups were on the cutting edge of early 1960s pop music. Leading performers included Darlene Love (who sang lead vocals on the records of a number of groups), the Ronnettes, the Supremes, and the Crystals. The girl groups had a clearly identifiable sound: 'girlish vocals fraught with adolescent idealism and pain, plus quirky arrangements embellished by strings and a dramatic drumbeat' (O'Brien, 1995: 68). The vocals were a combination of qualities: nasal, high-pitched, humming, and husky, they owed much to soul and gospel, yet were at the same time unique. Their song narratives were morality tales about the attractions and perils of 'first love', especially of the forbidden variety, primarily written by several youthful songwriting teams, including Gerry Goffin and Carole King. Many girl group releases were on independent labels, including Red Bird, Phillies, Scepter, and an ascendant Motown. The girl groups had considerable impact, articulating the optimism present in the US under the Kennedy administration, and providing the basis for the success of the 1960s British beat groups, including the Beatles. By the mid-1960s the girl group sound had been assimilated into mainstream pop, but they have continued to exercise a fascination, linked to a mythic status associated with innocence and optimism.

See also: **gender**

Further reading: Cyrus (2003); O'Brien (1995: ch. 3)

Listening: *The Best of the Crystals* (ABKCO, 1992); *The Best of the Ronnettes* (ABKCO, 1992); the Supremes, *Anthology* (Motown, 1974). There are a number of good compilations; see those issued by Rhino

Viewing: *Dancing in the Street* (1995), episode 2

GLAM ROCK; GLITTER ROCK

Also referred to as glitter rock, glam rock was a musical style/genre, and an associated subculture, which flourished in the early 1970s, especially in the UK. Glam was both a reaction against the seriousness of late 1960s progressive rock and the counter-culture, and an extension of it. It strongly emphasized the visual presentation of performers and their concerts, with vividly coloured hair, outrageous costumes, heavy make-up, and fire breathing (in the case of Kiss). In glam the music was almost secondary to the act itself, leading Frith (1988c: 42) to observe that 'the image of rock star – previously taken to be quite natural (rock was sincere) or entirely false (a cynical sales device) ... became part of musicians' creative effort'.

British glam pioneers were early period David Bowie and Gary Glitter, who had three British number one chart singles in the mid-1970s: 'With its mammoth drum beat, growling guitar, dumb instrumental hook, and incessant chorus of "hey", his debut single "Rock and Roll, Part Two" was a huge hit' (Erlewine *et al.*, eds, 1995: 342). In the United States, glam was represented by performers such as Kiss, with a huge fan following ('the Kiss Army') for their highly theatrical concerts, the punkish New York Dolls, and light heavy metal bands such as Bon Jovi. Other glam rockers included the more prosaic pop-oriented styles of Sweet and Slade, and the more art rock-oriented Roxy Music and Queen ('Bohemian Rhapsody' (1975)).

As the above list indicates, males dominated glam. The few prominent female performers adopted a blend of masculine and androgynous musical and performance styles, as did Suzi Quatro (see Auslander, 2004).

Elements of androgyny and bisexuality were a part of glam's image and appeal. The style of glam performers and their fans combined hippy sartorial elegance and skinhead hardness: 'Reminiscent of mods in their extravagant clothes, high heels and make up (often offset with tattoos), hard-working lads masculinized their decadent image composed of a collage of Berlin thirties and New York gay' (Brake, 1985: 76). Glam was part of the 1970s embourgeoisement of leisure in the UK, with new city centre leisure centres, and it influenced and merged into the new romantics; e.g. Adam and the Ants.

See also: **heavy metal; new romantics**

Further reading: Charlton (1994); Moore (1993); 'Glam', NME special edition, 2004

Listening: Kiss, *Double Platinum (Greatest Hits)* (Casablanca, 1978); New York Dolls, *Rock & Roll* (Mercury, 1994) (contains their 1973 and 1974 albums); David Bowie, *The Rise and Fall of Ziggy Stardust* (Rykodisc, 1972); *Rock'n'Roll: The Best of Gary Glitter* (Rhino, 1990); T-Rex, *Electric Warrior* (Reprise, 1972); *The Best of Sweet* (Capitol, 1993)

GLOBALIZATION

Refers to the increasing economic, social, cultural, and political global connections present internationally; the result of the world being shrunk into one communications system, dominated by international media conglomerates. Globalization emerged as a critical concept in the late 1980s. 'Patterns of population movement and settlement established during colonialism and its aftermath, combined with the more recent acceleration of globalization, particularly of electronic communications, have enabled increased cultural juxtaposing, meeting and mixing on a global scale' (Barker, 2002).

It was often used to argue that regional and local cultures are squeezed out, overwhelmed, or colonized and 'watered down' and commercialized for 'mainstream' global consumption. Although globalization was frequently used in association with **cultural imperialism**, it is distinguished from it as 'more complex and total, and less organized or predictable in its outcomes' (O'Sullivan *et al.*, 1994: 130; see also the discussion in Hesmondhalgh, 2002: ch. 6).

In relation to popular music, globalization has an economic and a cultural dimension, with the two closely linked. The dominance of the popular **music industry** and market by the **majors**, and the internationalization of music styles, can be viewed as examples of globalization.

Various authorities place the majors' market share of the global production, manufacture, and distribution of recorded popular music at between 80 and 90 per cent. In Europe, for example, the dominance of the multinationals was clear and increasing by the 1990s, with several of the majors having embarked on a concerted effort to absorb locally owned record companies and further increase their market share (Laing, 1992). The major companies also take major shareholdings in independent labels with promising artists, an investment which could pay off, as in Sony Music's 49 per cent ownership of key **Britpop** band Oasis's label Creation. The operation of such market dominance, however, is far from clear-cut, as studies of the development of 'international repertoire' demonstrate (Negus, 1999).

An important aspect of the role of the majors in national popular music markets is the question of the possible conflict between the local and the global, in relation to national musical vitality (see the examples in Robinson *et al.*, 1991). The basic concern is that the transnationals will promote their international artists at the expense of local artists, and international preferences and genres at the expense of more 'authentic' local popular music, and only develop those local talents and genres with global sales potential. At a more general level, it is noteworthy that English is the language of popular music, arguably a form of linguistic globalization. Do the policies and activities of the multinationals inhibit the development of indigenous music in local markets? The response is complex, and varies from country to country.

The musical interplay of the global and the local has been a central trope in recent scholarship. This has engaged with notions of **appropriation**, hybridity, and syncretism to demonstrate that the relationship is a negotiated rather than a deterministic one (see Born and Hesmondhalgh, eds, 2000; Steingress, 2003; and the related entries here). The playing out of such negotiations is particularly evident in diasporic communities, the internationalization of **rap** and hip-hop (Mitchell, 2001), and in **world music** more generally. The term 'glocalization' has been used to show how sharp distinctions between global and local are difficult to maintain (e.g. Taylor, 2003).

See also: **diaspora**

Further reading: Hull (2004); Negus (1992); Wallis and Malm, eds (1992)

GOSPEL

While its religious content has generally kept gospel from enjoying significant commercial success in the mainstream of popular music, it has been hugely influential, especially on **soul** and **R&B**. Garofalo (1997) refers to it the genre as 'sanctified R&B'. Gospel is a *Billboard* chart category, and features among the Grammy awards.

Black slaves in the US adapted the spiritual as part of the Protestant revival at the beginning of the nineteenth century, and gospel arose from the upsurge in fundamentalist churchgoing in black urban communities in the 1920s. Thomas Dorsey (b. 1899), a major composer and choir leader, is credited with inventing the term 'gospel'. Vocal call and response was an important element of gospel: the practice of singing in which the solo vocalist, the caller, is answered by a group of singers (for more contemporary examples, see the recordings of the Staples Singers). An intense spiritual 'feeling' was central to early gospel music, while the moaning, pleading, and supplicating vocals became part of the repertoire of jump blues and early soul singers. Gospel was an important part of the upbringing of many early rockabilly singers, and is evident in their vocal style; e.g. Elvis

Presley. During the late 1950s, Sam Cooke and Ray Charles performed gospel tunes with secular lyrics, or adapted gospel tunes, anticipating soul music. Other leading gospel performers were Mahalia Jackson, America's most popular gospel artist in the 1950s, and Aretha Franklin, who was a gospel star before singing more secular material. Gospel is clearly influential on the smooth harmonies and lead vocals of contemporary R&B.

See also: **doo-wop; R&B; soul**

Further reading: Cusic (1990); Ennis (1992); Gammond, ed. (1991); Hansen (1992)

Listening: Mahalia Jackson, *Gospels, Spirituals, Hymns* (CBS, 1991); Aretha Franklin, *Amazing Grace* (Atlantic, 1972); *Sam Cooke with the Soul Stirrers* (Specialty CD, 1991); Ray Charles, *The Right Time* (Atlantic, 1987) (especially 'I Got A Woman')

GOTH/GOTHIC ROCK; GOTHS

A musical genre, and associated subcultural style, goth was influenced by the proto-**punk** music of American band the Velvet Underground and the sound experiments of the rock **avant-garde**. The label goth, or gothic rock, was first applied in the 1970s to bands like Joy Division, Bauhaus, Siouxsie and the Banshees, and the Southern Death Cult. Siouxsie Sioux used the term 'gothic' to describe the orientation of her band, and may be the originator of the term. 'The music was generally a dark, angst-ridden and introspective alternative to the light-hearted disco sounds that were dominating that era' (*Music Central 96*), and combined gothic images (gloomy medieval castles, vampires, etc.) with a negative view of contemporary society. Goth was primarily an English phenomenon, though it developed internationally and remained evident in the 1990s.

Bauhaus' debut EP, *Bela Lugosi's Dead* (1979), is credited with introducing the genre in the UK; the nine-and-a-half-minute title track, with its lengthy haunting electronically produced sound effects, became a gothic rock anthem. (The thematic gothic connection lay in the fact that Lugosi played the lead part in the original *Dracula* film (1931).) While there was a variety of gothic bands and instrumental line-ups, the basic characteristics of the music remained fairly constant: a low bass pulse, pounding drumbeats, electronic sound effects, low pitched vocals, often spoken rather than sung, and with deep, dramatic vocal timbre. Performers such as the Sisters of Mercy used drum machines, low drones (long held notes), and made 'an almost minimalist use of short repeated melodic fragments' (Charlton, 1994: 280). Elements of an austere psychedelia were part of the music of Joy Division ('Love will Tear us Apart' on *Closer* (Qwest, 1980)) and the Jesus and Mary Chain. Into the 1980s and since, goth covers a broader spectrum of music, e.g. Robert Smith and the Cure.

Goth was also a cultural style, with goths characterized by their black clothes and the heavy use of dark eye/face make-up. The genre and its fans were associated with several **moral panics** around youth suicides in the late 1980s (see Shuker, 2001, for a New Zealand perspective). Such episodes were examples of the use of an **effects** argument to attack popular music.

Further reading: Charlton (1994); Thompson (2002)

Listening: Siouxsie and the Banshees, *Once Upon a Time: The Singles* (Geffen, 1984); the Jesus and Mary Chain, *Psychocandy* (Reprise, 1985); the Sisters of Mercy, *A Slight Case of Overbombing: Greatest Hits, Volume 1* (Warner Music, 1993); Robert Smith and the Cure, *Standing on the Beach: The Singles* (Geffen, 1984)

GRAMOPHONE *see* **phonograph**

GRUNGE

Grunge represented the mainstreaming of the North American indie rock ethic and style of the 1980s (Azerrad, 2001). As much a marketing device as an identifiable 'sound'; (cf. **alternative** music, which it is often conflated into), grunge initially developed in the Seattle area (USA) in the late 1980s, associated with the influential **indie** label Sub Pop. Pearl Jam and Nirvana were the two most influential bands credited with leading the commercial breakthrough of grunge/ alternative rock into a relatively moribund music scene in the early 1990s. Grunge became part of an international phenomenon (e.g. Britain's Bush, and Australia's silverchair), which briefly dominated the global music market in the mid-1990s.

The enormous worldwide response to the 1994 suicide of Kurt Cobain, Nirvana's lead singer, indicated the impact of grunge. The popularity of grunge was displaced by hip-hop and electronica at the end of the decade, with the 'death' of the style being heralded by the music press with the break up of Soundgarden in April 1997.

Grunge 'deemphasized appearance and polished technique in favour of raw, angry passionate songs that articulated the pessimism and anxiety of young people' (*Music Central 96*), fuelled by a broadly anti-establishment attitude. The speciality grunge/alternative albums, *The Trip, vols. 1–8*, show grunge to be musically a disparate genre, with noticeable differences in tempo, rhythm, and melody within a core structure of dominant guitar sounds and pessimistic lyrics. Many grunge performers straddle genres; e.g. Green Day are on the border between grunge and **punk**. While there was usually no 'grunge' category at the various music awards, those for **alternative** music were frequently won by bands identified with the genre (e.g. Pearl Jam at the 1995 MTV Awards). Grunge embraces clothing and attitude as well as music. The 'grunge look' includes flannel shirts, big baggy shorts, and opportunity shop clothing. But in reacting against commercialism and capitalism, grunge arguably established a new conformity, as both the music and clothing styles were soon **commodified**.

See also: **alternative music; Seattle sound**

Further reading: Shevory (1995); Tucker (1992) (includes discographies); Stanford (1996)

Listening: Nirvana, *Nevermind* (Geffen (US number 1 album 1991)); Pearl Jam, *Ten* (Epic, 1991); *The Trip, vols. 1–8* (Warner Music)

HARD ROCK

A loose, amorphous genre/style; hard rock is also referred to as heavy rock, stadium rock, or cock rock. The term has been applied since the late 1960s (the Small Faces, the Who) and early 1970s (Bad Company) to a variety of performers whose music was characterized by hard, driving rhythms, strong bass drum and use of backbeat (on snare), and short melodies, limited in pitch range. The formal structure of hard rock songs is largely verse-chorus-verse-chorus-solo section (usually played by the lead guitar) -verse-chorus.

Hard rock is also characterized by loud volume and assertive masculinity; evident in the personae of performers, especially vocalists (e.g. Roger Daltrey, Robert Plant, Axl Rose) and lead guitarists, and the genre's predominantly male following. Cock rock emerged as an alternative term for hard rock, highlighting the genre's often explicit and aggressive expression of male sexuality, its at times misogynist lyrics, and its phallic imagery. Cock rock performers were regarded as aggressive, dominating and boastful, a stance, it was argued, evident in their live shows (see Frith and McRobbie, 1990; Reynolds and Press, 1995).

Early hard rock styles drew on R&B (the Who), and overlapped with forms of heavy metal (Deep Purple). The Who fused melody and raw percussive power, extending the structural limitations of early rock'n'roll. In the USA in the 1980s, hard rock became associated with stadium rock, so-called because of large-scale concerts, held in sports stadiums, by bands such as Journey, Loverboy, and Foreigner. Other leading hard rock performers in the 1980s and 1990s included Bruce Springsteen, Australia's Cold Chisel (and a solo Jimmy Barnes), Van Halen, the Cult, Bon Jovi, and Aerosmith. Elements of hard rock are evident in the music of a range of current performers and styles, such as contemporary garage rock. Hard rock has become a staple part of the playlist for 'classic rock' radio.

See also: **garage rock**

Further reading: Dunbar-Hall and Hodge (1993); Marsh (1992)

Listening: Deep Purple, *Smoke on the Water: The Best of Deep Purple* (EMI, 1994); the Who, *Live at Leeds* (MCA, 1970; CD 1995); Guns N'Roses, *Appetite for Destruction* (Geffen, 1987); Bad Company, *10 From 6* (Atlantic, 1986); Paul Westerberg, *Come Feel Me Tremble* (Vagrant, 2003)

Viewing: *The Song Remains the Same* (Peter Clifton and Joe Massot, 1976) on Led Zeppelin; *The Kids Are Alright* (Polygram, 1984) on the Who

HARDCORE

In a general sense, hardcore is used to signify more extreme variants of a cultural form (e.g. hardcore pornography, with its explicit sexuality). Sometimes it is abbreviated to 'hard', as in 'hard trance', electronic music with higher beats per minute. Several extreme styles of **heavy metal** also draw on the concept (e.g. grindcore). Its more general use in popular music has been in relation to various styles of alternative and **indie music**. Part of the US underground in the late 1970s, hardcore developed out of punk and was linked with grunge and alternative rock. By the late 1990s the label had become a cliché, although it remains widely used.

'Uncompromising' is the word often used to characterize the genre. Originally harder and faster than its direct ancestor, punk rock, hardcore took punk music and 'sped up the tempos as fast as humanly possible, sticking largely to monochrome guitars, bass and drums, and favouring half-shouted lyrics venting the most inflammatory sentiments the singers and songwriters could devise' (Erlewine *et al.*, eds, 1995: 917). While internationally in evidence, hardcore's chief breeding ground was the United States. The genre was strongest in the San Francisco Bay area (the Dead Kennedys, Black Flag, the Circle Jerks), and Washington DC (Minor Threat, the Bad Brains). British hardcore/post-punk bands were noted for their melodically minimal, percussive structures (Wire, the Fall). Politics were left of centre, but enmeshed in a mass of contradictions, for instance that hardcore was against sexism and racism, but its performers were generally white and male. Nearly all (early) hardcore bands were on small, independent labels. A number of alternative bands had their roots in hardcore, before broadening the scope of their music and signing with major labels; e.g. Hüsker Dü, X, the Replacements. Some local alternative scenes cohered around hardcore musicians and their fans, notably the 'Straightedge' subculture in Washington DC.

See also: **alternative; independent; punk**

Further reading: Azerrad (2001); Lentini (2003); Tucker (1992) (includes discography)

Listening: The Dead Kennedys, *Fresh Fruit for Rotting Vegetables* (Alternative Tentacles, 1980); Black Flag, *Damaged I* (SST, 1981); Wire, *Pink Flag* (Restless, 1977)

Viewing: *The Decline of Western Civilization, Part One* (Penelope Spheeris, 1981): the Los Angeles punk/hardcore scene c. 1981, featuring Black Flag, the Circle Jerks, X, and the Germs

HEAVY METAL

The musical parameters of heavy metal as a genre cannot be comfortably reduced to formulaic terms. It is usually louder, 'harder', and faster-paced than conventional rock music, and remains predominantly guitar-oriented. The main instruments are electric guitars (lead and bass), drums and electronic keyboards, but there are numerous variants within this basic framework. Some forms of the genre have enjoyed enormous commercial success and have a large fan base; other, 'harder' subgenres have a cult following.

Heavy metal is frequently criticized as incorporating the worst excesses of popular music, notably its perceived narcissism and sexism, and it is also often musically dismissed. Even Lester Bangs, one of the few rock critics to view the emergence of heavy metal favourably, wrote of the genre:

> As its detractors have always claimed, heavy-metal rock is nothing more than a bunch of noise; it is not music, it's distortion – and that is precisely why its adherents find it appealing. Of all contemporary rock, it is the genre most closely identified with violence and aggression, rapine and carnage. Heavy metal orchestrates technological nihilism (Bangs, 1992c: 459).

Heavy metal was one of the main targets of moves to censor popular music in the 1980s (see **censorship**).

Until the publication of Weinstein's comprehensive sociological study (1991a), Walser's more musically grounded treatment (1993), and Arnett's study of its fans (1996), there were few attempts to seriously discuss the genre. Yet heavy metal displays a musical cogency and enjoys a mass appeal, existing within a set of social relations. There is a well-developed heavy metal subculture, predominantly working class, white, young and male, identifying with the phallic imagery of guitars and the general muscularity and oppositional orientation of the form (there is some debate here: see Walser, 1993). The symbols associated with heavy metal, which include Nazi insignia and Egyptian and Biblical symbols, provide a signature of identification with the genre, being widely adopted by metal's youth cult following (see Arnett, 1996). The genre has maintained a high market profile, despite critical derision and a negative public image.

Once established, heavy metal demonstrated the common pattern of **genre** fragmentation and hybridization. There are a number of identifiable heavy metal subgenres, or closely related styles. Although these are historically specific, each has continued to be represented in the complex range of contemporary heavy metal (now often referred to simply as 'metal'). These subgenres include:

(1) Heavy/**hard rock**: uses a classic guitar, drums, vocalist line-up (*Listening*: Def Leppard, *Hysteria* (Mercury, 1983); Aerosmith, *Pump* (Geffen, 1989)).

(2) Classic metal: emerged in the 1970s, partly as a 'return to basics' in the face of the excesses of progressive and art rock; it features high-pitched, often wailing, vocals and extended guitar solos (*Listening*: Black Sabbath, *Paranoid* (WB, 1971); AC/DC, *Back in Black* (Atco, 1980)).

(3) Soft/lite metal: a more accessible, commercial style, strong on visual impact, which draws on and intersects with **glam rock** (e.g. Poison, Kiss). The subgenre enjoyed huge commercial success in the late 1980s, and was largely responsible for breaking heavy metal with **MTV** and radio (*Listening*: Bon Jovi, *Slippery When Wet* (Mercury, 1986); Van Halen, *1984* (WB, 1984)).

(4) Funk metal: prominent in the 1990s; less structured than earlier forms of metal, with the bass guitar relied on more than the lead (*Listening*: Red Hot Chilli Peppers, *Blood Sugar Sex Magic* (WB, 1991)).

(5) Death metal: characterized by a grating vocal, though the music itself ranges from intensely **hardcore** to 'mellow' with samples (e.g. Death, Pestilence).

(6) Thrash/speed metal: largely a US phenomenon, thrash developed out of hardcore and punk, and became a journalistic convenience for guitar-based non-mainstream metal, usually played faster and louder. In the early 1990s, bands such as Metallica and Anthrax were seen as generating a new form of 'the true rock experience', which runs in direct contradiction to the 'the established expectation of pleasure and fun often associated with rock music' (Breen, 1991: 191). This new form was apocalyptic in its visions of negation, and constructed through the live concert as much as its recorded forms. The **crossover** success of Metallica brought the style to mainstream attention (see Kotarba, 1994). Speed metal remains popular, especially in Europe, where the names of leading bands indicate their social and musical stance: e.g. Sodom, Kreator, and Destuction (see *Record Collector*, January 2002: 'Speed Kills – Again') (*Listening*: Metallica, *And Justice for All* (Elektra, 1988); Destruction, *The Antichrist* (Nuclear Blast, 2000).

(7) Christian metal: lyrics drawing on the Bible and Christian values, but within a metal framework (see **Christian music**) (*Listening*: Stryper, *In God We Trust* (Hollywood, 1991) (the

band take their name from Isaiah 53:5: 'and with his stripes we are healed')).

(8) Industrial metal: greater use of sampling and computer technology (*Listening*: Ministry, *The Mind is a Terrible Thing to Taste* (Sire, 1989)).

This list is hardly exhaustive, with recent variants of metal including 'nu-metal', 'extreme metal', with a range of styles, including grindcore and Pagan metal (see McIver, 2000); and hybrids such as progmetal (see **progressive rock**). Reprising earlier controversies around heavy metal, but in more attenuated form, extreme metal raises questions of free speech, censorship, and 'the limits of musical expression' (Kahn-Harris, 2003).

A much-debated question is why a genre generally panned by the critics (and many other music fans) as formulaic noise, associated with a negative social stance and consequent public controversy, is so popular? Heavy metal fans are attracted by its sheer volume, the 'power' of the music, the genre's problem-oriented lyrics, at both the global and personal levels, and by its performers general lack of a commercialized image. This is a form of **authenticity**, with metal fans seeking greater 'substance' than available through mainstream chart-oriented music (Breen, 1991; Weinstein, 1991a: ch. 4).

Further reading: Arnett (1996); Bangs (1992c); Eddy (1992); Kahn-Harris (2003); Klosterman (2002); Kotarba (1994); McIver (2000); Walser (1993); Weinstein (1991a)

Viewing: *Dancing in the Street* (1995), episode 7: 'Hang on to Yourself'; *Decline of Western Civilization, Part Two: The Heavy Metal Years* (Penelope Spheeris, 1988)

Website: Keith Kahn-Harris provides an extensive bibliography on metal and related genres, and his own work on death metal (www.kahn-harris.org)

HEGEMONY

Italian Marxist theoretician Antonio Gramsci's concept of ideological (or cultural) hegemony was advanced to explain how a ruling class maintains its dominance by achieving a popular consensus mediated through the various institutions of society, including the mass media. Hegemony mystifies and conceals existing power relations and social arrangements. Particular ideas and rules are constructed as natural and universal 'common sense' and the popular media play a leading role in this process. Hegemony operates in the realms of consciousness and representations, making popular cultural forms important contributors to its formation and maintenance (Barker, 2002: ch. 3, gives a fuller discussion of the concept).

In relation to popular music, hegemony has been utilized to examine the manner in which song lyrics and music videos underpin dominant conceptions of gender, sexuality, and ethnicity; to investigate the cultural symbolic challenge offered by youth subcultures to mainstream, dominant society; and, most significantly, to analyse the Anglo-American international dominance of the music industry and its styles. This dominance has waned in recent years, with the reassertion of the European market and the emergence of Japanese media conglomerates as major players in the music industry, but the Anglo-American market remains of major importance, not least for its commercial legitimization of emergent trends. Aside from its market share, the Anglo-American music industries established and continue to privilege particular formats and working practices as 'natural' and accepted, especially those associated with 'international repertoire' (Negus, 1999).

See also: **cultural imperialism; globalization; subcultures**

HIGH CULTURE

The high culture tradition emerged during the nineteenth century; it was essentially a conservative defence of a narrowly defined high or elite 'culture', in the classic sense of 'the best that has been thought and said' (Arnold, 1869). This asserted an artistic conception of culture: the only real and authentic culture is art, against which everything else is set. It views the valued civilized culture of an elite minority as constantly under attack from a majority or mass culture which is unauthentic and a denial of 'the good life'. Its analytic emphasis is on evaluation and discrimination; a search for the true values of civilization, commonly to be found in Renaissance art, the great nineteenth-century novels, and so on. The high culture tradition includes the work of various cultural commentators, including F.R. Leavis, T.S. Eliot, Abbs, and Bloom. Elements of it are evident in Marxist-oriented critiques of mass culture: the **Frankfurt School**, Raymond Williams *et al.* ('left culturalism').

The high cultural critique of popular culture has frequently vehemently attacked popular music. While such a view can be traced back to Plato, it emerged more forcefully with the massive social changes of the nineteenth century. For example, writing in 1839, Sir John Herschel claimed: 'Music and dancing (the more's the pity) have become so closely associated with ideas of riot and debauchery among the less cultivated classes, that a taste for them, for their own sakes, can hardly be said to exist, and before they can be recommended as innocent or safe amusements, a very great change of ideas must take place' (cited in Frith, 1983: 39). A succession of commentators have regarded much popular music as mindless fodder, cynically manufactured for mindless youthful consumers. Bloom, for instance, claims that rock presents life as 'a nonstop commercial prepackaged masturbational fantasy' (1987) which he charges as responsible for the atrophy of the minds and bodies of youth.

Underpinning such views are assumptions about the potentially disruptive nature of 'the popular', and the need for social control and the regulation of popular pleasures. The high culture view of popular culture has been criticized for failing to recognize the active nature of popular culture consumption; failing to treat the cultural forms seriously on their own terms; biased by aesthetic prejudices, which are rarely explicated; and resting on outmoded class-based notions of a high–low culture split. The traditionally claimed distinctions between high and low culture have become blurred. High art has been increasingly commodified and commercialized, while some forms of popular culture have become more 'respectable', receiving state funding and broader critical acceptance.

The high culture perspective remains evident in the application of **aesthetics** to popular music, and the tendency of **musicology** to ignore or dismiss popular music genres. It also underpins some state attitudes towards the funding and regulation of cultural forms. At an everyday level, it is implicit in the manner in which musicians, fans, and critics make distinctions of value both between and within particular genres.

See also: **audiences; culture; Frankfurt School**

Further reading: Abbs (1975); Bloom (1987); Hall and Whannel (1964); Swingewood (1977)

HIP-HOP *see* **rap**

HISTORY

As a field of study, the history of popular music has been subject to internal critiques and debates in a similar manner to other forms of historical writing. At issue are the boundaries of the field, including its tendency to privilege Western developments; the treatment of various genres within it; and the emphasis which should be accorded to the context within which popular music is produced: the producers of music, the music, and its fans and the processes of consumption.

The history of popular music, especially in relation to the emergence of rock'n'roll and its subsequent generic development and mutation, has usually been presented in a fairly standard form, based around a chronological sequence of genres (see Bradley, 1992; Friedlander, 1996; Garofalo, 1997; Starr and Waterman, 2003). This sees it as essentially a Western tradition, and privileges rock'n'roll and the genres it mutated into. This tradition has been critiqued as 'rockist' (e.g. by Negus, 1996; on this point, see **popular music**). The various histories display a tendency to emphasize performers, genres, and texts, with rather less attention to the role of technology and economics. An example of this approach is the weight usually attached to the role of creative individuals in establishing rock'n'roll in the 1950s: Elvis Presley, Little Richard, Bill Haley, Buddy Holly, and Chuck Berry are seen to have virtually created the genre and revitalized popular music in the process. At one level, the impact of these performers is undisputed: even though they were adapting existing styles and forms, they were clearly innovative (see Gillet, 1983). But as Curtis observes, '*all* popular performers come along at the right time' and 'to explain the success of a given act, you need to make the social and cultural context of that success as specific as possible' (Curtis, 1987: 5). Accordingly, other writers have paid greater attention to the social, economic, and demographic situation in the US and the UK in the early 1950s, producing rather different accounts (e.g. Peterson, 1990).

'Framing' principles (other than chronology) used to outline and 'explain' the history of popular music include gender (e.g. O'Brien, 2002), technology (e.g. Millard, 1995, on sound recording), and its industrial organization, especially the role of independent labels (e.g. Kennedy and McNutt, 1999). Histories can also be situated around a particular musical genre or general style, as in Prendergast's sweeping study of ambient music (2003), or focus on a particular period and its broader culture, such as 'swinging London' and the 'innovation of cool' in the 1960s (Levy, 2003). There is a group of histories of popular music whose authors adopt a more idiosyncratic approach, often drawing on insider status. For example, Napier-Bell presents an historical account of the British music industry, tinged with cynicism reflecting his experiences in it (notably as manager for the Kinks in the 1960s). He attributes a key role to the use/abuse of drugs, as his title indicates: *Black Vinyl, White Powder* (2002).

The creation of a number of museums devoted to the history of popular music is part of the now prominent 'heritage industry'. Prominent examples in the United States include the Rock and Roll Hall of Fame (Cleveland), the Experience Museum (Seattle), and the Delta Blues Museum (Clarkesdale). The Delta Blues Museum, established in 1979, is typical of the approach and displays here, featuring vintage instruments and recording equipment, early recordings, and memorabilia. It has a library, a record collection, and an archive, including letters and photographs. Supported by performers such as ZZ Top, and the magazine *Living Blues*, the Delta Blues Museum seeks to preserve the music, and to raise the self-esteem of local people by reminding them of the important role the area has played in the development of the music. As do 'mainstream' museums, popular music museums raise questions on the selection of the material for inclusion (which artists, periods, styles, artefacts) and the manner in which these are to be contextualized and displayed. This process of reconstructing the musical past has created debate (see e.g. Strausbaugh, 2001; Santelli, 1999).

See also: **canon; discography***;* **documentary; memorabilia**

Further reading: Bradley (1992); Ennis (1992); Garofalo (1997); Negus (1996)

Viewing: *Dancing in the Street* (1995)

Websites: Rock and Roll Hall of Fame: www.rockhall.com; Delta Blues Museum: www.deltabluesmuseum.org

HOMOLOGY

In general terms, a reproduction or repetition of structure (O'Sullivan *et al.*, 1994), applied to popular music homology refers to the 'fit' between lifestyle/values and music preferences. The concept was central to the consideration of the place of music in youth **subcultures** by the subcultural analysts of the 1970s. Their answer to the question 'what specifically does a subcultural style signify to the members of the subculture themselves?' was to identify an homology between the 'focal concerns, activities, group structure and the collective self-image' of the subculture, and the cultural artefacts and practices adopted by the members of the subculture. The latter were seen as 'objects in which they could see their central values held and reflected' (Hall and Jefferson, eds, 1976: 56). The case of **skinhead** subculture was often used to demonstrate such an homology. The skins' style of heavy 'bovver' boots, braces, and drastically cropped hair communicated and asserted their values of 'hardness, masculinity and working-classness. The symbolic objects – dress, appearance, language, ritual occasions, styles of interaction, music – were made to form a unity with the group's relations, situation, experience' (ibid.).

The most extensive and theoretically sophisticated applications of the concept of homology to the preferred music of specific subcultures are Willis's study of bike boys (rockers) and hippies, *Profane Culture* (1978), and Hebdige's various case studies in his hugely influential study *Subculture: The Meaning of Style* (1979). Willis argued that there existed a 'fit' between certain styles and **fashions**, cultural values, and group **identity**; e.g. between the intense activism, physical prowess, love of machines, and taboo on introspection, of motor-bike boys, and their preference for 1950s rock'n'roll. For Hebdige, the punks best illustrated the principle.

> The subculture was nothing if not consistent. There was a homological relation between the trashy cut-up clothes and spiky hair, the pogo and the amphetamines, the spitting, the vomiting, the format of the fanzines, the insurrectionary poses and the 'soulless', frantically driven music. The punks wore clothes which were the sartorial equivalent of swear words, and they swore as they dressed – with calculated effect, lacing obscenities into record notes and publicity releases, interviews and love songs (Hebdige, 1979: 114).

Later writers on subcultures challenged the 'Birmingham position'. Writing at the end of the 1980s, Middleton concludes that subcultural analysis had drawn the connection between music and subculture much too tightly, 'flawed above all by the uncompromising drive to homology' (Middleton, 1990: 161). However, homology still has value as an analytical concept, particularly when used in conjunction with approaches to subculture derived from urban studies. Analyses of the cultural style and values provided in **hardcore** subcultures such as 'straightedge', and the cultural practices of **rap**, provide contemporary examples.

See also: **scenes; subculture**

Further reading: Gelder and Thornton, eds (1997); Hebdige (1979); Middleton (1990); Willis (1978)

HOUSE

House is a central style within the broad corpus of **dance music**. The various accounts of the origins of house music centre on its foundations in New York's underground dance scene in the 1970s. House was a direct descendant of **disco** and an important element of the dance **club** scene by the mid-1980s. House music got its name from the late-night parties held in warehouses, originally in New York, but then more prominently in Chicago, where 'DJs mixed the music in elaborate and lengthy sets in which segments of many songs were interspersed with one another. House music was propelled by the throbbing rhythms of disco, but with the emphasis less on lyrics and more on atmosphere and beat' (*Music Central 96*).

A number of identifiable variants of house developed (see the useful chart in Woodstra and Bogdanov, eds, 2001: 630). Two influential subgenres were Chicago house and acid house. In Chicago house, DJs combined German techno pioneers Kraftwerk with soul, drum machines. Influential pioneers included Frankie Knuckles at the Warehouse club (where Knuckles played from 1977 until 1983), and Francis Grosso at Sanctuary, a converted church: 'Grosso was the first DJ to segue records together into one, uninterrupted groove, emphasizing the hypnotic quality of the music's rhythm track and keeping the dancers locked on the floor' (Kempster, 1996: 11). Acid house saw musicians using Roland 303 and similar drum machines/ synthesizers, to produce dance music characterized by eclecticism and a splintering off into substyles (see Prendergast, 2003; Sicko, 1999). Acid house cross-fertilized with **indie music** in the UK in the late 1980s and early 1990s. For example, Primal Scream – originally the purveyors of prototypical indie 45s like 'All Fall Down' (Creation, 1985) – reinvented themselves with the release of *Screamadelica* (Creation, 1991). (See also **Madchester** and the **rave** scene.)

As Straw concludes: 'The most significant event in the history of dance music since 1980 has been the rise of house music' (Straw,

141

2001: 171). House was a musical style developed largely outside of rock and pop music; it laid the basis for the massive dance explosion of the 1990s; it gave dance a new rhythmic foundation; and it changed the nature of DJ work (ibid.).

A dimension of house music that has attracted considerable academic interest is the manner in which house music clubs represented 'temporary autonomous zones', largely free of outside surveillance, in which 'the public spectacle is abandoned' and displaced by a new 'tactile-audio space' (Rietveld, 1998: 204–5).

Further reading: Collins (1998); Gilbert and Pearson (1999); Kempster (1996); Reynolds (1998: ch. 3); Rietveld (1998); Straw (2001)

IDENTITY

Identity is the cultural descriptions of individuals (self and others), groups, and socio-political entities with which we identify. 'Identity is cultural since the resources that form the material for identity formation – language and cultural practices – are social in character' (Barker, 2002: 225). This emphasizes that identity, rather than being fixed and static, is a process of *becoming*, which is developed out of points of similarity and difference, involving both self-description and social ascription. Popular music is an aspect of attempts to define identity at the levels of self, community, and nation.

Self-identity can be expressed through the use of music consumption to indicate membership of constituencies based around class, gender, and ethnicity. At times, this is more loosely organized around particular scenes and sounds, as with **rave culture** and contemporary **dance music**. Self-identity can also be based on activities such as **fandom**, and practices such as **record collecting**. These identifications are not fixed and constraining; they produce differentially constructed *identities*, which can draw on an amalgam of factors, and which are subject to change. Self-identity also involves situating self in relation to competing discourses. For example, adherence to a musical genre can be used to distance oneself from the parent culture/community/social authority. In the 1950s, 'while rock 'n' roll was undoubtedly a moment in the expansion and technological development of the entertainment industry, it was also an instance of the use of foreign music by a generation as a means to distance themselves from a parental "national" culture' (Laing, 1986: 338).

Popular music plays a prominent role in the creation of community identity in the links between music and **locality**, especially in local scenes and subcultures. At the national level, identity is a part of cultural policies (e.g. quotas) aimed at promoting locally produced music, and the association of particular genres and national settings (e.g. salsa and the Caribbean).

National identity can be regarded as a social construct as much as a quality associated with a physical space. While such identities may be constructed or imagined (see Anderson, 1983), they are mobilized for particular interests, and emerge partly in relation to different 'others'. Popular music can be part of this, as evident in Nazi Germany in the 1930s (see Negus, 1996), and in various national cultural movements (see Garofalo, 1992b; Cloonan and Garofalo, 2003).

Further reading: Born and Hesmondhalgh (2000)

IDEOLOGY

Ideology can be understood 'in terms of ideas, meanings and practices which, while they purport to be universal truths, are better understood as maps of cultural significance. Above all, ideology is not separate from the practical activities of life but is a material phenomenon rooted in day-to-day conditions. Ideologies provide people with rules of practical conduct and moral behaviour' (Barker, 2002: 225). Various world views constitute ideologies, or, to put it another way, all social groups have ideologies. 'Ideology cannot be seen as a simple tool of domination but should be regarded as discourses which have specific *consequences* for relations of power at all levels of social relationships' (ibid.).

An example of ideology in popular music is provided by the emergence of rock in the 1960s. The subsequent use of the term 'classic rock' was confirmation of the status of the musical genre, with its associated values and set of practices: live performance, self-expression, and authenticity; the group as the creative unit, with the charismatic lead singer playing a key role, and the guitar as the primary instrument. This was a version of classic Romanticism, an ideology with its origins in art and aesthetics. Classic rock also produced a heavily gendered discourse, which celebrated a 'male homosocial paradigm of musicianship' (Den Tandt, 2004: 139). This ideology continued to dominate subsequent discourse, not just around rock music, but of popular music more generally (see **authenticity**).

Further reading: Gracyk (2001); Frith (1996); Grossberg (1992a)

INDEPENDENTS/INDIES; INDIE MUSIC

Indies are small record labels which are independent of the **majors** (at least in terms of the artist acquisition, recording, and promotion), though still reliant on a major for distribution. These labels are frequently considered to be more flexible and innovative in their roster of artists. They have been associated with the emergence of new genres: 'It is an attitude with a sound ... The heart and soul of it resides in record labels such as Creation, 4AD, Sub Pop, Demon, Stiff etc' (Larkin, ed., 1995).

It has been argued that independent record companies in the 1950s did not have the corporate hierarchy of the majors, and so had greater flexibility in picking up on and promoting new trends and talent, and a greater ability to adjust record production. In companies such as Sun, the owner, record producer, sound technician, and promoter often were the same person (as with Sam Philips at Sun). 'The 1950s decade was the golden era for small independents, which embraced blues, gospel, modern jazz, country, R&B, and rock'n'roll' (Kennedy and McNutt, 1999: xvii; this study provides an excellent history of the 'little labels' from 1920 to 1970). From 1948 to 1954, about one thousand new record labels were formed.

The independent sector continued to be an important part of the music industry, often acting as developers of talent for the majors. To maintain their market control, the larger companies have adopted several strategies in relation to the independents: buying out their artists' contracts (RCA and Elvis from Sun), or persuading artists to move labels; entering into marketing and other business arrangements with them, or simply buying them out. Several independents acquired a significant market share, as with **Motown** in the 1960s; these became mid-range companies, situated between the majors and the independents, and were subject to absorption by their larger rivals (see **market cycles**). At times, as in the 1950s, independent labels have been associated with the emergence of new styles of music: Stiff and British punk; Sub Pop and grunge; Def Jam and rap; Creation and Britpop; and Word and Christian music. While there are a huge number of independent labels, and they produce two-thirds of the titles released, their market share remains small, usually around 15 to 20 per cent (Hull, 2004).

The operation of the independents and the precise nature of their relationship with the majors has been debated. For example, in a case study of Wax Trax! Records, a Chicago-based industrial dance label, Lee argued that market expansion and the necessary links with majors for distribution force such indies to increasingly adopt the business practices of the majors, in the process moving away from their traditional cultural goals of artistry and creativity. The result is a 'hybrid label – a privately-held company that deals with a major for important production elements or that receives some of its operating funds from a major' (Lee, 1995: 196). The interaction between the majors and independents in such situations, however, remains a dynamic process. The examples of Creation and the career of Oasis (Harris, 2004), and Rough Trade (Hesmondhalgh, 1997) in the UK during the 1990s illustrated a definite blurring of the boundaries between the independents and the major companies.

The term **indie music** is used for a broad musical style, primarily equated with **alternative** music. This can be problematic, as in the case of the *Guinness Who's Who of Indie and New Wave* (Larkin, ed., 1995). Here, indie music is defined as 'music after the Sex Pistols played by creative on the edge musicians with lots of nice guitars that sound a bit like the Byrds, Velvet Underground and MC5'. Not only does this cover a considerable range of musical styles, but the volume includes 'electro synth' bands like Depeche Mode, 'basic rock bands' like the Del Lords and the Dead Kennedys, along with a large number of other punk performers.

Both senses of indie are linked to a set of dominant musical values, with **authenticity** at their core (Azerrad, 2001). These are cast as diametrically opposed to a stereotyped mainstream. Indie ideology views the music as raw and immediate, while mainstream music is processed and mediated by 'overproduction'; indie bands can reproduce their music in concert and even improve upon it, while mainstream bands use too many electronic effects to reproduce their music live. The crossover of indie bands from smaller labels into the mainstream music industry, as occurred with U2, R.E.M., and Nirvana, led to considerable debate among their fans.

See also: **alternative; authenticity**

Further reading: Hesmondhalgh (2002); Hull (2004); Kennedy and McNutt (1999); Shepherd *et al*. (2003: 683–776) contains an extensive list of record labels, including the main independents, which are often nationally based

INTERNET; NAPSTER

Created originally for military use, the Internet is a computer-linked global communications technology, with dramatically increasing numbers of people accessing it in the 1990s. The World Wide Web (WWW), a major part of the Internet, is the graphical network that contains websites dedicated to one topic, person, or company. These websites have homepages, which contain hyperlinks, which allow users to jump to other locations on the Internet. The Internet added a major new dimension to the marketing, accessing, reception, and consumption of popular music, while creating new problems for the enforcement of copyright.

The Web includes online music shops; sites for record companies and performers; online music journals; online concerts and interviews; Web radio, and bulletin boards. These represent new ways of inter-linking the audience/consumers of popular music, the performers, and the music industry. Discussions of the significance of such electronic commerce emphasize the business/economic aspects: the benefits to firms and consumers; the barriers and difficulties associated with doing business via the Net; the demographics of Net users; and the opportunities for companies on the Net. There are also significant cultural issues associated with popular music on the Net, which link up with on-going debates in the study of popular music, notably the relative importance (power) of the music industry and the consumers of popular music. The Net may create greater **consumer sovereignty** and choice by bypassing the traditional intermediaries operating in the music industry (primarily the record companies). The major record companies were initially slow to recognize its potential, but soon moved to create sites to showcase their activities and their artists (see Bibliography: websites). The nature and regulation of intellectual property rights was brought into even sharper focus with the electronic retrieval possibilities implicit in the Net. Beginning around 1999–2000, the mainstream music industry showed increasing alarm at the impact on their market share of operations such as Napster and practices such as the downloading of MP3s, and P2P (person-to-person) file sharing (see MP3). The accompanying debate is central to current popular music studies, as illustrated in the exchange between Marcus Breen and Eamonn Forde (*Popular Music*, 23, 1, 2004) and the contributors to a special issue of *Popular Music and Society* (27, 2, June 2004) on digital music delivery.

Napster software was introduced in 1999, 'designed as a combination search engine, communication portal, and file-sharing software that facilitated the sharing process by granting users access to all other Napster users and the MP3 files they chose to share' (Garofalo, 2003: 31). Within a few months, transfers of music files using Napster reached millions per day, and, at its peak, it was estimated that as many as 60 million people were using the service. The copyright violation and consequent loss of revenue led several artists (notably the band Metallica) and record labels to sue Napster for breach of copyright. The issues involved were complex and the litigation process was a lengthy and very public one. Napster was forced to close down, but was relaunched as a legitimate service in late 2003 (Napster 2.0). Newer technologies and providers moved things to another level: 'Whereas Napster required users first to log onto a central server to access other users' MP3 files, these newer networks allow direct user-to-user (peer-to-peer) (often abbreviated to P2P) connections involving multiple file types. These innovations expand the universe of file sharing activity and make it virtually impossible to track users or the files they choose to share' (Garofalo, 2003: 31). The battle over P2P file sharing continued, with the music industry targeting new, post-Napster services, and individual consumers whom they perceived as infringing copyright. An alternative industry strategy also emerged when in 2000 record companies began establishing copyright deals with Internet music producers. In 2003 the entry of Apple into the music marketplace, with its iTunes service, met with considerable success, encouraging the development of further such services.

There are several core issues in these developments and debates. At an immediate level has been the question of the impact of downloading on 'legitimate' recording sales. From the industry point of view, and some observers, downloading was clearly hurting the industry (e.g. Hull, 2004). Others were not so convinced, and there have been some interesting comparisons with similar earlier episodes, notably home taping (see Jones and Lenhart, 2004). Secondly, market control was central to the debate around Napster and its successors: were artists and the recording companies being *dis*empowered, and consumers (end-users) being *em*powered by the increasing availability of online music? A related aspect is the nature of the engagement of consumers with music through online practices, and the formats and artists downloaded.

Any new medium or technological form changes the way in which we experience music, with implications for how we relate to and consume music (see **technology**). In the case of the Net, an interesting question is what happens to traditional notions of the 'distance' between consumer and product, and its technological mediation?

In 2004, music buying looks set to continue to shift online. Legal downloading is taking an increasing market share (Hull, 2004: 258–9), made even more attractive by the development of the iPod and its competitors, portable music systems capable of storing huge numbers of songs in digital format.

See also: **MP3; piracy; technology**

Further reading: Garofalo (2003); Hull (2004); *Popular Music and Society*, 27, 2, June 2004 (special issue on digital music delivery)

JAM BANDS

A label applied to bands whose performances and recordings feature extended improvisation – 'jamming'. Associated originally with **jazz**, especially free and acid jazz, jamming was first evident in rock in the 1960s, especially in the work of the Grateful Dead, and in psychedelic styles more generally (e.g. Cream and Quicksilver Messenger Service). In the late 1960s and through into the 1970s it was central to **progressive** rock, although often in a more constrained fashion. Since the 1990s, the term has been used in the music press to refer to American bands such as Phish and the Dave Matthews Band, and the still active Grateful Dead (in several guises since the death of leader Jerry Garcia in 1995). The commercial and artistic status of these performers was based on their live shows, associated notions of musical authenticity, and a dedicated fan base. The **fans** of jam bands often traded concert tapes (see **bootlegs**), reflecting the different musical inflections in jam bands' performance of a standard set list.

Listening: Cream, *Wheels of Fire* (Polydor, 1968); the Grateful Dead, *Live Dead* (WB, 1969); Phish, *A Picture of Nectar* (Elektra, 1991)
Website: www.jambands.com

JAZZ

As a musical style and very broad metagenre, jazz is only very briefly considered here, primarily in terms of its links to and influence on more 'mainstream' popular music genres, fusing with these to create new forms: jazz rock fusion, jazz funk, and acid jazz. Jazz was also the first home for many musicians who moved over into other genres, notably **skiffle** in the 1950s.

Established at the beginning of the twentieth century, jazz was an American idiom developed from ragtime, blues, and the popular music of its day. The key component of jazz was improvisation, in which each performance represents an original and spontaneous creation (Gridley, 1997). Its subsequent genesis spawned increasingly varied and disparate subgenres, spreading regionally from Southern centres to generate distinct styles in St Louis, Kansas City, Chicago, New York, and beyond. The standard histories of jazz refer to a wide range of styles, including traditional (or Dixieland) jazz, swing, bebop, cool jazz, free jazz, and fusion. The music press and jazz collectors were important in the **canonization** of particular jazz styles and performers (Gabbard, ed. 1995; Gendron, 2002). The evolution of jazz has been punctuated by the renaissance of older styles and the creation of new fusions, most recently hip-bop and acid jazz in the 1990s. A popular dance genre, acid jazz combines elements of jazz, hip-hop, funk, and R&B. It has been primarily a singles medium. (For a representative compilation, see *Acid Jazz: Collection 1* (Scotti Brothers, 1997).)

Major jazz artists who at times shifted between these styles include Benny Goodman, Duke Ellington, Dave Brubeck, Ella Fitzgerald, Count Basie, Sarah Vaughan, Billie Holiday, Louis Armstrong, Miles Davis, John Coltrane, Thelonious Monk, Charlie Parker, and Wynton Marsalis.

Chronologically jazz styles are termed pre-modern (pre-1940) and the more diverse modern (post-1940). It is the latter which I am concerned with here, concentrating on two which exerted considerable influence on 'mainstream' popular music: bebop, and jazz rock/fusion. Bebop is an alliterative word possibly derived from the cry of 'arriba' heard in the Latin American bands of the period. Developed initially in New York, bebop was the popular name given to early modern jazz developments of the 1940s: 'a deliberate attempt by serious jazz musicians to move jazz away from the simple harmonies and basic rhythms of the earlier styles. Employing extended chordal harmonies and broken rhythms, bop changed the face of jazz' (Hardy and Laing, eds, 1990). Leading exponents included Dizzy Gillespie, Charlie Parker, and Thelonious Monk. The name fell out of use as the style became more broadly incorporated into modern jazz. Bebop's link with mainstream popular music was via the beats in the 1950s; its adoption as part of the musical palette utilized by some **progressive** and art rock performers in the 1960s and 1970s; and, more recently, as an element in some styles of **drum'n'bass**.

The term 'fusion' is variously used to designate the amalgamation of two styles of music, as in the fusion of folk and rock to form **folk rock**, a mix of electric and acoustic instrumentation and sounds. The term is most commonly applied to the music produced by the fusion of jazz and rock, jazz rock, which attempts to fuse elements of both styles. Jazz rock combines jazz improvisation with the instrumentation and rhythm of R&B, employing technology to a greater extent, including at times replacing the piano with the electric piano and the synthesizer. The more 'jazz-oriented' versions are usually referred to as fusion, while some commentators prefer the term jazz-rock fusion (Gammond, ed., 1991). The most critical and commercially successful United States exponents include Return to Forever, Blood, Sweat and Tears, and Weather Report, who had creative peaks in the early 1970s. In the UK the band Coliseum was the best-known exponent of the style, which was also an element in the work of guitarists such as Jeff Beck. Other musicians to work in a jazz rock vein include Stanley Clarke and Return to Forever, Chick Corea, Miles Davis, Larry Coryell, and John McLaughlin.

Further reading: Fordham (1991); Carr *et al.* (1988); Gridley (1997); Owens (1995)

Viewing: *Jazz* (Ken Burns, 2001), a ten-part, nineteen-hour documentary

Listening: *Ken Burns Jazz: The Story of America's Music* (5 CD boxed set; a twenty-track sampler is also available: *The Best of Ken Burns Jazz*) (Columbia/ Legacy and Verve Music Group joint release); Thelonious Monk, *Something in Blue* (Black Lion, 1972); Blood, Sweat & Tears, 'Spinning Wheel', *Greatest Hits* (CBS, 1972); Weather Report, *Mysterious Traveller* (Columbia, 1974); Jeff Beck, *Blow By Blow* (Epic, 1975)

KARAOKE

Karaoke can best be considered a performance/singing style, and a social experience. The karaoke machine is an electric (and, later, an electronic) apparatus designed especially for amateur 'hidden singers'. Karaoke involves people as singers, co-singers, and as listeners: 'It combines at the same time musical technologies, personal experiences and collective memories' (Mitsui and Hosokawa, eds, 1998: 3). It was first developed in Japan in the 1970s, where it became something of a social phenomenon over the following decade. Digital technologies, the advent of the CD, and the adding of a visual dimension all enhanced the appeal of karaoke. In the mid- to late 1980s, karaoke became internationalized, with karaoke bars appearing in the Pacific Rim, East Asia, North America and Europe. Reflecting this popularization, academic interest in karaoke grew in the 1990s. The practice was variously condemned as ephemeral and banal, or celebrated as democratic and pleasurable. In a key volume which synthesizes and moves beyond this work, Mitsui and Hosokawa (1998) and their contributors examine what underlies karaoke experiences, 'the cultural meanings produced by the resonance and dissonance between technology, place and behaviour' (Introduction).

Further reading: Mitsui and Hosokawa, eds (1998)

LANGUAGE

The issues here include language choice and dialect in popular music, with these related broadly to the politics of identity, multiculturalism, and the global dominance of English. These are evident in the work of a range of musical styles and artists, and also in listener and audience responses to them. The importance of language and lyrical realism is a feature of rap, reggae, and the blues (see **lyric analysis**), which also rely on particular oral styles: respectively rapping, toasting, and 'talkin' blues'. Considerations of which language will gain a wider audience, and the associated concerns of **authenticity** and musical meaning, has faced international variants of pop and rock (e.g. Cantonpop – see Mitchell, 1996; Europop – see Frith, 2001). Various styles of **world music** have been particularly conscious of the linguistic imperialism exercised by English, although these have also turned their exoticism to advantage in the marketplace, as a marker of authenticity. A similar concern also partly underpins national or regional cultural policies seeking to privilege and preserve linguistic identity, as in Francophone Quebec (see **policy**).

The appropriation of particular dialects, accents, and even specific vocabulary is evident in performers' vocal styles, punk rock, for example (see Laing, 1988). This can involve reappropriation of derogatory language, a process exemplified by black musicians (and audiences) in the United States using the term nigger (or 'nigga') to signify and affirm ethnic and community solidarity, compared with its historical use by whites. This can be in an ironic mode, as with Sly and the Family Stone's 'Don't Call Me Nigga Whitey' (1969). Reappropriation can also be gendered, as with **riot grrrl**'s use of 'slut' (Leonard, 1997) and women rappers use of 'bitch' and 'ho'.

See also: **lyric analysis**

Further reading: Berger and Carrol, eds (2003)

LISTENING

Listening is a physical process situated in social contexts and mediated by technology. Considerations of these aspects of listening have been a small but significant part of popular music studies. Listening to music is an activity which takes place with varying levels of intensity, influenced by the consumption context and the style of the performer: 'the "distracted" environment of many club settings and the hushed concentration typical of singer-songwriter concerts might represent two extremes' (Middleton, 1990: 95). More melodious and 'non-abrasive' styles of music form the staple of radio 'easy listening', and the loose genre of 'lounge music', while louder genres (heavy metal; hard rock) have been seen as dangerous to listeners' hearing. The development of headphones and the Walkman enabled different styles of listening, while reconfiguring the social locations and contexts within which it occurred (see Millard, 1995).

Negus identifies two groups of listeners focused on by Adorno and later theorists: those lost in the crowd, and easily manipulated into the collectivity, and obsessive individuals, alienated and not fully integrated into social life, with both types part of the anxieties of moral guardians (Negus, 1996). Adorno saw the mass culture products of the music industry as requiring very little effort on the part of listeners. He argued that it led to 'de-concentrated listening in which listeners rejected anything unfamiliar, regressing to "child-like" behaviour' (1991: 44–5). One facet of this was what Adorno termed 'quotation listening', where instead of listening to a piece of music and trying to grasp it as a whole, the regressive listener dwelt only on the most obvious aspects of melody. In the process listeners adopted a 'musical child's language' and responded to different works 'as if the symphony were structurally the same as a ballad' (1945: 213). Adorno referred disparagingly to the category of 'easy listening' as an example of the music industry's deliberately encouraging distracted audience activity, with an emphasis on the most familiar harmonies, rhythms and melodies, and producing a 'soporific' effect on social consciousness. Adorno saw this as fulfilling an ideological function in rendering the listening **audience** passive and making them unable to reflect critically on their world.

This view of passive listening has been challenged, especially by the active audience paradigm prominent in much recent media/cultural studies. Listening to particular musical styles requires distinct cultural capital, including, but not limited to, a knowledge of the sonic codes and conventions of the genre and the previous work of the performer and similar artists. Unfamiliar music requires 'work', musical labour to situate the piece in relation to other, already familiar music. Hennion (2003) has been prominent in developing what he calls a sociology of mediation, and a related history of listening. Undertaking fascinating empirical research into how people listen, he argues that listening technologies have transformed, and in a sense created, the act of listening (see also Tagg and Clarida, 2003).

Further reading: Gracyk (2001); Hennion (2003); Middleton (1990); Negus (1996)

LIVE; LIVE PERFORMANCE

Musical performance occurs in a wide variety of contexts. It can be impromptu and domestic, the classic singing in the shower, but the focus here is on public performance. This is either 'live' or a mediated form of the live (pseudo-live: experienced at one remove from the site of initial production). Live music, in the first sense of the term, is experienced in venues such as clubs, discos, and pubs; and through concerts and music festivals. The pseudo-live performance is through film, stage musicals, radio, and as music video. However, all of these forms mediate the music, creating a diegetic link between performer, text, and consumer. Their significance in determining cultural meaning lies in the interrelationship of ritual, pleasure, and economics. Popular music performance shapes audiences, fuels individual fantasy and pleasure, and creates icons and cultural myths. Investigating the processes involved in how performance communicates musical meaning to its constituent audiences in such different contexts has been a major preoccupation of popular music scholarship.

Historically, prior to the advent of recorded sound, all music was live, and was experienced as such. The term 'live' performance is now usually reserved for those situations where the audience is in physical proximity to the performance, and the experience of the music is contiguous with its actual performance. The status of live recordings is regarded as rather ambivalent, given that many are technologically sonically upgraded prior to their release.

For many critics, fans, and musicians there is a perceived hierarchy of live performances, with a marked tendency to equate the audiences' physical proximity to the actual 'performance' and intimacy with the performer(s) with a more authentic and satisfying musical experience. This view was central to the **ideology** of rock created during the

1960s, where it represented 'an ideologically invested practice whose value depends on a set of overlapping elements, including real-time interaction, a masculine mystique, work ideologies, and a realist aesthetic' (Den Tandt, 2004: ???).

This emphasis on the live as a key signifier of musical **authenticity** has since been undermined by performers who work primarily, and at times exclusively, in the studio setting. Some genres are now largely studio creations, especially recent styles of **techno**. At times, performance events have had the capacity to encapsulate and represent key periods and turning points in rock. Their significance is indicated by their use in a cultural shorthand fashion among fans, musicians, and writers (e.g. 'Woodstock') with an assumed set of connotations: the counter-culture, music festivals, youth, and 1960s idealism.

See also: **authenticity; concerts**

Further reading: Gracyk (1996)

LOCALITY

Locality has emerged as a key concept in contemporary popular music studies, picking up on well-established trends in cultural geography, and drawing on social anthropological methodology. Cultural geographers have been doing research on music since the late 1960s, seeking to establish 'the nexus between the social, cultural, economic and political in musical analysis' (Kong, 1995: 273). The breadth of this work can be seen in a recent edited collection which presents 'A Geography of American Music from Country to Classic and Blues to Bop' (subtitle), and includes a selected music geography bibliography (Carney, ed., 2003).

The geographical analysis of popular music has emphasized the dynamics and consequences of the geographical distribution of recorded popular music around the world, and how particular musical sounds have become associated with particular places (Carney, 1990; Kong, 1995). Locality has been used in a number of overlapping ways in popular music studies:

(1) To consider global processes of cultural homogenization and commodification, and the intersection of these with the local. The study of the global geographical distribution of recorded

popular music is concerned with the nature, status, and operation of cultural imperialism, and the relationship between local music and the international music industry. Here locality becomes a marker of political experience, juxtaposed against the other to ideologically valorize and support local music.

(2) The way in which music has frequently been used to express conceptions of homeland or national, regional, or community identity. This can take the form of sexual identity; e.g. the production of spaces of musical reception for the 'queer' community (Valentine, 1995).

(3) Locality as a social experience, linked to songwriters as a theme and as a means to authenticate their music (e.g. Bruce Springsteen).

(4) The notion of localized scenes/sounds. Histories of popular music will often refer to particular geographic locales, usually cities or regions, as being identified at a specific historical juncture with a sound; e.g. Chicago Blues. Somewhat contiguous with this usage is the application of the concept of scene; e.g. Athens, Georgia in the late 1980s. This implies a range of activities, loosely centred around and aligned to a particular style of music and its associated performers. Aside from exploring the characteristics of such scenes, a central interest in popular music studies has been the question of *why* they develop at a specific location at a particular time. Also 'we must question the underpinning assumption that sound and location are in some way connected' (Street, 1995: 256; for a fuller discussion, see **scenes**).

Cohen (1995: 65) suggests locality could be most usefully used in popular music studies in an anthropological sense:

to discuss networks of social relationships, practices and processes extending across particular places; to imply a methodological orientation concerned with the particular rather than the general, the concrete rather then the abstract. It could also emphasize interconnections and interdependencies between, for example, space and time, the contextual and the conceptual, the individual and the collective, the self and other.

Further reading: Carney, ed. (2003); Cohen (1995); Negus (1996: ch. 6); Street (1995); Whiteley *et al.* (2004). *Popular Music* 19, 1, 2000 is a special issue on place and scene

LYRIC ANALYSIS

In relation to song lyrics, the concept of realism asserts 'a direct relationship between a lyric and the social or emotional condition it describes and represents' (Frith, 1988b: 112; see also Middleton, 1990). This is evident in much study of folk song and the analysis of blues lyrics; e.g. interpreting American post-war urban blues lyrics as expressing their black singers' personal adjustment to urban ghetto-ization: 'a more detailed analysis of blues lyrics might make it possible to describe with greater insight the changes in male roles within the Negro community as defined by Negroes at various levels of socio-economic status and mobility within the lower class' (Keil, 1966: 74). Longhurst (1995) suggests that realism can also be applied to ska in the 1960s, with its concern for Jamaica's 'rude boys', and songs debating whether their activities could be considered a form of social and political protest, or simply anti-social, personally motivated criminality. Later **reggae** music, especially that of Bob Marley and the Wailers, was also strongly realist, addressing class struggle in Jamaica, and blacks' international situation in their struggle against the dominance of 'Babylon'. Black underclasses in Jamaica, and elsewhere, could readily identify with the issues in such songs.

Much **textual analysis** of popular music has been concerned with the lyrical component of songs. In a significant historical discussion, 'Why Do Songs Have Words?', Frith shows how through the 1950s and 1960s the sociology of popular music was dominated by the analysis of the words of songs. This was largely because such an approach was grounded in a familiar research methodology – content analysis – and assumed 'that it was possible to read back from lyrics to the social forces that produced them' (Frith, 1988b: 106). This approach has continued to be important, although its application has been tempered.

There are numerous examples of attempts to analyse song lyrics as examples of shifts in popular ideologies of sex, romance, and rela-tionships. These frequently emphasize lyrics as mirrors of social, political, and personal issues (e.g. Cooper, 1992). Given that **song-writers** are social beings, the words of the songs do express general social attitudes, and are worth study. But 'they treat lyrics too simply. The words of all songs are of equal value; their meaning is taken to be transparent; no account is given of their actual performance or their musical setting. Even more problematically, these analysts tend to equate a song's popularity to public agreement with the message' (Frith, 1988b: 107). Songs create identification through their emotional appeal, but this does not necessarily mean that they can be reduced to a simple slogan or message (see Gracyk, 2001, for an instructive discussion of this point).

Lyric analysis also tends to valorize certain forms of popular music, most notably blues, soul, and country, and some varieties of rock – the singer-songwriter – Dylan, Newman, etc. These are seen as 'the authentic expression of popular experiences and needs', whereas mainstream popular music song lyrics are largely seen in terms of mass culture arguments, and criticized for their banality and lack of depth (Adorno, 1941; Hoggart, 1957). In a left version of this critique, Harker (1980) reads off Tin Pan Alley lyrics as straightforward statements of bourgeois hegemony, equating pop's central themes of love and romance with the 'sentimental ideology' of capitalist society. Conversely, Harker argues for 'authentic' lyrics as the expression of 'authentic' relationships, with both reflecting direct experience, unmediated by ideology.

Part of the argument for rock music's superiority over pop and earlier forms of popular music rested on the claim that its major songwriters were poets. Richard Goldstein's *The Poetry of Rock* (1969) and similar anthologies helped popularize this view. Frith (1988b: 117) points out that this work has emphasized a particular form of rock lyrics – those akin to romantic poetry with lots of covert and obscure allusions. This approach attempts to validate rock in terms of established 'art' forms, elevating the role of the lyrical auteur figure and the ability to work in a recognizably high cultural mode. An extension of this position is the relegation of mainstream commercial rock/pop lyrics to banality and worthlessness. Yet clearly such lyrics do in some sense matter to their listeners: why else are they constantly reproduced in both album liner notes as social commentary from alternative bands and as the words of the latest chart entries in teen-oriented magazines such as *Smash Hits*? This provokes the more critical question posed by Frith: 'how do words and voices work differently for different types of pop and audience?' (ibid.: 121). This necessitates addressing how song lyrics work as ordinary language for variously located listeners and readers.

Further reading: Frith (1988b); Cooper (1992); Gracyk (2001); Harker (1980); Negus (1996)

MADCHESTER; MANCHESTER SOUND

A loose genre label, popularized by the British music press in the early 1990s, though more of a scene than a distinct sound. Since the late 1970s, Manchester had been associated with several styles of and prominent performers of indie/alternative music: in the late 1970s and early 1980s, the post-punk sound of Joy Division, who mutated into New Order; and 'bedsit blues' in the mid-1980s with the Smiths and James. In 1988, emerging out of acid house, the club-and-ecstasy sounds of 'Madchester became prominent, led by the Happy Mondays, the Stone Roses and the Inspiral Carpets. When the Happy Mondays' EP "Madchester Rave On" charted at the end of 1989, the scene was branded' (Garratt, 1998). The music fed off the association with Manchester: the songs often had included clear geographical references and reflected localized feelings and experiences; record covers and other promotional imagery incorporated place-related references; and a network of alternative record labels (especially Factory Records), venues, and an active local press created a supportive network for the bands and their followers.

See also: **house; locality**

Further reading: Garratt (1998); Harris (2004); Reynolds (1998: ch. 5); Rogan (1992)

Listening: The Smiths, *Strangeways Here We Come* (Rough Trade Records, 1987); the Stone Roses' self-titled debut (Silvertone, 1989); James, *Laid* (Polygram, 1993)

Viewing: *24 Hour Party People* (Michael Winterbottom, 2002)

MAJORS

The international record industry is dominated by a small group of large international companies, commonly referred to as the majors. In the late 1990s, there were six of these: Thorn/EMI (UK based); Bertelsmann (German); Sony (Japan); Time/Warner (USA); MCA (with a controlling interest purchased in 1995 by Canadian-owned company Seagrams); and Philips (Holland). Since then further consolidation and mergers have left four, all part of large international media conglomerates: Warner Music Group is part of AOL-Time Warner; Universal Music Group is owned by Vivendi Universal SA of France; Sony-BMG is jointly owned by the Japanese Sony Corporation and Bertelsmann AG in Germany; EMI Ltd is a UK firm (Hull, 2004: 125). 'Middle range' companies (Virgin, Motown, Island) have historically been absorbed by the majors, while the smaller **independents** are often closely linked to the majors through distribution deals. (For an outline of the organization and activities of each of the majors, and their websites, see Hull, 2004; for a comparison with the situation in the mid-1990s, see Burnett, 1996 and Barnett and Cavanagh, 1994. For a fuller listing of record labels, including the majors, with summaries of their history and operation, see Shepherd *et al.*, 2003.)

The music majors are part of a battle for global dominance of media markets, reflecting attempts by companies to control both hardware and software markets, and distribute their efforts across a range of media products – a process labelled 'synergy' – which enables maximization of product tie-ins and marketing campaigns and, consequently, profits. Each major is part of a larger communications or electronics conglomerate. Each major has branches throughout the Americas and Europe, and, in most cases, in parts of Asia, Africa, and Australasia. Each embraces a number of record labels: the Philips labels include Polydor, Deutsche Grammophon, Phonogram, and Decca; Sony includes CBS, Epic, and Def Jam.

The market share exercised by the majors varies from country to country, but in some cases is over 90 per cent. There is considerable debate over the economic and cultural implications of such market dominance, especially the strength of local music industries in relation to marked trends toward the **globalization** of the **culture industries**. Some commentators see the natural corollary of such concentrations of ownership as an ability to essentially determine, or at the very least strongly influence, the nature of the demand for particular forms of popular culture. On the other hand, more optimistic media analysts, with a preference for human agency, emphasize individual consumers' freedom to choose, their ability to decide how and where cultural texts are to be used, and the meanings and messages to be associated with them. The debate in this area is one of emphasis since clearly both sets of influences/determinations are in operation.

See also: **globalization; music industry**

Further reading: Burnett (1996); Hull (2004); Negus (1992); Wallis and Malm, eds (1992)

MANAGERS

In industrial organizations which are part of the **culture industries**, those working in management act as important **cultural intermediaries**.

Although not directly integrated into the **music industry**, managers operating within it play an active role in the production of particular artists and styles of music. Indeed, such managers often have the reputation of being 'starmakers and Svengalis', manipulating their artists' music and image. In the 1950s and 1960s, several UK managers (e.g. Larry Parnes) were dominating father figures for their artists, but managers more usually operate as representatives and advisers, handling the myriad details of daily business decisions, including arranging media interviews and promotional appearances, dealing with correspondence, maintaining record company relations, and organizing tours/concerts. Ideally, managers contribute to the formation of career strategies, resolve conflict and ambiguity, communicate effectively with the different parties involved, control the allocation of resources wisely, shield artists from criticism, and generally provide knowledgeable leadership and advice to artists. In the process, they can be influential in determining the prevailing climate of the music industry within which they function.

Further reading: Cusic (1996); Napier-Bell (2002); Negus (1996); Rogan (1988)

MARKET CYCLES

An influential attempt to explain both the emergence of rock'n'roll in the 1950s and subsequent shifts in popular music, is the market cycles explanation developed initially by Peterson and Berger (1975). This suggests that original musical ideas and styles, generated more or less spontaneously, are taken up by the record industry, which then popularizes them and adheres to them as the standard form. Meanwhile new creative trends emerge which have to break through the new orthodoxy.

Thus develops a cycle of innovation and consolidation, a cycle reflected in the shifting pattern of economic concentration and market control in the **music industry**. Media conglomerates are formed during periods of market stability, and inhibit the growth of **independents**, who are usually the source of new ideas. Yet under conditions of oligopoly there is also a growing unsatisfied demand from those who are not satisfied with the prevailing product available. Bursts of musical innovation – rock'n'roll, the San Francisco sound, punk – are often associated with youth subcultures, which help draw attention to them. Small record labels emerge to pioneer the new sound and style, followed by reconcentration and market stagnation once more as the **majors** regain control. The main evidence used by Peterson and Berger is the relative **chart** shares (in the top twenty) of the competing labels and the relative chart performance of established artists, and new and emerging artists. Subsequent research used a similar approach, but with conflicting conclusions (see **music industry**).

While the market cycles thesis offers an economic rationale for the bewildering historical shifts in popular music tastes, there have been a number of criticisms of it. There are methodological difficulties posed by its reliance on commercially successful singles, with the underlying assumption that the diversity of popular music is to be found in the hit parade. This overlooks the predominance of album sales over singles since the early 1970s, and the generally accepted tendency to accord greater aesthetic weight to the longer format. Further, it sees market diversity as a direct function of the number of individual hit records in any one year. To confirm this argument it would be necessary to undertake a critical stylistic analysis of the actual recordings that were hits on the basis of their musical features rather than the companies that released them. It could also be argued that the products of the independents are by no means always characterized by innovation. Indeed, frequently they themselves copied styles already popularized by their major competitors. Finally, as Peterson and Berger themselves acknowledge, the distinction between majors and independents has not been clear-cut since about 1970, while the two tiers of the industry have historically been linked through the majors' control of distribution. While oligopoly persists, the impact of the **Internet** and new relationships between the independent sector and the majors have radically changed the music industry, making the market cycles model less applicable.

See also: **independents; majors; music industry**

Further reading: Peterson and Berger (1975)

MARKETING

Marketing has come to play a crucial role in the circulation of cultural commodities. It is a complex practice, involving several related activities: research, product planning and design, packaging, publicity and promotion, pricing policy, and sales and distribution, and is closely tied to merchandising and retailing. Central to the process is product positioning and imbuing cultural products with social significance to make them attractive to consumers. (For insightful discussions of this, see Ewen, 1988; Ryan, 1992.) In popular music this has centred on the marketing of genre styles and stars which have come to function in a similar manner to brand names, 'serving to order demand and stabilize sales patterns' (Ryan, 1992: 185). **Fashion** is a crucial dimension: the commodity is designed to attract the attention and interest of shoppers: 'commodity aesthetics' necessitate the construction of a desirable appearance around the commodity, to stimulate the desire to purchase and possess. In the marketing process, cultural products are a contested terrain of signification.

It is noteworthy that by the 1990s the cant term for music within the industry was 'product'. This relates to popular music being an increasingly commodified product: merchandise to be packaged and sold. The music can be reproduced in various formats – vinyl, **cassette audio tape**, **CD**, DAT, and video – and variations within these: the dance mix, the cassette single, the limited collector's edition, and so on. These can then be disseminated in a variety of ways – through radio airplay, discos and dance clubs, television music video shows and MTV-style channels, and live concert performances. Accompanying these can be **advertising**, reviews of the record or performance, and interviews with the performer(s) in the various publications of the music press. In addition there is the assorted paraphernalia available to the fan, especially the posters and the T-shirts. Further, there is the use of popular music within film soundtracks and television advertising. The range of these products enables a multimedia approach to the marketing of the music, and a maximization of sales potential, as exposure in each of the various forms strengthens the appeal of the others. The marketing of popular music includes the use of genre labels as signifiers, radio formatting practices, and standardized production processes (e.g. Stock, Aitken, Waterman and dance pop in the 1980s). Above all, it involves utilizing star images, linking stars and their music with the needs/demands/emotions/desire of audiences.

In terms of the everyday operation of the **music industry**, marketing has been examined in several studies, with particular attention paid to industry personnel responsible for advertising and sales, and the promotional role of radio, music video, and the music press. There is less critical examination of aspects such as packaging (e.g. **album covers**, performer's dress codes), and the retailing of popular music.

On this last point, as du Gay and Negus observed, 'profound transformations in the distribution system have led to retailers exercising an increased influence within the music industry' (1994: 396). The deployment of new technologies in electronic data processing, combined with greater concentration of music retailing, permitted retail, distribution, and production 'to be arranged as an interconnected logistic package', allowing 'music retailers to delineate, construct and monitor the "consumer" of recorded music more intricately than ever before' (ibid.). This trend continued in the mid-1990s, exemplified by the rise of megastores. Traditional music retail has now been undermined by the rise of online music (see **Internet**).

See also: **advertising; commercialism; stars**

Further reading: Featherstone (1987); Chapple and Garofalo (1977); Hull (2004); Negus (1992)

MARXISM

A social theory based on the nineteenth-century views of Karl Marx and Friedrich Engels, who saw human history as a process rooted in people's material needs and changing modes of production (historical materialism), which 'in the last analysis' determine the nature of **class** structure. Class struggle and the emergence of socialism were central to this classic Marxist analysis. A very influential critique of capitalism, and imperialism as its highest form, Marxism has informed the subsequent development of social theory, mutating into a range of Marxist perspectives on society. The major variants of Marxism differ in terms of their relative emphasis on base (the classical Marxist term for economic structures – the forces of production, relations of production, and modes of production), and superstructure (the family, schools, the church, etc.), the role of social class as a determinant, and the nature and operation of **ideology**. Marxism has been a major theory informing media and **cultural studies**, especially through **political economy**.

The validity of Marxist approaches, especially in their classical variants (Adorno's views), have been the subject of extended debate within popular music studies. While few writers on popular music would consider themselves 'Marxist', Marxist perspectives and concepts have informed the field in discussions of the music industry and its international operation (see **cultural imperialism** and **globalization**); the examination of the constitution of popular music audiences and subcultures; and studies of the constitution of individual subjectivity and social structures, through the intersection of popular music with class, ethnicity, and gender.

See also: **cultural studies; Frankfurt School; political economy**

Further reading: Barker (2000); Boyd–Barrett and Newbold (1995); Chapple and Garofalo (1977); Harker (1980); Hesmondhalgh (2002); Rosselson (1979); Smith (2001); Stevenson (2002: ch. 1); Storey (1993)

MASS CULTURE/SOCIETY *see* **culture; Frankfurt School**

MEMORABILIA

Generally, memorable things not to be forgotten, regarded as worthy of preservation and collection. 'Rock and pop memorabilia has become the fastest growing field of collecting', claimed a Phillips auction house writer in 1988 (Fox). The first such auction, in London in 1981, included John Lennon's upright Steinway piano. As major auction houses included such items, this field of collecting gained credibility and respectability, and prices began to rise. In 1988 a guitar used by John Entwistle, the Who's bass player, on the group's BBC *Top of the Pops* appearances in the early 1970s fetched £15,000. Audio tapes of very early Rolling Stones and Beatles 'performances' have also realized high prices. The majority of early interest was in items related to the Beatles and Elvis Presley, but other artists soon attracted interest, especially those from the 1950s and 1960s. The death of a prominent artist lends great appeal to their collectability. Leading auction houses in London and New York (Phillips, Sothebys, etc.) now conduct regular sales.

There are a large range of collectable memorabilia: various records, including promotional copies and gold discs, musical instruments, autographs, tour programmes, posters, tour jackets, and concert tickets and T-shirts, plus novelty toys and a whole range of ephemera marketed around major artists like the Beatles. **Record collecting** is a major aspect of memorabilia, supported by a network of collector magazines, discographies and price guides, record fairs, and second-hand shops. The motivations for such collecting include investment, cultural preservation, nostalgia, and the desire to acquire **cultural capital** (see Belk, 2001; Pearce, 1995).

See also: **fans; record collecting**

Further reading: Fox (1988); Kay (1992)

MERSEYBEAT

Historically, the Merseybeat (or Liverpool) sound emerged with the Beatles *et al.* in the early 1960s. It was marketed as such, especially as part of the **British invasion** of the American market, although its performers were mainly part of British **beat music**. The musical characteristics and general coherence of Merseybeat are debated. Cohen has conceptualized the (contemporary as well as historical) sound as a complex amalgam of factors, incorporating a variety of regional, national, and international influences, but all particular to Liverpool, and reflecting 'a range of social, economic and political factors peculiar to the city' (1994a: 117). She relies on the way in which Liverpool musicians situate themselves and their music, especially in relation to other **sounds/scenes**. Negus, on the other hand, argues that this is to 'impose a meaning on the music that is grounded more in inter-city rivalries than actual sounds' (1996: 185).

See also: **British invasion; locality**

Further reading: Clayson (1995); Cohen (1994); Negus (1996)

MOD

A youth subculture, which began in London around 1963, mod was basically a working-class movement with a highly stylized form of dress, the fashions of which changed frequently, and an interest in R&B music. Originally called 'modernists' (a bebop jazz phrase), mods were influenced by the urban fashions of young American blacks. Mods wore their hair short and well cut in a series of changing styles. Mod transport was highly decorated motor scooters, and their clothes were casual and a parka when out riding, or expensive suits with a specific length of sidevent and the latest Italian shoes. Living for weekend partying, mods took pep pills, particularly 'purple hearts' (amphetamines). Several class-based strains of mod appeared, each with distinctive styles: an art school, high camp version; mainstream mods; scooter boys; and the hard mods, who developed into skin-heads. The mod lifestyle parodied and subverted the respectable conventions of their class backgrounds and the relatively unskilled office jobs many of them held.

The Who and the Small Faces were favourite mod groups, along with Tamla Motown artists, and ska and blue beat in the late 1970s.

The Who's rock opera *Quadrophenia* (1973) (later filmed) celebrates mod, as does the stutter vocal of the group's classic single 'My Generation' (1965) (see Shuker, 2001). Mods clashed with the rockers in a series of holiday weekends in the mid–1960s, giving rise to a media-fuelled **moral panic**. There was a revival of the subcultural style in the late 1970s and the UK two-tone groups used a combination of mod dress with ska and blue beat rhythms. There is a continued interest in mod style, exemplified by the successful 2004 mod retrospective in London.

Further reading: Barnes (1979); Brake (1985); Hebdige (1979)

MORAL PANIC

Moral panic is a sociological concept applied to community over-reaction to new media forms and (often associated) deviant subcultural groups. The popular media are seen to amplify and exaggerate episodes/phenomena out of proportion to their actual scale and significance, thereby contributing to the construction of a moral panic. Historically, concern over the impact of popular **culture** has emerged periodically with the advent of each new mass medium: silent cinema and the talkies, dime novels and comics, television, and video. The moral panics around these were episodes in cultural politics, in part representing struggles to maintain dominant norms and values. Popular culture was seen by its critics as diametrically opposed to **high culture** and something to be regulated, particularly in the interests of the susceptible young.

The concept of moral panic was utilized in the British sociology of deviance and new criminology studies of the 1970s. The writing on deviance and moral panic drew on labelling theory, associated with the work of the American sociologist Howard Becker. He argued that societies and social groups 'create deviance by making those rules whose infraction comprises deviance and by applying them to particular people, and labelling them as outsiders' (Becker, 1997: 9); that is, deviance is considered to be a social construct. The mass media are a major source for the labelling process, as they transmit and legitimate such labels, e.g. Cohen's 'folk devils', and contribute to the operation of social control. Labelling theory is evident in popular music studies of various **audiences** and their perceived 'antisocial' behaviours.

Popular music has had its own succession of moral panics, with particular genres and youth subcultures attracting controversy and opposition, both upon their emergence and sporadically since: jazz in the 1920s, rock'n'roll and the teds in the 1950s, the mods and rockers of the 1960s, punk in the 1970s, goths, heavy metal, and rap in the 1980s, and British rave culture in the 1990s. In such moral panics, criticism has centred variously on the influence of such genres on youthful values, attitudes, and behaviour through the music's (perceived) sexuality and sexism, nihilism and violence, obscenity, black magic, or anti-Christian nature. The political edge of popular music has been partly the result of this hostile reaction often accorded to the music and its associated causes and followers, helping to politicize the musicians and their fans. The best-known application of moral panic to episodes featuring a popular music connection is Stanley Cohen's classic study of the clashes between mods and rockers at several seaside resorts in the mid-1960s (Cohen, 1980).

Critcher (2003) provides a thorough and insightful discussion of studies drawing on the concept, and the application of moral panic to various social episodes of the past thirty years. He concludes that a moral panic has three dimensions: it involves an identifiable process of definition and action; it marks the boundaries of society; and it is a set of discourses of various kinds and levels (Criticher, 2003: 1, ch. 12).

Further reading: Cohen (1980); Critcher (2003); Shuker (2001: ch. 12)

MOTOWN; MOTOWN SOUND

Motown was the black music company founded by Berry Gordy in Detroit (Motor Town) in 1959, and the first black-owned record company to achieve major chart success in the United States. Gordy deliberately targeted the white **crossover** market. Motown represented a blander, more commercial version of the **soul** music associated with artists at Atlantic and Stax. By 1973 the company had effectively relocated to Los Angeles, but declined as its roster of artists weakened. Motown was sold to MCA in 1988 (for US$61 million), although Gordy retained the lucrative publishing rights to Motown's **back catalogue**. In 1993 Motown was acquired from MCA by Polygram.

The 'Motown sound' had a pounding beat, strong bass lines, hooks from keyboards and guitars, and 'vocals stripped of ghetto inflections' (McEwen and Miller, 1992). In the best of several studies of the company, George (1985) views it as a team effort of performers, songwriters, producers, and session players, with Gordy overseeing and coordinating. Songwriters/producers Holland, Dozier, Smokey Robinson, and Norman Whitfield 'combined evocative relationship based lyrics with gospel elements, while avoiding the raw sounds of black R&B which white audiences were reluctant to embrace' (Fitzgerald, 1995). Motown recordings utilized a core of creative session musicians – the Funk Brothers – drawn from the Detroit jazz scene (see the film documentary, *Standing in the Shadows of Motown*).

Motown had considerable commercial success during the sixties, with artists such as the Miracles, the Four Tops, the Temptations, Marvin Gaye, and Stevie Wonder. The Supremes had five consecutive US number one hits in 1964–5, while the Jackson Five enjoyed similar chart success in the1970s.

See also: **soul**

Further reading: Early (2004); George (1985); Hirshey (1985); McEwen and Miller (1992) (includes a discography)

Viewing: *Dancing in the Street* (1995), episode 4; 'Standing in the Shadows of Motown' (Paul Justman, 2002)

Listening: The Temptations, *Anthology* (Motown, 1973); Marvin Gaye, *Super Hits* (Motown, 1973); Stevie Wonder, *Looking Back* (Motown, 1977); the Four Tops: 'I Can't Help Myself (Sugar Pie, Honey Bunch)' (1965) on *The Greatest Hits* (Motown, 1967)

MP3

MP3 is a recorded sound that is technologically encoded so that it takes up much less storage space than it would otherwise. MP3 files are small enough to make it practical to transfer (download) high-quality music files over the **Internet** and store them on a computer hard drive: CD-quality tracks downloadable in minutes (see Mann, 2000). Hardly surprisingly, MP3 soon became very popular as a way to distribute and access music. According to Media Matrix, the number of people listening to digital music (primarily but not exclusively MP3) in the United States in June 1999 was four million, having grown from only a few thousand in June 1998 (Mann, 2000: xxi). It was widely claimed that MP3 had become the word most searched for on Web search engines.

For consumers, MP3 enables access to a great variety of music, most of it free, and they can selectively compile their own collections of songs by combining various tracks without having to purchase entire albums. For artists, MP3 means they can distribute their music to a global audience without the mediation of the established **music industry**. Yet MP3 also raises concerns about potential loss of income. For Internet music publishers, MP3 opens up opportunities for smaller, more innovative companies.

For the major record companies, MP3 challenges their control over distribution and, since the format has no built-in way to prevent users from obtaining and distributing music illegally, can represent considerable lost royalties. The **majors** joined together to create the Secure Digital Music Initiative (SDMI; see www.sdmi.org) in an attempt to reassert control over music distribution. Alongside these misgivings, the music industry is now making considerable use of MP3, setting up its own online subscription services. Many online music retailers offer tracks for download by MP3, hoping these will act as a 'taster' for listeners' purchases. Recording companies have recognized the need to utilize the new **technology** to maintain their market dominance in the new world of online audio music, looking for new concepts in packaging and marketing to digitally retail songs via the Internet.

See also: **Internet; Napster**

Further reading: Garofalo (2003); Hull (2004); Jones and Lenhart (2004)

MTV

The American cable **television** channel MTV (Music Television), founded in 1981, has become virtually synonymous with **music video** as a cultural form. Originally owned by the Warner Amex Satellite Company, but subsequently sold to Viacom International, the channel became enormously popular during the 1980s, and has been credited with boosting a flagging music industry. MTV captured a considerable share of the advertising directed at the youth and young adult/'yuppie' market, and solved the perennial problem of cable television – how to generate enough revenue for new programming – by having the record companies largely pay for the 'programmes' by financing the video clips. In the late 1980s it was reaching nearly 20 million American homes, and was regularly watched by 85 per cent of 18- to 34-year-olds.

By 1991 MTV had 28 million subscribers, and was adding between one and three million new subscribers every year. MTV's success spawned a host of imitators in the United States, and a number of national franchises and imitations around the globe, including MTV Europe (1988–) and MTV Asia (1991–). After an initial struggle to untangle cable and satellite regulations in dozens of countries, MTV Europe broke even for the first time in 1993, and became the continent's fastest growing satellite channel, with its twenty-four-hours-a-day music video programming available in more than 44 million homes. Thirty per cent of its airtime is reserved for European performers, and a genuine effort was made to play a substantial number of 'European' music videos (Burnett, 1990). MTV Asia reached more than three million households in over thirty countries, from Japan to the Middle East. The channel featured English-language broadcasts, and programming dominated by music videos from Western stars, but it also had a quota of approximately 20 per cent for Asian performers.

The influence of MTV on the US music industry was enormous during the 1980s. Getting a music video on regular MTV play became necessary to ensure **chart** success, while the channel became the most effective way to 'break' new artists, and to take an emerging artist into star status. Performers who received considerable exposure on MTV before they were picked up by radio include Madonna, Duran Duran, the Thompson Twins, and Paula Abdul. The successful 1980s 'invasion' of the American charts by style-conscious and photogenic British groups, was directly attributed by some analysts to MTV (see **new romantics**). Innovative videos and MTV helped consolidate American performers such as Paula Abdul, and Talking Heads, and pushed sales of Michael Jackson's albums – over 40 million copies of *Thriller*.

Given their crucial role in determining commercial success in the 1980s, a key question was how particular music videos were chosen for the MTV playlist. Kaplan's (1987) study of the channel ignored the selection issue, as did most early commentators, who remained preoccupied with the videos as texts. Rubey (1991) noted that MTV's top twenty lists were compiled from national album sales, video airplay, and the channel's own research and requests, building circularity and subjectivity into the process. In the most thorough study of the operation of MTV, Banks (1996: ch. 9) examined the **gatekeeper** role of the American MTV channel, the role of its Acquisitions Committee and the standards, both stated and unstated, which they applied. He concluded that the **major** music companies willingly edited videos on a regular basis to conform to MTV's standards, even coercing artists into making changes to song lyrics, while smaller, **independent** companies cannot usually get their videos on MTV.

The influence of MTV channels waned during the 1990s, as the format lost its freshness and was becoming clichéd. While newly popular genres such as hip-hop featured strongly on MTV, other styles such as dance music developed largely independently of music video. Perhaps reflecting this, there is a lack of academic literature on the current operation of MTV. A good deal of information on its present scheduling, along with video clips, can be seen on its website.

Further reading: Banks (1996); Den Tandt (2004); Goodwin (1993); Hanke (1998); Kaplan (1987); Lewis (1990); Sturmer (1993)

Website: www.mtv.com

MULTIMEDIA

While this term is frequently loosely used, it generally refers to the communication of messages or information through the combined use of text, graphics, animation, audio, and motion video. In the modern sense, it goes with another basic concept of new technology – interactivity. Multimedia has come to imply more than just the convergence of voice, music, alpha–numeric text and so on, it also implies that the user has some degree of interactive control over these, instead of being a passive viewer, as with broadcast television.

In a broader perspective, multimedia is a synonym for convergence: major media companies working together, often under corporate umbrellas. Thus any product system or venture agreement or technology that brings together components of more than one previously distinct sector of the media industry – be it publishing and computers or TV and computers – can be described as multimedia. This was facilitated by the on-going convergence of the electronics and music industries, which began in the 1980s. There is an associated drive for control of both the hardware and software dimensions of the marketplace, along with the cross-fertilization and maximization of texts (one text, many forms).

In the early 1990s, record companies, including EMI and the Warner Music Group, began forming multimedia distribution divisions to explore the possibilities of new technologies, including music CD ROMs, music- or artist-specific computer screensavers and video/computer games, complete with soundbites.

Further reading: Hesmondhalgh (2002: ch. 7); Stevenson (2002: ch. 6)

MUSIC INDUSTRY; RECORDING COMPANIES

Music industry

There is a tendency, especially in general discourse, to equate the 'music industry' with record companies, when the latter are only one part of it. The *music industry* embraces a range of institutions and associated markets: the recording companies and the retail sector, producing and selling recordings in their various formats; the **music press**; music hardware, including musical instruments and sound recording and reproduction **technology**; merchandising (posters, T-shirts, etc.); and royalties and rights and their collection/licensing agencies. These facets are increasingly under the ownership/control of the same parent company, enabling the maximum exploitation of a particular product/performer.

The increased concentration of the **culture industries** is a feature of late capitalism, and the music industry has been part of this process of consolidation. A small group of internationally based large corporations have spread their interests across a variety of media, resulting in multimedia conglomerates, such as Time-Warner. (Barnet and Cavanagh term these 'imperial corporations' (1994: 14) and provide several instructive case studies of their operations around that time; for a more current discussion, see Hull, 2004.) At issue is the consequent question of control of the media and whose interests it operates in, and the relationship between diversity and innovation in the market. Free-market economists argue that innovation will occur more frequently under conditions of oligopoly (increased concentration, fewer producers), since larger firms are better able to finance innovation and pass the costs and benefits along to consumers. Conversely, other analysts argue that conditions of oligopoly mean a lack of incentive for firms to depart much from the tried and tested, resulting in a high level of product homogeneity. The crucial question in this debate is how does such concentration affect the range of opportunities available to musicians and others involved in the production of popular music, and the nature and range of products available to the consumers of popular music? In other words, what is the cultural significance of this situation, and what role does it play in the creation of meaning in popular music?

Initial analyses of the relationship between concentration, innovation, and diversity in popular music suggested a negative relationship between concentration and diversity in the recording industry, relating this to a cyclical pattern of **market cycles** (Peterson and Berger, 1975).

The basis for this analysis was the proportion of top-selling records (as indicated by the American *Billboard* singles charts) sold by the leading companies (the **majors**). During periods of greatest market concentration, there were fewer top-selling records. Conversely, during periods of greater market competition, with marked competition from newer/smaller record companies (the **independents**), there were a greater number of top-selling records in the **charts**. Rothenbuhler and Dimmick (1982) showed that relationship continued to hold between 1974 and 1980, confirming Peterson and Berger's thesis. However, this view was challenged by Burnett (1996) and Lopes (1992), who both argued that a high level of concentration was in fact accompanied by a high level of diversity. 'Major record companies find it advantageous to incorporate new artists, producers and styles of music to constantly reinvigorate the popular music market and to ensure that no large unsated demand among consumers materializes' (Lopes, 1992: 70). An important consideration here is the role of **gatekeeping**, the filtering processes at work before a particular piece of music reaches the charts. Building on Lopes, Christianen (1995: 91) points out the importance of the number of decision-makers within a firm as a variable explaining the diversity and innovation generated by a major record company. In a sophisticated study of the Dutch music industry, he argues that the pattern between innovation and diversity is more complex than previous analysts had suggested.

Hull (2004) argues that the recording industry is now entering a new post-industrial phase, characterized by decentralizing of the means of recording, reproduction, and distribution. At the same time, there is increasing consolidation of the music industry as a whole. These trends have brought about complex patterns of ownership and business practices.

See also: **culture industries; market cycles**

Further reading: Burnett (1996); Christianen (1995); Hesmondhalgh (2002); Hull (2004)

Recording companies

The sound recording companies, often referred to in shorthand fashion as 'record companies' (or labels), are at the centre of the music industry. They range in size from small-scale local operations to those which are part of international media conglomerates. This standard

division into **majors** and **independents** reflects not simply economics, but ideological weight (see the entries on each type), and has
often been viewed in dichotomous terms. However, this is to simplify
what is a complex situation of interdependence and frequently similar
operations (not in terms of scale, but rather in terms of organization
and process). Record companies exhibit the defining characteristics of
the **culture industry**, usually being hierarchically organized business
structures with clearly demarcated roles. In a larger enterprise these
would include management, producers, marketing and public relations, publicity, promotion, business affairs, finance and legal, manufacture and distribution, administrative and secretarial (see Negus,
1992: 38ff.; Hull, 2004). The major problem faced by record companies is the uncertainty of the music market: only one in eight of the
artists A&R sign and record will achieve sufficient sales to recoup the
original investment and start to earn money for the artists and generate
a profit for the company. This situation has led to major record
companies looking for acts already partially developed and indicating
commercial potential.

See also: **A&R; culture industries**

Further reading: Barrow and Newby (1995); Burnett (1966); Cusic (1996);
Hull (2004); Negus (1992). Shepherd *et al.* (2003) provides an extensive
outline of the majors and the leading independent labels internationally

MUSIC PRESS; MUSIC JOURNALISM; MUSIC MAGAZINES

The music press includes a wide range of publications. Many general
magazines and newspapers cover popular music, with regular review
columns. There has been little critical analysis of how these publications construct popular music and influence the reception of genres
and performers. (A notable exception is Stratton, 1982, but the music
industry has changed substantially since he wrote.) More specifically,
the music press refers to specialized publications, lifestyle magazines
with major music coverage, music trade papers, and weekly and
monthly consumer magazines devoted to popular music, or particular
genres within it. In addition to these are privately published **fanzines**
(as these are usually peripheral to the market economy of commercial
publishing they are considered separately). There is also a variety of
book-length writing on popular music.

An extensive, annotated bibliography covering the writing on popular music since 1955, published in 1985, revealed a considerable body of literature, which had increased dramatically during the early 1980s. Subsequently published bibliographic guides show rapid growth continued during the following decade (see Taylor, 1985; Gatten, 1995; Leyser, 1994; Shepherd *et al.*, 1997). Although categories frequently overlap, we can distinguish between popular (auto)**biographies**, histories and **genre** studies; and various forms of consumer guides, including encyclopedias and dictionaries, **chart** listings and discographies: bibliographies of records or other musical texts, usually organized by artist, genre, or historical period. The last represent an important aspect of popular music history, which they constitute as well as record, and are important texts for **fans** and **aficionados**. There are also more esoteric publications, such as **rock** quiz books, genealogical tables plotting the origin and shifting membership of groups, and 'almanacs' dealing with the trivia and microscopic detail of **stars**' private lives. Taylor's summary of all this is apposite: 'The variety of these publications is matched by the variation in the quality of their writing, accuracy and scholarship, which means one must approach them with a degree of discrimination and care' (Taylor, 1985: 1). This judgement still stands.

Popular **music journalism** includes the proliferation of 'quickie' publications aiming to cash in on the latest **pop** sensation. Reading like press releases and emphasizing the pictorial aspect rather than any extended critical commentary, these are often little more than pseudo-publicity. They reinforce the public preoccupation with **stars**, feeding **fans**' desire for consumable images and information about their preferred performers. In these respects, they complement those popular music magazines aimed at the **teenage** market (see below). McRobbie's edited collection, *Zoot Suits and Second-Hand Dresses* (1988) showed serious popular music journalism changed dramatically during the 1980s, 'with interest shifting from the music itself to a more general concern with the cultural phenomena which accompany it'. This new focus was strongly evident in the new 'style bibles' of the 1980s, notably *The Face*. Some of this journalism also colonized the 'mainstream' press and the more 'serious' weekly and monthly magazines.

Alongside this is a similar, though more historically situated, body of journalistic work on popular music which is not only aimed at a broader readership, but is also thoughtful and critically analytical of its subjects: the work of critics like Greil Marcus, Lester Bangs, Robert Christgau, and Dave Marsh in the United States, and Jon Savage, Dave

Rimmer, Nik Cohn, and Charles Shaar Murray in the United Kingdom. Indicative of the commercial and ideological significance of this work is its appearance in book form as sustained in-depth studies of genres and performers, exemplified by Savage, 1991, on the Sex Pistols and **punk rock**; collected reviews and essays (Murray, 1991; Christgau, 1990); the publication of several encyclopedias of popular music (e.g. Clarke, ed., 1990; Gammond, ed., 1991); and anthologies (e.g. Heylin, 1992). McRobbie noted the overlap between this work and academia, and the closing together of the two forms: 'while pop journalism has moved towards a more serious mode, academic writing has, to some extent, shifted towards a lighter, more essayistic style' (McRobbie, 1988: xvii). This in part reflects the proliferation of journals which have grown up around **cultural studies**, which have frequently provided a forum for shorter pieces and work-in-progress statements, and been more receptive to more 'journalistic' contributions. This is work in a more exploratory mode, 'where theoretical questions inform a piece of work without necessarily overwhelming it' (ibid.: xix). This pattern continued through the 1990s, with a number of established critics continuing to publish on emergent trends and performers, as well as reassessing previous ones (see Leonard and Strachan, 2003).

Popular music magazines have received surprisingly little attention in popular music studies. General accounts of the development of popular music (Chambers, 1985; Szatmary, 1991; Garofalo, 1997) make considerable use of the music press as a source, while largely ignoring its role in the process of **marketing** and cultural legitimization. The music press is absent from otherwise far-ranging anthologies, studies of the music business, and even encyclopedias of popular music. While there is obvious overlap – and market competition – amongst the various types of music magazine, they do have distinctive qualities. The music trade papers keep industry personnel informed about changes in the record and media industries, including copyright and regulatory legislation and policies; advise retailers about marketing campaigns, complementing and reinforcing their sales promotions; and provide regular chart lists based on extensive sales and radio play data (the main publication is *Billboard*). Musicians' magazines, *Guitar Player*, *Keyboard*, etc., inform their readers about new music technologies and techniques, thereby making an important contribution towards musicianship and musical appropriation (see Théberge, 1991; this analysis is still valuable, but needs updating).

The various consumer or fan-oriented music magazines play a major part in the process of selling music as an economic commodity, while at the same time investing it with cultural significance. Such magazines don't simply deal with music, through both their features and advertising they are also purveyors of style. At the same time, these magazines continue to fulfil their more traditional function of contributing to the construction of audiences as consumers. The majority of popular music magazines focus on performers and their music, and the relationship of consumers/**fans** to these. These magazines fall into a number of fairly clearly identifiable categories, based on their differing musical aesthetics or emphases, their socio-cultural functions, and their target audiences. 'Teen glossies' emphasize vicarious identification with performers whose music and image is aimed at this youth market; *Smash Hits* is the market leader here. The 'inkies' (*Melody Maker*) have historically supported a tradition of critical rock journalism, with their reviewers acting as the gatekeepers for that tradition. The 'style bibles' (exemplified by *i-D* and, before its demise in April 2004, *The Face*) construct popular music as part of visual pop culture, especially fashion. More recent magazines offer a combination of the inkies' focus on an extensive and critical coverage of the music scene and related popular culture, packaged in a glossier product with obvious debts to the style bibles (*The Source*, MOJO, UNCUT).

Reviews in the music press form an important adjunct to the **marketing** of recordings, providing the record companies (and artists) with critical feedback on their releases. In the process, they also become promotional devices, providing supportive quotes for advertising, including stickers added to record covers ('the year's best release', says magazine X), and forming part of press kits sent to radio stations and other press outlets. Both the press and critics also play an important ideological function, distancing consumers from the fact that they are essentially purchasing an economic commodity, by stressing the product's cultural significance. This is reinforced by the important point that the music press and critics are not, at least directly, vertically integrated into the **music industry** (i.e. not owned by the record companies). A sense of distance is thereby maintained, while at the same time the need of the industry to constantly sell new images, styles, and product is met. There has been some attention to the nature and role of reviews in music magazines, showing that they are involved in constructing a discourse which **canonizes** and legitimizes particular performers and their work (Kembrew, 2001; Evans, 1998).

See also: **fanzines**

Further reading: Barrow and Newby (1996); Leonard and Strachan (2003); Shuker (2001)

MUSIC VIDEO

Music video is a hybrid cultural form, encompassing elements of both **television** and **radio**. Individual music video clips provide the content for long-form music video and DVD compilations, available for hire or purchase, individual music video programmes within general broadcast television channel schedules, and **MTV** and similar cable/ satellite music channels.

Individual music video clips follow the conventions of the traditional 45 single: they are approximately two to three minutes long, and function, in the industry's own terms, as 'promotional devices', encouraging record sales and chart action. While these clips are the staple component in MTV-style television; individual music programmes on television, and the long form music videos, their place in each case is different, as are their associated patterns of **consumption**.

The analysis of music video clips was a major growth area in both television studies and the study of popular music in the 1980s, and into the 1990s (see the bibliography in Shepherd *et al.*, 1997). This body of work focused largely on the visual aspect of music videos, their perceived violence and sexuality/sexism, and their significance as a central postmodern cultural artefact. Situating themselves in film studies rather than music studies, these analyses accordingly focus on music videos as discrete, self-contained, essentially visual **texts**. They frequently largely ignored considerations such as music videos' industrial and commercial dimensions, their placement in the flow of television programming, and the links between music videos and music stardom.

For a fuller understanding of music videos it is necessary to consider their production process and their commercial function for the music industry, the institutional practices of channels such as MTV, and their reception as polysemic texts, open to varying audience interpretations. Music video is both an industrial/commercial product and a cultural form. Since the late 1990s, with MTV less prominent, and new genres of dance music not reliant on music video for their popularity, academic interest in the format has waned. Close readings of music videos continue to be made, but are more cognizant of these considerations, and have accorded greater attention to their production processes (Vernallis, 1998; 2004).

The long-form music video cassette or (increasingly) DVD, available for hire or purchase, has become an increasingly important part of the popular music market (see Hull, 2004), as retail outlets clearly demonstrate. However, there is a dearth of research on these products, their production and marketing, their purchasers, and the uses they make of such formats.

See also: **MTV; television**

Further reading: Goodwin (1993); Kaplan (1987); Shore (1985); Vernallis (2004)

MUSICALS

Stage musicals are a historically well established and popular cultural form. While they are part of popular music in a general sense, only a small proportion of such musicals are thematically based on those popular musical genres considered here. There have been successful shows based on the lives and music of Elvis Presley, Buddy Holly, Abba, and the Beatles; 'rock operas' such as *Tommy*, which has periodically been resurrected; and nostalgia-oriented musicals drawing on particular historically situated genres, notably disco. These productions are often termed 'rock musicals', to distinguish them from the classic musicals which dominate the Broadway and West End theatres. Musicals featuring popular music and star performers serve similar purposes to popular music **films**: they help create and popularize ideologies, for instance *Hair* and the counter-culture of the 1960s, and mythologies of real life stars or those they historically portray: *The Rocky Horror Show* (London, 1973–80, and internationally), and its subsequent film version (1975), exemplifies the cult status rock musicals can attain (see Shuker, 2001). Despite the commercial and critical success of a number of 'rock musicals', they remain an oddly neglected subject within popular music studies.

See also: **film**

MUSICIANS; MAKING MUSIC

The bulk of the popular writing on musicians is on those considered **stars/auteurs**. Academic study has focused on identifying those who are considered 'musicians', especially within particular social and community settings, the processes whereby musicians 'make music'; and the hierarchies of musician (and associated forms of musicianship) which are held among critics, fans, and musicians themselves.

Musicians

'Musician' covers a range of people creating music, from the purely recreational player of a musical instrument through to those who make a specialized contribution to the recording process. With the advent of new technologies, and the importance of sound mixers and producers as creators of recordings, the term has taken on a more flexible and diffuse meaning. Playing music is for the majority of those who do so an essentially 'amateur' activity, which may become a career option. However, while the term musician is usually equated with a full-time professional, various studies have found it difficult to distinguish 'amateur' from 'professional' musicians. Finnegan's local musicians tended to use the term professional in an evaluative rather than an economic sense, to refer to a player's standard of performance, musical knowledge and qualifications, and regular appearances with musicians themselves regarded as professional (Finnegan, 1989). More recent studies show that this perception remains prevalent (e.g. McIntyre, 2003).

Making music

Accounts of how musicians create their music demonstrate a complex process of musical composition, rehearsal, and performance. The musical world of the two bands that Cohen studied was based around a series of polarities: creativity/commerce; musical content and quality/ image and superficiality; honest and natural/false and deceitful; artistic integrity/selling out; independent record companies/major record companies; live music for community, experimentation and indulgence/ recorded music for profit and for a mass market. The bands situated themselves into a combination of these various factors, with tension, constant debate, and shifting allegiances evident among their members. Their creative process was typically incremental and participatory (Cohen, 1991: 134; see also Bennett, 1990). Ethnographic work on performers working within a range of musical styles and social contexts suggest that this picture remains valid, especially for guitar-based bands in 'rock' and related genres. The situation is different in the cases of **DJ** 'turntabilists' and those working in **dance musics**. The nature of musical creativity, and the social contexts which it operates in, are beginning to be more systematically addressed (see e.g. Negus and Pickering, 2004; Toynbee, 2000).

There are clear hierarchies of musician(ship), although these vary according to genre. Value distinctions are evident in the terms used by critics and fans to label various performers as auteurs, 'journeymen', session musicians, or members of cover bands. For example, session musicians, performers who are contracted to studios or particular recording projects, function as the pieceworkers of the music industry and rarely attain wider critical recognition for their efforts.

See also: **covers; tribute bands**

Further reading: Cohen (1991); Bennett (1990); Finnegan (1989); Hatch and Millward (1987); Shuker (2001: ch. 6)

MUSICOLOGY; POPULAR MUSICOLOGY

In broad terms, musicology is

> the whole body of systematized knowledge about music which results from the application of a scientific method of investigation or research, or of philosophical speculation and rational systematization to the facts, the processes and development of musical art, and to the relation of man in general (*Harvard Dictionary of Music*; cited in Middleton, 1990: 103).

A major debate in popular music studies has been around the value of a musicological approach to music **texts**. Indeed, there is an argument as to whether popular music even merits such a 'serious' analysis, a question related to the **high culture** and mass society critiques of popular music. Until recently, academic musicologists have generally neglected rock/pop music (notable early exceptions include Mellers, 1974, 1986; Shepherd, 1991) in part out of an unwillingness to engage with a form of music which is accorded low cultural value in comparison with 'serious' music. At the same time, many sociologists writing on popular music were wary of musicology. For example, the application of traditional musicology to **rock** music has frequently provided a rich source for ridicule. This was due to its tendency to be distant from the mechanics of much actual composition of rock, its 'vague pretentiousness' and 'chronic failure to address what is really at stake in the tunes' (McClary and Walser, 1990: 277). As Frith observed, both rock musicians and rock commentators generally lack formal musical training: 'They lack the vocabulary and techniques of musical analysis, and even the descriptive words that critics and fans do use – harmony, melody, riff, beat – are only loosely understood and applied' (Frith, 1983: 13; also Frith and Goodwin, eds, 1990: Pt. 5).

Frith saw rock critics as essentially preoccupied with sociology rather than sound, and there has been too ready a willingness to dismiss musicology as having little relevance to the study of rock. The arguments here were well rehearsed through the 1980s: traditional musicology neglects the social context, emphasizes the transcription of music (the score), and elevates harmonic and rhythmic structure to pride of place as an evaluative criterion. Popular music, on the other hand, emphasizes interpretation through performance, and is received primarily in terms of the body and emotions rather than as pure text. Many rock musicians observed that classical music operated according to a different set of musical criteria, which has little validity for their own efforts (e.g. Pete Townshend; in Palmer, 1970: 131).

In the early 1990s, there were signs that the largely negative attitude toward musicology (in relation to popular music) was changing. Several musicologists engaged with popular music (e.g. Walser, 1993; McClary, 1991; Middleton, 1990), while popular music scholars generally began to accord musicology more weight in their analyses. This work varied in the degree to which such analysis simply takes as a given the concepts and tools of traditional (e.g. more classical music-oriented) musicology (e.g. Mellers, 1974, 1986), or modifies these in relation to popular music (e.g. Moore, 2001). The past decade has produced a substantial body of what can be termed 'popular musicology' (including Brackett, 1995a; Hawkins, 2002; Moore, 2001; Hawkins provides a helpful overview and critique).

Much of this work demonstrates that the traditional conception of musicology remains inadequate when applied to popular music in any straightforward manner (equating the two forms). For example, a concentration on technical textual aspects alone – the score – is inadequate, since it fails to deal with how the **effects** listeners celebrate are constructed, what McLary and Walser (1990: 287) term 'the dimensions of music that are most compelling and yet most threatening to rationality'. This takes into consideration the role of pleasure, the relationship of the body, feelings and emotions, and sexuality in constructing responses to rock music. Recent popular musicology has engaged further with the more affective domains of the relationship between the text and its listeners, and into the generic and historical locations of the text and its performer(s). Genre study usefully moves us beyond the music as pure text, alerting us once again to the value of context and consumption. So too does the study of narrative structures and representations in popular music, particularly the ideological and contextual aspects of these.

It is worth remembering that people are more 'musical' than is usually credited. Radio listening – switching stations in search of something recognizable or engaging – and selecting which music to play on one's stereo involves an ability to distinguish between different types of music. This is to utilize a more extended definition of 'musical' (Tagg, 1990: 104), where what is crucial is the link between musical structures and people's use of them. As Hawkins observes, 'the task of interpreting pop is an interdisciplinary task that deals with the relationship between music and social mediation. It is one that includes taking into account the consideration of the sounds in their relationship to us as individuals' (2002: 3).

Musical analysis

A number of authors have argued, with reference to detailed examples, that musical analysis of selected compositions is a workable approach to studying the nature and evolution of popular music; with such analysis presupposing a basic knowledge of the elements of music (e.g. Brown, 1994; Moore, 2001; Hatch and Millward, 1987; Vulliamy and Lee, 1982). The main sonic elements of music are rhythm (beat); melody; harmony; and, in songs, the **voice** (especially timbre). Of particular relevance in popular music are the related elements of riffs, hooks, and lyrics. These are considered briefly here in relation to their applicability in popular musicology. Fuller accounts of them, and other musical terms, can be found in the glossaries and accompanying discussions in Brown, 1992; Charlton, 1994; Middleton, 1990; Moore, 2001; and, especially helpful, Tagg (website).

Rhythm is the beat patterns underlying most forms of communication, pulses of varying lengths of time. Rhythms are often recurring or repetitive (as in a heartbeat) and follow a consistent pattern. In music, rhythm patterns generally indicate the emotional feel of different types of song; e.g. slow connotes emotional. A rhythm section is the group of musical instruments that maintain the beat pattern and the harmonic flow of a piece of music; these usually include drums, bass, and guitar/keyboards. The tempo is the pace of the beat. With popular music styles that include percussion, rhythm is best followed by listening to the drums, and counting the beat aloud. The backbeat is beats two and four of a four-beat pattern, the accenting of which creates rock's basic rhythm.

Melody is an organized set of notes consisting of different pitches (high or low sounds). The melody of a song is what we would be singing if we substituted the syllable 'la' for all the regular syllables. Melody is the variation in the lead singer's voice, without accompaniment. Various melodies are present in popular music forms: the main melody (sung by the lead singer); background melodies (sung by other group members, or backup singers); and bass melodies.

Harmony is the simultaneous sounding of two or more different notes at the same time, e.g. guitar chords, blocks of notes on the piano, and the sounds of a chorus. The easiest place to hear harmonies is in the background melodies. Harmony varies from simple to complex, and often delineates one style from another. Harmony is important in popular music because it provides the texture of the total sound; it has been prominent in genres emphasizing vocals, such as **a cappella** and **doo-wop**.

Related to rhythm and harmony are riffs and hooks. The *hook* is the melodic or rhythmic pattern that is catchy and 'hooks' or attracts the listener to want to listen to the rest of the song, and, more importantly, want to hear it repeated. Hooks are central to commercially oriented popular music (see Burns, 1987). A *riff* is a short melodic or rhythmic pattern repeated over and over while changes take place in the music along with it. This 'sonic repetition' is a feature of number of 'classic' popular music records, most notably in the Rolling Stones' 'Satisfaction'.

Further reading: Hatch and Millward (1987); Hawkins (2002); Moore (2001); Tagg and Clarida (2003)

MUZAK

Muzak is the term applied, rather negatively, to 'functional' or 'background' music. Muzak accounts for the greatest proportion of the music we are exposed to in our daily lives, though we are rarely consciously aware of it. It is used in a deliberate attempt to influence, or manipulate, the buying patterns of supermarket shoppers, the eating habits of restaurant patrons, etc. Muzak is also used as background, or 'piped music', music in places such as airport lounges, doctors' waiting rooms, and lifts (elevator music), to 'soothe' the mood of people in such public spaces, and similarly in workplaces to enhance worker satisfaction and output.

Functional music is economically very significant: Muzak Corporation, the largest of the programmed-music companies, grossed over $50 million in 1990, when it had ninety-six franchises supplying 'programmed music' to 135,000 businesses in sixteen countries. Such companies have been paying enormous sums to acquire copyrights to songs, rearrange them, and profile and track the behaviour of various consumer groups. Muzak has been critiqued on aesthetic and musical grounds as a form of banal 'wallpaper' music; or as an example of bureaucratic rationalism, linked to post-Fordist industrial practices perpetuating the alienation of workers. Jones and Schumacher 'examine the practices and discourses of functional music, how they have evolved historically, their role in the regulation of work and consumption, and their reproduction of particular kinds of economic, spatial, and symbolic power relations' (1992: 157).

Kassabian (1999) uses the more appropriate term 'ubiquitous music' for such sounds, which are beginning to receive greater attention (see e.g. the work of Tagg and Clarida, 1990; 2003).

See also: **listening**

Further reading: Jones and Schumacher (1992); Kasabian (1999); Tagg and Clarida (2003)

NEW AGE

A marketing label as much as a truly distinguishable musical **genre**. 'More of a mood than a style, new age was soothing instrumental music of the 1980s, based on the softer kinds of classical, jazz and folk' (Hardy and Laing, eds, 1990). New age is characterized by having precious little vocal accompaniment and making considerable use of **ambient** (natural) sounds, synthesizers, and **samplers**. 'New Age music is commonly marked by minute variations and an abundance of repeats. This music is all middle; it starts and stops, it is turned on and off, but one does not get a distance sense of beginnings and endings' (Hall, 1994: 14). It is almost exclusively recorded music, produced and consumed via audio tape and CD. The Wyndham Hill label was prominent in popularizing the genre, which has its own specialist radio programmes, and is a genre sales category in many retail outlets.

New age is sometimes scorned as 'yuppie muzak' (Gammond, ed., 1991), in part because of its appeal amongst relatively well-off and liberally educated listeners. Hall claims new age to be a **postmodernist** musical style, 'due to its eclectic, constantly shifting character and confusion of boundaries; its spirit of playfulness, taste for irony, and textual looting; its aggressive multiculturalism; and its anti-intellectualism yet devotion to learning' (see Hall, 1994, for an elaboration of these claims). Other observers regard the genre as musically a heavily conservative one, leaning towards the formulaic, and oriented toward private introspection.

Further reading: Hardy and Laing (1990: entries on John Fahey, Ian Mathews); Hall (1994); Schaefer (1987)

Listening: Oldfield, *Tubular Bells* (Virgin, 1973)

NEW ROMANTICS

A rather general label or movement, applied to British synthesizer-based bands of the mid-1980s who did well in the US market partly because of extensive exposure on MTV. The term is often used interchangeably with (British) new pop. The new romantics frequently adopted extravagant dress, make-up and period clothes (e.g. Adam and the Ants). Other leading performers included Soft Cell, Duran, Duran, Culture Club, Howard Jones, and the Human League.

See also: **MTV; glam rock**

Further reading: Rimmer (1985); Hill (1986)

Listening: *At Worst … The Best of Boy George and Culture Club* (Virgin, 1993); Duran Duran, *Notorious* (Capitol, 1986)

NEW WAVE

The origins of the term lie with its application to avant-garde French film-makers of the 1950s to signal a radical break with dominant conventions. Musically new wave performers were innovative and progressive, but not necessarily threatening (cf. **punk**). New wave was usually more melodic and more accessible, in some cases with a greater emphasis on song lyrics.

New wave embraced a wide range of styles: in the UK, the Police (with reggae associations), XTC, Elvis Costello, and Graham Parker and the Rumour; in the US, Devo, the Cars, the B-52s, Talking Heads, Blondie (overlayed with disco), Tom Petty and the Heartbreakers (with rock'n'roll antecedents), and Jonathan Richman and the Modern Lovers. Especially in the US, new wave was used by record companies to avoid the negative connotations of punk; accordingly, bands which were stylistically and ideologically 'punk' were marketed as new wave, e.g. Blondie. The term is also sometimes used to refer to new strains of British **heavy metal** in the 1980s.

See also: **punk**

Further reading: Erlewine et al., eds (1995); Heylin (1993); Larkin (1995)

Listening: Elvis Costello, *The Best of Elvis Costello & the Attractions* (CBS, 1985); *The Best of Blondie* (Chrysalis, 1981); Talking Heads, *More Songs about Buildings & Food* (Sire, 1978)

NORTHERN SOUL

Northern soul was (and is still) a regional cult in the UK Midlands, based around ballroom/**club culture** and all-night dancing to 1960s Motown and independent label (e.g. Cameo Parkway, Verve) **soul** records chosen for their 'danceability', e.g. the Exciters. Northern soul became prominent in the early 1970s, with the Wigan Casino, a First World War dance hall, being declared by *Billboard* to be the world's best discotheque. The **subculture** maintained itself, with **fanzines**, continued all-nighters, and record compilations.

Hollows and Milestone's fascinating case study of the phenomenon challenges orthodox subcultural theory, and its preoccupation with music as a symbol and the homology between musical style and subcultural values. Northern soul produces a sense of **identity** and belonging based on the **consumption** of 'music as music', based around a club scene. Here the records have value both as commodities and as bearers of musical meaning. The exchange, buying, and selling of records is an important part of the Northern soul scene. Indeed, the use of 'white labels' represents a unique form of fetishization of black musical culture by white consumers (Hollows and Milestone, 1998).

Further reading: Garratt (1998: ch. 5); Hollows and Milestone (1998)

Listening: *Once Upon a Time in Wigan*, Kent (2004; compilation soundtrack to the play of the same name)

PAYOLA

A term used for the offering of financial, sexual, or other inducements in return for promotion. In 1955 the US House of Representatives Legislative Oversight Committee, which had been investigating the rigging of quiz shows, began looking at pay-to-play practices in rock music **radio**. Payola, as the practice was then known, had long been commonplace, but was not illegal. 'Song plugging', as the practice was originally termed, had been central to **music industry marketing** since the heyday of Tin Pan Alley and was central to the marketing of radio in the 1930s (Ennis, 1992: 43–4; 66–8). By the 1950s, **DJs** and radio station programmers frequently supplemented their incomes with 'consultant fees' and musical credits on records, enabling them to receive a share of songwriting royalties.

The United States Congress investigated the practice, and legislation was introduced making it illegal. During the Congressional committee hearings, Dick Clark admitted to having a personal interest in around a quarter of the records he promoted on his influential show. He divested himself of his music business holdings and was eventually cleared by the committee. A clean-cut figure, Clark survived the scandal because he represented the acceptable face of **rock'n'roll**. Pioneer DJ Alan Freed was not so fortunate; persecuted and eventually charged with commercial bribery in 1960, his health and career were ruined.

Payola did not target all music radio, but was rather 'the operative strategy for neutralizing rock'n'roll' (Garofalo, 1997: 170), and part of a conservative battle to return to 'good music'. The campaign against payola was underpinned by economic self-interest. ASCAP supported it by attacking rivals BMI, whose writers were responsible for most rock'n'roll; the **majors** supported it as part of a belated attempt to halt the expansion of the **independents**. Hill goes so far as to conclude that one way to see the payola hearings was as an attempt – ultimately successful – 'to force a greater degree of organization and hierarchical responsibility onto the record industry so that the flow of music product could be more easily regulated' (1991: 667). The involvement of conservative government officials, and a number of established music figures (including Frank Sinatra), was largely based on an often intense dislike of rock'n'roll, a prejudice with only loosely concealed racist overtones given the prominence of black musicians in the genre.

The practice of payola continued in other guises. During the 1980s and 1990s, major labels spent millions of dollars in the US on 'independent promotions' people, or song pluggers, in an attempt to guarantee radio airplay for their records. Despite adverse publicity and the occasional lawsuit, the practice was still prevalent in 2001–2 (Hull, 2004).

See also: **charts; DJs; radio**

Further reading: Ennis (1992); Friedlander (1996); Garofalo (1997)

PHONOGRAPH; GRAMOPHONE CULTURE

Edison invented the phonograph, a 'talking machine', in November 1877. The phonograph represented the true beginning of recorded sound technology, replacing 'the shared Victorian pleasures of band-stand and music hall with the solitary delight of a private world of sound' (Millard, 1995: 1). Edison's phonograph used cylinders and was able to record and reproduce sound. Other researchers developed the new technology further: Berliner developed the gramophone (1888), using a disk instead of a cylinder, while Edison considerably improved on his original in 1887. The phonograph and the gramophone are the forerunners of contemporary home stereo systems.

The phonograph was originally intended primarily as a business tool, but moved into entertainment initially through coin-operated phonographs (from 1889). With the development of pre-recorded cylinders in the early 1900s, the phonographic industry took off. While in 1897 only about 500,000 records (78s) had been sold in the United States, by 1899 this number had reached 2.8 million, and continued to rise. The phonograph, as various historians of recorded sound have observed, played a role in defining modernity, being put to use in ways that sharply changed the culture of music in the home, turning music into a 'thing'. The domestication of recorded sound increased the musical repertoire available to the home listener, while freeing up the experience of music from its physical location. As Gronow and Saunio put it: 'the musician became immortal' (1983: 213).

In 1896 the first machines aimed at the home entertainment market were introduced by Edison and the Columbia label in the United States. By 1900 the gramophone (the term later came to denote all forms of 'record player') had emerged as the fashion accessory of the day and was recognized as a familiar feature in most homes. The recording industry took off around the turn of the century. In 1899, 151,000 phonographs were produced in the US alone, and there was now a 'steady if limited supply of discs and pre-recorded cylinders' (Gronow, 1983: 54–5). By 1900, several large commercial recording companies were operating on a stable national basis, and listening to the various new 'talking machines' was a popular pastime. A strong link between hardware and software was established from the start of sound recording, with companies marketing both their models of the phonograph and the recordings to be played on it.

Various commentators have identified a succession of phases in the technological history of the phonograph: an acoustic one from 1877 to the 1920s; the use of electrical/magnetic tape from the 1920s; and the digital age, with the CD, from 1982: 'the industry built on the pho-nograph was driven forward by the constant disruption of innovation: new systems of recording, new kinds of machine, and newer types of recorded music' (Millard, 1995: 5–6; see also Read and Welch, 1977). By the 1970s, most homes in 'developed' countries had a home stereo, the modern phonograph, consisting of an amplifier, a record turntable, tape recorder, and radio.

See also: **sound recording**

Further reading: Eisenberg (1988), esp. ch. 8; Jones (1992); Millard (1995)

PIRACY

Piracy is usually simply regarded as a form of theft, and the music industry has generally favoured this definition. However, there has been considerable debate around the various practices associated with music piracy, and whether these are indeed a form of theft. It is probably circumspect, therefore, to always signal this ambivalence by using the term in quote marks: 'piracy'.

The same technologies that have made commercially recorded popular music a global commodity have also made it one of the world's most vulnerable to 'piracy'. There are a number of practices involved here, and it is important to distinguish between, first, the multiple copying and subsequent on-selling for profit of copyrighted recordings in various formats; and, second, copying by individuals on a 'one off' basis, primarily but not exclusively for personal use. This includes **cassette audio** home taping; downloading recordings from the **Internet**, as **MP3s**, via services such as **Napster**; and practices including file sharing.

A third form of 'piracy' is the unauthorized recording of **concerts**: **bootlegs**, usually for personal use or trading among fans; due to their particular cultural nature, these have been considered separately.

The International Federation of the Phonogram Industry (IFPI), the 'watchdog' of the global **music industry**, noted that worldwide **CD** piracy had doubled during the mid–1990s, and put the retail value of pirate sales in 1994 at some 6 per cent of legitimate sales. Recent estimates suggest an increase in the volume and 'market share' of such copies (Hull, 2004).

New reproductive technologies make many of these pirated editions almost indistinguishable from the originals. In some countries in Asia, Africa, the Middle East, and Latin America the proportion of pirated copies is considerably higher, with China a major offender. The IFPI has had only limited success in curbing these activities, since many governments are reluctant to act against their own bootleggers, who are part of an important 'informal economy', providing a major source of income and jobs.

'One off' copying of recordings, while also in a strict sense 'piracy', poses a different set of issues. The first major controversy here arose around home taping in the 1970s. A practice enabled by the development of (increasingly cheap) cassette audio tape and the cassette tape player, home taping is *individual* copying (to audio or video tape) from existing recordings, or off–air. Making *multiple* copies is considered piracy, although both forms breach **copyright**. Home taping was frequently criticized by the mainstream music industry, and many artists, because of the perceived loss of revenue involved. Others regarded home taping as a legitimate cultural practice, asserting consumer autonomy. The IFPI and the music industry called (unsuccessfully in most national contexts) for a levy on blank tapes.

The arguments around home taping rehearsed many of those surrounding the subsequent use of the Internet to access music 'for free', by downloading MP3s into home computers. (see Internet; Napster). Once again, there has been vigorous and extensive debate over the economic and cultural implications for music posed by a new **technology**.

See also: **bootlegs; copyright**

Further reading: Burnett (1996); Hull (2004)

PIRATE RADIO

Pirate broadcasts are alternatives to licensed, state–run or commercial **radio** programming. However, the pirate stations usually rely on the same popular music that is programmed on commercial radio, rarely programming music other than the main **pop** and **rock styles**. A major exception was in the 1960s, when the British pirates challenged the

BBC's lack of attention to pop and rock music. British pirate radio in its heyday, 1964–8, was an historical moment encapsulating the intersection of rock as cultural politics and personal memory with market economics and government intervention. Twenty-one different pirates operated during this period, representing a wide range of radio stations in terms of scale, motives, and operating practices.

Chapman argues that the myth of the pirates is that they were about providing pop music to the disenfranchised youthful listeners, representing a somewhat anarchic challenge to radio convention and commerce, but the reality was rather more commercial. However, given that the BBC's popular music policy was woefully inadequate in the early 1960s, the pirates did cater for a largely disenfranchised audience; they also pioneered some innovative programmes and boosted the careers of leading **DJs** Kenny Everett and John Peel. As their programming indicated, they were never predominantly about popular music, and were heavily oriented towards **advertising**. All the pirates were commercial operations: 'though work place and legal judicial circumstances were not typical, in all other respects these were entrepreneurial small businesses aspiring to become entrepreneurial big businesses' (Chapman, 1992: 167). This was particularly evident in the case of Radio London, set up with an estimated investment of £1.5 million, whose 'overriding institutional goals were to maximize profit and bring legal commercial radio to Great Britain' (ibid.: 80). In this respect, the station succeeded, with the BBC's Radio One, established in 1967 as the pirates were being closed down, borrowing heavily from the practices of pirate radio, and hiring ex-pirate DJs. In New Zealand, prominent pirate radio station Radio Hauraki was inspired by the British pirates (see Blackman, 1988).

In contrast to the UK pirates, US pirate radio stations operate on shoestring budgets, broadcast irregularly, rarely attempt to turn a profit, do not solicit advertising, and keep a very low profile. The Federal Communications Commission has an attitude of 'selective enforcement', meaning that it acts on complaints and interference, but does not seek out pirate broadcasters.

Further reading: Chapman (1992); Jones (1992)

POLICY

Policy in relation to popular music is formulated and implemented at the levels of the international community, the nation state, regions, and local government. It includes regulation and stimulation of aspects of the production and consumption of music. At an international level there are agreements on market access and **copyright** provisions. At the state level policies include the regulation/deregulation of **broadcasting**; the use of tax breaks and content quotas; support for local copyright regulation, and **censorship**. The local level involves venue-related regulations.

The state has often been ignored in analyses of popular music, though there is a tradition of work on cultural policy, at both the central and local state level. The call in the early 1990s for popular music researchers to pay more attention to the state (see Bennett *et al.*, 1993; Negus, 1996) has since been addressed by a range of work. Studies of local policy include Kenney's history of the evolution of Chicago **jazz**, which details how a mix of council regulations, licensing law, moral watchdog organizations, and police practices influenced the particular genre form taken by jazz in that city (Kenney, 1993). In a similar project, Chevigny (1991) shows how successive New York City Councils applied a network of zoning, fire, building, and licensing regulations to discipline the venues and styles of jazz within the city. Homan (1998) demonstrated the complex relationship between city zoning, licensing, and noise regulations in Sydney and the venues for **rock** and **dance**, and the styles of music associated with them.

In social and political theory there are two major competing theories of the nature of the state (broadly defined as the government and its institutional agents, especially the civil service) and its operation: liberal, pluralist views, which see the state as operating neutrally in 'the public interest'; and Marxist-oriented views, which see the state as upholding the interests of the ruling or dominant groups in society. Within these two extremes, there is a continuum of views (see O'Sullivan *et al.*, 1994 for a succinct overview).

State cultural policies have been largely based on the idealist tradition of **culture** as a realm separate from, and often in opposition to, that of material production and economic activity. This means that government intervention in its various forms — subsidy, licensing arrangements, protectionism through quotas, and so on — is justified by the argument which has been clearly elaborated by Garnham:

> that culture possesses inherent values, of life enhancement or whatever, which are fundamentally opposed to and in danger of damage by commercial forces; that the need for these values is universal, uncontaminated by questions of class, gender and ethnic origin; and that the market cannot satisfy this need (1987: 24).

A key part of this view is the concept of the individual creative artist, with the associated cultural policy problem defined as 'one of finding audiences for their work rather than vice versa' (ibid.). This **ideology** has been used by elites in government, administration, intellectual institutions, and broadcasting to justify and represent sectional interests as general interests, thereby functioning as a form of cultural **hege-mony**. Seeing classical music, ballet, and the theatre as **high culture** or 'the arts' legitimizes both their largely middle-class **consumption** and their receipt of state subsidy. Popular culture is then constructed in opposition to this, as commercial, inauthentic, and so unworthy of significant government support. Such a dichotomized high–low culture view is unsustainable, yet it nonetheless remains a widely held and still powerful ideology.

State attitudes and policies toward popular culture are a significant factor in determining the construction of meaning in popular music. At the level of attitudes, state cultural policies are indicative of the various views held about the very concept of culture itself, debates over government economic intervention in the marketplace versus the operation of the 'free market', the operation of **cultural imperialism**, and the role of the state in fostering national **cultural identity**. There have been notable attempts on the part of the state to use particular forms or **genres** of popular music to foster a particular ideology and engender national solidarity, while at the same time marginalizing, or actively persecuting, other genres (e.g. the suppression of 'non Ayan' jazz and the elevation of the nationalistic composer Wagner in Nazi Germany in the 1930s – see Negus, 1996; for other examples, see Garofalo, 1992b). The use of national anthems is a small but significant part of such efforts.

In the case of popular music, government attitudes have generally, but not exclusively, tended to reflect a traditional conservative view of 'culture' (see the high culture tradition), which is used to justify non-intervention in the 'commercial' sphere. Yet this non-intervention exists in tension with frequent governmental concern to regulate a medium which, at times, has been associated with threats to the social order: moral panics over the activities of youth subcultures, the sexuality and sexism of rock, and obscenity. There have been a number of cases where the state has played a significant role in relation to popular music through economically and culturally motivated regulation and intervention. This has usually been to defend national cultural production against the inflow of foreign media products, using trade tariffs, industry incentives, and suchlike, and is focused on popular rather than high culture (see **cultural imperialism**).

The past decade has seen increased governmental (state) interest in the economic possibilities inherent in the social and economic value of the arts and creative industries, and popular music has been a significant part of this discourse. State and local governments have increasingly recognized the economic and social potential of popular music. Their intervention 'is becoming increasingly explicit, increasingly programmatic and institutional ... the role of government has become a crucial factor in the structural organization of rock music at the local, the national and ultimately at the global level' (Bennett *et al.*, 1993: 9). Government music policy has been evident in the former East Germany, Holland, Canada, Australia, New Zealand, and the United States. The issues raised include the defence of national identity, the music industry as a site for youth employment, and the protection of local markets (see the contributions to Bennett *et al.*, 1993; also Berland, 1991; Breen, 1999; Shuker, 2001).

State regulation/deregulation of broadcasting occurs with governmental regulation of the airwaves, through: (i) limiting the available radio frequencies or television channels, through licensing policies; (ii) broadcasting codes of practice, which may serve to restrict exposure of 'offensive' material (see **censorship**); and (iii) content quotas: legislated provisions for a minimum fixed proportion of local content on radio (and, sometimes, television) programming. Such quotas are designed to protect local culture industries from the perceived negative influence of imported, largely US, popular culture. Examples of the application, or the attempted application, of music quotas include New Zealand, Australia, Canada, and France.

British state policy on music in the 1990s was a local phenomenon, with a proliferation of regional and city-based music projects; several writers raised the cultural implications of these initiatives (especially Cohen, 1991; Street, 1993). While such initiatives are still evident, there has recently been greater attention to the question of national policy. An instructive discussion of the current engagement of popular music scholars with the development of governmental policy is provided by Cloonan *et al.* (2004). Reflecting on their commissioned report for 'Scottish Enterprise: Mapping the Music Industry in Scotland', their study raises four issues common to such projects: (1) the lack of comprehensive official data, and the associated question of what constituted 'the music industry', including the difficulty of quantifying the cultural value of musical activity; (2) the need to relate the 'local' or national situation to the issue of market size and the role of key global players; (3) the competing expectations (of such reports) of political stakeholders and 'industry' personnel; and (4) the policy role of the academic in attempting to provide 'public knowledge'.

See also: **broadcasting; censorship; cultural imperialism**

Further reading: Garnham (1987); Negus (1996); Shuker (2001)

POLITICAL ECONOMY

Political economy was used in the eighteenth century to describe what became 'economics' in the late nineteenth century. The field developed in response to the emergence of mercantile capitalism as the dominant economic force, the expansion of markets, and the growth of the state. These changes raised questions of the relationship of the individual to the social order. The theoretical bases of political economy embraced the concepts of social class, the value and division of labour, and moral dimensions such as the nature and operation of self-interest.

Political economy became associated with particular variants of economics, and was often used as a code word for Marxism. Early (classic) Marxist political economy tended to devalue the significance of culture, seeing it primarily as the reflection of the economic base. In relation to the mass media, this view was given its fullest expression in the work of the **Frankfurt School**, especially Adorno. Later variants of political economy aspired to develop 'an integrated field that encompasses the specialised disciplines of politics, economics and international relations' (Gill and Law, 1988: xviii; see also Garnham, 1990; Jhally, 1989). Contemporary political economy is interested in the relationship between economic organization and political, social, and cultural life. Such an approach frequently labels itself 'critical political economy' to distinguish and distance itself from what it considers the 'cruder' formulations of classical (Marxist) political economy.

All variants of political economy require analysis of the way politics shapes the economy, and of the way in which the economy shapes politics. Accordingly, current political economy has explored issues such as the place of the economy within the larger social system, the importance of market institutions for individual autonomy, private enterprise and capitalism as a system of economic development, poverty and inequality in market economies, global patterns of wealth and inequality, and the limits of the market and the role of government (Levine, 1995).

Political economy is a major dimension of critical media and communications studies, embodying a scepticism toward business and the state and embracing a commitment to greater social equality and democracy. The application of political economy to the study of the media has as its starting point the fact that the producers of mass media are industrial institutions, essentially driven by the logic of capitalism: the pursuit of maximum profit. That these **culture industries** are owned and controlled by a relatively small number of people and show a marked tendency towards increased concentration is regarded as a situation involving considerable ideological power: the media as 'consciousness industries'. Schiller (1996) has traced the pervasive and increasing inequality in access to information and cultural products due to the commercialization and privatization of broadcasting, libraries, higher education, and other areas of public discourse. Commenting on the United States, Bagdikian (1997) observes how 'a small number of the country's largest industrial corporations have acquired more public communications power than any private business has ever before possessed in world history', together creating 'a new communications cartel within the United States'. The **music industry** has been part of this process of con- solidation of 'imperial corporations' (Barnet and Cavanagh, 1994). At issue is the consequent question of control of the media and whose interests it operates in, and the relationship between diversity and innovation in the market.

In popular music studies, political economy is a central feature of analyses of the operation of the music industry, especially its sound recording companies; studies of music and cultural imperialism/ globalization; MTV; and central and local state policy toward popular music (see the separate entries on each of these). One example of such work must suffice as an illustration here.

Drawing on political economy as an explanatory framework for her analysis, Gaines (1992) examines intellectual property law and the contradictions in legal attempts to accommodate late capitalism. Her study attempts to explain how external changes in material production are reflected within internal structures of law and culture. She rejects Marxian political economy, with its emphasis on the determining role of the economic base, and proposes a more complex view of 'political, social, economic, legal and cultural forms as connected yet disconnected' (p. 16) Gaines utilizes a dichotomy of 'circulation-restriction' of cultural commodities to show how the corporate power of monopoly capit- alism over signs, images, and meanings is in contest with the doctrine of free enterprise within law.

Political economy continues to inform popular music studies, but in a more complex fashion than was present in the economic determinism of earlier studies. Contemporary approaches involve examining popular music by asking of the music industry, and governmental institutions: Who produces the popular music text? For what audience, and in what physical contexts? In whose interests? What is privileged, and what is excluded? Such interrogation necessitates examining popular music media institutions in terms of their production practices, financial bases, technology, legislative frameworks, and their construction of audiences.

See also: **cultural imperialism; globalization; MTV; music industry**

Further reading: Bennett *et al*. (1993); Frith, ed. (1993); Negus (1992)

POLITICS; SOCIAL MOVEMENTS

In the general sense of the word, politics permeates popular music studies. Practically every aspect of the production and consumption of popular music involves theoretical debates about the dynamics of economic, cultural, and political power and influence, and the reproduction of social structures and individual subjectivities (see **Frankfurt School; political economy; cultural studies; feminism; structuralism**). In a more specific sense, politics is reflected in direct state intervention in the cultural sphere, e.g. via forms of censorship, and the regulation of broadcasting. Here the discussion focuses rather on the question of the role of popular music in creating social change, and its mobilization within social movements.

A central problem in social theory has been to explain how cultures change, and to identify the forms of social activity at work in processes of social transformation. While there is considerable theoretical debate over the relative importance of social structures and human agency, a key part of social change are changes in the cognitive identity of the individuals involved. Popular music has played a prominent role in articulating this process, at both the individual and collective group level. At various historical points, popular music has translated political radicalism into a more accessible idiom, identifying social problems, alienation and oppression, and facilitating the sharing of a collective vision. Performers and songs contribute to forging a relationship between politics, cultural change, and popular music. Popular music has frequently acted as a powerful means of raising both consciousness about and funds for political causes. At the same time, however, there is a tendency for such popular music forms to be co-opted, commodified, and watered down or neutralized by the music industry.

Examples of popular music playing an overt political role include campaigns and interventions at several levels. Internationally, the global phenomenon of Live Aid in 1985 addressed the issue of famine in Africa; the Mil Foundation and the Concerts for Tibet, initiated by the Beastie Boys, raised issues of repressive Chinese government policies in that country. Examples at a national level include the Campaign for Nuclear Disarmament movement in the UK in the late 1950s; Civil Rights in the US in the 1960s, Rock Against Racism in the UK in the late 1970s and early 1980s, and Rock Against Bush in 2004. (As Rock Against Racism is one of the most fully documented of these campaigns, it is considered separately below.) Many artists have individually used their music to make political statements on a variety of issues, including racism, class, gender politics, sexuality, and environmental concerns. These are frequently within the strong historical tradition of protest song, particularly in folk music, which has been carried on in genres such as reggae, punk, and alternative music.

There is disagreement as to the cultural significance and force of such statements and campaigns. For Grossberg, 'on the one hand, so much activity is attempting to explicitly articulate rock to political activism; on the other hand, this activity seems to have little impact on the rock formation, its various audiences or its relations to larger social struggles' (Grossberg, 1992a: 168). This argument rests on a perceived 'radical disassociation' of the political content of the music of bands such as U2, R.E.M. and Midnight Oil 'from their emotionally and affectively powerful appeals' (ibid.). It is clear that many listeners derive pleasure from such performers without either subscribing to their politics, or, indeed, even being aware of them. On the other hand, a variety of examples can be adduced to illustrate that many listeners *do* have their ideological horizons both confirmed and extended by association with political rock. This can also have practical benefits – the Amnesty International tours of 1988 are estimated to have added some 200,000 new members to the organization in the USA alone (see Garofalo, 1992b; Street, 1986; Denselow, 1990).

Rock Against Racism is an example of such an association between music and politics. It was a partially successful mass campaign to confront the racism arising in the harsh urban landscapes of inner city Britain in the 1970s. Rock Against Racism used demonstrations, concerts, a magazine, and records to mobilize upwards of half a million people: 'black and white people, outside conventional politics, inspired by a mixture of socialism, punk rock and common humanity, got together and organized to change things' (Widgery, 1986: 8). In February 1981 *Rock Against Racism's Greatest Hits* (Virgin Records) was the first album done as a political gesture, providing a precedent for the subsequent efforts of organizations such as Band Aid. Leading groups and artists (Tom Robinson Band, the Clash) contributed to mass concerts and carnivals, and anti-National Front rallies, which served to politicize while entertaining. While the campaign failed to stop racist attacks, far less racism, it was a factor in the sharp decline of the National Front's share of the vote in the general election of 1979, following the fascist organization's surge of support in the mid-1970s.

Rock Against Racism strengthened the idea that popular music could be about more than entertainment, and in a sense provided the inspiration for similar campaigns in the 1980s. But as Street (1986) notes, the Rock Against Racism campaign illustrates 'the delicacy of the relationship between a cause and its music', as the reliance on the music as the source of unity and strength threw into sharp relief differences of stylistic affiliations. Political strategies were 'played out and resolved in terms of musical choices', a process which indicated 'the limitations of a politics organized around music' (Street, 1986, p. 78). Similar difficulties were evident in attempts to harness rock to the cause of the striking British miners in 1984–5, and with Red Wedge, the opposition Labour Party's attempt to use rock to win the youth vote in the 1987 UK general election. In both cases, strongly held views about the correct relationship of political principle and musical style arguably seriously limited the impact of the efforts (see Denselow, 1990: ch. 8; Frith and Street, 1992).

It has been argued that the history of such attempts to use popular music to forge mass movements will always face two problems. First, the power of popular music is transitory by nature, novelty and shock value have a short lifespan, and routinization and disempowering follows. Second, there is the confused nature of musical power's 'collectivity': 'The power of mass music certainly comes from its mobilization of an audience; a series of individual choices (to buy this record, this concert ticket) becomes the means to a shared experience and identity. The question, though, is whether this identity has any political substance' (Frith and Street, 1992: 80).

A further dimension of this question is the tendency of many commentators to incorrectly assume that 'youth' represent some sort of 'natural left' political constituency. Yet popular music is hardly the preserve of the political left and broadly progressive politics. It can, and has been, used to support a broad range of political positions. President

Bush's inaugural performances included an impressive line-up of blues and soul artists; white supremacist organizations like the National Front in the UK and neo-Nazi groups in Germany have used punk rock and hardcore bands to attract new recruits; and US anti-abortion activists have co-opted 'We Shall Overcome' to maintain solidarity at sit-ins outside abortion clinics.

See also: **censorship; concerts**

Further reading: Garofalo (1992b); Eyerman and Jamison (1995); Pratt (1990)

POP; DANCE POP

Musically pop is defined by its general accessibility, its commercial orientation, an emphasis on memorable hooks or choruses, and a lyrical preoccupation with romantic love as a theme. The musical aesthetics of pop are essentially conservative: 'It is about providing popular tunes and clichés in which to express commonplace feelings – love, loss, and jealousy' (Frith, 2001: 96). Along with songwriters, producers are often regarded as the main creative force behind pop artists (e.g. Stock, Aitken, and Waterman; Chinn and Chapman, Phil Spector).

Accordingly, as a genre in the marketplace, pop's defining feature is that 'It is music produced commercially for profit, as a matter of enterprise not art' (ibid.: 94). Pop has a long, although largely unacknowledged, musical history predating the 1950s. Over the past half century it has been a metagenre, frequently collapsed into and equated with 'popular', but including a range of styles under labels such as 'chart pop' and 'teen pop'. Much of pop is regarded as disposable, for the moment, dance music; the best of it survives as 'golden oldies'.

'The abbreviation "pop" was not in use as a generic term until the 1950s when it was adopted as the umbrella name for a special kind of musical product aimed at a teenage market' (Gammond, 1991: 457). Nonetheless, as Ennis documents, pop music was evident in three of the defining 'streams' which eventually overlap and fuse in the evolution of American *popular* music:

(1) Pop as the commercial music of the nation, associated with Tin Pan Alley, musical theatre, the motion picture, and the rise of radio.
(2) 'Black pop', the popular music of black Americans, commercially domesticated around 1900, and from 1920 to 1948 known as 'race music'.

(3) 'Country pop', the popular music of the American white south and southwest.

Alongside these were three smaller streams: jazz, folk, and gospel. Collectively, these six streams were the basis for the emergence of (what Ennis terms) 'rocknroll' in the 1950s. **Rock'n'roll** was created by the grafting together of the emotive and rhythmic elements of the **blues**, the folk elements of country and Western music, and **jazz** forms such as **boogie woogie**. Pop is seen to have emerged as a somewhat watered-down, blander version of this, associated with a more rhythmic style and smoother vocal harmony – the period of **teen idols** in the late 1950s and early 1960s (e.g. Bobby Vee).

Reflecting the dominance of teen pop in the late 1950s, pop became used in an oppositional, even antagonistic sense, to **rock** music. This was linked to notions of art and commerce in popular music, e.g.

> 'Pop implies a very different set of values to rock. Pop makes no bones about being mainstream. It accepts and embraces the requirement to be instantly pleasing and to make a pretty picture of itself. Rock on the other hand, has liked to think it was somehow more profound, non-conformist, self-directed and intelligent'
>
> (Hill, 1986: 8).

Subsequently the term pop was used to characterize chart- and teenage audience-oriented music, particularly the genres of dance pop, **bubblegum**, **power pop**, and the **new romantics**, and performers such as the **girl groups** of the 1960s, their 1990s equivalents, and the ubiquitous **boy bands** of the modern era. Pop is also currently the dominant style in reality television shows such as *Pop Idol* (see **television**). The most significant of these styles has been chart-oriented, dance pop. As with pop generally, dance pop is often maligned, in part because of its perceived commercial orientation and its main audience of adolescent girls – teenyboppers (for a positive analysis of such consumption, see Baker, 2002). Commercially highly successful exponents include Kylie Minogue (in the 1980s); Paula Abdul, Bananarama, and the Spice Girls in the 1990s; and, most recently, Britney Spears and Hillary Duff.

The success of these performers was frequently attributed to the Svengali-like influence of producers (e.g. Stock, Aitken, and Waterman and Kylie Minogue), and exposure through MTV and high-energy videos (e.g. Paula Abdul), as much as or more than talent. In 1989, after Milli Vanilli had won the Grammy Award for Best New Group, there was an uproar when it emerged that the duo did not sing on their records (see Martin, 1993). Nonetheless, dance pop is a continuing staple of contemporary popular music, and is due for a critical reappraisal as part of audience-oriented cultural studies analysis.

The debate around the Spice Girls, who had enormous international success in the late 1990s, exemplified the discourse around dance pop, especially regarding its commodification and authenticity. The Spice Girls 'introduced the language of independence to a willing audience of preteen and teenage girls – girl power' (Whiteley, 2000: 215); stressing female bonding, a sense of sisterhood, friendship, and self-control in their personas, press interviews, and the lyrics to their songs. However, critics pointed to the contradictions between the Spice Girls' professed self-expression and their subversion to standard sexualized 'feminine' images, and their incorporation into a male-dominated music industry, thereby sustaining dominant gender ideologies (see Lemish, 2003).

See also: **authenticity; producers**

Further reading: Baker (2002); Frith (2001); Hawkins (2002); Hill (1986)

Listening: Paula Abdul, *Forever Your Girl* (Virgin, 1988); Bananarama, *Greatest Hits Collection* (London, 1988); Britney Spears, *Baby One More Time* (Zomba, 1999); Hilary Duff, *Metamorphosis* (Buena Vista, 2003)

POPULAR CULTURE *see* **culture** ·

POPULAR MUSIC

Historically, the term popular has meant 'of the ordinary people'. It was first linked in a published title to a certain kind of music that conformed to that criterion in William Chapple's *Popular Music of the Olden Times*, published in instalments from 1855. Not until the 1930s and 1940s did the term start to gain wider currency (Gammond, ed., 1991; see also Williams, 1983).

Popular music defies precise, straightforward definition. As Negus observes, unlike film studies, 'popular music is broader and vaguer in scope and intentions. The moving media image can be traced to particular social and technological developments within a particular period of history, and this provides a boundary for study in a way that has no parallel in popular music studies' (1996: 5; and see Hayward, 1996). Such difficulties lead some writers on popular music to slide over the question of definition, and take a 'common–sense' under-standing of the term for granted. This aside, various attempts to provide a definition can be identified.

Definitions placing an emphasis on 'popular'

Middleton observes that the question of 'what is popular music' is 'so riddled with complexities ... that one is tempted to follow the example of the legendary definition of folk song – all songs are folk songs, I never heard horses sing 'em – and suggest that all music is popular music: popular with someone' (1990: 3). However, the criteria for what counts as popular, and their application to specific musical styles and genres, are open to considerable debate. Classical music clearly has sufficient following to be considered popular, while, conversely, some forms of popular music are quite exclusive (e.g. death metal).

Definitions based on the commercial nature of popular music, and embracing genres perceived as commercially oriented

Many commentators argue that it is commercialization that is the key to understanding popular music, e.g. 'When we speak of popular music we speak of music that is commercially oriented' (Burnett, 1996: 35). This approach is related to the emphasis on the popular, arguing that such appeal can be quantified through charts, radio air-play, and so forth. In such definitions, certain **genres** are identified as 'popular music', while others are excluded (e.g. Clarke, ed., 1990; Garofalo, 1997; and of course the same process of selection is at work in this volume). However, this approach can suffer from the same problems as those stressing popularity, since many genres, especially metagenres such as world music, have only limited appeal and/or have had limited commercial exposure. Moreover, popularity varies from country to country, and even from region to region within national markets. It needs to also be noted that this approach is largely con-cerned with *recorded* popular music.

Identification by general musical and non–musical characteristics

Tagg (1982), in an influential and much–cited discussion, characterizes popular music according to the nature of its distribution (usually mass);

how it is stored and distributed (primarily recorded sound rather than oral transmission or musical notation); the existence of its own musical theory and aesthetics; and the relative anonymity of its composers. The last of these is debatable, and I would want to extend the notion of composers and its associated view of the nature of musical creativity (see **auteurs**; **producers**; **songwriters**). However, musicologists have usefully extended the third aspect of this definition, while sociologists have concentrated on the first two dimensions.

It seems that a satisfactory definition of popular music must encompass both musical and socio–economic characteristics. Essentially, all popular music consists of a hybrid of musical traditions, styles, and influences, and is also an economic product which is invested with ideological significance by many of its consumers. At the heart of the majority of various forms of popular music is a fundamental tension between the essential creativity of the act of 'making music' and the commercial nature of the bulk of its production and dissemination (see Frith, 1983: ch. 1).

Further reading: Burnett (1996); Frith *et al.*, eds (2001); Longhurst (1995); Middleton (1990); Negus (1996); Tagg (1982)

POSTMODERNISM; POSTMODERN ROCK

Postmodernism is a 'portmanteau term encompassing a variety of developments in intellectual culture, the arts and the fashion industry in the 1970s and 1980s' (O'Sullivan *et al.*, 1994: 234). Postmodernism seeks to blur, if not totally dissolve the traditional oppositions and boundaries between the aesthetic and the commercial, between art and the market, and between high and low culture. The precise nature of postmodernism, however, proves hard to pin down, and there is a marked lack of clarity and consistency in all the varying usages of the term.

In a key contribution to early theoretical discussion around the concept, Fredric Jameson overviews postmodernism as the cultural expression of a new phase of capitalism, characterized by communications technologies facilitating the virtually instantaneous shifting of international capital, the emergence of new centres of capital (e.g. Japan) in a global economy, new class formations breaking with the traditional labour/capital division, and a consumer capitalism which markets style, images, and tastes as much as actual products. He argued that the commodification of culture has resulted in a new populism of the mass media, a culture centred around the marketing and consumption of surfaces and appearances, epitomized by the ubiquity of commercial television (Jameson, 1984). Despite its obvious plausibility as a general explanation of developments in popular culture, postmodernism suffers from a number of difficulties, including its frequent lack of specificity; its overpreoccupation with texts and audiences at the expense of locating these within their economic/productive context within which cultural products reside; its reduction of history and politics and its propensity to ignore 'traditional' sociological notions of production, class and ideology. (For a useful general discussions of the debates surrounding postmodernism, see Stevenson, 2002: ch. 5 and Smith, 2001: ch. 13.)

The postmodernist view of popular music generally regards it as exemplifying the collapse of traditional distinctions between art and the commercial, the aesthetic and the unaesthetic, and the authentic and unauthentic. This view has been prominent in discussions of **music video**, with its affinities to advertising (Kaplan, 1987); and, during the 1980s, with commentators on popular music, especially rock, who saw the music once associated with youthful rebellion and political activism as now thoroughly commercialized and incorporated into the postmodernist capitalist order. Frith (1988a, 1988b) suggested the arrival of a curious entity, postmodernist pop, a value-free zone where aesthetic judgements are outweighed by whether a band can get its video on MTV and its picture in *Smash Hits*. In an analysis of a number of major 1980s pop stars, Hill echoed Adorno's critique of popular music as manufactured mass culture. Appropriately subtitled 'Manufacturing the 1980's Pop Dream', Hill's study of performers such as Michael Jackson, Duran Duran, Wham, and Madonna demonstrated that 'this fresh species of genuinely talented practitioners are *ready and willing* to manufacture themselves' (his emphasis), and that 'never before have commerce and creativity so happily held hands' (Hill, 1986: 9; see **commercialism**). While both Frith and Hill conceded that popular music had always been about style as well as music, they argued that it was now increasingly subverted to the services of commercialism.

Aside from general production and marketing tendencies in popular music being drawn on to elaborate a postmodern view of the cultural form, postmodernism has also been applied to particular styles of music, treating them almost as a form of **genre** category: postmodern rock defined by Goodwin (1991) to include: (1) music that is outside the mainstream of popular music and is to be taken seriously; (2) music that is created by musicians who come chronologically after 'modern rock'; and (3) music that has evolved from **punk** rock. He observed that because popular music is conceptually used to define theory, culture, and practice, 'further analysis of its relation to music will have to take account of this epistemological feedback loop'. A number of contemporary genres demonstrate such characteristics (see **rap, dance music**), although these could no longer be regarded as outside of the mainstream; indeed, they have to a considerable extent become the mainstream.

Further reading: Gracyk (1996); Longhurst (1995)

POWER POP

The term power pop has a long history, being applied to various performers since the 1960s. The genre has been subject to considerable denigration, being viewed as a lightweight pop style, associated primarily with a teenage audience. In the early 1980s, power pop was a somewhat cynical major record company label to market post-punk styles, further undermining any claim it had to critical authenticity. However, while the style has its share of pale imitators, power pop has produced some excellent bands and much memorable music, and remains strongly present in contemporary pop and rock music.

The musical source point for nearly all power pop is the Beatles, who established its style, a combination of lyrics about young love, distinctive vocal harmonies, strong melodies, and catchy guitar riffs (e.g. 'From Me To You'). Other major performers credited with developing the genre in the 1960s included the Who, the Kinks, and the Move, who juxtaposed aggressive melodies and loud, distorted guitars (the 'power'). Leading American power pop bands during the same period were the Byrds, who originally modelled themselves on the Beatles, and several performers whose recordings were often denigrated as **bubblegum** music (lightweight commercial pop), but which have held up as examples of power pop, such as Tommy James and the Shondells, and Paul Revere and the Raiders.

Subsequent British exponents of power pop included the under-rated Beatles-influenced and highly melodic Badfinger (e.g. the singles 'No Matter What' and 'Baby Blue'), Nick Lowe, Gary Glitter, Slade, and Sweet, the last three with strong **glam/glitter** associations. For example, Slade mixed upfront lead vocals, a basic footstomping beat, anthemic choruses, and loud, distorted guitar chords to produce six number one UK singles in the early 1970s (though with little impact in the US).

In the United States, the label was applied to the Raspberries and Big Star in the early 1970s. Big Star's founders Chris Bell and former Box Top vocalist Alex Chilton were fans of 1960s British **beat music**, especially the Beatles, and combined to produce effervescent guitar pop. Their two studio albums were well received by the music press, but poor distribution and promotion curtailed the commercial impact of their recordings. Big Star nonetheless became one of the most influential cult bands in the history of popular music, and their repackaged albums and compilations reflect continued interest in them.

Other major American power pop performers included Cheap Trick, the Knack (largely for the huge success of their sleazy but hook-filled single 'My Sharonna' (1979), which sold over five million copies), the rockabilly-tinged Dwight Twilly Band ('I'm on Fire' (1975)), and, in the 1980s, the Byrds-influenced R.E.M. All were strongly influenced by the 1960s pioneers of the style, producing clever lyrics, strong harmonies, and punchy guitar hooks.

During the 1980s and into the 1990s, many of the new wave and post-punk British and American bands incorporated elements of power pop (e.g. the Replacements, the Stone Roses), as did the bands identified with the New Zealand Flying Nun label sound, notably the Chills. Contemporary **Britpop** owes major musical debts to it (Oasis), as do 'alternative rock' bands such as Echobelly, Elastica, and Nirvana – Kurt Cobain acknowledged the Beatles and Big Star as major influences.

Further reading: Charlton (1994); Erlewine *et al.*, eds (1995) (for updates, see www.allmusic.com); Weisband and Marks (1995)

Listening: The Move, *Great Move! The Best of the Move* (EMI, 1994); the Raspberries, *Raspberries Best* (Capitol, 1975); Big Star, *#1 Record/Radio City* (Stax, 1992; originally released on Ardent, 1972, 1974); Dwight Twilley, *Sincerely* (DDC, 1976); Slade, *Best of Slade* (Polydor, 2000); Cheap Trick, *In Colour* (Epic, 1977)

PRODUCERS

The occupation of producer emerged as a distinct job category and career path in the popular **music industry** during the 1950s, initially as someone who directed and supervised recording sessions. Successful producers (e.g. songwriters Leiber and Stoller at Atlantic; George Martin at EMI) began exerting pressure on their recording companies to receive credits (on recordings) and royalties. By the mid-1960s, the studio producer had become an **auteur** figure, an artist employing multitrack technology and stereo sound to make recording 'a form of composition in itself, rather than simply as a means of documenting a performance' (Negus, 1992: 87). The main example of a producer with this new status was Phil Spector. In the 1970s and 1980s, the role of the producer as a cultural intermediary was consolidated with the creative freedom accompanying the development of new **technology**: synthesizers, samplers, and computer-based sequencing systems such as Pro Tools. Producers are now central figures in genres such as dub and electronic/techno dance music, and have played a major role in many contemporary pop and rock chart successes (e.g. the Matrix in Avril Lavigne's singles and first album). Identifiable by particular musical imprints on their work, such producers are a new type of star figure in music (see 'Superproducers' in *The Wire*, October 2003: 124–37; this profiles a number of leading producers, working across a range of genre styles; see also the appendix to Zak, 2001).

The way producers operate, their contribution to the session, and the level of reward they are accorded vary widely, depending on the stature of the musicians they are working with and the type of music being recorded (see e.g. Butch Vig's account of his work on Nirvana's *Nevermind* album in Berkenstadt and Cross, 1998). Producers' approaches to recording vary from the naturalistic, 'try it and see what happens', to a more calculated, entrepreneurial attitude. Production practices represent an amalgam of established techniques and the possibilities offered by the new technologies.

See also: **auteurs; cultural intermediaries; sound recording**

Further reading: Negus (1992); Millard (1995); Schloss (2004); Zak (2001)

PROGRESSIVE ROCK; ART ROCK

A broad musical genre, progressive and art rock are frequently conflated (e.g. Moore, 2001) and incorporated in designations such as 'space rock' and 'Kraut rock'. (For convenience I will use 'progressive' here as a collective descriptor.) Progressive rock was associated with attempts to combine classical, **jazz**, and rock forms, and many of the performers were classically trained musicians. Progressive rock was initially part of the **counter–culture**/underground movement of the mid- to late 1960s, especially in the UK, where it soon became a marketing category, with a number of commercially successful performers (e.g. Traffic). It acquired its paradigmatic form and flourished with early 1970s groups such as the Nice, Yes, and ELP (Emerson, Lake and Palmer); then with Eno (early Roxy Music, etc.), Pink Floyd, and Genesis. The genre was prominent primarily in the UK, where it had a strong art-school connection, and in Europe (Tangerine Dream, Kraftwerk, Can: Krautrock). In the US, bands such as Kansas, Styx and Boston fall into the genre. Procol Harum's single, 'A Whiter Shade of Pale' (1967), whose distinctive organ sound was based on Bach's Suite No. 3 in D Major, is much cited as the classic example of art rock.

Progressive rock 'is marked, above all, by its diversity, a diversity suggestive of a constellatory, rather than a linear, account' (Moore, 1993: 101–2). The music is primarily not intended for dancing, so largely avoids the standard rock beat, with timbre and texture more important. Macan (1997) stresses progressive rock musicians' conscious imitation of classical music prototypes, and experiments in longer instrumental forms, borrowed from symphonic forms (as with Yes). Space and science-fictional themes were a feature of song titles and lyrics (e.g. Pink Floyd, 'Set the Controls for the Heart of the Sun' (1968)), with such variants being labelled space rock (e.g. by Downing, 1976; Thompson, 1994). In performance, progressive rock forged connections with the broader art scene (Walker, 1987), and made considerable use of theatrical conventions, as in Hawkwind's 'Space Ritual' stage show (1969–). The genre embraced the use of fantastic and obscure imagery, mixing conventions from disparate styles. This is evident in the names of several of the key albums, e.g. King Crimson's *Lark's Tongues in Aspic*, and the album cover art.

Several progressive rock performers integrated their work with classical music (e.g. Rick Wakeman, *Journey to the Centre of the Earth* (A&M, 1974)), although the results were frequently scorned by critics: 'classical pastiche ... genuinely appalling' (Rockwell, 1992); 'brutally synthesiser overkill' (DeCurtis, 1992, on ELP). Conversely, classical composers have adapted progressive rock to symphonic conventions: in 1995 Jaz Coleman arranged *The Symphonic Music of Pink Floyd*. Recorded with the London Philharmonic Orchestra, the album spent thirty-six weeks at the top of the *Billboard* crossover charts in the US and sold nearly 750,000 copies.

The merits of progressive rock have been much debated. Early critics saw it as emphasizing musical virtuosity over emotional intensity (central to sixties rock's authenticity), and frequently lapsing into pretentiousness and self-indulgence. **Punk** rock was in part a reaction against the perceived excesses of what punks derogatorily called 'prog rock'. The style's commercial appeal waned in the 1980s, although it emerged in hybrid genres such as progressive metal (Queensryche; Dream Theatre). Progressive rock nonetheless maintained a dedicated fan base, underpinned by **fanzines** (Atton, 2001). It underwent something of a largely positive academic reassessment in the late 1990s (see further reading), and continued interest has led to a reissuing of the work of several of its key performers, notably Yes.

Further reading: Holm–Hudson (2002); Macan (1997); Martin (1998); Moore (1993: 79–87); Rockwell (1992) (includes a useful discography)

Listening: Pink Floyd, *Dark Side of the Moon* (Harvest, 1973); Emerson Lake and Palmer, *The Best of ELP* (Atlantic, 1980); Procul Harum, 'A Whiter Shade of Pale', *The Best of Procul Harum* (A&M, 1972); Yes, *The Yes Album* (Atlantic, 1971) (CD reissue with bonus tracks, Rhino, 2004); Hawkwind, *In Search of Space* (One Way, 1971); King Crimson, *In the Court of the Crimson King* (1969; EG, 1989); *Kansas, The Best of* (CBS, 1984)

PSYCHEDELIC/ACID ROCK

A musical style usually regarded as a genre, which emerged in the mid-1960s, psychedelic rock described music inspired by or related to drug-induced experience, with the term used more or less inter-changably with acid rock (e.g. Whiteley, 1992) (the label 'acid' was the common name for the mind-expanding drug LSD). Various artists recorded songs assumed to refer to drugs (e.g. Jefferson Airplane, 'White Rabbit' (1967)). Whiteley provides extensive discussions of several key releases, including the Beatles' 'Tomorrow Never Knows' and 'Strawberry Fields Forever' singles, referring to 'the LSD coding' in these.

Musicians used fuzztone, feedback, synthesizers, and sheer volume, mimicking the supposedly mind-expanding properties of marijuana and LSD. Much of the music was characterized by experimentation and indulgence, with an emphasis on albums rather than singles (though there were some chart successes, e.g. Jefferson Airplane's 'Somebody to Love' (1967)). Psychedelic/acid rock was related to fashion, poster, and record design, and concert visual effects as well as the music, and was broadly linked with the youth counter-culture and, more specifically, with the hippy subculture.

Psychedelic rock had two main focii in the mid- to late 1960s: the US west coast and London, UK. In San Francisco around 1967–9, a psychedelic scene emerged, based around the Haight-Ashbury area, and free, open-air gatherings and commercial Fillmore concerts. With the success of the Monterey Pop Festival, US record companies realized the commercial potential of the genre. The main performers included Jefferson Airplane, the Grateful Dead, Moby Grape, and Quicksilver Messenger Service.

In the UK, psychedelic rock was linked to the 'swinging sixties' London-based scene. Tending to be conflated with progressive rock, it featured prominently in the charts in the late 1960s. Major artists included Cream, Arthur Brown, and Jimi Hendrix; and psychedelia also influenced the leading groups of period: the Beatles (with *Sergeant Pepper* (1967)) and the Rolling Stones (*Satanic Majesties* (1967)).

Psychedelic rock strongly influenced the subsequent development of other genres, especially alternative, art rock, heavy metal, and progressive rock; its more contemporary influence is clear in Britpop and styles of dance music, such as acid house.

See also: **counter-culture**

Further reading: Hicks (1999); Perry (1992); Puterbaugh (1992); Selvin (1994); Whiteley (1992)

Listening: Cream, *Disraeli Gears* (Polydor, 1967); Jefferson Airplane, *Surrealistic Pillow* (RCA, 1967); the Grateful Dead, *Anthem of the Sun* (WB, 1968); Quicksilver Messenger Service, *Happy Trails* (Capitol, 1969)

PUB ROCK

Initially a musical style and music press and record marketing label, pub rock is now identified more in terms of the pub as a context for the performance and consumption of popular music. The term originated in England during the early 1970s, when some musicians reacted to the excesses of glam/glitter rock by forming energetic bands that derived their sound from early rock'n'roll and R&B; they played primarily in 'pubs', licensed premises similar to US bars, hence the label. Pub rock was important because it brought music back into small venues, closing the distance between band and audience. The style tended to be a muscular, white male-dominated musical form, and the everyday image of the performers was inseparable from the style of their fans. These characteristics, and the discourse of fans and the music press surrounding them, constructed pub rock as a more **authentic** musical style.

Pub rock had little commercial impact (until the advent of **punk**, which it clearly influenced, and provided many of the musicians for) although a number of bands recorded/charted. The term also gained some currency in Australia and New Zealand, due to the significance of the pub (and the pub circuit supported by major breweries and their hotels) as a venue for live music (see Hayward, ed, 1992). Major performers included Brinsley Schwarz, Ducks Deluxe, Dr Feelgood, Eddie and the Hot Rods, and the Motors.

Further reading: Turner (1992); Tucker (1992); Bennett (1997)

Listening: *Brinsley Schwarz* (Capitol, 1970); Dr Feelgood, *Malpractice* (UA, 1975)

PUNK; PUNK ROCK

A youth subculture, closely associated with punk rock, during 1977–80 punk became the most visible youth subculture in the UK and in most Western metropolitan centres (notably Los Angeles and Melbourne). In part, punk was a reaction to hippy romanticism, and a lack of social status – some commentators saw punks as unemployed youth, celebrating their unemployability. There were several strata: middle-class, art school influenced punks, influenced by bohemianism; and working-class 'hard' punks. Punk style was very 'DIY' (do it yourself): old school uniforms, plastic garbage bags, and safety pins combined to present a shocking, self-mocking image. Punks adopted the swastika as an element of their style, though removed from its Nazi setting and adopted as shock-provoking jewellery. Hairstyles were either close shaved and dyed in bright colours, or (later) Mohican haircuts: spiked up into cockatoo plumes. Punk dances were the robot, the pogo, and the pose: 'collages of frozen automata' (Brake, 1985: 78). Hebdige (1979) stresses the **homology** of these elements in the subculture. Punks tended to align themselves with Rock Against Racism, but theirs was more a cultural than a political phenomenon, operating at the level of symbolic resistance.

While punk rock is conventionally linked to the UK 'punk explosion' of c. 1977–9, it clearly had its antecedents in the **garage rock** bands of the late 1960s, such as the Troggs, and early 1970s

American bands, most notably the Velvet Underground, Iggy and the Stooges, and the New York Dolls. Stylistically, much punk music was loud, fast, and abrasive. The myth endures that it was all three chords and an attitude, but the performers actually included some very capable and experienced musicians (in the case of the UK, many were from the **pub rock** scene of the mid-1970s), although 'the issue of skill and competence in punk rock remains ideologically charged' (Laing, 1988: 83). Punk bands relied on **live** shows to establish an identity and build a reputation, consequently 'techniques of recording and of arrangement were adopted which were intended to signify the "live" commitment of the disc' (ibid.: 74). In short, punk records generally sound 'live', as if the studio had not come between the intentions of the musicians and their listening audience. Aggressive, often shouted or snarled vocals blurred song **lyrics**. Punk emphasized an overall sound (voice plus instruments), rather than lyrical meaning. The ideology of sincerity was central to punk; in interviews 'the stated beliefs of musicians, and their congruence with the perceived messages of their lyrics, became routine topics' (ibid.: 90). But, as various analyses demonstrate, in many cases punk lyrics are like collages, a series of often fractured images, with no necessarily correct reading (see Sabin, 1999). Although a male-dominated form, 'punk's emphasis on eccentric self expression and its immediate availability to prospectus participants opened the genre to women' (O'Meara, 2003: 303). Female punk performers included Patti Smith in the US and the Raincoats in the UK.

The tempo of punk is usually described using terms such as 'basic' and 'primitive'. As a minimalist musical style, punk rock eschewed the growing use of electronic instruments associated with **progressive rock**, and featured a strict guitar and drums instrumental line-up: 'this was a sound best suited to expressing anger and frustration, focusing chaos, dramatizing the last days as daily life and ramming all emotions into the narrow gap between a blank stare and a sardonic grin' (Marcus, in DeCurtis, 1992: 595). The lack of importance of virtuosity in instrumental solos, reflected punk's frequent association of skill with glibness. Punk's attitude to rhythm was crucial to its sense of difference from other popular genres. It tended to submerge syncopation in its rhythmic patterns – the main reason for the 'un-dance-ability' of much punk rock.

There were marked differences between late 1970s British and American punk, especially in terms of their antecedents and class associations (see Shevory, 1995: 25ff.; also Heylin, 1993). UK punk emerged in the mid- to late 1970s, with major performers including the Sex Pistols, the Stranglers, the Clash, the Damned, and the Buzzcocks. Marcus (1992) links the Sex Pistols and punk rock to the French avant-garde (the Situationist internationale) and Dada cultural movements. Other commentators place it against the Thatcher government's new-right economic and social policies (although Thatcher was not elected until 1979), and the alienation and disenchantment of many British youth, especially, but not exclusively, working-class males.

The 'origins' of the punk rock subculture and its influence and longer-term legacy continue to be debated. Some commentators regard the subculture and its music as originating in England, and then being taken up internationally, others make a strong case for it originating rather in New York's alternative scene in the 1970s. Lentini moves past this preoccupation with locating a single national source, arguing that 'punk evolved as a hybrid musical genre and subcultural entity through a process of American and British cultural exchanges' (2003: 153), most notably the 1976 UK tours by several American bands, and the Sex Pistols 1978 US tour.

The mid- to late 1970s US boasted an influential punk scene of its own, especially in New York, and arguably one at times with a higher level of musical sophistication than its British counterparts; leading performers included the Ramones, the New York Dolls, Richard Hell and the Voidoids, Television, and Talking Heads (although marketed as **new wave**). American punk had more bohemian, non-working-class associations than its English counterparts. While US punk enjoyed little commercial success in its heyday, it has persisted and mutated in the last thirty years, being influential on various **alternative** performers, particularly **hardcore** and thrash.

Punk went underground or was subsumed into indie and alternative styles in the 1980s. It has maintained itself as a subcultural and musical style through into the present, with a continuing emphasis on a DIY authenticity. Punk continues to be part of various music scenes in larger metropolitan centres, with elements of punk style present in a variety of genres (see e.g. O'Connor, 2002, on DC punk).

See also: **hardcore**

Further reading: Marcus (1992); McNeil and McCain (1996); O'Hara (1995); Sabin (1999); Savage (1991)

Viewing: *Sid and Nancy* (1986); *The Decline of Western Civilization: Part One* (1982)

Listening: *UK punk* – The Buzzcocks, 'Orgasm Addict' (1977) on *singles going steady* (EMI, 1980); Sex Pistols, *Never Mind the Bollocks* (WB, 1977); the Clash, *London Calling* (Epic, 1979); *US punk* – 'White Light, White Heat' (1968) on *Velvet Underground Live* (Polygram, 1974); *Ramones* (self-titled debut) (Sire, 1976); Richard Hell and the Voidoids, 'Blank Generation' on the album of the same name (1977); Television, *Marquee Moon* (Elektra, 1977)

R&B *see* **rhythm & blues**

RACE *see* **ethnicity**

RADIO

Until the advent of MTV in the late 1980s, radio was indisputably the most important broadcast medium for determining the form and content of popular music. The organization of radio broadcasting and its music formatting practices have been crucial in shaping the nature of what constitutes the main 'public face' of much popular music, particularly rock and pop and their associated subgenres. Radio has also played a central role at particular historical moments in popularizing or marginalizing music genres. The discussion here provides a brief history of radio in relation to popular music, and sketches the current state of 'music radio'.

Radio developed in the 1920s and 1930s as a domestic medium, aimed primarily at women in the home, but also playing an important role as general family entertainment, particularly in the evening. Radio in North America was significant for disseminating music in concert form, and helped bring regionally based forms such as western swing and jazz to a wider audience. Historically the enemy of the record industry during the disputes of the 1930s and 1940s around payment for record airplay, radio subsequently became its most vital promoter. The reshaping of radio in the 1950s was a key influence in the advent of rock'n'roll. Radio airplay became central to commercial success, especially through the popular new chart shows. Hit radio was 'one of America's great cultural inventions', revitalizing a medium threatened by television (Barnes, 1988: 9). The DJ (disc jockey) emerged as a star figure, led by figures such as Bob 'Wolfman Jack' Smith and Alan Freed.

FM radio was developed in the early 1930s, using a frequency modulation (hence FM) system of broadcasting. It did not have the range of AM, and was primarily used by non-commercial and college radio until the late 1960s, when demand for its clearer sound quality and stereo capabilities saw the FM stations become dominant in the commercial market. They contributed to what became a dominant style of music radio in the 1970s and 1980s (radio friendly; high production values; relatively 'easy listening'; classic rock). With the appeal of FM, the 1970s witnessed a consolidation of the historically established role of radio in chart success: 'Independent programme directors became the newest power brokers within the industry, replacing the independent record distributors of the early sixties' (Eliot, 1989: 169). This reflected the way in which most radio stations now followed formats shaped by consultants, with a decline in the role of programme directors at individual stations, a situation that persisted into the 1990s. Though video became a major marketing tool in the 1980s, radio continued to play a crucial role in determining and reflecting chart success (see Hendy, 2003).

Radio stations are distinguishable by the type of music they play, the style of their DJs, and their mix of news, contests, commercials, and other programme features. We can see radio broadcasts as a flow, with these elements merging. The main types of radio station include college, student, pirate, and youth radio (e.g. the US college stations; New Zealand's campus radio, and Australia's Triple J network); state national broadcasters, such as the BBC; community radio; and, the dominant group in terms of market share, the commercial radio stations. (Due to its unique nature, and historical significance, **pirate radio** has been considered separately.) There is a long-standing contradiction between the interests of record companies, who are targeting radio listeners who buy records, especially those in their teens and early twenties, and commercial radio's concern to reach the older, more affluent audience desired by advertisers. To some extent, this contradiction has been resolved by niche marketing of contemporary music radio.

Station and programme directors act as gatekeepers, being responsible for ensuring a prescribed and identifiable sound or format, based on what the management of the station believes will generate the largest audience – and ratings – and consequent advertising revenue. The station's music director and the programme director – at smaller stations the same person fills both roles – will regularly sift through new releases, selecting three or four to add to the playlist. The criteria underpinning this process will normally be a combination of the reputation of the artist; a record's previous performance, if already released overseas; whether the song fits the station's format; and, at times, the gut intuition of those making the decision. In the case of the first of these factors, reputation and previous track record, publicity material from the label/artist/distributor plays an important role, jogging memories or sparking interest in a previously unknown artist. This process is examined by Hendy (2003) on UK Radio One's playlist, and by Neill (2000) on New Zealand's commercial networks. Chart performance in either the US or UK is especially significant where the record is being released in a 'foreign' market. In choosing whether or not to play particular genres of popular music, radio functions as a gatekeeper, significantly influencing the nature of the music itself. This is illustrated in the shifting attitude of radio to heavy metal (outlined by Weinstein, 1991b: 149–61).

Historically, radio formats were fairly straightforward, and included 'top 40', 'soul', and 'easy listening'. Subsequently formats were more complex, and by the 1980s included 'adult-oriented rock', classic hits (or 'golden oldies'), contemporary hit radio, and urban contemporary (Barnes, 1988). Urban contemporary once meant black radio, but now includes artists working within black music genres. In the USA, black listeners constitute the main audience for urban contemporary formats, but the music also appeals to white listeners, particularly in the 12- to 34-year-old age group. Today, radio in most national contexts includes a range of formats: the dominant ones, reflecting historical developments in addition to current demographics, are rock, contemporary chart pop, adult contemporary, and classic hits.

As channel switching is common in radio, the aim of programmers is to keep the audience from switching stations. Common strategies include playing fewer commercials and running contests which require listeners to be alert for a song or phrase to be broadcast later, but the most effective approach is to ensure that the station does not play a record the listener does not like. While this is obviously strictly impossible, there are ways to maximize the retention of the listening audience. Since established artists have a bigger following than new artists, it makes commercial sense to emphasize their records and avoid playing new artists on high rotation (i.e. many times per day) until they have become hits, an obvious catch-22 situation. The most extreme example of this approach is the format classic rock, or classic hits, which only plays well-established hits from the past. This format remains very popular, capitalizing on the nostalgia of the demographic bulge who grew up during the 1960s, and who now represent a formidable purchasing group in the marketplace.

The concern to retain a loyal audience assumes fairly focused radio listening. Paradoxically, while the radio is frequently 'on', it is rarely 'listened' to, instead largely functioning as aural wallpaper, a background to other activities. (On this point, and *who* is listening to the radio, see **consumption**.) Yet high rotation radio airplay remains vital in exposing artists and building a following for their work, while radio exposure is also necessary to underpin activities like touring, helping to promote concerts and the accompanying sales of records. The very ubiquity of radio is a factor here; it can be listened to in a variety of situations, and with widely varying levels of engagement, from the Walkman to background accompaniment to activities such as study, domestic chores, and reading. (For a succinct discussion of the characteristics of radio, see Crisell, 1994.)

The state regulates radio in two ways. First, in shaping the commercial environment for radio, primarily through licensing systems, but also by establishing codes of practice – a form of **censorship**. This state practice has at times been challenged, most notably by pirate radio. Second, the state has at times attempted to encourage 'minority' cultures, and local music, (with the two frequently connected), through quota and other regulatory legislation. Examples of this include government support of Maori (iwi or tribal) radio in New Zealand (Shuker, 2001); and attempts to include more French-language music on Canadian radio, a case which illustrates the difficulties of conflating 'the national' in multicultural/bilingual settings (see Dorland, 1996).

The advent of Web radio (see **Internet**) and new broadcasting technologies have fostered an explosion of radio stations, even although many have a very localized signal. In the commercial sector, digital technologies have produced new production aesthetics, and reshaped the radio industry (Dunaway, 2000; Hull, 2004).

See also: **pirate radio**

Further reading: Barnard (1989); Berland (1993); Crisell (1994); Hendy (2003)

RAGTIME

A piano style developed around the turn of the twentieth century, ragtime was primarily a **black music** genre with prominent European influences present. Ragtime is a composed music although it originated in oral, unwritten traditions; its musical features are a left hand based on chords, which are broken up differently on each beat (commonly in a four-beat phrase); a melodic right hand with complex figuration; and uneven accenting between the two hands (syncopa-tion). Its most famous practitioner was Scott Joplin, whose 'Maple Leaf Rag' remains one of the best-known ragtime compositions. Ragtime was an important formative influence in **jazz** and **R&B**.

Further reading: Gammond, ed. (1991); Clarke, ed. (1990)

Listening: Scott Joplin never recorded. The recordings attributed to him are made from piano rolls he cut; his compositions are to be found on a variety of piano music

RAP; HIP-HOP

Rap has been regarded as the most popular and influential form of African-American music of the past two decades: 'black America's most dynamic contemporary popular cultural, intellectual, and spiri-tual vessel' (Rose, 1994: 19), and 'the dominant cultural voice of urban black youth' (Forman, 2002: Introduction). In the early 1990s, the study of rap was regarded as holding the promise of reinvigorating black studies in the US (Baker, 1993), while rap and hip-hop's con-cerns with pastiche, collage, and bricolage are seen to exemplify **postmodernist** cultural tendencies (Potter, 1995). At the same time, rap music has been highly controversial, with its musical and social merits fiercely debated. During the late 1990s, rap became main-streamed in the United States music market, and increasingly inter-nationalized.

The antecedents of rap lie in the various storytelling forms of popular music: talking blues, spoken passages and call-and-response in gospel. Its more direct formative influences were in the late 1960s, with reggae's DJ toasters, and stripped-down styles of funk music, notably James Brown's use of stream-of-consciousness raps over ele-mental funk back-up.

Initially a part of a **dance** style which began in the late 1970s among black and Hispanic teenagers in New York's outer boroughs, rap became the musical centre of the broader cultural phenomenon of hip-hop: clothing, attitude, talk, walk, and other collaged cultural elements (see below). Rappers made their own mixes, borrowing from a range of musical sources – sampling – and talking over the music – rapping – in a form of improvised street poetry. This absorption and recontextualization of elements of popular culture marked out rap/hip-hop as a form of pop art, or postmodern culture. The style was also commercially significant, as black youth were 'doing their own thing', bypassing the retail outlets. 'By taping bits of funk off air and recycling it, the break–dancers were setting up a direct line to their culture heroes. They were cutting out the middlemen.' (Hebdige, 1990: 140). Many of the early rappers recorded on **independent** labels, initially on twelve-inch **singles**, most prominently Sugar Hill Records in New York. The genre was soon taken up by white youth, white artists, and the **major** record labels, in a familiar process of the **appropriation** of black musical styles.

As with other maturing musical styles, a number of identifiable subgenres emerged within rap (see Toop, 1991). In the early to mid-1990s these included:

(1) *Gangsta rap*, which is machismo in orientation, and includes themes of gang violence, drugs, and the mistreatment and abuse of women, often with explicitly violent/sexual lyrics; e.g. Snoop Doggy Dog; Ice T. Musically, a heavy bass is prominent.
(2) *Hardcore rap*, which focuses on serious political messages aimed at the black community as a whole; e.g. Public Enemy.
(3) *Reggae rap*, which has a distinctive reggae-style beat and rhythm, with the lyrics spoken rather than sung; e.g. Snow, 'Informer'; Shinehead, 'Jamaican in New York'.
(4) *Female rap*: female vocalists emphasizing gender solidarity/ power over men; strong beat, heavy bass; e.g. Salt n Peppa; Monie Love.

Rap demonstrated continued vitality, although it was increasingly reshaped for a broader (and whiter) market, with the blander commercial rap of performers such as M.C. Hammer, Kris Kross, and Vanilla Ice. Contemporary rap is often conflated with and marketed as 'hip-hop', and includes a wide range of hybrid musical styles.

Rap has been subject to both critical denigration and **censorship** (especially gangsta rap), and cultural praise. Early 1990s rap scholarship was preoccupied with the politics of the genre, seeing it as providing a narrative about race, resistance, and empowerment (Boyd, 1994; Cross, 1993). The social commentary of 'hardcore' rappers such as Public Enemy saw them considered in Gramscian terms, as a politically significant form of organic intellectual (see Abrams, 1995). There was debate over the identification of rap and hip-hop as specifically **black music**/culture, which presents itself as a unitary cultural movement (Rose, 1994). This raised questions about the diasporic nature of rap, and the role played by non-black youth in its development. Many of the essays in Ross and Rose (eds, 1994) used rap and hip-hop as points of departure to examine cultural practices among youth **subcultures** generally. These themes remained part of subsequent critical discourse, with black **identity** a major theme.

Although generally used as synonymous with rap, hip-hop is the broad term that encompasses the social, fashion, music, and dance subculture of American's urban, black and Latin (mainly, but not exclusively) youth of the 1980s and 1990s. It embraces rap, break-dancing, graffiti art, music clubs with DJs, athletic attire (baseball caps; basketball boots, etc.). Potter claims that hip-hop culture constitutes a 'highly sophisticated postmodernism' (1995: 13), a self-conscious political practice, reclaiming, recycling, and reiterating the past for the common people. Potter calls hip-hop a 'cultural recycling center' and a 'counter-formation' of capitalism (108). Here the central reference point is Michel de Certeau's theory that consumers trace their own paths through the commodity relations with which they are presented. Other observers, including Mitchell (1996), critiqued such grand claims being made (often by white intellectuals) for hip-hop/rap, seeing it in more prosaic terms as a form of black street culture.

By the late 1990s, rap and hip-hop became bracketed together as part of mainstream American culture. A *Time* magazine cover story, featuring Lauryn Hill, proclaimed the arrival of the 'Hip Hop Nation', referring to 'the music revolution that has changed America' (*Time*, 8 February 1999: 40–57). The Fugees, *The Score* (Sony/Columbia, 1996), was a huge international success (sales of 7 million by early 1997). In adding elements of **R&B**, **soul**, and ragga rock to the genre, it foreshadowed the contemporary orientation of rap.

By 1998, rap had become the top-selling music format in the US market, passing country. Its influence pervaded fashion, language, and street style. The *Time* story noted that the two terms, rap and hip-hop, were now 'nearly, but not completely, interchangeable' (ibid.). In 2004, this conflation appears almost complete.

Forman (2002) provides a detailed and sophisticated analysis of rap/hip-hop's cultural practices, with a focus on the manner in which 'Rap music takes the city and its multiple spaces as the foundation of its cultural production', making the genre 'an important site for the examination and critique of power and authority in the urban context' (ibid.: Introduction). Krims (2002) took a similar stance, emphasizing 'the poetics of its functioning in the formation of ethnic and geographic identities'. Such analyses have interesting links with the semiotic approach to youth subcultures of earlier writers such as Hebdige (1979), and the emerging literature on music and urban **scenes**.

Rap also became globalized. In a major edited study, *Global Noise*, Mitchell argued that 'Hip-hop and rap cannot be viewed simply as the expression of African–American culture; it has become a vehicle for global youth affiliations and a tool for reworking local identity all over the world' (2001: Introduction). His contributors engage with issues of language, identity, and location in creating and maintaining hip-hop communities from New Zealand to the Netherlands.

Further reading: Forman (2002); Mitchell (2001); Potter (1995); Rose (1994)

Listening: *Genius of Rap: The Sugar Hill Story* (Castle, 1987); Run DMC, *Raising Hell* (London, 1986) (the first rap album to **cross over** to the pop charts, and thereby bring rap into wider public consciousness); Public Enemy, *It Takes a Nation of Millions to Hold Us Back* (Def Jam/Columbia, 1988); Outkast, *Speakerbox* (Arista, 2003)

RASTAFARI *see* **reggae**

RAVES; RAVE CULTURE

Raves grew out of semi-legal warehouse parties organized by young entrepreneurs in the UK and US in the late 1980s. Raves are clubs held outside established dance venues in unconventional places, such as disused warehouses, aircraft hangers, and tents in farmers' fields; these gathering attracted up to 15,000 people in the UK in the early1990s (Thornton, 1995). Rave culture is the general term applied to youth associated with raves, ecstasy use, and the various dance musics, especially house, from the mid-1980s onward, especially in the UK. The use of the drug ecstasy provoked a **moral panic** in the UK, and a number of other countries during the early 1990s, with draconian legislation to regulate raves (Critcher, 2003: ch. 4).

The discourse surrounding rave culture offers two broad explanations for the phenomenon: a hedonistic 'rush culture' of escapism, and the pursuit of a transcendental higher consciousness: 'Rave is more than the music plus drugs; it's a matrix of lifestyle, ritualized behaviour, and beliefs. To the participant, it feels like a religion' (Reynolds, 1998: Preface).

See also: **house**

Further reading: Garratt (1998); Reynolds (1998); Thornton (1995)

REALITY TELEVISION *see* **television**

RECORD COLLECTING

We can point to the development of a collecting sensibility, linked to possessive individualism, historically present since the Greeks, but more fully realized under contemporary capitalism: 'collecting has long been the strategy for the deployment of a possessive self, culture, and authenticity' (Clifford, 1988: 218). Today, 'the gathering together of chosen objects for purposes regarded as special is of great importance, as a social phenomenon, as a focus of personal emotion, and as an economic force' (Pearce, 1995: Preface). As such, collecting has been the subject of considerable theoretical speculation and empirical study, with major contributions from sociology, anthropology, history, social psychology, museum studies, and market research, especially consumer studies.

The literature on collecting embraces a now fairly standard set of motifs and an associated vocabulary. Collectors and the collecting process are variously associated with longing, desire, and pleasure; ritualistic, near-sacred, and repetitive acquisition; passionate and selective consumption; stewardship and cultural preservation; and obsession and linked pathologies such as completism, accumulation, and a pre-occupation with collection size. Collectables can be of almost infinite type, but are usually regarded as 'things removed from ordinary use and perceived as part of a set of non-identical objects or experiences' (Belk, 2001: 67), thereby placing a premium on their intrinsic value. The collection exhibits a series of attributes: it is a source of pleasure; an economic investment; an exhibition of logic, unity and control; an indicator of cultural and social capital; and a socially sanctioned form of materialist and competitive **consumption**, consumer culture taken to excess.

Record collecting is a major activity, yet a relatively neglected aspect of the consumption of popular music. 'Record collecting' can be considered shorthand for a variety of distinct but related practices. Foremost is the collection of sound recordings, in various formats, by individuals. Such recordings include various official releases, in a variety of formats; bootleg recordings (largely of concerts); radio broadcasts, and sound with visuals – the music video or DVD (see **record formats**). Individual collecting also frequently includes the collection of related literature (music books and magazines) and music **memorabilia** (e.g. concert tickets and programmes, tour posters).

The interest from both private collectors and the Hard Rock Café chain have stimulated interest – and prices – in the collecting of such memorabilia, with several major auction houses starting to conduct regular sales during the 1980s (see Kay, 1992). There is also the record collecting undertaken by institutions, which frequently includes sheet music and other printed music literature, in addition to recordings, musical instruments, and popular music ephemera.

Record collecting has a now extensive, although largely unexplored history. During the mid- to late nineteenth century, a mix of capitalism and consumerism, increased leisure time and disposable income, and nostalgia made collecting a significant aspect of social identity for the new middle classes of Europe, Britain and its colonies, and the United States. Record collecting as a social practice was a logical extension of such activities. The commodification of sound and its reproduction as a cultural and economic artefact around the turn of the century produced the 'sound recording' in its various historical formats. Cylinders and their successors, 78s, along with the equipment necessary to play them, became an important part of mass, popular culture. The gramophone became a major fashion accessory of the day, and sound recordings became collectables.

Today, record collecting is a major form of collecting, with its own set of collecting practices. It includes an associated literature (the music press generally, but especially the specialist collector magazines, fanzines, discographies, and general guidebooks); the recording industry's targeting of collectors (reissue labels, promotional releases, remixes, boxed sets); and dedicated sites of acquisition (record fairs, second-hand and specialist shops, e-bay, and high-profile auctions).

While general studies of music consumption, especially fandom, provide some insights, more extended critical discussion of record collecting is sparse. Indeed, the best-known representation of record collectors is arguably that provided in Nick Hornby's best-selling novel *High Fidelity* (1995), and the subsequent film of the same name, directed by Stephen Frears and starring John Cusack, released in 2000. Both book and film portray record collectors as obsessive males, whose passion for collecting is often a substitute for 'real' social relationships, and who exhibit a 'trainspotting' mentality toward popular music.

While this image has much in common with some academic discussions of collectors and collecting, it represents only a partial account of record collectors. A study of self-identified record collectors (Shuker, 2004) showed that they demonstrate a complex mix of characteristics, including a love of music, obsessive-compulsive behaviour, accumulation and completism, selectivity and discrimination, and self-education and scholarship. As a social practice, record collecting presents itself as a core component of individual social identity and a central part of the life cycle.

See also: **consumption; fans; memorabilia**
Further Reading: Belk (2001); Pearce (1995); Shuker (2004); Straw (1997)

Viewing: *High Fidelity* (2000); *Ghost World* (2001); *Vinyl* (2000) (documentary)

RECORD FORMATS

Formats are a significant part of popular music, providing empirical data for historical studies of market cycles, shifting consumer tastes, and changing opportunities for musicians. Formats have exercised a significant influence on the marketing of particular genres and their associated artists and audiences. Changing **technologies** and their associated formats usually appeal to consumers wanting better sound, and to those who possess a 'must have' consumerist orientation to such new technologies, thereby creating fresh markets as older consumers upgrade both their hardware and their record collections (see Eisenberg, 1988).

The major record(ing) formats are the shellac 78; the various forms of vinyl: **albums**, **singles** and **EPs**; the compact disc (**CD**); and the **cassette audio tape**. The importance of several of these warrants their separate consideration. The discussion here considers the initial historical development of these various formats, and the economic and cultural significance of subsequent shifts in their relative importance.

The first major recording/phonograph companies (Columbia, established in 1889; RCA, 1929, incorporating Victor formed in 1901; and Decca, 1934 in the United States) were engaged from the inception of the industry in a battle over alternative recording and reproducing technologies. At stake was the all-important market share. The ten-inch 78 rpm shellac disc emerged as the standard by the 1930s, but experimentation and research continued. Not only was sound quality a consideration, but arguably even more important was the amount of music that could be placed on a record, offering the consumer 'more value for money'. In the early post-war years, Columbia developed a long-playing high-fidelity record using the newly developed vinyl. In 1948 Columbia released its twelve-inch $33\frac{1}{3}$ rpm LP. Refusing to establish a common industry standard, RCA responded by developing a seven-inch vinyl record, with a large hole in the middle, that played at 45 rpm. After several years of competition between the two speeds, the companies pooled their talents and agreed to produce in both formats. By 1952, the LP had become the major format for classical music and the 45 the format for single records for popular radio airplay, jukeboxes and retail sales.

Since the 1950s, there have been marked shifts in the popularity of various recording formats. The 1980s saw the decline of the vinyl single, worldwide sales of which dropped by a third from 550 million in 1980 to 375 million in 1988. The global sales of vinyl LPs continued their decline into the 1990s, while CD sales continued to show a significant increase. In the major United States market, which accounts for one third of global sales, unit sales in 2004 were 766.9 million album-length CDs; 5.2 million album-length cassettes; and 1.3 million vinyl albums (data from Recording Industry Association of America). Vinyl made a limited 'comeback' in the mid-1990s in the US market: the number of vinyl albums sold nearly doubled to 2.2 million in 1995, with several major artists choosing to release albums on vinyl before the CD (e.g. Pearl Jam, Hootie and the Blowfish).

Plasketes suggests that the rise of the CD 'simultaneously laid the foundation for a new subculture of vinyl collectors', and that the market for vinyl, although diminished, remains viable (1992: 109). But most observers regard the vinyl LP as now clearly outmoded, particularly since 'the future (geographic) growth areas for sound carriers are Asia and Africa, both continents where mass markets have been created by the compact cassette' (Laing, 1990: 235). Vinyl, however, retained its appeal to collectors and twelve-inch singles remained central to **dance music**. New technologies such as erasable compact disc hold out the quality of digital sound with the additional cachet of the ability to record, although they are also accompanied by industry concerns over **piracy**.

Performers are affected by the shifts in formats. Historically, with a few significant exceptions (Led Zeppelin), performers have generally relied on the single to promote their album release. Commercial success without a single now became more common. Whatever the aesthetic status of the vinyl single, its material significance lay in its availability to artists with limited resources. The seven-inch 45 and the twelve-inch dance single, with their specialist market tied to the **club scene**, offer such performers only a partial substitute.

See also: **albums; cassette audio tape; CD; charts; singles**

Further reading: Millard (1995); Sanjek (1988)

RECORDING *see* **sound recording**

REGGAE; SKA; RASTAFARI

The collective term for a number of successive forms of Jamaican popular music, including ska and rocksteady, picked up in the West since the 1960s, reggae has had an influence on popular music vastly disproportionate to its limited commercial success.

Reggae initially developed in the 1950s when Jamaican musicians combined indigenous folk music with jazz, African and Caribbean rhythms, and New Orleans R&B. The resultant hybrid was ska. In the early 1960s, ska was exported to the UK, with some chart success: the Skatalites; Millie Small. In the mid-1960s, influenced by American soul music, ska's hyper rhythms gave way to the slower, loping beats of rocksteady. Around the end of the 1960s, these styles of Jamaican popular music came to be known as reggae, which 'embellished the bedrock rhythms of ska and rocksteady with political and social lyrics, often influenced by Rastafarianism, racial pride, and the turbulent Jamaican political climate. The rhythms ebbed and flowed with the hypnotic, jerky pulse that has become reggae's most identifiable trademark' (Erlewine, *et al.*, eds, 1995: 938), along with the bass and choppy rhythm tracks. Key early figures included Toots & the Maytals, the Wailers, Burning Spear, and Jimmy Cliff.

While the influence of ska and reggae were evident in some Western popular music, for instance the Spencer Davis Group's hit 'Keep on Running' (1967), the genre had only a cult following outside Jamaica. This changed in the 1970s, with Island Records' astute marketing of Bob Marley and the Wailers (Shuker, 2001: 46–9). Marley himself became a cult figure, revered among many young blacks, even more so after his death in 1981 (see White, 1989), and reggae was influential on many 'white' performers (e.g. the Police, the Clash, UB40). Reggae continued to evolve, with toasting (a DJ talkover style) and dub forms in the 1980s, both of which demonstrated the importance of the record **producer** and the Jamaican **sound system** to the genre.

There was a ska revival in the UK in the late 1970s, primarily associated with Coventry and the Two Tone record label. Bands with both black and white members worked with elements of reggae, ska, dub, and rock, in bands including UB40, the Specials, Madness, Selector, and Bad Manners. Their record **lyrics** were politically and socially conscious, often containing British working-class themes and criticizing the 'establishment'.

Reggae is strongly associated with **Rastafari**, variously considered as a social movement, a religious cult, and a youth **subculture**, which came out of the ghettos of Kingston, Jamaica in the 1950s. Rastafarianism preaches the divinity of Haile Selassie of Ethiopia, characterizes white domination as 'Babylon', and advocates a black return to Africa, focused on Ethiopia. Rastafarian males grow their hair in long, plaited dreadlocks while women cover their heads, use no cosmetics and wear long modest dresses. Rastas wear woollen caps coloured green (Ethiopia), red (for the blood of their brothers), yellow (the sun), and black (their skin). The use of marijuana (ganja) is given a religious significance (see Gilroy, 1993 for elaboration). Rasta, at least at the level of cultural style, was widely adopted among 'black' groups internationally; e.g. Maori in New Zealand. Reggae plays a major role in communicating the ideals of the movement, through reggae artists acting as role models, and through the themes and lyrics of the music.

Reggae has maintained a commercial and artistic presence through into the 1990s, often forming an important constituent of other popular music genres. Fan and collector interest in reggae's back catalogue have boosted reissue labels, such as Trojan. The genre remains a minority taste, although several contemporary reggae-pop hybrids (Aswad, UB40) have achieved chart success, as have some **rap** performers who utilize reggae rhythms; e.g. Shinehead, *Unity* (Elektra, 1988). Contemporary dance music draws on reggae as part of its eclectic musical palette (see **drum'n'bass**).

Listening: Toots and the Maytals, *Funky Kingston* (Island, 1973); Bob Marley and the Wailers, *Legend* (Island, 1984) ('greatest hits'); Peter Tosh, *Equal Rights* (Columbia, 1977); Glen Brown and King Tubby, *Termination Dub 1973–1979* (Blood & Fire/Chant, 1996); Lee Perry, *The Producer Series/Words of My Mouth* (Trojan, 1996) (compiles Perry's 1970s work); Madness, *Complete Madness* (Stiff, 1982); The English Beat, *I Just Can't Stop It* (IRS, 1980); The Specials, 'Ghost Town' (1981 UK number one) on the album *The Specials: The Singles Collection* (Chrysalis, 1991)

Further reading: Barrow and Dalton (1997); Bishton (1986); Davis (1992); Jones, Simon (1988); Ward (1992b) (includes discography)

REISSUES *see* **back catalogue**

RETAIL *see* **marketing**

RHYTHM & BLUES (R&B)

In its earliest forms, R&B was one of the most important precursors of **rock'n'roll**, and a crucial bridge between blues and soul. George (1989: Introduction) accords R&B a socio-economic as well as a musical meaning, linking it to a black community sense of identity 'forged by common political, economic and social conditions'.

The earliest R&B artists emerged from the American big band and swing jazz era (in the 1930s and 1940s), playing dance music that was louder, used more electric instrumentation, especially the new bass guitar, and accentuated riffs, boogies, and vocals. The first popular style of R&B was jump blues, which blended a horn-dominated line-up with swing rhythms from jazz, and general chord structures and riffs from blues. Several different styles evolved: vocal 'shouters' (e.g. Big Joe Turner); instrumentalists, especially saxophonists, with strong jazz connections; and smoother, urbane vocal styles. Associated with independent labels, such as Speciality, jump blues was popular in cities with growing black communities, especially Los Angeles. Louis Jordan was the most prominent performer, enjoying considerable **crossover** success through the 1940s and early 1950s.

In 1949, 'race music' as it was termed in the industry, was renamed R&B by *Billboard* magazine. While popular on its own charts, and black radio stations, it received little airplay on white radio stations. Indeed, R&B records were sometimes banned because of their explicit sexual content, including Hank Ballard's 'Work With Me Annie', Billy Ward's 'Sixty Minute Man', and the Penguin's 'Baby Let Me Bang Your Box'. Jerry Wexler, an **A&R** man at Atlantic, helped shape jump blues into more commercial styles, which pointed the way for rock'n'roll. Around the same time, piano-based New Orleans R&B also crossed over, especially with the success of Fats Domino ('Ain't That a Shame' (1955)).

R&B was a major part of rock'n'roll. Some would argue that it *was* rock'n'roll, appropriated by white musicians and record companies, for a white audience. R&B elements were merged into the various styles of **rock**, including British R&B of the 1960s (e.g. the Rolling Stones; the Pretty Things; Them); and subsequently into **disco**, **funk**, and **rap**. R&B was also central to soul music in the sixties. In the 1990s R&B 'swingbeat' groups like Boyz II Men can be regarded as examples of the genre returning to its black roots. R&B remains an important radio format in the US, and a category at the Grammy awards, and is part of contemporary styles of rock and hip-hop. An example of such hybridity is Erykah Badu, whose blend of elements of Afro-mysticism, R&B, and jazz has been labelled 'neosoul' (*Rolling Stone*, 20 February 2003: 72).

Indeed, so broad has been the presence of R&B that the term is sometimes used as a general name for the corpus of **black music**.

Further reading: George (1989); Gillet (1983)

Listening: Ray Charles, *Best of Atlantic* (Rhino, 1994) (his groundbreaking 1950s singles); Sam Cooke, *The Man & His Music* (RCA, 1986); Dr John, *Anthology* (Rhino, 1996) (New Orleans piano-based R&B)

RIOT GRRRL

Initially based in Washington DC and Olympia, Washington, riot grrrl quickly became the focus of considerable media attention. Through **fanzines** and sympathetic role models among female musicians, riot grrrls asserted the need to break down the masculine camaraderie of the **alternative** and **hardcore** music scenes, which marginalized girls and young women. They drew on **feminism** and **punk** DIY ideology to question conventional ideas of femininity, and rejected 'rockist' ideas of cool and mystique, challenging the view that enhanced technical virtuosity is necessary to create music (see **ideology**). Some writers referred to them as 'punk feminists' (see Leonard, 1997, on the discourse surrounding riot grrrl). Riot grrrls aimed to create a cultural space for young women in which they could express themselves without being subject to male scrutiny and domination. They played with conflicting images and stereotyped conventions, as with their appropriation of 'girl' and their assertive use of the term 'slut'. Musically, the performers linked to the riot grrrl movement sounded very like traditional **hardcore** and late 1970s punk bands, but their emphasis was on the process rather than the product. Performers and supporters included L7, Bikini Kill, and Kim Gordon of Sonic Youth. Inspired in part by the riot grrrls, a number of prominent women-led bands emerged during the 1990s, e.g. Hole, Veruca Salt, and Echobelly. Performers associated with 'the angry women in rock' media tag of the mid-1990s, notably Alanis Morissette and Fiona Apple, selectively appropriated key concepts from the riot grrrl movement, with considerable commercial success. Schilt (2003) argues that this represented the incorporation of riot grrrl, and a dilution of its oppositional politics.

Further reading: Leonard (1997); Schilt (2003)

Listening: L7, *Bricks Are Heavy* (Slash/WB, 1992); Bikini Kill, *Pussywhipped* (Kill Rock Stars (the group's own label, which also puts out material from like-minded bands), originally an EP, 1992, reissued on CD 1993)

ROCK *see* **rock'n'roll**

ROCKABILLY

An early fusion of **black** and **country** musics in the American South, pre-dating (just) and overlapping with **rock'n'roll**, with its peak in the mid-1950s. **Blues**-inspired and **bluegrass**-based, rockabilly was described by exponent Carl Perkins as 'blues with a country beat'. Primarily a male form, its key figures included Perkins, Gene Vincent, Eddie Cochrane, Elvis Presley (the Sun sessions). Guralnick claims the form started and ended with Elvis, but its influence has endured. Initially a US style, rockabilly was picked up by British fans, notably the teddy boys, providing an interesting example of cross-national **appropriation** (see Gracyk, 2001, 1116–19**)**.

Rockabilly tended to be a rigid and strictly defined form, with imitation at its core (at least in the 1950s): 'Its rhythm was nervously up tempo, accented on the offbeat, and propelled by a distinctively slapping bass. The sound was always clean, never cluttered, with a kind of thinness and manic energy that was filled by the solid lead of Scotty Moore's guitar or Jerry Lee's piano. The sound was further bolstered by generous use of echo' (Guralnick, 1989: 68).

Rockabilly was subsequently carried on by late 1950s and 1960s performers such as Roy Orbison and the Everley Brothers, and into the 1980s by revivalists like the Stray Cats and the Blasters. Rockabilly was an influence on the work of many rock'n'roll performers, including the early Beatles, and on 1970s **punk** bands, such as the Clash. In the 1980s, bands like the Blasters, the Cramps, and Jason and the Scorchers played a style of rock infused with elements of rockabilly, country & western, and punk.

Further reading: Guralnick (1992) (includes discography); Morrisson (1996)

Listening: The Blasters, 'Marie Marie' (c. 1981) from *The Blasters Collection* (Slash/WB, 1990); *Rock This Town: Rockabilly Hits*, Volumes 1 and 2 (Rhino, 1991); Elvis Presley, *The Complete Sun Sessions* (RCA, 1987)

ROCK'N'ROLL; TEDDY BOYS; ROCKERS; ROCK; CLASSIC ROCK

Rock'n'roll was the genre of popular music that emerged when black **R&B** songs began to get airplay on radio stations aiming at a wider, predominantly white audience, and when white artists began re-recording black R&B songs. R&B, American **country** music, and 1940s and 1950s **boogie-woogie** music are all elements of early rock'n'roll. Some writers (e.g. Gammond, ed., 1991; Garofalo, 1997) conflate it with **rock**, which became the more general label for the various styles which mutated from rock'n'roll. Two main youth **subcultures** were associated with **rock'n'roll**: teddy boys and rockers.

Alan Freed, a Cleveland **DJ**, is usually given credit for coining the phrase 'rock'n'roll' in the early 1950s. However, as Tosches (1984) documents, the style had been evolving well before this time. The term 'rock'n'roll', with its sexual connotations, was popularized in the music of the 1920s. In 1922, blues singer Trixie Smith recorded 'My Daddy Rocks Me (With One Steady Roll)' for Black Swan Records, and various lyrical elaborations followed from other artists through the 1930s and 1940s. In April 1954, Bill Haley and the Comets made 'Rock Around the Clock'. The record was a hit in America, then worldwide, eventually selling 15 million copies. It represented a critical symbol in the popularization of the new musical form. Subsequent major figures included Chuck Berry, Little Richard, and, in particular, Elvis Presley.

The new music provoked considerable criticism, with many older musicians contemptuous of rock'n'roll. British jazzman Steve Race, writing in *Melody Maker*, claimed:

> Viewed as a social phenomenon, the current craze for rock 'n' roll material is one of the most terrifying things ever to have happened to popular music ... Musically speaking, of course, the whole thing is laughable ... It is a monstrous threat, both to the moral acceptance and the artistic emancipation of jazz. Let us oppose it to the end (cited in Rogers, 1982: 18).

Other criticism focused on the moral threat, rather than the new teenage music's perceived aesthetic limitations. To many, rock'n'roll appeared hostile and aggressive, epitomized by Elvis Presley's sensual moves. *Music Central* sums up the contemporary status of the genre:

The prominence of the guitar, a substantial beat, the orientation to young people, and the blatant sexuality of the songs and the performers were, and still are, some of the basic building blocks of rock 'n' roll. Since the 1950s, the phrase has come to mean many different things and encompass a wide assortment of sub-genres: progressive rock, punk rock, acid rock, heavy metal, country rock, glitter rock, new wave, alternative rock … all variations on a 40-year old theme

(*Music Central* 96).

Originally a British phenomenon, teddy boys, or 'teds', first appeared in the mid-1950s. Mainly from unskilled backgrounds, the teds had been left out of youth's new affluence. Their style included hair worn in elaborate quiffs (the DA, etc.), dressed with grease, long, pseudo-Edwardian drape jackets (hence the name), thick crêpe-soled shoes ('brothel creepers') and thin string ties: 'the "Teddy boy" appropriation of an upper-class style of dress "covers" the gap between largely manual, unskilled near-lumpen real careers and life chances, and the "all-dressed-up-and-nowhere-to-go" experience of Saturday evening' (Hall and Jefferson, eds, 1976: 48). The teds' music preferences were early rock'n'roll and **rockabilly**. New Zealand and Australian imitative version of the teds in the 1950s were termed 'bodgies'.

The teddy boys' activities centred around rock'n'roll music, coffee bars and cafes with juke boxes, and pubs. They were involved in riots in cinemas and dance halls during the advent of rock'n'roll, and in the 1958 UK race riots: 'the ted was uncompromisingly proletarian and xenophobic' (Hebdige, 1979: 51). There were teddy boy revivals in the 1970s and 1980s, although the dress and demeanour of the 'modern teds' carried rather different connotations, being more reactionary and closer to their working-class machismo parent culture.

In Britain in the 1960s, the teds evolved into rockers (also known as bikers, or greasers, especially in the US). The rockers wore black leather jackets, jeans and boots, had greased hair and rode motorbikes. Largely low-paid unskilled manual workers, they were a male-oriented sub-culture; female followers rarely rode. Willis saw a **homology** between the rocker's masculinity, rejection of middle-class lifestyle, the motorbike, and the preference for rock'n'roll. The rockers' key value was freedom, and their preferred music was 1950s rock'n'roll: Elvis, Gene Vincent, and Eddie Cochrane. The rockers clashed violently with the **mods** in 1963–4 at southern English holiday resorts, producing a **moral panic**. They have never entirely vanished as an identifiable subculture. Contemporary bikers show a preference for **heavy metal**.

Rock is the broad label for the huge range of styles that have evolved out of rock'n'roll. Rock is often considered to carry more 'weight' than pop, with connotations of greater integrity, sincerity, and authenticity. **Classic rock** is a term originally used for a **radio** format concentrating on playing 'tried and proven' past chart hits which will have high listener recognition and identification (see Barnes, 1988). Also known as 'oldies' or 'gold', classic rock playlists are largely drawn from the Beatles to the end of the 1970s, and emphasize white male rock performers such as Cream, the Doors, Led Zeppelin, Creedence Clearwater Revival, and the Who. The format became prominent in part because of the consumer power of the ageing post-war 'baby boomers', and the appeal of this group to radio advertisers. Classic rock has also become a loosely defined **genre** and a general marketing category.

See also: **hard rock**

Further reading: on rock'n'roll, rock, and classic rock: Brown (1992); Cohn (1970); Gillet (1983); DeCurtis and Henke (1992a); Tosches (1984); on teddy boys and rockers: Brake (1985); Cohn (1970); Gelder and Thornton, eds (1997); Hebdige (1979); Willis (1978)

Listening: Elvis Presley, 'Heartbreak Hotel' (1956) and 'Hound Dog' (1956) on *The Top Ten Hits* (RCA, 1987), a double album compilation

ROOTS; ROOTS MUSIC

'Roots' is variously used to refer to: (i) an artist's sociological and geographical origins, and the relationship between these and their music; (ii) the audience/environment in which the artist's career is rooted; and (iii) more generally, for artists who are considered the originators of musical styles/genres (as in Guralnick's study (1991) of 'major roots musicians' in **rockabilly**, **country**, and **blues)**. Roots is often a genre-specific term, being most frequently used in relation to styles such as folk, the blues, and various world musics. It is also often a constituent of populist notions of authenticity. Musically, roots is based on the notion that the sounds and the style of the music should continue to resemble its original source. Acceptance of this can lead to a questioning of 'traditional' artists using musical high-tech instruments and equipment. Increasingly, roots music has been used as a stylistic label by the music press, where it is often conflated with alt.country and Americana; see e.g. UNCUT's regular column.

See also: **alt.country; authenticity; folk culture**

Further reading: Redhead and Street (1989)

SALSA

Salsa is Spanish for 'sauce' or 'spice', and has been used in relation to music since the 1920s in a similar fashion to 'funky'. For many musicians and commentators, salsa is a euphemism for Cuban music. The word salsa was used for many years by Cuban musicians before the genre became popularized in New York in the late 1960s, and salsa provided a neutral marketing label to bypass the United States economic blockade of Cuba following the Castro-led revolution of 1959. Concord Picante, the salsa label of the Concord jazz company, helped popularize the genre in the 1980s. Historically significant salsa musicians include Celia Cruz, the Queen of Salsa, and mambo bandleader Tito Punte, while Reuben Blades is the most prominent contemporary salsa performer.

The staple musical elements present in salsa – the son and the clave – are derived from essentially Cuban styles. However, this direct link between salsa and Cuba is problematic, given that salsa is produced mainly by Cubans and Puerto Ricans living in New York and Puerto Rico. Further, a number of other features have been detected in the music, including Puerto Rican 'folkloric' forms such as the bomba, big-band jazz, soul, call-and-response patterns from work songs, and even funk and rock elements (Negus, 1996: 117). Accordingly, it seems more appropriate to consider salsa as a hybrid genre.

The association between salsa and working-class Puerto Ricans has been argued using content analysis of song **lyrics** (e.g. Padilla, 1990). This assumes an intrinsic connection between social context, the production and reception of the music, and song lyrics. Claims for salsa's expression of a pan-Latin consciousness are similarly based. Negus shows how the case of Reuben Blades shows the difficulties with any such straightforward correspondences, arguing instead for a more complex process of mediation of the music. Blades, who was born in Panama, educated at Harvard, and lives in New York writes and performs socially committed songs, which began to reach a wider audience following his signing to Elektra in 1984.

Further reading: Padilla (1990); Negus (1996: 113–22); Hardy and Laing, eds (1991: entries on Reuben Blades, Celia Cruz, Tito Punte)

Listening: Reuben Blades, *Nothing But the Truth* (Elektra, 1988) and *Buscando America* (Elektra, 1994); Celia Cruz, *Celia and Johnny* (Voya, 1975)

SAMPLING

The practice of using computer **technology** to take selected extracts from previously recorded works and using them as parts of a new work, usually as a background sound to accompany new vocals. Sampling has been the subject of considerable controversy, with debate around issues of authorship and creativity, the nature of musicianship, the **authenticity** of the recordings it produces, and the legality of the practice. Sampling can be viewed as part of rock's historic tendency to constantly 'eat itself', while also exemplifying its **postmodern** tendencies: 'The willful acts of disintegration necessary in sampling are, like cubism, designed to find a way ahead by taking the whole business to pieces, reducing it to its constituent components. It's also an attempt to look to a past tradition and to try and move forward by placing that tradition in a new context' (Beadle, 1993: 24).

Digital sampling allows sounds to be recorded, manipulated, and subsequently played back from a keyboard or other musical device (see Théberge, 1999). Introduced in the late 1970s and subsequently widely used, digital sampling illustrates the debates surrounding musical technologies. Its use is seen variously as restricting the employment of session musicians, and as enabling the production of new sounds, e.g. the use of previously recorded music in the creation of rhythm tracks for use in **rap** and dance remixes. The increasing emphasis on new such technologies is significantly changing the emphases within the process of producing popular music: 'As pop becomes more and more a producer's and programmer's medium, so it increasingly is a sphere of composition, as opposed to performance' (Goodwin, 1998: 130).

The process of 'digging in the crates' for rare vinyl records to provide the raw material for sample-based hip-hop, illustrates the point that sampling is very much a social practice: 'digging serves a number of other purposes for the production community. These may include such functions as manifesting ties to hip-hop deejaying tradition, "paying dues", educating producers about various forms of music, and serving as a form of socialization between producers' (Schloss, 2004: 79).

See also: **copyright; dance music; rap; technology**

Further reading: Beadle (1993) (includes a useful discography); Goodwin (1990); Jones (1992); Lysloff and Gay (2003)

Listening: The Jams, *Shag Times* (KLF, 1988); De La Soul, *3 Feet High and Rising* (Tommy Boy, 1989); Jive Bunny and the Mixmasters, *Jive Bunny The Album* (Telestar, 1989)

SCENES

As indicated elsewhere (see **locality**), there is considerable exploration of the role and effectiveness of music as a means of defining identity. Situated within this, the concept of scene has become a central trope in popular music studies, a key part of the 'spatial turn' evident in urban and cultural studies generally. To an extent, scene, as an analytical concept of greater explanatory power, is now regarded as having displaced **subcultures**. The rhetoric of the **music press** commonly identifies artists with scenes, while **fans** and **musicians** both uphold the notion of a correspondence between local sounds and scenes.

Scene can be understood as 'a specific kind of urban cultural context and practice of spatial coding' (Stahl, 2004: 76). A basic reference point for later discussion was an essay by Straw (1992), which argued for greater attention to scene in popular music studies, defined as the formal and informal arrangement of industries, institutions, audiences, and infrastructures. Also influential were Cohen's study of 'rock culture' in Liverpool (1991), and Shank's study of the rock'n'roll scene in Austin, Texas (1994). Researchers subsequently engaged with, refined, and applied the concept of scene to a wide range of settings and locales (e.g. Bennett, 2000; O'Connor, 2002; Stahl, 2004); much of this work, along with theoretical discussion of the concept of scene(s) can be found in several edited collections (Whitelely *et al.*, 2004 and Bennett and Kahn-Harris, 2004), while the journal *Popular Music* devoted an issue to the theme (19: 1, 2001). To provide just one example from among many, locality, scene, and youth culture are fruitfully brought together in the work of Bennett (2000), in a series of ethnographic case studies. His study of urban dance music (including house, techno, and jungle) in Newcastle upon Tyne, England, shows how, through their participation in club events and house parties, 'the members of this scene celebrate a shared underground sensibility that is designed to challenge the perceived oppression and anarchism of Newcastle's official night-time economy and the coercive practices of the local police force'(ibid.: 68).

A particular focus, in part arising from the earlier fascination with subcultures, has been on **alternative** music scenes. (The term 'underground' is also used for non-commercialized alternative scenes, since the performers in them are hidden from and inaccessible to people who are not 'hooked into' the scene.) Alternative music scenes fall into two basic categories. They are either college (US tertiary institutions) or university towns, or large cities that are somehow 'alternative', usually to even larger urban centres nearby (e.g. Minneapolis and Chicago). Most important American college towns had local music scenes self-consciously perceived as such in the 1980s, with these linked as part of an American **indie** underground (see Azerrad, 2001). The most prominent were Athens, Georgia (source of the B-52's, Love Tractor, Pylon, and R.E.M); Minneapolis (source of the Replacements, Hüsker Dü, Soul Asylum, and Prince), and **Seattle**. Sometimes a small college town and nearby large city have contributed to a shared scene; e.g. Boston and Amherst, MA (sources of Dinosaur Jr., the Pixies, Throwing Muses, and the Lemonheads), with bands moving back and forth between the two centres. Alternative scenes worldwide appear to conform to this basic pattern.

While alternative music is often linked to particular local scenes, the question is why then and there? Such scenes have generally developed out of a combination of airplay on the local college radio stations, access to local live venues, advertisements and reviews in local **fanzines** and free papers and, especially, the existence of local **independent** record companies (see e.g. **Seattle** and **Dunedin**). Bertsch (1993) argues that there are fundamental links between alternative music scenes and high-tech areas, with both sharing a decentralized, do-it-yourself approach to production, and with **indie** isolationism not far removed from the entrepreneurial spirit of capitalism, with 'every one out for himself'. Music-making, equipment design and programming are undertakings one person or a small group can succeed at without much start-up capital.

The specific configuration and dynamics of particular alternative scenes have been examined in numerous ethnographically oriented studies. A few brief examples must suffice here: Takasugi (2003) studied the development of underground musicians in a Honolulu (Hawaii) scene in the mid-1990s. His interest was in the values and norms shared by members of the scene, the relationship of these to the socialization and identity formation of the musicians involved, and 'how the resulting networks serve to sculpt and reinforce the identity of the band members within the scene' (74). This was to conceptualize the scene as 'a kind of social movement' (ibid.), one in which the distinction between fans and musicians was not always clear, with both integral to the scene. O'Connor, in a study of contemporary **punk** scenes in four cities (Washington, DC, Austin, Texas, Toronto, and Mexico City), shows that clear differences exist between such scenes, explicable in terms of the social geography of each city. For the punks involved, these scenes were identified with the active creation of infrastructure to support punk bands and other forms of creative activity.

The relationship of the local to the global is a key part of the dynamic of local music scenes, alternative or otherwise. For many participants in alternative local scenes, the perceived dualities associated with **indie** and **major** record labels are central to their commitment to the local. Here 'the celebration of the local becomes a form of fetishism, disguising the translocal capital, global management, and the transnational relations of production that enables it' (Fenster, 1995: 86). However, the 'local' is increasingly allied with other localities, for both economic and affective reasons. Fenster notes 'the degree to which "independent" non-mainstream musics, while clearly based upon local spaces, performances and experiences, are increasingly tied together by social networks, publications, trade groups and regional and national institutions in ... locally dispersed formations' (ibid.: 83). This internationalization of the local is a process encouraged and fostered economically by the major record companies, who place particular local sounds within larger structures, reaching a larger market in the process; e.g. the marketing of the Seattle sound (see **globalization**). Similarly, local sounds/scenes and their followers are ideologically linked through internationally distributed **fanzines**, **music press** publications, and the **Internet**.

See also: **locality; Seattle sound; Dunedin sound**

Further reading: Bennett (2000); Fenster (1995); Jipson (1994) (on Athens, Georgia); Olson (1998); Straw (1992)

SEATTLE SCENE; SEATTLE SOUND

In 1992 the Seattle music scene came to international prominence, closely linked with the mainstream breakthrough of **alternative** music promoted by American college **radio**. Nirvana's second album and major-label debut *Nevermind* (Geffen, 1991) topped the *Billboard* charts; Pearl Jam and Soundgarden were major draw cards at the second Lollapalooza **touring** music **festival** in 1992, and both bands enjoyed huge record sales. The Seattle sound broadly referred to a group of bands initially recording with Seattle's Sub Pop **independent** record label, which were known for their **grunge** sound.

The Seattle scene and the grunge music with which it was associated became the most written about phenomenon in contemporary popular music since the birth of punk. Major labels scoured Seattle for unsigned bands or internationally sought out grunge-oriented performers (e.g. Australia's silverchair). The film *Singles* (Cameron Crowe, 1992), set amidst the Seattle scene, was widely publicized and commercially successful. The popularization of grunge-related **fashion** saw spreads in *Elle* and *Vogue* touting $1000 flannel shirts from the world's most famous designers. The Seattle sound became a marketing ploy for the **music industry,** as well as an ideological touchstone for 'Generation X'. '"Seattle" defines the source of the phenomenon and organizes its often disparate expression. In writing about the Seattle scene, critics are not just chronicling a random success story. They are grappling with the notion of a geographically specific scene itself' (Bertsch, 1993).

A combination of factors explained why 'Seattle' occurred at that time and place: the ability of Sub Pop to feed into the **majors**; many good bands of a similar style; the strong local alternative scene, linked to the Universities of Washington and Evergreen State (the latter a progressive, no-grades school with an alternative-oriented radio station); and the city's geographical separation from LA (Kirschner, 1994). Critics emphasized the purity and **authenticity** of the Seattle scene as a point of origin, defining bands like Nirvana in opposition to the mainstream. The foundations for the success of bands such as Nirvana and Soundgarden were laid throughout the 1980s by earlier alternative music scenes (Azerrad, 2001). What had changed was that by the early 1990s it had become easier and quicker for new alternative or indie bands to attract the attention of major labels or commercial radio, and to move to major labels and achieve some mainstream success: 'By the summer of 1991, the reasonably rapid rise of Jane's Addiction and popularity of the "alternative" Lollapalooza rock festival that lead singer Perry Farrell organized clearly heralded a significant change in the "natural laws" of commercial success. The success of the Seattle scene is thus neither an accident of fate, nor a testament to the superiority of Seattle bands' music. It is, rather, the product of many different scenes and the labor that went into them'

(Bertsch, 1993). Seattle was part of a nationwide American indie alternative scene.

See also: **locality; scenes**

Further reading: Azerrad (2001); Bertsch (1993); Garofalo (1997); Kischner (1994)

Viewing: *Hype!* (Doug Pray, 1996) (documentary)

SEMIOTICS *see* **structuralism**

SEXUALITY

Sexuality refers to the expression of sexual **identity**, through sexual activity, or the projection of sexual desire and attraction; this is primarily in relation to other people, but can also be related to material/cultural artefacts. Sexuality and desire are central human emotions, or drives, which have been an essential part of the appeal of the **culture/entertainment industries**, including popular music, and the social processes whereby performers and their texts operate in the public arena. Popular music is also a significant area of culture in which sexual politics are struggled over.

Sexuality is central to discussions of how male and, more frequently, female performers, are conceived of – socially constructed – as sex objects or symbols of desire. Here certain forms of subjectivity/identity are projected as 'normal', traditionally white, male sexuality. The operation of this process is a major focus in studies of **music video** and **stars/stardom**, and in relation to particular **genres**. It involves consideration of the nature of spectatorship and the (gendered) gaze, utilizing conventions primarily developed in film studies (see e.g. Kaplan, 1987, on **music video**).

Sexual ambiguity is central to many forms of popular music, which has frequently subverted the dominant sexuality constructed around male–female binaries. Discussion has concentrated on exploring the relationship between sexual orientation, public personas, and a performer's music. Some performers openly represent or subvert and 'play with' a range of sexualities. Others constitute themselves, at times very self-consciously, as objects of heterosexual desire, or as icons for different ('deviant'?) sexualities and their constituencies. Early 1950s male stars were 'adored objects', catering to both homosexual desire and female consumption; e.g. Elvis Presley. Later performers include representations of the homoerotic (e.g. Madonna, Morrissey, Suede); androgyny (Bowie during the Ziggy period), the effeminate (the Cure), and asexuality (Boy George); bisexuality (Morrissey, Suede); and gay and lesbian (Freddie Mercury; k.d. lang). The application of such labels, their connotations, and their relationship to 'real' gay communities have been at times strongly contested (see Geyrhalter, 1996; Hawkins, 2002; Whiteley *et al.*, eds, 2004).

Some genres/performers are linked to particular sexualities/communities; e.g. **disco** generally celebrates the pleasure of the body and physicality, and is linked to the gay community and specific **club scenes**; **heavy metal** has traditionally been associated with overt masculinity (though see Walser, 1993, who contends that the genre has historically been actively *made* as male), as have some forms of rock (e.g. **hard rock**).

The **lyrics** of many mainstream **pop** songs deal with heterosexual love, desire, longing, and lust; some deal with other sexual orientations and sexual practices; e.g. the Kinks, 'Lola'. Some songs function at an ironic, 'in joke' level; e.g. the Village People's 'In the Navy' and 'YMCA'. Some openly support or express solidarity with particular sexualities; e.g. Tom Robinson, 'Glad to be Gay'. Other musical **texts** criticize non-heterosexuality or openly express homophobic or misogynist views (see **rap**). There is considerable argument over whether these texts are 'read' by their **listeners**, **audiences**, and **fans** in any straightforward manner, or whether the artists' intended or preferred readings, embedded in the text, are acknowledged, let alone assimilated into individual and social values and meanings.

See also: **gender; lyric analysis**

Further reading: Baker (2002); Frith and McRobbie (1978); Negus (1996: 123–33); Press and Reynolds (1995); Savage (1988)

Listening: Little Richard, 'Tutti Frutti' on *18 Greatest Hits*, (Rhino, 1985); Frankie Goes to Hollywood, 'Relax' on *Bang! Greatest Hits*, (ZIT/Island, 1994); Suede, 'Pantomime Horse' and 'Animal Nitrate' on *Suede* (1993)

SINGLES; EPS

Historically often referred to as 45s (the rpm), the single is a **record(ing) format** of considerable historical importance, though its contemporary status and influence is at issue. The single was originally a seven-inch vinyl format, with an 'A' side, the recording considered most likely to receive radio airplay and chart 'action', and a 'B' side, usually seen as a recording of less appeal. A few 'B' sides have achieved chart success along with their 'A' counterparts: 'double-sided hits', e.g. several of the Beatles' singles. An **EP** is an 'extended play' single, a vinyl seven inch, usually with four songs. In the UK the EP represented an early form of 'greatest hits' package, with attractive covers, and outsold **albums** until the early 1960s.

In the early 1950s, the vinyl single overtook its shellac 78 counterpart as the dominant **music industry marketing** vehicle. Singles became the major selling format, the basis for radio and television programming, and the most important **chart** listing, with the last two in an apparently symbiotic relationship. Singles appealed to young people with limited disposable income. For the record companies, singles were cheaper to produce than an album, and acted as market 'testers'. While a single's success was important for performers and the record companies in itself, it was also important as a means of drawing attention to the accompanying, or subsequent album, with the release of both being closely related. With a few significant exceptions (e.g. Led Zeppelin), performers generally relied on the single to promote their album release. This approach became the 'traditional' construction of record marketing through the 1960s and 1970s. Album compilations of singles, either by one performer or from a genre or style of music became an important market. While some performers with high-charting singles were 'one-hit wonders', singles success frequently launched careers, leading to an album deal and moves from independent to major labels.

In the 1980s new single formats gained an increasingly significant market share. There was a massive increase in sales of **cassette** singles in America, with sales of 32.7 million alone in the first half of 1989, already surpassing the 1988 full-year total of 22.5 million. In 1990, Swedish band Roxette's 'Listen to Your Heart' became the first single to hit number one in the United States without being released as a vinyl 45. Twelve-inch singles, including remixes, became an important part of the **dance music** scene, and, accompanying the general rise of the **CD** format, the CD single also began to emerge as a popular marketing form and consumer preference.

At the same time, the single increasingly became a device for marketing an album. Negus (1992: 65) documents the decline of the vinyl single through the 1980s. In the US sales of singles from 1979 to 1990 declined by 86 per cent (from 195.5 million to 27.6 million units), and despite the growth of new formats, total sales of singles declined by 41 per cent. In Britain the single's decline was less dramatic, with total sales falling by 21 per cent, from 77.8 million in 1980 to 61.1 million in 1989. This reflected the continued industry practice in the UK of releasing one or two singles *prior* to the issue of an album. The relative decline of the single reflected the higher costs of the new formats, and the pressure to produce a video to accompany a single, a practice which was regarded as necessary for supporting radio airplay and chart success (see **music video**).

Performers were affected by the shift to the CD format. Whatever the aesthetic status of the rock/pop single, its material significance lay in its availability to artists with limited resources. The seven-inch 45 and the twelve-inch dance single, with their specialist market tied to the **club scene** (Straw, 2001), offer such performers only a partial substitute. Linked to this is the point that many of the independent record companies can't afford CDs, restricting the market options available to their artists.

The appeal of particular singles is assessed primarily by the placing achieved on the charts, as well as the record's longevity there. (It should be noted that these are not quite the same thing.) Making subsequent assessments of the commercial, and thereby presumed cultural, impact of a single on the basis of total sales and the length of time spent in the charts is a common practice (see Whitburn, 1988). The single is now less important, with sales in all formats having declined in the past decade, but remains crucial to commodifying **pop** music for the **teen** market.

See also: charts; record formats

Further reading: Frith (1988b: 11–23); Hull (2004)

SKA *see* **reggae**

SKIFFLE

A musical **genre** which emerged out of **jazz** in Britain in the early 1950s, skiffle was arguably more significant as a catalyst than as a musical style. Skiffle appealed as a 'do it yourself' style of music, and thousands of groups sprang up. It had a simple rhythm section (homemade string bass and washboard), augmented by banjo and guitars. The most successful performer was Lonnie Donnegan, who drew on American **blues** and **folk**, especially the work of Woody Guthrie and Leadbelly; e.g. 'Rock Hardin' Line'. By the early 1960s skiffle had developed into **beat** with instrumental groups (such as the Shadows) using electric instrumentation. Skiffle was influential as a training ground for beat musicians; e.g. John Lennon's Quarrymen.

See also: **beat music**

Further reading: Bradley (1992); Longhurst (1995)

Listening: Lonnie Donnegan, *The EP Collection* (See For Miles, 1992): remasters of his work up to 1962, this includes a substantial biography

Viewing: *Dancing in the Street* (1995), episode 3

SKINHEADS

A youth **subculture**, first appearing in Britain in the late 1960s, skinheads were a working-class reaction to the hippy **counter–culture** and their own social marginalization. They made a virtue of working classness: hair cropped to the scalp, working shirts and short jeans supported by braces, heavy boots (cherry red Dr Martens; accordingly, skinheads were sometimes referred to as 'bootboys') was the standard uniform. Often associated with football hooliganism, skinheads became increasingly racist, and were involved in attacks against immigrants, especially Asians. While targets for neo-Nazi recruitment by the National Front, skinheads were largely apolitical. By the late 1960s they had become highly visible and a clear example of 'folk devils'. English skinheads espoused traditional conservative values: defence of their local territory, hard work, and extreme patriotism; essentially they attempted to 'magically recover the traditional working-class community' (Clarke, 1976). Skinheads became an international phenomenon, present in North America, Europe (especially Germany, where they were linked to Nazi revivalism), and Australia and New Zealand, though these were groups essentially derivative of their British counterparts. Skinheads remained a visible subculture into the twenty-first century.

Originally skinheads' musical preferences embraced **black music** genres: ska, bluebeat, and **reggae**, in contradiction to their racism; and subsequently Oi! Oi! first appeared in 1981, as a manifestation of

British **punk rock**; it was characterized by a loud, driving guitar sound, basic, abrasive, nihilistic, and often racist lyrics. Oi! groups adopted skinhead dress style, and played at National Front meetings. The most prominent performers were the 4 Skins, though they attained only limited commercial success. Sham 69, though not normally considered an Oi! band, also developed a strong skinhead–National Front following. Oi! was often denigrated: 'violent, ugly, unintelligent' music (Taylor, 1985: 69); and 'yob rock' (Larkin, ed., 1995: 153; referring to the 4 Skins).

See also: **moral panic; subcultures**

Further reading: Clarke (1976); Larkin, ed. (1995)

Listening: The 4 Skins, *The Good, The Bad, And The 4 Skins* (Secret, 1982); Sham 69, *The First, The Best, And The Last* (Polydor, 1980)

Viewing: *Romper Stomper* (Australia, 1992)

SONGWRITERS; SONGWRITING; SINGER-SONGWRITERS

In comparison with the writing on other roles in the music industry, and the nature of the creative process in popular music, the role of the songwriter has not received much sociological or musicological attention. The limited amount of published work has concentrated on song composition, the process of songwriting, and the contributions of leading songwriters, especially those associated with the Brill Building in New York. Some songwriters have been accorded **auteur** status, especially when they have later successfully recorded their own material (e.g. Carole King), or are performing as singer–songwriters.

There are numerous examples of songwriters exercising considerable influence over artists/styles. In the 1950s Leiber and Stoller got an unprecedented deal with Atlantic to write and produce their own songs; the resulting collaborations with performers such as the Drifters and Ben E. King produced sweet **soul**, a very self-conscious marriage of **R&B** and classical instruments, notably the violin. In the 1960s Holland, Dozier, Holland contributed to the development of the **Motown** sound. In the1970s Chinn and Chapman composed over fifty British top ten hits in association with **producers** Mickie Most and Phil Wainman, 'using competent bar bands (Mud, Sweet) on to whom they could graft a style and image' (Hatch and Millward, 1987: 141), to produce highly commercial **power pop**, **glitter rock**, and **dance music**.

In the late 1950s and early 1960s a factory model of songwriting, combined with a strong **aesthetic** sense, was evident in the work of a group of songwriters (and music publishers) in New York's Brill Building: 'the best of Tin Pan Alley's melodic and lyrical hall marks were incorporated into r&b to raise the music to new levels of sophistication' (Erlewine *et al.*, eds, 1995: 883). The group included a number of outstanding songwriting teams: the more pop-oriented Goffin and King; Mann and Weil; and Barry and Greenwich; the R&B-oriented Pomus and Sherman, and Leiber and Stoller. Several also produced, most notably Phil Spector, Bert Berns, and Leiber and Stoller, who wrote and produced most of the Coasters' hits. One factor which distinguished the group was their youth: mainly in their late teens or early twenties, with several married couples working together, the Brill Building songwriters were well able to relate to and interpret teenage dreams and concerns, especially the search for identity and romance. These provided the themes for many of the songs they wrote, especially those performed by the **teen idols** and **girl groups** of the period. Pomus and Sherman and Leiber and Stoller wrote some of Elvis Presley's best material. Collectively, the Brill Building songwriters were responsible for a large number of chart successes, and had an enduring influence. The role of such song-writers, however, was undermined with the **British invasion** and the emergence of a tradition of self-contained groups or performers writing their own songs (most notably the Beatles), which weakened the songwriting market.

The term **singer–songwriter** has been given to artists who both write and perform their material, and who are able to perform solo, usually on acoustic guitar or piano. An emphasis on lyrics has resulted in the work of such performers often being referred to as song poems, accorded auteur status, and made the subject of intensive **lyric analysis**. The **folk** music revival in the 1960s saw several singer-writers come to prominence: Donovan, Phil Ochs, and, especially, Bob Dylan. Singer-songwriters were a particularly strong 'movement' in the 1970s, including Neil Young, James Taylor, Joni Mitchell, Jackson Browne, and Joan Armatrading, most of whom are still performing/recording. In the 1980s the appellation singer–songwriter was applied to, among others, Bruce Springsteen, Prince, and Elvis Costello; and in the 1990s to Tori Amos, Suzanne Vega, Tanita Tikaram, Tracy Chapman, and Toni Childs and most recently, to David Gray,

Shania Twain, and Norah Jones. This recent female predominance led some observers to equate the 'form' with women performers, due to its emphasis on lyrics and performance rather than the indulgences associated with male-dominated styles of **rock** music. The application of the term to solo performers is problematic, in that most of those mentioned usually perform with 'backing' bands, and at times regard themselves as an integral part of these groups. Nonetheless, the concept of singer-songwriter continues to have strong connotations of greater **authenticity** and 'true' **auteurship**.

See also: **auteur**

Further reading: Flanaghan (1987); Groce (1991); McIntyre (2003); MOJO, October 2003 (excellent profile of Holland–Dozier–Holland); Shaw (1992) (includes discography); Sicoli (1994); Zollo (1997)

Listening: Carole King, *Tapestry* (Ode, 1971) (songwriter turned recording artist, and one of the best selling albums of the period); Neil Young, *Harvest Moon* (WB, 1992); Tracy Chapman, *Matters of the Heart* (Elektra, 1992); Alanis Morissette, *Jagged Little Pill* (WEA, 1996)

Viewing: *Dancing in the Street* (1995), episode 2 (Leiber and Stoller)

SOUL

Originally a secular version of **gospel**, soul was the major black musical form of the 1960s and 1970s. Soul had originally been used by **jazz** musicians and listeners to signify music with a greater sense of **authenticity** and sincerity. As it developed in the 1960s, soul was a merger of gospel-style singing and **funk** rhythms. Funk was originally used in the 1950s to describe a form of modern jazz which concentrated on 'swing' and became used in the 1960s in **R&B** and soul music, especially for the recordings of 'Soul Brother Number One' by James Brown.

Guralnick defines soul as 'the far less controlled, gospel based, emotion-baring kind of music that grew up in the wake of the success of Ray Charles from about 1954 on and came to its full flowering, along with Motown, in the early 1960s' (1991: 2). The genre was often ballad in form, with love as a major theme. Soul became closely identified with several **independent** record labels: Atlantic, Stax/Volt, and **Motown**, each with its own 'stable' of performers and an identifiable sound, and associated with particular geographic locations and music **scenes**: e.g. Detroit; Philadelphia; Southern. Soul was politically significant through the 1960s, paralleling the civil rights movement. Soul singers of note to emerge in the 1950s included Sam Cooke and Jackie Wilson; in the 1960s James Brown, Bobby Bland, Aretha Franklin, Otis Redding, and Percy Sledge.

Soul had ceased to be an identifiable genre by the late 1970s, gradually being absorbed into various hybrid forms of **black music** and **dance music** more generally. Its major performers and their records still enjoy a considerable following, indicated by the sales of soul compilation albums, and the international success of the film *The Commitments* (1991) and its soundtrack of soul **covers**.

See also: **Motown; Northern soul**

Further reading: Garofalo (1997); Guralnick (1991); Hirshey (1985); Ritz (1985)

Listening: James Brown, *Live at the Apollo* (*Polydor*, 1963); Aretha Franklin, *30 Greatest Hits* (Atlantic, 1986); Al Green, *I Can't Stop* (Blue Note, 2003); Otis Redding, *The Very Best of Otis Redding* (Rhino, 1993); Percy Sledge, 'When a Man Loves a Woman' (1966) (the first southern soul record to cross over and top both the R&B and pop charts; available on various compilations)

SOUND; SOUND PRODUCTION; SOUND RECORDING; SOUND REPRODUCTION; SOUND SYSTEMS

In physical, scientific terms, sound is the sensation caused in the ear by the vibration of the surrounding air, or what is or may be heard. Musical sound is produced by continuous and regular vibrations, compared to 'noise' as disorganized sound (although 'noise' has been appropriated by **avant-garde** and experimental musicians). In popular music studies, primary interest has been on changes in the nature of sound reproduction and recording, especially the manner in which new technologies have influenced the nature and product.

New technologies of **sound production** are democratizing, opening up performance opportunities to players and creating new social spaces for listening to music. However, these opportunities and spaces are selectively available, and exploited by particular social groups. There are a number of excellent studies of these developments and their implications. Historical examples include the impact of nineteenth-century brass band instruments; the microphone in the 1930s; and the electric guitar in the early 1950s; these are sketched here.

Victorian England saw an unprecedented expansion in participative music, with brass bands a major part of this. Herbert (1998) examines how and why brass bands developed, their distribution and extent, and the nature and significance of their impact. In doing so he illustrates the complex intersection of **technology**, urbanization, and musical forms at work in shaping the brass band movement. The first half of the nineteenth century was the peak period of brass bands. They emerged as a new form of leisure activity, with the development of new brass instruments made possible by the invention of the piston valve: 'Suddenly brass instruments possessed a new musical facility, and potentially a new social identity' (ibid.: 110). The advent of new instruments made possible new musical techniques, and an expanded brass band repertoire. The microphone, introduced in the 1920s, revolutionized the practice of popular singing, as vocalists could now address listeners with unprecedented intimacy. This led to new musical creativities and sites of authorship. Johnson traces the emergence of the microphone as a 'performance accessory' in Australia, showing how it was inscribed by gender politics. Masculinist resistance to this 'artificial' aid left it primarily to women singers to exploit its possibilities in the 1930s. 'In particular, they experimented with projection, timbre and sensibility in a way that placed the intimate "grain of the voice" in the public arena, laying the foundations for the distinctive vocalisation of rock/pop' (Johnson, 2000: ch. 4; see also Chanan, 1995: ch. 7). The use of electrical signals to increase (amplify) the loudness of sounds, amplification was especially important in the history of popular music, enabling larger live audiences and contributing to the development of new instruments, especially the electric guitar, and new musical styles. Amplification of the guitar 'allowed guitarists to play fluid and hornlike solos, while the country and jump **blues** genres popular in the late Forties ecouraged them to elaborate a more percussive and riffing style' (Miller, 1999: 41; see also Waksman, 2003). The Fender Esquire in 1950, the first mass-produced solid-body electric guitar, changed the range and variety of people who could play, reducing the importance of controlling each string's resonance precisely, covering fingering mistakes. *Non*-amplification is sometimes associated with an ideology of **authenticity**; e.g. **folk music**'s traditional privileging of acoustic instruments, and the largely negative response from the folk music community to Bob Dylan's 'going electric' in the mid-1960s.

The advent of MIDI (Musical Instrument Digital Interface) and digital electronics completely restructured music production from

1983 onwards and has been regarded as 'a watershed in the history of popular music' (Théberge, 1997: 5). The new generation of instruments and software expanded styles and concepts of production, and raised the status of **producers**. For **musicians** and producers, 'the sound possibilities arising from the new modes of technical production would redefine compositional thinking' (Hawkins, 2002: 4).

Sound recording is the process of transferring '**live**' musical performance on to a physical product (the recording). The history of sound recording is one of technical advances leading to changes in the nature of the process, and the tasks and status of the associated labour forms. Such changes are not narrowly technical, as different recording technologies and their associated working practices (e.g. multitracking, overdubbing, tape delay) enable and sustain different aesthetics (for a detailed history, see Cunningham, 1996; for a concise overview, see Millard, 1995: ch. 14). Major sound studios have historically been linked to particular production aesthetics and personnel; Cogan and Clark (2003) profile a number of these fascinating 'Temples of Sound', as they term them. In the recording studio, the work of the sound mixer, or sound engineer, 'represents the point where music and modern technology meet' (Kealy, 1979). Initially designated as 'technicians', sound mixers have converted a craft into an art, with consequent higher status and rewards. Zak refers to them as 'both craftsmen and shamans' (2001: 165), who are now responsible for much of what we hear on a recording, acting as a kind of translator for the other members of the recording team (including the musicians). Through the 1980s and into the 2000s new recording technologies have continued to open up creative possibilities and underpinned the emergence of new genres, notably the variants of **techno** and **hip-hop**.

Particular recordings demonstrate advances in sound recording, at times accompanied by greatly increased use of studio time. For example, Les Paul and Mary Ford, 'How High is the Moon', which occupied the number one position on the *Billboard* chart for nine weeks in spring 1951, launched the concept of sound-on-sound recording, coupled with Paul's discovery of tape delay (Cunningham, 1996: 25). Pink Floyd's *Dark Side of the Moon* (Harvest, 1973) set a new precedent in sound recording techniques, including its use of noise gates, devices which allow audio signals to be heard once they rise above a pre-determined volume threshold, and an extensive use of synthesizers. Approaching the history of popular music from this perspective creates quite a different picture of artistic high points and **auteur** figures, in comparison with the conventional chronologies (see Cunningham, 1996; Zak, 2001).

Sound reproduction as part of home entertainment had its origins in the late nineteenth century (see **phonograph**), with an on-going history of gradual improvements in fidelity, realism, and portability. Stereophonic sound was first developed for use in film theatres in the 1930s, with home stereo systems as scaled down versions. In 1931 the first three-way speaker systems were introduced. The sound was divided into high, middle, and low frequencies, with each band sent to three different transducers in the loud speaker, each designed to best facilitate that part of the sound spectrum: the large 'woofer' for the bass, a mid-range driver, and the smaller 'tweeter' for the treble. Due to the depression, and the difficulty of reaching agreement on a common stereo standard (compare the battle over **recording formats**), this system was not turned into a commercial product until the late 1950s. In the 1950s, tape was the format to first introduce stereo sound into the home. Read and Welch (1977: 427) observe that the 'introduction of the stereo tape recorder for the home in 1955 heralded the most dramatic increase ever seen for a single product in home entertainment'. The increased sales of magnetic tape recorders and pre-recorded tape forced the record companies to develop a competing stereo product, particularly for the classical music audiophile. By the 1960s, stereo sound was incorporated into the loudspeakers used in home stereos. December 1957 saw the first stereo records introduced to the market. These were not intended for the mass market, and sales were initially not high, but home stereos became popularized during the 1960s, in part based on the technological breakthrough of the transistor, invented in 1948.

In addition to home stereo systems, and their predecessors the **phonograph**, there are more mobile forms of sound reproduction, important to particular lifestyles. The transistor **radio** deserves a history of its own, along with the radio. Another mobile form of sound system is the Walkman, which had a major impact when it was introduced during the 1980s (see Negus, 1992). Currently, iPods, mobile phones (which can also play music and use jingles to alert their owners to incoming calls), and suchlike have become fashion accessories for many young people.

A further example of a socially situated playing/listening technology is the 'sound system', a term given to large, heavily amplified mobile discos and their surrounding **reggae** culture. These initially emerged in Jamaica from the 1950s onwards, and were subsequently transplanted to Britain with the influx of Caribbean immigrants. 'The basic description of a sound system as a large mobile hi-fi or disco does little justice to the specificities of the form. The sound that they generate has its own characteristics, particularly an emphasis on the reproduction of bass frequencies, its own aesthetics and a unique mode of consumption' (Gilroy, 1993; in Gelder and Thornton, eds, 1997: 342).

Further reading: Beadle (1993) (includes a useful discography); Gelatt (1977); Millard (1995: ch. 10); Jones, Steve (1992); Read and Welch (1977); Théberge (1997); Zak (2001)

SOUNDS *see* scenes

SOUNDTRACKS

There are three main types of music soundtrack: in feature **film** and **documentary**; in **television**; and in video/electronic games. Mainstream narrative cinema has used two types of musical soundtrack to complement the filmic text: (i) theme music, usually composed specifically for the film (e.g. *Star Wars*, *Jaws*, *Lord of the Rings*); (ii) a soundtrack consisting of selected popular music, usually contemporary with the temporal and physical setting of the film, or representative of the period evoked (e.g. *The Big Chill*, *Singles*, *American Graffiti*). Occasionally, there may be two 'soundtracks' released, and the two approaches are sometimes combined (e.g. *Dead Man Walking* (1996)). The emphasis here is on the second of these forms (for a consideration of the first, see Wojcik and Knight, 2001).

Rock Around the Clock (1956) and many of the films featuring Elvis Presley demonstrated the market appeal of popular musical soundtracks, as indeed had many Hollywood musicals before them. Mainstream narrative cinema has increasingly used popular music soundtracks to great effect, with accompanying success for both film and record. The film to first demonstrate the commercial possibilities here was *Saturday Night Fever* (1977). Later examples of such successful marketing tie-ins and media cross-fertilization include *The Commitments* (1991), with a soundtrack featuring some impressive **covers** of soul classics and the powerful voice of Andrew Strong (who plays the part of the lead singer Deco); and *The Lord of the Rings* films, soundtracks, video games, and merchandise, along with the reissues of the original books.

Such soundtracks feature popular music composed specifically for the film, or previously recorded work which is thematically or temporally related to the film; e.g. *The Big Chill* (1983); *Boyz N The Hood* (1991). This enables **multimedia marketing**, with accompanying commercial success for both film and record. Prince's soundtrack for the film *Batman* (1989) was part of a carefully orchestrated marketing campaign, which successfully created interest in the film and helped break Prince to a wider audience, primarily through exposure (of the promotional video clip) on **MTV** (Shuker, 1994).

Video game music is emerging as a major form of revenue for the music industry. Symphonic video game soundtracks have been big business in Japan for some time, where they regularly feature in album charts, and the European and North American markets are now picking up on them. The 2003 *seven*-CD soundtrack to *Grand Theft Auto: Vice City* includes 1980s songs such as Ozzy Osbourne's 'Bark at the Moon' and Grandmaster Flash's 'The Message'. The popularity of the games (*Vice City* has sold 10.5 million copies worldwide) encourages interest in the music CDs, which include the added enticement of 'secret' game codes. An increasing number of established musicians are now writing music for games, and the British Academy of Film and Television Arts recently added an awards category for video game soundtracks. The nature and impact of them is a subject for investigation.

Further reading: Mundy (1999); Wojcik and Knight (2001)

STARS; STARDOM

Stars are individuals who, as a consequence of their public performances or appearances in the mass media, become widely recognized and acquire symbolic status. Stars are seen as possessing a unique, distinctive talent in the cultural forms within which they work. Initially associated with the Hollywood film star system, stardom is now widely evident in sports, television, and popular music. While there is a large body of theoretically oriented work on film stars (see Hayward, 1996 for a helpful overview), the study of stardom in popular music is largely limited to personal biographies of widely varying analytical value.

The important question is not so much 'what is a star?' but how do stars function within the **music industry**, within textual narratives, and, in particular, at the level of individual fantasy and desire. What needs to be explained is the nature of emotional investment in pleasurable images. 'Stars are popular because they are regarded with some form of active esteem and invested with cultural value. They resonate within particular lifestyles and cultures' (O'Sullivan *et al.*, 1994: 207), and represent a form of escapism from everyday life and the mundane.

Stardom in popular music, as in other forms of popular culture, is as much about illusion and appeal to the fantasies of the audience as it is about talent and creativity. Stars function as mythic constructs, playing a key role in the ability of their **fans** to construct meaning out of everyday life. Such stars must also be seen as economic entities, who are used to mobilize audiences and promote the products of the music industry. They represent a unique commodity form which is both a labour process and product. Audience identification with particular stars is a significant marketing device, making stars as much as an economic entity as a purely cultural phenomenon. For example, over the course of her career Madonna has generated more than US$500 million in worldwide music sales for Time-Warner. She represents a bankable image, carefully constructed in an era of media globalization. Several popular music stars have continued to generate enormous income after their death, which freezes their appeal in time while enabling their continued **marketing** through both the **back catalogue** and previously unreleased material. Elvis Presley was still ranked number one in Forbes's 2004 list of 'dead celebrity earners', with an annual income of US$ 40 million (derived from admissions to Graceland, licensing and merchandising), while John Lennon, George Harrison, Bob Marley, and composer Irving Berlin also made the top ten. *Dead Elvis* (Marcus, 1991b) offers a fascinating account of the on-going cultural preoccupation with 'the King' since his death in 1977.

The enormous fascination with stars' personal lives suggests a phenomenon which cannot be simply explained in terms of political economy. **Fans** both create and maintain the star through a ritual of adoration, transcending their own lives in the process. Stars appeal because they embody and refine the values invested in specific social types; e.g. Kylie Minogue in the 1980s as the wholesome but sexual girl next door, and Bruce Springsteen, with an image founded on **authenticity**. Contemporary 'established' stars are frequently at pains to exercise considerable control over their artistic lives, perhaps because this has often been hard won; all have an ability to retain an audience across time, either through reinventing their persona and image, or through exploring new avenues in their music. Many have produced a substantial body of work, often multimedia in form, while seeking, to varying degrees, new ways of reinterpreting or reaffirming popular music styles and traditions. In these respects, such stars are frequently considered to be **auteurs**.

The construction of a popular music star's persona/image may change across time, at times in a calculated attempt to redefine a performer's audience and appeal. A number of commentators have observed how Madonna has been able to constantly reinvent her persona, and retain a high degree of creative control over her work. Her audience appeal and commercial success lies primarily in performance, through both concerts and music video, and her ability to keep herself in the public eye, and the creation and maintenance of image is central to her success.

Springsteen and Madonna are the popular music stars of the past fifteen years who have generated the greatest amount of academic (and popular) analysis and discussion. In sum, the discourse surrounding them shows how stardom has become a construct with a number of dimensions: the economic, the cultural, and the aesthetic or creative – the relationship between stardom and **auteurship**.

See also: **fans**

Further reading: on stardom generally, and in relation to film stars, see Hayward, S. (1996); on Madonna, see Schwichtenberg, ed. (1993); on Springsteen, the various biographies by Marsh; for bibliographic guidance on particular 'rock stars/pop stars', see Leyser (1994)

STRUCTURALISM; POST-STRUCTURALISM; SEMIOTICS

'An intellectual enterprise characterized by attention to the systems, relations and forms – the structures – that make meaning possible in any cultural activity or artifact. Structuralism is an analytical or *theoretical* enterprise, dedicated to the systematic elaboration of the rules and constraints that work, like the rules of a language, to make the generation of meanings possible in the first place' (O'Sullivan *et al.*, 1994: 302). Structuralists' attempts to establish such 'rules of meaning' led to several distinct approaches during the 1970s: semiotics; deconstruction (overwhelmingly a mode of literary analysis, derived from the work of Derrida); and post-structuralism.

'Structuralist' views of popular culture and media forms concentrate on how meaning is generated in media texts, examining how the 'structure' of the text (visual, verbal, or auditory) produces particular ideological meanings. Such study is primarily through **semiotics**, the study of signs, which has been applied widely in the study of communications, providing a method for the analysis of both verbal and non-verbal messages. Semiotics distinguishes between signifier, signified, and sign. The signifier can be a word, an image, or a physical object; the signified is the mental concept associated with the signifier; the sign is the association of signifier and signified. Signs may be organized into linked codes, as with dress **fashions**. Social convention may influence the precise nature and strength of the relationship between signifier and signified. Barthes argued that signs can form myths, in that a sign may represent a whole range of cultural values. In addition to associating an image or an object with a concept (denotation), signs also carry connotations, engendering emotions.

Post-structuralism 'is hard in practice to separate from structuralism. It is more alert to psychoanalytic theories and the role of pleasure in producing and regulating meanings than was the highly rationalist early structuralism. Post-structuralism is also more concerned with the external structures (social process, class, gender, and ethnic divisions, historical changes) that make meaning possible' (O'Sullivan *et al.*, 1994: 304). This shifted the focus from the text to the reader/viewer/listener. Within popular music studies, post-structuralist ideas have informed discussions on the nature and significance of **class**, **gender**, and **ethnicity** in relation to changes in the production and **consumption** of music.

In popular music studies, semiology has been used in analyses of song **lyrics**, **music videos**, **album covers**, youth **subcultures**, and photographs (see Longhurst's instructive decoding of a press photograph of Courtney Love and Sinead O'Connor at the 1993 MTV awards, to show how such images/texts contain different levels of meaning (1995: 163–4)). The **musicological** approach can be loosely regarded as a structuralist form of cultural analysis, since it privileges the text by placing the emphasis firmly on its formal properties. Musicologists tackle popular music as music, using conventional tools derived from the study of more traditional/classical forms of music: harmony, melody, beat, rhythm, and the lyric. However, this preoccupation with the text in and of itself has been critiqued for its lack of consideration of music as a social phenomenon. In traditional musicology, the music itself becomes a disembodied presence, lacking any social referents. The concept of musical codes is a structuralist approach to investigating how meaning is conveyed in musical texts, and has also been used to inform discussions of competence, the differing ability of listeners to decode or interpret musical texts (see Middleton, 1990).

Further reading: Middleton (1990); Longhurst (1995)

STYLE *see* **fashion; genre; subculture**

SUBCULTURE

As the contributors to a major edited reader demonstrate, while there is no consensus about the definition of a subculture, they can be broadly considered to be social groups organized around shared interests and practices (Gelder and Thornton, eds, 1997: Pt. 2). Subcultures often distinguish themselves against others; factions of the larger social group, they usually set themselves in opposition to their parent culture, at least at a cultural level.

In the mid-1970s, rather than being part of a coherent youth culture, it seemed to many observers that youth consisted of a 'mainstream' majority, and minority subcultures whose distinctiveness was shaped largely by the social class and ethnic background of their members (cf. the **counter-culture** of the 1960s, and the view of youth as a generational unit). Sociological interest concentrated on the various youth subcultures, whose members were seen to rely on leisure and style as a means of winning their own cultural space, and thus represented cultural politics at an oppositional, symbolic, level.

Music is one of a complex of elements making up subcultural style. Its role in terms of pleasure and cultural capital is similar to that played out among more mainstream youth, but in an accentuated form. The relationship between popular music and youth subcultures was comprehensively explored in a number of influential studies during the 1970s and early 1980s. Collectively, these argued what became a frequently asserted thesis: that youth subcultures appropriate and innovate musical forms and styles as a basis for their **identity**, and, in so doing, assert a counter-cultural **politics**. This perspective was primarily associated with writers linked to the UK's influential Birmingham Centre for Contemporary Cultural Studies, whose views became more widely accepted. (*Further reading*: Gelder and Thornton, eds (1997: Pt. 2); Hall and Jefferson (1976); Hebdige (1979); and Willis (1978); and see **cultural studies**.)

For the writers associated with the BCCCS, subcultures were regarded as 'meaning systems, modes of expression or life styles developed by groups in subordinate structural positions in response to dominant meaning systems, and which reflect their attempt to solve structural contradictions rising from the wider societal context' (Brake, 1985: 8). Hebdige starts from the premise that style in subculture is 'pregnant with significance', illustrating this through a comprehensive analysis of various spectacular subcultural styles: beats and hipsters in the 1950s; teddy boys in the 1950s and 1970s; mods in the early 1960s; skinheads in the late 1960s; Rastas in the 1970s; glam rockers in the early to mid-1970s; and, most visible of all, punks in the mid-1970s. In his analysis, subcultures rely on leisure and style as a means of making their values visible in a society saturated by the codes and symbols of the dominant culture. The significance of subcultures for their participants is that they offer a solution, albeit at a 'magical' level, to structural dislocations through the establishment of an 'achieved identity' – the selection of certain elements of style outside of those associated with the ascribed identity offered by work, home, or school. The expressive elements of this style offer 'a meaningful way of life during leisure', removed from the instrumental world of work: 'Subcultures are therefore expressive forms but what they express is, in the last instance, a fundamental tension between those in power and those condemned to subordinate positions and second class lives. This tension is figuratively expressed in the form of subcultural style' (Hebdige, 1979: 132).

The majority of youth were seen to pass through life without any significant involvement in such subcultures. Associated aspects of subcultural fashion and musical tastes may be adopted, but for 'respectable' youth these are essentially divorced from the lifestyle and values of the subculture. Members of youth subcultures, on the other hand, utilize symbolic elements to construct an identity outside the restraints of class and education, an identity which places them squarely outside of conservative mainstream society. Membership of a subculture was seen to necessarily involve membership of a class culture and could be either an extension of, or in opposition to, the parent class culture (e.g. the skinheads). Writers such as Hebdige were at pains not to overemphasize this class dimension, and to accord due analytical weight to gender and ethnic factors.

Youth subcultures in the 1970s and early 1980s were an international phenomenon, but with marked differences. Subcultural styles in both Britain and the United States essentially developed out of their immediate social context, reworking commercial popular culture into a subcultural style which reflected and made sense of their structural social location. This process was not so clear cut in more culturally dependent societies. For example, in Canada the situation was confused by the nation's historical links with Britain and France and the marked contemporary influence of its close proximity to the United States, a situation contributing to Canada's problem of finding a sense of national identity. Canadian youth cultures were consequently largely derivative and any potential oppositional force in them was highly muted (Brake, 1985).

The BCCCS writers' socio-cultural analyses represented an original and imaginative contribution to the sociology of youth cultures, but were critiqued for their overemphasis on the symbolic 'resistance' of subcultures, which was imbued with an unwarranted political significance; romanticizing working-class subcultures; their neglect of ordinary or conformist youth; and a masculine emphasis, with little attention paid to the subcultural experiences of girls. And while music was regarded as a central aspect of subcultural style, its homological relation to other dimensions of style was not always easy to pin down. For example, the skinheads' preferred music changed over time, making problematic any argument for its homological role in skinhead culture. As Hebdige observed, the 'early' skinheads preference for elements of black style, including reggae and ska music, is contradictory considering their racial stance. At times, stylistic attributes were too quickly attributed to a specifically subcultural affiliation, rather than recognizing their generalizability (see **homology**). In part, this arises from the problematic subculturalist dichotomizing of mainstream and oppositional musics, locating itself 'within the broader terrain of the ideological politics of style organized around an opposition of center and margin' (Grossberg, 1992a: 145).

While this convergence between music and cultural group values is evident in some contemporary youth subcultures, most notably **heavy metal** and **grunge**, subsequent theoretical discussions and case studies suggest that the degree of homology between subcultures and music had been overstated. Indeed the very value of the concept 'subcultures', and particularly its conflation with oppositional cultural politics, became seriously questioned. Dick Hebdige, one of the central figures of 1970s subcultural theory, concluded that 'theoretical models are as tied to their own times as the human bodies that produce them. The idea of subculture-as-negation grew up alongside punk, remained inextricably linked to it and died when it died' (Hebdige, 1988: 8; see also Bennett, 2000, Grossberg, 1992a; Redhead, 1990).

Redhead's detailed reading of post-punk events in the UK suggested that the very notion of 'subculture', and the emphasis on it as part of a tradition of 'rock authenticity' and opposition at the level of cultural politics, were in need of revision: 'Such notions are not capable of capturing the changes in youth culture and rock culture from at least the late 1970s onwards. They are, moreover, unsatisfactory as accounts of pop history and youth culture in general' (Redhead, 1990: 41–2). For many youthful consumers during the 1980s and 1990s, the old ideological divides applied to popular music had little relevance, with their tastes determined by a more complex pattern of considerations than any 'politically correct' dichotomizing of genres. This is most evident in the constituencies for **alternative** and **dance music**.

Recent research in popular music has retained elements of the subculturalist approach, but has moved towards a more sophisticated understanding of the activities of music **audiences**, drawing heavily on the concept of **scenes**.

See also: **bricolage; goth; mod; punk; homology; scenes**

Further reading: Gelder and Thornton, eds (1997); Muggleton (2000)

SURF MUSIC

A short-lived but influential musical phenomenon, surf music was a regional **scene** associated with a **subculture**, which became a marketing label. The majority of surf music recordings were issued between 1961 and 1965, with their chart success largely confined to southern California. The style has continued as something of a cult **genre**.

Surf music was the most guitar-oriented style of early **rock'n'roll**, and had enormous influence on subsequent electric guitar playing styles. Dick Dale was the acknowledged father of surf rock, developing a reverb guitar sound which evoked the waves and 'runs' of surfing, a teenage subculture which initially developed in California and Hawaii in the late 1950s. Dale developed a technique based on the tremeloe playing used in Middle Eastern plucked instruments such as the bouzouka, sustaining notes by plucking strings up and down. The surf music craze was sparked by Dale and the Del-Tones' 1961 single 'Let's Go Trippin' (subsequently covered by the Beach Boys on their album *Surfin USA*), with hundreds of surf bands emerging.

Surf was Californian good time music, with references to sun, sand, and (obliquely) sex; also hot rods and drag racing. Surf music provided the soundtrack for the beach movies of the period, and for documentaries celebrating surfing and the associated lifestyle (e.g. *The Longest Wave*; *Crystal Voyager*).

There was a strong surf instrumental vein, with the Surfaris' 'Wipe Out' (1963), the Chantays' 'Pipeline' (1963), and the Ventures all making the national charts. The most commercially successful surf performers were vocal duo Jan and Dean, and the Beach Boys, who became the leading and most enduring of the surf bands. Creatively led by Brian Wilson, the Beach Boys were heavily influenced by the 1950s vocal group style and harmonies of the Four Freshmen and Chuck Berry's **rock'n'roll**. Their early hit 'Surfin USA' is based on Berry's 'Sweet Little Sixteen'. The Beach Boys largely abandoned surfing themes and broadened their scope after 1963, with the thematically linked album *Pet Sounds* (1966) and the single 'Good Vibrations' (1966) their crowning achievements.

Surf music experienced a revival in the 1980s, and continues to maintain a cult status associated with specialist labels (e.g. Surfdog); though now only rarely played, it has become an element of more contemporary genres, while its guitar sound continues to be influential.

Further reading: Charlton (1994); Garofalo (1997); Jim Miller (1992) (profile of the Beach Boys including a discography); White (1994)

Listening: 'Surfin USA' (1963) on *The Beach Boys Twenty Golden Greats* (Capitol/EMI, 1978); *King of Surf Guitar: Best of Dick Dale* (Rhino, 1989); *MOM: Music for Our Mother Ocean* (Surfdog/Interscope, 1996) (includes Pennywise covering 'Surfin USA', Pearl Jam covering 'Gremmie Out of Control' an obscure 1964 surf single, and other contemporary alternative bands performing songs with surf theme and guitar sound: Soundgarden, 'My Wave', silverchair, 'Surfin Bird', and the Ramones 'California Sun')

Viewing: *Dancing in the Street* (1995), episode 2

SYNCRETISM *see* **appropriation**

TASTE; TASTE CULTURES

Taste refers to our cultural preferences, and is usually used in the sense of 'good taste'. Particular activities, practices, and cultural texts have acquired a higher status than others (see **culture**). Those who consume these are viewed as having 'good taste', being regarded as culturally and aesthetically discerning. Related to this are notions of a **canon** of cultural **texts**, underpinned by **ideology** and **aesthetics**. However, there are problems posed by the subjectivity of the discourse surrounding taste, and the shifting historical nature of what constitutes taste. Further, texts connoting 'good taste' are usually validated by those who are considered to have such taste, a process of self-confirmation. In short, what constitutes taste is socially constructed. In its contemporary formulations, taste is frequently conflated with the concept of **cultural capital**. Fiske (1992) suggests that there is an equivalent popular culture capital that establishes its own hierarchy of taste.

American sociologist Herbert Gans developed the concept of taste cultures in the 1960s to refer to the differentiation of cultural **consumption** among social groups, and the manner in which such patterns were shaped. A taste culture is a group of people making similar choices, with these being related to similar backgrounds: class and education are the key determinants of membership in taste cultures. This has much in common with the notion of lifestyles: distinctive configurations of cultural identity and sets of social practices which are associated with particular consumption groups, taste cultures, and subcultures. There is debate over the degree of individual autonomy/choice involved in the construction of lifestyles, and the extent to which they allow for a genuine plurality of expression, including resistance. In an anthropological sense, both taste cultures and lifestyles refer to particular forms of symbolic consumption, along with the rhetorics and discourses in play in the production or regulation of modern cultural life.

These concepts, and the associated debates, have informed popular music studies of **audiences** and consumption. Much of this work takes musical taste/cultural capital as central to identity formation, situating this in relation to **gender**, adolescent peer group identity, and social context (e.g. Koizumi, 2002; Baker, 2002). Grossberg (1992a), on the other hand, suggests that music for youthful consumers no longer operates with the same 'differentiating logic' as it did previously.

Further reading: Featherstone (1987)

TECHNO

Techno emerged as a musical style and metagenre in the 1980s, partly associated with new, computer-generated, **sound**/composition technologies available to musicians. Techno is often conflated with **house** and **ambient** music, or used contiguously with the whole corpus of electronic **dance music**. Techno became closely associated with a particular social setting, being the staple music at large-scale parties –

raves – which, with the associated use of the drug ecstasy, generated considerable controversy (and **moral panic**) in the early to mid-1990s in the UK.

The defining musical characteristics of techno are, in most cases: a slavish devotion to the beat, and the use of rhythm as a hypnotic tool (usually 115–60 bpm); these are primarily, and often entirely, created by electronic means; a lack of vocals; and a significant use of **samples**.

There are a number of variants, or subgenres within techno, often linked with particular record labels/regional **scenes**. The 'proto-techno' of the original Detroit (US) creators of techno shows a mixture of influences, especially influential German electronic band Kraftwerk's 'assembly line technopop', and the **funk** of George Clinton and Parliament. From this basis came 'Detroit techno', a stripped-down, aggressive funk sound, played mostly on analogue instruments and characterized by a severe, pounding rhythm, and 'hardcore techno', speed metal tunes played on Detroit techno instrumentation. Subsequent variants included the more accessible and commercial 'techno-rave'; 'breakbeat', a style using sped-up hip-hop beat samples; and 'tribal', with rhythm patterns and sounds drawing on Native American and world music. Some techno performers have moved progressively with and through a number of these styles; e.g. the Shamen's initial recordings combined psychedelic rock with hardcore **rap** rhythms, while their later work makes greater use of samples, drum machines, and heavily amplified guitar sounds.

See also: **dance music**

Further reading: Reynolds (1998); Sicko (1999) (includes discography); Woodstra and Bogdanov (2001)

Listening: The Shamen, *Boss Drum* (Epic, 1992); Leftfield, *Leftism* (Hard Hands/Columbia, 1995); Underworld, 'Born Slippy' on *Trainspotting: Original Soundtrack* (EMI, 1996)

TECHNOLOGY

In sociological usage technology embraces all forms of productive technique, including hand-craft, but the more popular use of technology is synonymous with machinery. Both understandings of the term are evident in considerations of the relationship between popular music and technology. However, as Théberge observes, 'technology' is not to be thought of simply in terms of 'machines', but rather in terms of practice, the uses to which **sound recording** and playback devices, **recording formats**, and **radio**, computers, and the **Internet** are put: 'in a more general sense, the organization of production and consumption' Théberge (1999: 216–17).

The history of music is in part one of a shift from oral performance to notation, then to music being recorded, stored, and disseminated utilizing various mediums of sound (and visual) transmission. These are hardly discrete stages, but they do offer an organizing logic for the overview here. Any new medium of communication or technological form changes the way in which we experience music, and this has implications for how we relate to and consume music. Technological changes in recording equipment pose both constraints and opportunities in terms of the organization of production, and the development of new forms of musical instruments allowed the emergence of 'new' sounds. New recording formats and modes of transmission and dissemination alter the process of musical production and **consumption**, and raise questions about authorship and the legal status of music as property. While the creation of music and technological innovation have historically always been related, discussions of this relationship have been conscious to avoid overbalancing into technological determinism: the notion that the form(s) of technology are the principal factor producing cultural/social change.

These topics have been the subject of intensive study (major books include Jones, 1992; Cunningham, 1996; Millard, 1995; Chanan, 1995; Théberge, 1997). The importance of these topics has warranted separate treatment in each case, and they are simply indicated here:

(1) *Sound production*: the influence of new instrumentation (e.g. the microphone; the electric guitar).
(2) *Sound recording*: the role of the recording studio; the importance of amplification; the changing status of formats.
(3) *Sound reproduction*: the **phonograph** and its descendants.
(4) *Sound dissemination*: the historical impact and contemporary importance of radio, and the Internet and **MP3**.
(5) The combination of sound and visuals – **film**, **television** and **MTV**, **music video**, and **multimedia**.
(6) The deployment of new technologies in the area of music retail (see **marketing**).

It is also important to acknowledge that prior to recorded sound, print was central to the transmission of music. Even before the invention of the printing press, handwritten songs were circulated. The printing press facilitated the circulation of Broadside ballads from the early sixteenth century, and sheet music, which peaked at the end of the nineteenth century (see Negus, 1996).

Technology is an inherent part of some definitions of popular music, with attempts to maintain a distinction between a 'folk mode' predicated on live performance, and a mass culture form associated with recording. The latter is criticized as 'only commercial, leaving the profound and innate potential of the medium for cultural and aesthetic expression still undeveloped' (Cutler, 1985: 142). However, 'the widespread use of inexpensive multitrack recorders and the spread of homemade cassette networks are giving rise to another form of folk music that fits neither category. Likewise the use of turntables and microphones in rap music contradicts the easy combination of recording and mass culture' (Jones, 1992: 5). Innovations such as music video and electronic technologies of composition have generated a certain amount of 'technophobia'. Negus makes an intriguing comparison between contemporary antipathy to such developments and the hostile reception initially accorded the piano (Negus, 1992: 31).

The discourse surrounding music and technology embraces divergent views about creativity and musicianship, artistic freedom, and property rights (particularly **copyright**). New technologies are variously seen as democratizing or consolidating established **music industry** hierarchies; rationalizing or disruptive of distribution processes; confirming or challenging legal definitions of music as property; and inhibiting or enabling new creativities and sites of authorship (Thornton, 1995: 31).

Further reading: Jones (1992); Lysloff and Gay, eds (2003); Millard (1994); Negus (1992); Théberge (1997); Zak (2001)

TEENAGERS; TEENYBOPPERS; TEEN IDOLS

A teenager is a person in their teens (13–19 years of age), and a teenybopper is a teenage girl who follows the latest **fashions** in clothes, hairstyles, and pop music. First used in the late 1950s, teenybopper soon acquired strongly derogatory connotations, being applied to girl **fans** and their preferred artists and musical styles: teen idols and 'teen rock'. Teen idols represented a blander, less rebellious version of rock'n'roll, and the music of Paul Anka, Booby Vee, Bobby Vinton, and Tommy Sands prospered in the charts in the early 1960s.

Successful female singers following 'the same pallid formula' (Fried-lander, 1996: 72) included Lesley Gore and Connie Francis. The clean-cut teen idols projected a mixture of sexual appeal and innocent youth to a receptive teenage market.

Academic analysis has concentrated on the social construction of teenagers as an identifiable social group, their musical preferences, and their (declining) significance as a market (see **demographics**). Profiles of popular music **consumption** show a clear pattern of age- and **gender**-based **genre** preferences. Teenagers are traditionally a major audience for, and consumers of, popular music, especially pop, dance **music**, **bubblegum**, and **power pop**. (Other genres will frequently include variants and performers aimed at the teenage market: e.g. the 'lite' heavy metal of Bon Jovi in the 1980s; the 'soft' rap of Kriss Kross and Snow in the 1990s). That girls enjoy commercial pop music more than boys reflects the segmented nature of the market, with certain performers having a clear appeal for younger listeners, particularly girls, and being marketed as such; e.g. Kylie Minogue, Duran Duran, and Bananarama in the 1980s; the Back Street Boys and the Spice Girls in the 1990s; Hilary Duff and and Beyonce more recently. There is a major genre of music magazines aimed at the teenybopper/younger market (e.g. *Smash Hits*). The majority of their readers are girls, who buy them partly for their pin-up posters, reflecting their frequent obsession with particular **stars** and what has been termed teenybopper bedroom culture.

See also: **boy bands; girl groups; pop**

Further reading: Ennis (1992); Friedlander (1996); Frith and McRobbie (1990)

Listening: *The Very Best of Connie Francis* (Polydor, 1963); *Bobby Vee* (Legendary Masters Series, EMI, 1990)

TELEVISION; REALITY TELEVISION

Television has been an important mode of distribution, promotion, and formation for the music industry. The discussion here is of free-to-air, broadcast television, and the popular music programmes which form part of its schedules (**MTV** and similar cable channels are dealt with separately). Included here are light entertainment series based around musical performers, music documentaries, and the presentation of musical acts as part of television variety and chat/interview shows. It is also worth noting that popular music plot themes, music segments and signature tunes are also an important part of many television genres, especially those aimed at children (e.g. *Sesame Street*) and adolescents (*The Simpsons*, *The X Files*), but also 'adult' dramas such as *The Sopranos* (with the accompanying release of **soundtrack** albums from such series).

A contradictory relationship has traditionally existed between television and popular music. Television is traditionally a medium of family entertainment, collapsing class, gender, ethnic, and generational differences in order to construct a homogeneous audience held together by the ideology of the nuclear family. In contrast, many forms of popular music, especially **rock'n'roll** and its various mutations, have historically presented themselves as being about 'difference', emphasizing individual tastes and preferences. The rock tradition viewed television as 'always after the event – young viewers might have learned to move and dress directly from the TV screen, but the assumption was that it was a window on the real youth world that was somewhere out there' (Frith, 1988c: 212).

The introduction of public broadcast television in the United States and the UK in the 1950s coincided with the emergence of rock'n'roll. Television helped popularize the new music, and established several of its performers, most notably Elvis Presley, as youth icons. Indeed, as Grossberg observes, 'television has been, for some fans, their only access to "live" performance' (1993: 189). Television was quick to seize the commercial opportunities offered by the emergent youth culture market of the 1950s. 'Television became devoted, at least in part, to the feature of televisual musical products for an audience that spent much of its leisure time and money in the consumption of pop music goods' (Burnett, 1990: 23). This led to a proliferation of television popular music shows. The better-known of these on US television included *American Bandstand*, one of the longest running shows in television history (1952–), *Your Hit Parade* (1950–9), and *The Big Record* (1957–8). Britain had *Juke Box Jury* and *Top of the Pops*, both starting in the late 1950s, and *The Old Grey Whistle Test* (launched by the BBC in 1971, and aimed at more album-oriented older youth). In 1963 *Ready Steady Go!* began showcasing new talent, who usually performed live, compared to the *Top of the Pops'* staid studio lip-synchs with backing from a house orchestra. In addition to the music, such shows have acted as influential presenters of new dances, images, and clothing styles. Several of these shows have recently been marketed as sell-through videos or DVDs (e.g. *The Best of the Old Grey Whistle Test*, BBC DVD, 2001). They are valuable documents of historically significant performers and styles.

Television's presentation of rock music prior to the advent of music video was generally uninspiring. Performers either straightforwardly performed, even if at times in an impressively frenetic manner (as with the Who's debut effort on *Ready Steady Go!*) or mimed to their recordings in a pseudo-live setting. There were a few notable experiments through the 1960s and 1970s to incorporate additional visual elements (see Shore, 1985, for a full history of the development of **music video** in relation to television). The 1980s success of MTV boosted televised music videos, reshaping the form and the broadcast programmes that relied on music videos for their content. In the United States and Canada, nearly every major city had its own televised music video show, with several nationally syndicated. Music video programmes also became a stock part of television channel viewing schedules in the UK and Western Europe, and New Zealand and Australia. Only in the latter two countries, which have only recently acquired cable television and do not yet have widely available satellite reception, have such programmes retained the high audience ratings they achieved during the 1960s. Popular music programmes are competing against other genres for scheduling space, while the demographic significance of the youth audience has declined since the 1990s.

Mainstream television's music video shows remain significant primarily because of their importance to advertisers, as they draw a young audience whose consuming habits are not yet strongly fixed. A number of studies have illustrated the factors at work in the emergence and nature of popular music programmes on commercial television, particularly their place within scheduling practices and the process of selection of the music videos for inclusion on them. Of particular interest are the links between such programmes, **advertising**, and record sales. While it is difficult to prove a direct causal link, as with radio airplay and chart 'action' there is evidence that exposure on such programmes has an influence on record purchases. The nature of such shows, and their tendency to play music videos which are shortened versions of the associated song, have exercised considerable influence over the way in which videos are produced and their nature as audio-visual and star texts (see Negus, 1992: 97). Also significant, especially in small nations such as Australia, New Zealand, and the Netherlands, is the status of locally produced music videos compared with their imported counterparts, who are competing for space on such programmes, a form of **cultural imperialism**. (On Australia, see Stockbridge, 1992; on New Zealand, Shuker, 2001.)

'Reality television' is used to describe a variety of programming ranging from crime and emergency-style shows, to talk shows, docusoaps, and some forms of access–style programming. Emerging in the 1980s in the United States, it established itself as a central part of mainstream, popular television by the mid–1990s. In the 2000s reality television has become the leading programme format, with many shows internationally franchised (e.g. *Survivor; Big Brother*). A hybrid genre, reality television draws on and reworks generic codes and conventions from a variety of sources, using new technology (e.g. camcorders) to convey a sense of immediacy and authenticity to viewers. Reality television has been criticized for being reliant on shock value and pandering to viewer voyeurism and the lowest common denominator; and celebrated as a form of 'democratainment', with its emphasis on viewer participation (Casey *et al.*, 2002).

Popular music has provided a significant vehicle for reality television. Popular series like *The Monkees* in the 1960s (Stahl, 2002) and *S Club 7 in Miami* in the late 1990s (Shuker, 2001: ch. 10) reinforced the public profiles and commercial success of their performers. In their use of manufactured groups, they foreshadowed the recent *Pop Idol* and *Popstars* series. These musical talent quests, based on audience votes but with a key role played by judging panels (especially in the initial selection of participants), have become an international phenomenon. They have created new pop stars in a number of countries, although the career of some has been short-lived (e.g. True Bliss in New Zealand). Hear'Say, put together through *Popstars*, topped the UK album and singles charts in 2001. *Pop Idol* launched the careers of Will Young and Gareth Gates in the UK, and Ruben Studdard in the US (the popularity of the television show led *Rolling Stone* to do a cover story, featuring Ruben: 21 August 2003).

The popularity of such shows, their audience, and the discourse (notably of **commodification** and **authenticity**) surrounding them are topics yet to be investigated academically.

See also: **music video; MTV**

Further reading: Frith (2002); Fryer (1998); Grossberg (1993); Mundy (1999); *Popular Music*, 21, 3, 2001 (music and television special issue)

TEX-MEX

A genre associated with Chicano, Mexican and Texan musicians, Tex-Mex is very eclectic, blending rock, country, R&B, blues, and traditional Spanish and Mexican music (e.g. Sir Douglas Quintet).

Although the genre had a much longer history, it emerged as a marketing label in the 1980s, primarily with the commercial success of Los Lobos ('one of America's most distinctive and original bands' (Erlewine *et al.*, eds, 1995: 484)).

Further reading: Lipsitz (1994); Miguel (2002)

Listening: Los Lobos, *How Will the Wolf Survive* (Slash, 1984); Sir Douglas Quintet, *Mendocino* (Acadia/Evangeline, 2002) (original release 1969; now with bonus tracks)

TEXT; TEXTUAL ANALYSIS; INTERTEXTUALITY

The term text has traditionally been used to refer to an author's original words, or a prose work – especially one recommended for student reading. More recently, as a cultural studies term, text refers to any media form that is self-contained, e.g. television programmes, recordings, films, and books. Popular music texts are quite diverse, and include recordings, record sleeve covers, and music videos. The most prominent are sound recordings, in various formats, and their packaging (album covers, boxed sets, etc.). In addition there are several other important forms of popular music texts: musical performances, especially concerts; DJ discourse, music videos, music magazines, posters, T-shirts, tour brochures, and fan club merchandise. These texts are frequently interconnected and mutually reinforcing.

Textual analysis is concerned with identifying and analysing the formal qualities of texts. their underpinning structures and constituent characteristic. As such, it has become closely associated with **semiotic** analysis, often linked to psychoanalytical concepts. In the case of popular music, textual analysis takes several forms. The most important is the examination of the musical components of songs, including their lyrics, in their various recorded formats (see **musicology**).

Other forms of popular music texts, such as record covers, concerts, music video, lyric analysis, and DJ talk have been examined through various approaches to content and discourse analysis. For example, album covers convey meaning through the semiotic resources they draw on and display, via language, typography, images, and layout. While texts are usually analysed independently, they can also be considered collectively, as with content analysis of chart share in terms of genres, record labels (majors compared to independents: see

market cycles), and the proportion of artists who are women. A similar approach has been applied to radio and MTV airplay.

Intertextuality is 'a blanket term for the idea that a text communicates its meaning only when it is situated in relation to other texts ... often characterized as meaning that "arises" between texts' (Gracyk, 2001: 56). Examples of this process are the dialogue that occurs between cover versions of songs and their antecedents, and fan discourse around preferred styles and performers. Intertextuality is also implicit in the repackaging of recordings as generic compilations and boxed sets. Gracyk (ibid.: ch. 3) provides a number of interesting musical examples, making the point that such 'influences, connections, and allusions create nuances of meaning that cannot be grasped simply through a general intertextuality' (ibid.: 59).

A point of debate around popular culture is its ideological role in reinforcing/reproducing dominant values through their representation in popular texts. Critics who concentrate on the text itself, often using concepts from semiotic and psychoanalytic analysis, argue that there frequently exists in the text a preferred reading, that is, a dominant message set within the cultural code of established conventions and practices of the producers/transmitters of the text. However, while many consumers may, at least implicitly or subconsciously, accept such preferred readings, it must be kept in mind that it is not necessarily true that the audience as a whole do so. In particular, subordinate groups may reinterpret such textual messages, making 'sense' of them in a different way. This opens up the idea of popular resistance to, and subversion of, dominant cultures. This notion has informed analysis of the nature and reception of popular song lyrics, and music videos.

Further reading: Butler (2003); Gracyk (2001); Jenkins (1997)

TIN PAN ALLEY

In the late 1800s, songwriters and publishers began congregating in a section of New York which became known as Tin Pan Alley from the 'tinny' sound of the upright pianos used there. Tin Pan Alley dominated mainstream American popular music from around 1900 through to the late 1940s. 'Tin Pan Alley songs were for white, urban, literate, middle- and upper-class Americans. They remained practically unknown to large segments of American society, including most blacks ... and the millions of poor, white, rural Americans ... clustered in the South and scattered across the lower Midwest. These two groups had their own distinctive types of music, oral tradition music' (Charles Hamm; quoted in Garofalo, 1997: 43).

Tin Pan Alley was characterized by its association with sheet music, as composing and publishing were the main sources of revenue for those involved. It catered to popular tastes, incorporating and homogenizing elements of new musical styles as they emerged, especially ragtime, blues, and jazz. The overwhelming proportion of its songs focused on romantic love, and helped celebrate and legitimize changes in sexual codes of behaviour in America in the 1920s. Tin Pan Alley songs catered to young women, often from middle-class families, who in the 1920s and 1930s were moving for work in the larger American cities: 'female record purchasers and radio listeners could appreciate the exhilaration of finding "someone" in the newly freed social space of the impersonal city' (Horowitz, 1993: 39).

In the early 1950s, the transition from Tin Pan Alley to rock'n'roll reflected important demographic, social, and cultural shifts in American society.

Further reading: Ennis (1992); Garofalo (1997); Horowitz (1993)

TOURS; TOURING

A tour is a scheduled, consecutive series of **concerts** in different centres; tours can be of short duration, with a small number of concerts over a period of several weeks, or can be world affairs, lasting for up to two years. For the band or performer who has risen beyond the purely local, further commercial success is closely linked to touring, which is especially necessary to promote a new release and build up an **audience**. Tour schedules are frequently extremely gruelling, resembling 'package' vacation tours, with performers playing different cities each night and much of the intervening time consumed by travel. Tour books, band **biographies**, and many classic songs document 'life on the road', with its often attendant excesses, and exhilaration at audience enthusiasm coupled with fatigue.

Tours expose performers and their music to potential **fans** and purchasers, building an image and a following. Tours were important historically for helping 'break' English bands in the United States at various times, and this remains more generally true for the present national and international touring scenes. The nature of tour concerts is an oddly ambivalent one. On the one hand, for the fans it is a rare opportunity to see a favoured performer, especially for those living in locations where the opportunity may be literally a once in a lifetime one. On the other hand, for the performer each concert blurs into a series of 'one night stands' and the challenge is to maintain a freshness to each performance. There exists a clear hierarchy of tours. For a relatively unknown act, seeking to publicize a new or first release and create an audience, opportunities for live work will be few, and pub and university/polytechnic campus circuits remain essential. The scale of most 'national' tours is very localized, covering only main urban centres. For established visiting bands, and local acts which have 'broken' into the charts and the marketplace, there are larger scale 'national' tours. These still largely play selected cities, where venues and audiences are large enough to (hopefully) make the exercise economic. At the top end of the scale, are the global tours of the top international acts, which are massive exercises in logistics and **marketing** – and also hugely profitable; e.g. the Rolling Stones' Voodoo Lounge tour of 1994–5, and the Kiss tour of 1996–7. On the other hand, punk tours in North America in the 1980s relied on a nexus of local promoters, venues, and fan support (O'Connor, 2002; Azerrad, 2001), a situation that has continued as part of the indie/ alternative ethic.

During the record industry's affluent years of the early 1970s, tours by major acts were associated with legendary excesses and expenses. Eliot cites one publicity manager: 'I was working with Zeppelin, Bad Company, the Rolling Stones. It was the heyday of rock excess, when everybody was rolling in money and there were limousines to take you to the bathroom. The company rule was "Whatever it takes, you do it to keep everyone happy"' (Eliot, 1989: 173) This was unsustainable when the record industry retrenched in the mid-1970s, and companies began to cut back on tour support and set such expenditure off against a band's future earnings. Nevertheless, through the 1980s and into the 1990s, touring remained the best way to maintain audience interest in a successful act and a key factor in breaking a new one. These tours are about promotion as much as performance. The performers appear on radio and TV shows, make personal appearances at record stores, and generally help promote sales. Such tours work to strictly controlled budgets, with the act usually paying for everything out of record sales before the allocation of royalties.

While most tours by popular musicians are commercial affairs, there have been significant tours supporting political causes; e.g. the Amnesty International tour of North America in 1988, in support of the human–rights organization, which is estimated to have added some 20,000 new members to the organization in the United States alone;

and the Red Wedge tour in support of the British Labour Party's election campaign in 1987 (see Denselow, 1990; Garofalo, 1992b; Street, 1986). Another variant is the package tour, where a group of artists are placed on the same bill. This was a popular style of tour during the 1960s, when it was important for internationally popularizing British beat performers, and has resurfaced with the successful Lollapalooza tours of 1991 onward, which put together a number of alternative acts.

See also: **documentaries**

Further reading: The monotony of touring is captured in Bruce Thomas, *The Big Wheel* (1990), a 'novel' about a band's tour of America. Thomas was bass player with Elvis Costello and the Attractions.

TRIBUTE BANDS

The extreme example of **covers** bands are those performers who not only directly model themselves on established bands, but actually copy them, presenting themselves as simulacra of the originals – and in the process demonstrating a high level of musical competence. Often referred to as tribute bands, these have become big business; e.g. Bjorn Again, the Australian Abba tribute band, who take their name from a member of the original band. Supporters of these performers argue that the imitators are bringing the music to a new audience of under twenty-fives, opening it up to a generation who never saw the originals, and thereby encouraging them to seek out their material. In some cases, tribute performers are filling 'gaps created by the inactivity or demise of the original artists, as occurred with metal tribute bands in the early 1990s' (Weinstein, 2000: ch. 8). Their detractors point to the difficulties in policing copyright and regard it as at best unfortunate that the original artists are now forced to share audiences with their imitators.

As a largely imitative culture, with little room or audience desire for tributes that include 'twists' upon the original performers, tribute bands raise a number of interesting questions for investigation: the bases of their appeal; their popularity with music venue booking agents; the types of acts chosen for imitation; the composition of their audience; their international nature (e.g. Beatles tribute bands exist in Christchurch [New Zealand], Sydney, London, and Tokyo; Madonna acts perform in Thailand, Japan, Germany and North America); and music industry and musicians attitudes toward them. (These are addressed in a forthcoming edited volume: Homan, 2005.)

Further reading: Bennett (2000: ch. 7); Homan (2002; 2005)

Viewing: *Tribute* (Richard Fox; Kris Curry, 2004) (a documentary that traces the fortunes of Kiss, Queen, Judas Priest, and competing Monkees tribute bands in the United States)

TRIP-HOP

Trip-Hop began to circulate as a term in the British music press during the mid-1990s for a 'movement' led by Massive Attack, Portishead, and Tricky. Trip-hop was **dance music** which was 'a dark, seductive combination of **hip-hop** beats, atmospheric reverb-laden guitars and samples, soul hooks, deep bass grooves and ethereal melodies' (Erlewine *et al.*, eds, 1995: 506). The style had actually been around for several years, in several mutating guises, all forms of a slowed-down hip-hop.

Further reading: Reynolds (1998); Sicko (1999) (includes discography); Woodstra and Bogdanov, eds (2001)

Listening: Massive Attack, *Blue Lines* (Virgin, 1991); Portishead, *Dummy* (Polygram, 1994)

VOICE

'Popular music is overwhelmingly a "voice music". The pleasures of singing, of hearing singers, is central to it', and 'there is a strong tendency for vocals to act as a unifying focus within the song' (Middleton, 1990: 261, 264). Discussions of the role of the voice within popular music have focused on the relationship between lyrics, melodic types, and the singing styles (and vocal timbres: tone quality as it relates to the characteristic differences among singing voices) characteristic of various genres and performers. A key semiological notion is the 'grain' of the voice (very broadly its feeling), as opposed to the direct meaning of lyrics, and the way in which particular styles of voice convey certain sets of emotions, often irrespective of the words they are singing.

A number of authors have discussed how the voice is used in popular music, particularly with regard to rock. Three main aspects are evident. First, attempts to distinguish between 'black' and white' voices, which tend to see the 'black' voice as demonstrative and communicating through a variety of vocal techniques, and the 'white' voice as more restrained and restricted. A second distinction is between 'trained' and 'untrained' voices, with the former found in a range of older popular musics rather than more contemporary forms (e.g. minstrel shows). The 'untrained' voice is important in signifying **authenticity** in rock, e.g. the 'straining' quality of high voices as indicating great effort, naturalness, and a lack of artifice. A third approach has been to associate specific genres with vocal styles, which are linked in turn to gender. The main example of this is the discussion of 'cock rock' (as male) and 'teenybop' (as female) by Frith and McRobbie (1978), which has been built upon by others (e.g. Shepherd, 1991). Shepherd notes that the hard, rasping vocal sound typical of 'cock' or hard rock is 'produced overwhelmingly in the throat and mouth, with a minimum of recourse to the resonating chambers of the chest and head'; he contrasts this with the 'typical vocal sound of woman-as-nurturer: soft and warm, based on much more relaxed use of the vocal cords and using the resonating chambers of the chest', present in much pop music (ibid.: 167).

Moore argues that such distinctions are problematic because of their essentialist assumptions: 'they emphasise only one aspect of vocal production, and attempt to read meaning into the voice's presence on the basis of that single aspect', ignoring that a multitude of factors characterizes a vocal style (1993: 42). He suggests and elaborates four such factors: the register and range which any particular voice achieves; its degree of resonance; the singer's 'heard attitude' to pitch; and the singer's heard attitude to rhythm. Moore usefully illustrates these through a discussion of the vocal styles of Bill Haley, Little Richard, Fats Domino, and Elvis Presley.

As Frith and McRobbie (1990) observe, it is the way in which singers sing, rather than what they sing, that is central to their appeal to listeners. Compare, for instance, the vocal styles of Elvis Presley, Bjork, Margot Timmins (the Cowboy Junkies), Johnny Rotten (Sex Pistols), and Mick Jagger.

See also: **hard rock; heavy metal; punk**

Further reading: Middleton (1990); Moore (1993); Shepherd (1991); Tagg and Clarida (2003)

WORLD MUSIC

While it can be considered a metagenre, world music is really more of a marketing category. World music became prominent in the late 1980s as a label applied to popular music originating outside the Anglo-American nexus. The term was launched in 1987 as a new category of popular music by eleven independent British, European, and American record labels specializing in music from Third World countries, including Earthworks. In the United States, the term 'world beat' was sometimes used for world music. It is necessary to distinguish between world music situated within the Western music industry and 'world musics which are defined as objects of ethnomusicological study' (Mitchell, 1996: 118).

World music was encouraged by the interest in, enthusiasm for, and borrowings from non-Western national musical styles by Western artists such as David Byrne, Peter Gabriel, and Paul Simon – though Simon's use of African forms, notably in *Graceland* (1986), has proved contentious (see **appropriation**). World music was popularized and defined by musical **festival** programming, especially WOMAD: World of Music Arts, and Dance, established by Peter Gabriel in 1982, and general media and public interest in the 'exotic'.

In an early attempt to 'map' the field, Sweeney defined world music primarily through a series of exclusions: world music is not part of the Anglo-American pop and rock mainstream, nor local re-creations of it; not artificially preserved folklore; and not North American roots music like country and blues. He sees it as popular through its regular use by ordinary people, being performed and danced to, and listened to, especially via radio or cassette (Sweeney, 1981). The subsequent internationalization of world music undermined such clear distinctions (see Broughton *et al.*,1994) Ling draws an interesting parallel between the development of Viennese classical music in the eighteenth century, and the current status and nature of world music. The current mainstreaming of world music is indicated by review sections in the music press, and dedicated journals such as *Froots*.

The marketing of world music, and the guides to it, usually construct the category around national **identity**, even though that is clearly tenuous, given the diversity of styles within particular countries. As such, discussions of world music will embrace, among others, Rai music from Algeria, Nigerian juju, Caribbean Zouk (for an instructive genre study, see Guilbault, 1993), and Brazilian bossa nova. Hybrid forms like the Anglo-Indian **bhangra**, and Franco-American Cajun and Zydeco are also included under the broad rubric.

Perhaps more so than other forms of popular music, world music is open to processes of hybridization and musical acculturation. Reflecting this, the metagenre has received considerable academic attention. The discourse here is rather polarized between celebration of its musical attributes, and condemnation of its appropriation by the global music industry (Frith, 2003).

Further reading: Born and Hesmondhalgh, eds (2000); Barrett (1996); Ling (2003); Mitchell (1996); Steingress (2003)

FURTHER RESOURCES

In addition to the books and articles listed here, I have made extensive use of music magazines and the Internet. These provide current and often extensive information on current developments.

1. MUSIC MAGAZINES

Billboard
Guitar Player
ICE: The CD News Authority
Melody Maker
MOJO
Music Week
NME
Q
Record Collector
Rip It Up (New Zealand)
Rolling Stone (US and Australian editions; especially the annual
   yearbook)
UNCUT

In addition to their print versions, several of these have websites. *Addicted to Noise* is online only; see below.

2. SELECTED WEBSITES

Note that these are subject to change; an enormous number of other sites can be accessed through these. More specialist websites have been indicated with their related entries.

(i) Labels

AOL Time Warner: www.timewarner.com
Bertelsmann A.G.: www.bertelsmann.com
EMI Group: www.emigroup.com
Island Records: www.islandrecords.com
Rhino Records: www.rhino.com
Sony Music: www.sonymusic.com
Warner Music Group: www.wmg.com

(ii) Periodicals; Music Press

UNCUT: www.uncut.net
Perfect Beat: The Pacific Journal of Research Into Contemporary Music and Popular Culture: www.ccms.mq.edu/perfectbeat
NME: www.nme.com
Q: www.q4music.com
Vibe: www.vibe.com

(iii) General

ASCAP: www.ascap.com
APRA (Australia): www.apra.com.au
IASPM: www.iaspm.net
Internet Underground Music Archive, an excellent starting point: www.iuma.com/
Music Resources on the Internet: www.music.indiana.edu
Performing Arts Reading Room, Library of Congress, which has excellent music resources and links: www.loc.gov/rr/perform/
Tagg Philip: www.tagg.org

BIBLIOGRAPHY

Abbs, P. (1975) *Reclamations: Essays on Culture, Mass-Culture and the Curriculum*, London: Heinemann.

Abrams, N. (1995) 'Antonio's B–Boys: Rap, Rappers, and Gramsci's Intellectuals', *Popular Music and Society*, 19, 4: 1–20.

Adorno, T. with the assistance of G. Simpson (1941) 'On Popular Music', reprinted in Frith, S. and Goodwin, A. (eds) *On Record: Rock, Pop, and the Written Word*, New York: Pantheon Books.

——(1976) 'Perennial Fashions: Jazz', in *Prisms*, London: Neville Spearman; trans. S. and S. Weber (first published 1955).

——(1991) *The Culture Industry: Selected Essays on Mass Culture*, ed. J. Bernstein, London: Routledge.

Agger, B. (1992) *Cultural Studies as Critical Theory*, London: Falmer Press.

Aikat, D.D. (2004) 'Streaming Violent Genres Online: Visual Images in Music Videos on BET.com, Country.com, MTV.com, and VH1.com', *Popular Music*, 27, 2: 221–40.

Aizlewood, J. (ed.) (1994) *Love is the Drug*, London: Penguin.

Anderson, B. (1983) *Imagined Communities*, London: Verso.

Ang, I. (1991) *Desperately Seeking the Audience*, London and New York: Routledge.

Arnett, J. (1996) *Metalheads: Heavy Metal Music and Adolescent Alienation*, Boulder, CO: Westview Press.

Arnold, M. (1869) *Culture and Anarchy*, reprinted 1993, Cambridge: Cambridge University Press.

Ash, J. and Wilson, E. (1992) *Chic Thrills: A Fashion Reader*, London: Harper-Collins.

Atton, C. (2001) '"Living in the Past"?: Value Discourses in Progressive Rock Fanzines', *Popular Music*, 20, 1: 29–46.

Auslander, P. (2003) 'Good Old Rock and Roll: Performing the 1950s in the 1970s', *Journal of Popular Music Studies*, 15, 2

——(2004) 'I Wanna Be Your Man: Suzi Quatro's Musical Androgyny', *Popular Music*, 23, 1: 1–16.

Azerrad, M. (2001) *Our Band Could Be Your Life: Scenes from the American Indie Underground 1981–1991*, Boston: Little, Brown and Company.

Bagdikian, B.H. (1997) *The Media Monopoly*, 5th edn, Boston: Beacon Books.

Bailey, S. (2003) 'Faithful or Foolish: The Emergence of the "Ironic Cover Album" and Rock Culture', *Popular Music and Society*, 26, 2: 141–60.

Baker, H., Jr (1993) *Black Studies, Rap and the Academy*, Chicago: University of Chicago Press.

Baker, S. (2002) 'Bardot, Britney, Bodies and Breasts: Pre-teen girls' Negotiations of the Corporeal in Relation to Pop Stars and their Music', *Perfect Beat*, 6, 1: 3–17.

Bangs, L. (1990) *Psychotic Reactions and Carburetor Dung*, ed. G. Marcus, London: Minerva.

——(1992a) 'The British Invasion', in DeCurtis, A. and Henke, J. (eds) *The Rolling Stone Illustrated History of Rock and Roll*, 3rd edn, New York: Random House, pp. 199–208.

——(1992b) 'Bubblegum', in DeCurtis, A. and Henke, J. (eds) *The Rolling Stone Illustrated History of Rock and Roll*, 3rd edn, New York: Random House, pp. 452–4.

——(1992c) 'Heavy Metal', in DeCurtis, A. and Henke, J. (eds) *The Rolling Stone Illustrated History of Rock and Roll*, 3rd edn, New York: Random House, pp. 459–64.

——(1992d) 'Protopunk: the Garage Bands', in DeCurtis, A. and Henke, J. (eds) *The Rolling Stone Illustrated History of Rock and Roll*, 3rd edn, New York: Random House, pp. 357–61.

Banks, J. (1996) *Monopoly Television: MTV's Quest to Control the Music*, Boulder, CO: Westview Press.

Barker, C. (2002) *Making Sense of Cultural Studies: Central Problems and Critical Debates*, London: Sage Publications.

Barlow, W. (1989) *Looking Up At Down: The Emergence of Blues Culture*, Philadelphia: Temple University Press.

Barnard, S. (1989) *On the Radio: Music Radio in Britain*, Milton Keynes: Open University Press.

Barnes, K. (1988) 'Top 40 Radio: A Fragment of the Imagination', in Frith, S. (ed.) *Facing the Music*, New York: Pantheon Books.

Barnes, R. (1979) *Mods*, London: Eel Pie Publishing.

Barnett, R. J. and Cavanagh, J. (1994) *Global Dreams: Imperial Corporations and the New World Order*, New York: Simon & Schuster.

Barrett, J. (1996) 'World Music, Nation and Postcolonialism', *Cultural Studies*, 10, 2 (May): 237–47.

Barrow, S. and Dalton, P. (1997) *Reggae: The Rough Guide*, edited by Buckley, J., London: The Rough Guides.

Barrow, T. and Newby, J. (1996) *Inside the Music Business*, London and New York: Routledge.

Bayton, M. (1990) 'How Women Become Musicians', in Frith, S. and Goodwin, A. (eds) *On Record: Rock, Pop, and the Written Word*, New York: Pantheon Books.

Beadle, J. (1993) *Will Pop Eat Itself?: Pop Music in the Soundbite Era*, London: Faber and Faber.

Beattie, K. (2004) *Documentary Screens: Non-Fiction Film and Television*, London: Palgrave Macmillan.

Becker, H. (1997) 'The Culture of a Deviant Group: The "Jazz" Musician', in Gelder, K. and Thornton, S. (eds) *The Subcultures Reader*, London and New York: Routledge (first published 1963).

Beebe, R., Fulbrook, D., and Saunders, B. (eds) (2002) *Rock Over the Edge: Transformations in Popular Music Culture*, Durham and London: Duke University Press.

Belk, R.W. (2001) *Collecting in a Consumer Society*, 2nd edn, London: Routledge.

Bennett, A. (1997) "Going Down to the Pub!": The Pub Rock Scene as a Resource for the Consumption of Popular Music', *Popular Music*, 16, 1: 97–108.

——(2000) *Popular Music and Youth Culture: Music, Identity and Place*, London: Macmillan.

Bennett, A. and Dawe, K. (eds) (2001) *Guitar Cultures*, Oxford: Berg.

Bennett, A. and Kahn-Harris, K. (eds) (2004) *After Subcultures*, London: Ashgate.

Bennett, H.S. (1990) 'The Realities of Practice', in Frith, S. and Goodwin, A. (eds) *On Record: Rock, Pop, and the Written Word*, New York: Pantheon Books.

Bennett, T., Frith, S., Grossberg, L., Shepherd, J., and Turner, G. (1993) *Rock and Popular Music: Politics, Policies, Institutions*, London: Routledge.

Berger, H. and Carroll, M. (2003) *Global Pop, Local Language*, Jackson: University Press of Mississippi.

Berkenstadt, J. and Cross, C.R. (1998) *Nevermind: Nirvana*, New York: Schirmer Books.

Berland, J. (1991) 'Free Trade and Canadian Music', *Cultural Studies*, 5, 3: 317–25.

——(1993) 'Radio Space and Industrial Time: The Case of Radio Formats', in Bennett, T. *et al.* (1993) *Rock and Popular Music: Politics, Policies, Institutions*, London: Routledge.

Bertsch, C. (1993) 'Making Sense of Seattle', *Bad Subjects*, 5 (March/April).

Bishton, D. (1986) *Black Heart Man*, London: Chatto & Windus.

Blackman, A. (1988) *The Shoestring Pirates*, Auckland: Hauraki Enterprises.

Blake, A. (1992) *The Music Business*, London: Batsford.

Bloom, B. (1987) *The Closing of the American Mind*, New York: Simon & Schuster.

Bloomfield, T. (1993) 'Resisting Songs: Negative Dialectics in Pop', *Popular Music*, 12, 1: 13–31.

Bloustein, G. (ed.) (1999) *Musical Visions*, Sydney: Wakefield Press.

Bordo, S. (1993) '"Material Girl": The Effacements of Postmodern Culture', in Schwichtenberg, C. (ed.) *The Madonna Connection: Representational Politics, Subcultural Identities, and Cultural Theory*, St Leonards, NSW: Allen & Unwin, pp. 265–90.

Born, G. and Hesmondhalgh, D. (eds) (2000) *Western Music and its Others: Difference, Representation, and Appropriation in Music*, Berkeley: University of California Press.

Bourdieu, P. (1984) *Distinction: A Social Critique of the Judgement of Taste*, London: Routledge & Kegan Paul.

Bowman, R. (1997) *Soulsville, USA: The Story of Stax Records*, London: Books With Attitude.

Boyd, T. (1994) 'Check Yo Self, Before You Wreck Yo Self: Variations on a Political Theme in Rap Music and Popular Culture', *Public Culture*, 7: 289–312.

Boyd–Barrett, O. and Newbold, C. (1995) *Approaches to Media: A Reader*, London: Arnold: New York: St Martin's Press.

Brackett, D. (1995a) *Interpreting Popular Music*, Cambridge: Cambridge University Press.

——(1995b) 'The Politics and Musical Practice of Crossover', in Straw, W. *et al.* (eds) *Popular Music: Style and Identity*, Montreal: Centre for Research on Canadian Cultural Industries and Institutions.

Bradley, D. (1992) *Understanding Rock'n'Roll: Popular Music in Britain 1955–1964*, Buckingham: Open University Press.

Brady, L. (1994) *Rock Stars/Pop Stars: A Comprehensive Bibliography, 1955–1994*, Westport, CT: Greenwood Press.

Brake, M. (1985) *Comparative Youth Culture*, London: Routledge & Kegan Paul.

Brand, G. and Scannell, P. (1991) 'Talk, Identity and Performance: *The Tony Blackburn Show*', in Scannell, P. (ed.) *Broadcast Talk*, London: Sage, pp. 201–26.

Brantlinger, P. (1990) *Crusoe's Footprints: Cultural Studies in Britain and America*, London and New York: Routledge.

Breen, M. (1991) 'A Stairway to Heaven Or a Highway to Hell?: Heavy Metal Rock Music in the 1990s', *Cultural Studies*, 5, 2 (May): 191–203.

——(1992) 'Global Entertainment Corporations and a Nation's Music: The Inquiry into the Prices of Sound Recordings', *Media Information Australia*, 64 (May), pp. 31–41.

——(1993) 'Making it Visible: The 1990 Public Inquiry into Australian Music Copyrights', in Frith, S. (ed.) *Music and Copyright*, Edinburgh: Edinburgh University Press, ch. 6.

——(1995) 'The End of the World as We Know It: Popular Music's Cultural Mobility', *Cultural Studies*, 9, 3 (October): 486–504.

——(1999) *Rock Dogs*, London: Pluto Press.

——(2004) 'Busting the Fans: The Internet's Direct Access Relationship' *Popular Music*, 23, 1: 79–82.

Brennan, S. (1996) 'Student Radio: An Alternative Culture', SITES, 33: 87–101.

Brewster, B. and Broughton, F. (1999) *Last Night a DJ Saved My Life: The History of the Disc Jockey*, New York: Grove Press.

Broughton, S., Ellingham, M., Muddyman, D., and Trillo, R. (eds) (1994) *World Music: The Rough Guide*, London: The Rough Guides.

Brown, C.T. (1992) *The Art of Rock and Roll*, 3rd edn, Englewood Cliffs, NJ: Prentice-Hall.

Burnett, R. (1990) 'From a Whisper to a Scream: Music Video and Cultural Form', in Roe, K. and Carlsson, V. (eds), *Popular Music Research*, NORDI-COM, University of Goteborg.

——(1996) *The Global Jukebox: The International Music Industry*, London and New York: Routledge.

Burns, G. (1987) 'A Typology of "Hooks" in Popular Records', *Popular Music and Society*, 6, 1: 1–20 (also on Tagg website).

Butler, M. (2003) 'Taking it Seriously: Intertextuality and Authenticity in Two Covers by the Pet Shop Boys', *Popular Music*, 22, 1: 1–20.

Carney, G. (1990) 'Geography of Music: Inventory and Prospect', *Journal of Cultural Geography*, 10, 2: 35–48.

——(ed.) (2003) *The Sounds of People and Places: A Geography of American Music from Country to Classical and Blues to Bop*, 4th edn, Lanham: Rowman & Littlefield Publishers, Inc.

Carr, I., Fairweather, D., and Priestley, B. (1988) *Jazz: The Essential Companion*, London: Paladin.

Carson, M., Lewis, T., and Shaw, S.M. (2004) *Girls Rock! Fifty Years of Women Making Music*, Lexington, Kentucky: The University Press of Kentucky.

Casey, B., Casey, N., Calver, B., French, L., and Lewis, J. (2002) *Television Studies: The Key Concepts*, London and New York: Routledge.

Cavicchi, D. (1998) *Tramps Like Us: Music and Meaning Among Springsteen Fans*, New York: Oxford University Press.

Cawelti, J. (1971) 'Notes Toward an Aesthetic of Popular Culture', *Journal of Popular Culture*, 5, 2 (fall): 255–68.

Chambers, I. (1985) *Urban Rhythms: Pop Music and Popular Culture*, London: Macmillan.

——(1986) *Popular Culture: The Metropolitan Experience*, London: Methuen.

Chanan, M. (1995) *Repeated Takes: A Short History of Recording and its Effects on Music*, London: Verso.

Chapman, R. (1992) *Selling the Sixties: The Pirates and Pop Music Radio*, London and New York: Routledge.

Chapple, S. and Garofalo, R. (1977) *Rock'n'Roll is Here to Pay: The History and Politics of the Music Industry*, Chicago: Nelson-Hall.

Charlton, K. (1994) *Rock Music Styles: A History*, 2nd edn, Madison, WI: Brown & Benchmark.

Chester, A. (1990) 'Second Thoughts on a Rock Aesthetic: The Band', *New Left Review*, 1970, 62, London; reprinted in Frith, S. and Goodwin, A. (1990) *On Record: Rock, Pop, and The Written Word*.

Chevigny, P. (1991) *Gigs: Jazz and the Cabaret Laws in New York City*, New York: Routledge.

Christenson, P.G. and Roberts, D.F. (1998) *It's Not Only Rock & Roll: Popular Music in the Lives of Adolescents*, Cresskil, NJ: Hampton Press, Inc.

Christgau, R. (1982) *Christgau's Guide: Rock Albums of the '70s*, London: Vermillion.

——(1990) *Christgau's Record Guide: The '80s*, London: Vermillion.

——(1998) *Grown Up All Wrong: 75 Great Rock and Pop Artists from Vaudeville to Techno*, Cambridge and London: Harvard University Press.

Christianen, M. (1995) 'Cycles of Symbolic Production? A New Model to Explain Concentration, Diversity and Innovation in the Music Industry', *Popular Music*, 14, 1: 55–93.

Citron, M. (1993) *Gender and the Musical Canon*, Cambridge: Cambridge University Press.

Clarke, D. (ed.) (1990) *The Penguin Encyclopedia of Popular Music*, London and New York: Penguin.

Clarke, D. (1995) *The Rise and Fall of Popular Music*, London: Viking/The Penguin Group.

Clarke, J. (1976) 'The Skinheads and the Magical Recovery of Community', in Hall, S. and Jefferson, T. (eds) *Resistance Through Rituals: Youth Subcultures in Post-War Britain*, London: Hutchinson/BCCCS.

Clayson, A. (1995) *Beat Merchants*, London: Blandford.

Clayton, M., Herbert, T., and Middleton, R. (eds) (2003) *The Cultural Study of Music: A Critical Introduction*, New York and London: Routledge.

Clifford, J. (1988) *The Predicament of Culture*, Cambridge, Mass: Harvard.

Cline, C. (1992) 'Essays from Bitch: The Women's Rock Newsletter with Bite', in Lewis, L.A. (ed.) *The Adoring Audience: Fan Culture and the Popular Media*, London: Routledge.

Cloonan, M. (1996) *Banned! Censorship of Popular Music in Britain: 1967–92*, Aldershot: Arena.

Cloonan, M. and Garofalo, R. (eds) (2003) *Policing Pop*, Philadelphia: Temple University Press, 2003.

Cloonan, M., Williamson, J. and Frith, S. (2004) 'What is music worth? Some reflections on the Scottish experience', *Popular Music* 23, 2, 205–12.

Cogan, J. and Clark, W. (2003) *Temples of Sound: Inside the Great Recording Studios*, San Francisco: Chronicle Books.

Cohen, Sarah (1991) *Rock Culture in Liverpool: Popular Music in the Making*, Oxford: Clarendon Press.

——(1993) 'Ethnography and Popular Music Studies', *Popular Music*, 12, 2: 123–38.

——(1994a) 'Identity, Place and the "Liverpool Sound"', in Stokes, M. (ed.) *Ethnicity, Identity and Music*, Oxford: Berg.

——(1995) 'Localizing Sound', in Straw, W. *et al.* (eds) *Popular Music: Style and Identity*, Montreal: Centre for Research on Canadian Cultural Industries and Institutions.

——(1998) 'Sounding Out the City: Music and the Sensuous Production of Place', in Leyshon, A., Matless, D. and Revill, G. (eds), *The Place of Music*, New York: The Guilford Press, pp. 269–90.

——(1999) 'Scenes', in Horner, B. and Swiss, T. (eds), *Key Terms in Popular Music and Culture*, Malden, MA and Oxford: Blackwell, pp. 239–50.

Cohen, Stanley (1980) *Folk Devils and Moral Panics*, Oxford: Robertson.

Cohn, N. (1970) *WopBopaLooBopLupBamBoom: Pop From the Beginning*, St Albans: Paladin/Granada.

——(1992) 'Phil Spector', in DeCurtis, A. and Henke, J. (eds) *The Rolling Stone Illustrated History of Rock and Roll*, 3rd edn, New York: Random House, pp. 177–88.

Collis, J. (ed.) (1980) *The Rock Primer*, Harmondsworth: Penguin.

Cook, N. and Everist, M. (eds) (1999) *Rethinking Music* (reprinted with corrections in 2001), Oxford: Oxford University Press

Cooper, B.L. (1981) 'A Popular Music Perspective: Challenging Sexism in the Social Studies Classroom', *The Social Studies*, 71: 1–8.

——(1992) 'A Review Essay and Bibliography of Studies on Rock'n'roll Movies, 1955–1963', *Popular Music and Society*, 16, 1: 85–92.

Cooper, K. and Smay, D. (eds) (2001) *Bubblegum Music is the Naked Truth*, Los Angeles, CA: Feral House.

Corner, J. (2002) 'Sounds Real: Music and Documentary', *Popular Music*, 21, 3: 357–66.

Covach, J. and Boone, G.M. (eds) (1997) *Understanding Rock: Essays in Musical Analysis*, New York: Oxford University Press.

Cowen, T. (1998) *In Praise of Commercial Culture*, Cambridge, Mass. and London: Harvard University Press. (esp. ch. 4: 'From Bach to the Beatles: The Developing Market for Popular Music').

Coyle, M. and Dolan, J. (1999) 'Modelling Authenticity, Authenticating Commercial Models', in Kevin, J.H., Dettmar, K., and Richey, W. (eds) *Reading Rock and Roll: Authenticity, Appropriation, Aesthetics*, New York: Columbia University Press, pp. 17–35.

Crafts, S.D., Cavicchi, D., and Keil, C. and the Music in Daily Life Project (1993) *My Music*, Hanover and London: Wesleyan University Press.

Crisell, A. (1994) *Understanding Radio*, 3rd edn, London and New York: Routledge.

Critcher, C. (2003) *Moral Panics and the Media*, Buckingham and Philadelphia: Open University Press.

Cross, B. (1993) *It's Not About a Salary: Rap, Race and Resistance in Los Angeles*, New York: Verso.

Cunningham, M. (1996) *Good Vibrations: A History of Record Production*, Chessington: Castle Communications.

Cupitt, M., Ramsay, G., and Shelton, L. (1996) *Music, New Music and All That: Teenage Radio in the 90s*, Sydney: Australian Broadcasting Authority.

Curran, J., Morley, D., and Walkerdine, V. (eds) (1996) *Cultural Studies and Communications*, London and New York: Edward Arnold.

Curtis, J. (1987) *Rock Eras: Interpretations of Music and Society 1954–1984*, Bowling Green, OH: Bowling Green State University Press.

Cusic, D. (1990) *The Sound of Light: A History of Gospel Music*, Bowling Green, OH: Bowling Green State University Press.

——(1996) *Music in the Market*, Bowling Green, OH: Bowling Green State University Press.

Cutler, C. (1985) *File under Popular*, London: November Books.

Cyrus, C. (2003) 'Selling an Image: Girl Groups of the 1960s', *Popular Music*, 22, 2: 173–94.

Dancing in the Street (1995), BBC ten-part series on the history of rock.

Dannen, F. (1991) *Hit Men: Power Brokers and Fast Money Inside the Music Business*, New York: Vintage Books.

Davis, S. (1992) *Reggae Bloodlines: In Search of the Music and Culture of Jamaica*, New York: Da Capo Press.

DeCurtis, A. (ed.) (1991) 'Rock and Roll Culture', *South Atlantic Quarterly*, 90, 4.

——(1992) 'Bruce Springsteen', in DeCurtis, A. and Henke, J. (eds) *The Rolling Stone Illustrated History of Rock and Roll*, 3rd edn, New York: Random House, pp. 619–25.

DeCurtis, A. and Henke, J. (eds) (1992a) *The Rolling Stone Illustrated History of Rock and Roll: The Definitive History of the Most Important Artists and their Music*, 3rd edn, New York: Random House.

DeCurtis, A. and Henke, J. (eds) (1992b) *The Rolling Stone Album Guide: Completely New Reviews*, New York: Random House.

Den Tandt, C. (2004) 'From Craft to Corporate Interfacing: Rock Musicianship in the Age of Music Television and Computer-Programmed Music', *Popular Music and Society*, 27, 2: 139–60.

Denisoff, R.S. (1986) *Tarnished Gold: The Record Industry Revisited*, New Brunswick, NJ: Transaction.

Denselow, R. (1990) *When The Music's Over: The Story of Political Pop*, London: Faber and Faber.

DeRogatis, J. (1996) *Kaleidoscope Eyes: Psychedelic Rock from the '60s to the '90s*, NJ: Citadel Press/Carol Publishing.

Dettmar, K. and Richey, W. (eds) (1999) *Reading Rock and Roll: Authenticity, Appropriation, Aesthetics*, New York: Columbia University Press.

Deuleuze, G. (1994) *Difference and Repetition*, London: Athlone Press.

Dickerson, J. (1998) *Women On Top: The Quiet Revolution that's Rocking the American Music Industry*, New York: Billboard Books.

Dixon, W. with D. Snowden (1989) *I Am the Blues: The Willie Dixon Story*, London: Quartet Books.

Doggett, P. (2000) *Are You Ready for the Country Elvis, Dylan, Parsons and the Roots of Country Rock*, London: Viking/Penguin Group.

Doherty, T. (1988) *Teenagers & Teenpics: The Juvenilization of American Movies in the 1950s*, Boston, MA: Unwin Hyman.

Dorland, M. (ed.) (1996) *The Cultural Industries in Canada: Problems, Policies and Prospects*, Toronto: James Lorimer & Company.

Doss, E. (1999) *Elvis Culture: Fans, Faith and Image*, Lawrence, KS: University Press of Kansas.

Downing, D. (1976) *Future Rock*, St Albans: Panther.

Draper, R. (1990) *Rolling Stone Magazine: The Uncensored History*, New York: Doubleday.

Du Gay, P. and Negus, K. (1994) 'The Changing Sites of Sound: Music Retailing and the Composition of Consumers', *Media, Culture and Society*, 16, 3: 395–413.

Duffett, M. (2003) 'False faith or False Comparison: A Critiique of the Religious Interpretation of Elvis Fan Culture', *Popular Music and Society*, 26, 4: 513–22.

Dunaway, D. (2000) 'Digital Radio Production: Towards an Aesthetic', *new media & society*, 2, 1: 29–50.

Dunbar-Hall, P. and Hodge, G. (1993) *A Guide to Rock'n'Pop*, 2nd edn, Marrickville, NSW: Science Press.

Dyer, R. (1990) 'In Defence of Disco', in Frith, S. and Goodwin, A. (eds) *On Record: Rock, Pop, and the Written Word*, New York: Pantheon Books.

Early, G. (2004) *One Nation Under a Groove. Motown and American Culture*, 2nd edn, Ann Arbor: University of Michigan Press.

Eddy, C. (1992) 'The Metal Explosion', in DeCurtis, A. and Henke, J. (eds) *The Rolling Stone Illustrated History of Rock and Roll*, 3rd edn, New York: Random House, pp. 465–73.

Edgar, A. and Sedgwick, P. (eds) (1999) *Key Concepts in Cultural Theory*, London and New York: Routledge.

Ehrlich, D. (1997) *Inside the Music: Conversations with Contemporary Musicians about Spirituality, Creativity, and Consciousness*, Boston, MA and London: Shambhala.

Einarson, J. (2001) *Desperados: The Roots of Country Music*, New York: Cooper Square Press.

Eisenberg, E. (1988) *The Recording Angel: Music, Records and Culture from Aristotle to Zappa*, London: Pan Books.

Eliot, M. (1989) *Rockonomics: The Money Behind the Music*, New York and Toronto: Franklin Watts.

Endres, T.G. (1993) 'A Dramatic Analysis of Family Themes in the Top 100 Country Songs of 1992', *Popular Music and Society*, 17, 4: 29–46.

Ennis, P.H. (1992) *The Seventh Stream: The Emergence of Rock'n'Roll in American Popular Music*, Hanover and London: Wesleyan University Press.

Epstein, J.S. (ed.) (1994) *Adolescents and their Music: If It's Too Loud, You're Too Old*, New York and London: Garland Publishing.

Erlewine, M., Bogdanov, V., and Woodstra, C. (eds) (1995) *All Music Guide to Rock*, San Francisco: Miller Freeman.

Evans, L. (1994) *Women, Sex and Rock'n'Roll: In their Own Words*, London: Pandora/HarperCollins.

Evans, M. (1998). 'Quality Criticism: Music Reviewing in Australian Rock Magazines', *Perfect Beat*, 3, 4 (January): 38–50.

Ewen, S. (1988) *All Consuming Images: The Politics of Style in Contemporary Culture*, New York: Basic Books.

Eyerman, R. and Jamison, A. (1995) 'Social Movements and Cultural Transformation: Popular Music in the 1960s', *Media, Culture and Society*, 17: 449–68.

Fabbri, F. (1999) *Browsing Music Spaces: Categories and the Musical Mind* (paper delivered at IASPM (UK) conference. Reproduced online by permission of the author (www.tagg.org)).

Fairchild, C. (1995) '"Alternative" Music and the Politics of Cultural Autonomy: The Case of Fugazi and the D.C. Scene', *Popular Music and Society*, 19, 1: 17–36.

Farrell, G. (1998) 'The Early Days of the Gramophone Industry in India: Historical, Social, and Musical Perspectives', in Leyshon, A., Matless, D., and Revill, G. (eds), *The Place of Music*, New York: The Guilford Press, pp. 57–82.

Fast, S. (2001) *In the Houses of the Holy: Led Zeppelin and the Power of Rock Music*, Oxford: Oxford University Press.

Featherstone, M. (1987) 'Lifestyle and Consumer Culture', *Theory, Culture and Society*, 4: 55–70.

Felder, R. (1993) *Manic, Pop, Thrill*, Hopewell, NJ: Eco Press.

Fenster, M. (1995) 'Two Stories: Where Exactly is the Local?', in Straw, W. *et al.* (eds) *Popular Music: Style and Identity*, Montreal: Centre for Research on Canadian Cultural Industries and Institutions.

Fink, M. (1989) *Inside the Music Business: Music in Contemporary Life*, New York: Schirmer/Macmillan.

Finnegan, R. (1989) *The Hidden Musicians: Music-Making in an English Town*, Cambridge: Cambridge University Press.

Fiske, J. (1989) *Understanding Popular Culture*, Boston: Unwin Hyman.

——(1992) 'The Cultural Economy of Fandom', in Lewis, L. (ed.) *The Adoring Audience: Fan Culture and the Popular Media*, London: Routledge.

Fitzgerald, J. (1995) 'Motown Crossover Hits 1963–66 and the Creative Process', *Popular Music*, 14, 1: 1–11.

Flanaghan, B. (1987) *Written in my Soul: Rock's Great Songwriters Talk about Creating their Music*, Chicago: Contemporary Books.

Fong-Torres, B. (1991) *Hickory Wind: The Life and Times of Gram Parsons*, New York: Pocket Books.

Ford, C. (2002) 'The Very Best of James Brown?', *Popular Music*, 21, 1: 127–31.

Forde, E. (2004) 'So, What Would the Music Industry Say? Presenting a Case for the Defence', *Popular Music*, 23, 1: 82–5.

Fordham, J. (1991) *Jazz on CD: The Essential Guide*, London: Kyle Cathie.

Forman, M. (2002) *The Hood Comes First: Race, Space, and Place in Rap and Hip-Hop*, Middletown, Connecticut: Wesleyan University Press.

Fornas, J., Lindberg, U., and Sernhelde, O. (1995) *In Garageland: Rock, Youth and Modernity*, London: Routledge.

Fowles, J. (1996) *Advertising and Popular Culture*, Thousand Oaks: Sage.

Fox, A. (1988) *Rock and Pop: Phillips Collectors Guides*, London: Boxtree.

Friedlander, P. (1996) *Rock and Roll: A Social History*, Boulder, CO: Westview Press.

Friedman, T. (1993) 'Milli Vanilli and the Scapegoating of the Inauthentic', *Bad Subjects*, 9.

Frith, S. (1978) *The Sociology of Rock*, London: Constable.

——(1983) *Sound Effects: Youth, Leisure and the Politics of Rock'n'Roll*, London: Constable.

——(1987) 'Towards an Aesthetic of Popular Music', in Leppert, R. and McClary, S. (eds) *Music and Society*, Cambridge: Cambridge University Press, pp. 133–49.

——(ed.) (1988a) *Facing the Music*, New York: Pantheon Books.

——(1988b) *Music for Pleasure: Essays in the Sociology of Pop*, Cambridge: Polity Press.

——(1988c) 'Video Pop: Picking up the Pieces', in Frith, S. (ed.) *Facing the Music*, New York: Pantheon Books, pp. 88–130.

——(ed.) (1989) *World Music, Politics and Social Change*, Manchester: Manchester University Press.

——(ed.) (1993) *Music and Copyright*, Edinburgh: Edinburgh University Press.

——(1996) *Performing Rites: On the Value of Popular Music*, Cambridge, MA: Harvard University Press.

——(2001) 'Pop Music', in Frith, S., Straw, W. and Street, J. (eds), *The Cambridge Companion to Pop and Rock*, Cambridge: Cambridge University Press, pp. 93–108.

——(2002) 'Look! Hear! The Uneasy Relationship of Music and Television', *Popular Music*, 21, 3: 277–90.

Frith, S. and Goodwin, A. (eds) (1990) *On Record: Rock, Pop, and the Written Word*, New York: Pantheon Books; London: Routledge.

Frith, S. and Horne, H. (1987) *Art Into Pop*, London: Methuen.

Frith, S. and McRobbie, A. (1990) 'Rock and Sexuality', in Frith, S. and Goodwin, A. (eds) *On Record: Rock, Pop, and the Written Word*, New York: Pantheon Books, pp. 371–89 (first published 1978).

Frith, S., Straw, W., and Street, J. (eds) (2001) *The Cambridge Companion to Pop and Rock*, Cambridge: Cambridge University Press.

Frith, S. and Street, J. (1992) 'Rock against Racism and Red Wedge', in Garofalo, R. (ed.) *Rockin' the Boat: Mass Music and Mass Movements*, Boston: South End Press.

Fryer, P. (1998) 'Everybody's on Top of the Pops: Popular Music on British Television 1960–1985', *Popular Music and Society*, 21, 2: 71–90.

Gaar, G. (1992) *She's a Rebel: The History of Women in Rock & Roll*, Seattle: Seal Press.

Gabbard, K. (ed.) (1995) *Jazz Among the Discourses*, Durham and London: Duke University Press.

Gaines, D. (1991) *Teenage Wasteland: Suburbia's Dead End Kids*, New York: HarperCollins.

Gaines, J. (1992) *Contested Culture: Image, Voice and the Law*, London: British Film Institute.

Gambaccini, P., Rice, T., and Rice, J. (1995) *The Guinness Book of British Hit Singles: Every Hit Single Since 1952*, 10th edn, Enfield: Guinness Superlatives.

Gamman, L. and Marshment, M. (1988) *The Female Gaze: Women as Viewers of Popular Culture*, London: The Women's Press.

Gammond, P. (ed.) (1991) *The Oxford Companion to Popular Music*, Oxford: Oxford University Press.

Garnham, N. (1987) 'Concepts of Culture: Public Policy and the Cultural Industries', *Cultural Studies*, 1, 1 (January): 23–37.

——(1990) *Capitalism and Communication: Global Culture and the Economics of Information*, London: Sage.

Garofalo, R. (1992a) 'Understanding Mega-Events', in Garofalo, R. (ed.) *Rockin' the Boat: Mass Music and Mass Movements*, Boston: South End Press.

——(ed.) (1992b) *Rockin' the Boat: Mass Music and Mass Movements*, Boston: South End Press.

——(1993) 'Whose World, What Beat: The Transnational Music Industry, Identity and Cultural Imperialism', *The World of Music*, 35, 2: 16–32.

——(1994) 'Culture versus Commerce: The Marketing of Black Popular Music', *Public Culture*, 7: 275–87.

——(1997) *Rockin' Out: Popular Music in the USA*, Needham Heights, MA: Allyn & Bacon.

——(2003) 'I Want My MP3: Who Owns Internet Music?', in Cloonan, M. and Garofalo, R. (eds) *Policing Pop*, Philadelphia: Temple University Press.

Garon, P. (1975) *Blues and the Poetic Spirit*, London: Eddison.

Garratt, S. (1998) *Adventures in Wonderland: A Decade of Club Culture*, London: Headline.

Gass, G. (1991) 'Why Don't We Do It in the Classroom?', *South Atlantic Quarterly*, 90, 4.

Gatten, J. (1995) *Rock Music Scholarship: An Interdisciplinary Bibliography*, Westport, CT: Greenwood Press.

Gelatt, R. (1977) *The Fabulous Phonograph, 1877–1977*, New York: Macmillan.

Gelder, K. and Thornton, S. (eds) (1997) *The Subcultures Reader*, London and New York: Routledge.

Gendron, B. (1986) 'Theodor Adorno Meets the Cadillacs', in Modleski, T. (ed.) *Studies in Entertainment*, Bloomington: Indiana University Press, pp. 18–36.

——(2002) *Between Montmartre and the Mudd Club: Popular Music and the Avant-Garde*, Chicago and London: The University of Chicago Press.

George, N. (1985) *Where Did Our Love Go?*, New York: St Martin's Press.

——(1989) *The Death of Rhythm & Blues*, New York: Pantheon Books.

Geyrhalter, T. (1996) 'Effeminacy, Camp and Sexual Subversion in Rock: The Cure and Suede', *Popular Music*, 15, 2: 217–24.

Gilbert, J. and Pearson, E. (1999) *Discographies: Dance Music, Culture and the Politics of Sound*, London and New York: Routledge.

Gill, R. (1996) 'Ideology, Gender and Popular Radio: A Discourse Analytic Approach', in Baehr, H. and Gray, A. (eds) *Turning It On: A Reader in Women and Media*, London: Arnold.

Gill, S. and Law, D. (1988) *The Global Political Economy: Perspectives, Problems, and Policies*, London: Wheatsheaf.

Gillet, C. (1983) *The Sound of the City: The Rise of Rock and Roll*, revised edn, London: Souvenir Press.

Gilroy, P. (1993) *The Black Atlantic: Modernity and Double Consciousness*, Cambridge, MA: Harvard University Press.

——(1997) 'Diaspora, Utopia, and the Critique of Capitalism', in Gelder, K. and Thornton, S. (eds) *The Subcultures Reader*, London and New York: Routledge.

Goertzel, B. (1991) 'The Rock Guitar Solo: From Expression to Simulation', *Popular Music and Society*, 15, 1: 91–101.

Golding, P. and Murdoch, G. (1991) 'Culture, Communications and Political Economy', in Curran, J. and Gurevitch, M. (eds) *Mass Media and Communications*, London: Edward Arnold, pp. 15–32.

Goode, E. and Ben-Yehuda, N. (1994) *Moral Panics: The Social Construction of Deviance*, Oxford and Cambridge, MA: Blackwell.

Goodwin, A. (1990) 'Sample and Hold: Pop Music in the Digital Age of Reproduction', in Frith, S. and Goodwin, A. (eds) *On Record: Rock, Pop, and the Written Word*, New York: Pantheon Books, pp. 258–74.

——(1991) 'Popular Music and Postmodern Theory', *Cultural Studies*, 5, 2 (May): 174–90.

——(1993) *Dancing in the Distraction Factory: Music Television and Popular Culture*, Oxford, Minn.: University of Minnesota Press.

——(1998) 'Drumming and Memory: Scholarship, Technology, and Music-Making', in Swiss, T., Sloop, J., and Herman, A. (eds), *Mapping the Beat: Popular Music and Contemporary Theory*, Malden, MA and Oxford: Blackwell, pp. 121–36.

Gorman, P. (2001) *In Their Own Write: Adventures in the Music Press*, London: Sanctuary Publishing Limited.

Gracyk, T. (1996) *Rhythm and Noise: An Aesthetics of Rock*, Durham and London: Duke University Press.

——(2001) *I Wanna Be Me: Rock Music and the Politics of Identity*, Philadelphia: Temple University Press.

Grant, B. (1986) 'The Classic Hollywood Musical and the "Problem" of Rock'n'Roll', *Journal of Popular Film and Television*, 13, 4 (winter): 195–205.

Greco, A.N. (ed.) (2000) *The Media and Entertainment Industries: Reading in Mass Communications*, Boston, MA: Allyn & Bacon.

Green, L. (2001) *How Popular Musicians Learn: A Way Ahead for Music Education*, Aldershot: Ashgate.

Gribin, A.J. and Schiff, M. (1992) *Doo-Wop: The Forgotten Third of Rock 'N' Roll*, Iola, WI: Krause Publications (includes a huge 'sonography').

Gridley, M. (1997) *Jazz Styles: History and Analysis*, Upper Saddle River, NJ: Prentice-Hall.

Groce, S.B. (1991) 'On the Outside Looking In: Professional Socialization and the Process of Becoming a Songwriter', *Popular Music and Society*, 15, 1.

Gronow, P. and Saunio, I. (1998) *An International History of the Recording Industry*, London and New York: Cassell.

Grossberg, L. (1986) 'Teaching the Popular', in Nelson, C. (ed.) *Theory in the Classroom*, Urbana, IL: University of Illinois Press.

——(1992a) *We Gotta Get Out of this Place: Popular Conservatism and Postmodern Culture*, New York: Routledge.

——(1992b) 'Is There a Fan in the House? The Affective Sensibility of Fandom', in Lewis, L. (ed.) *The Adoring Audience: Fan Culture and Popular Media*, London and New York: Routledge.

——(1993) 'The Media Economy of Rock Culture: Cinema, Post-Modernity and Authenticity', in Frith, S. *et al.* (eds) *Sound and Vision: The Music Video Reader*, London: Routledge, pp. 185–209.

——(2002) 'Reflections of a Disappointed Popular Music Scholar', in Beebe, R., Fulbrook, D., and Saunders, B. (eds) *Rock Over the Edge*, pp. 25–59.

Grossberg, L., Nelson, C., and Treichler, P. (eds) (1992) *Cultural Studies*, London and New York: Routledge.

Guilbault, J. (1993) *Zouk: World Music in the West Indies*, Chicago: University of Chicago Press.

Guralnick, P. (1989) *Feel Like Going Home*, London: Omnibus Press.

——(1991) *Sweet Soul Music: Rhythm and Blues and the Southern Dream of Freedom*, London: Penguin.

——(1992) 'Rockabilly', in DeCurtis, A. and Henke, J. (eds) *The Rolling Stone Illustrated History of Rock and Roll*, 3rd edn, New York: Random House, pp. 67–72.

——(2003) *Lost Highway: Journeys and Arrivals of American Musicians*, Edinburgh: Canongate.

Gurevitch, M., Bennett, T., Curran, J., and Woollacott, J. (eds) (1982) *Culture, Society and the Media*, London: Methuen.

Gurley, T. and Pfefferle, W. (1996) *Plug In: The Guide to Music on the Net*, Englewood Cliffs, NJ: Prentice-Hall.

Guterman, J. (1992) *The Best Rock-and-Roll Records of All Time: A Fan's Guide to the Stuff You Love*, New York: A Citadel Press Book.

Guterman, J. and O'Donnell, O. (1991) *The Worst Rock and Roll Records of All Time: A Fan's Guide to the Stuff You Love to Hate*, New York: Carol.

Haggerty, G. (1995) *A Guide to Popular Music Reference Books: An Annotated Bibliography*, Westport, CT: Greenwood Press.

Hakanen, E. and Wells, A. (1993) 'Music Preference and Taste Cultures Among Adolescents', *Popular Music and Society*, 17, 1: 55–69.

Hall, D. (1994) 'New Age Music: A Voice of Liminality in Postmodern Popular Culture', *Popular Music and Society*, 18, 2: 13–21.

Hall, S. (1993) 'Minimal Selves', in Gray, A. and McGuigan, J. (eds) *Studying Culture*, London: Edward Arnold, pp. 134–8.

Hall, S. and Jefferson, T. (eds) (1976) *Resistance Through Rituals: Youth Subcultures in Post-War Britain*, London: Hutchinson/BCCCS.

Hall, S. and Whannel, P. (1964) *The Popular Arts*, London: Hutchison.

Hall, S., Critcher, C., Jefferson, T., Clarke, J., and Roberts, R. (1978) *Policing the Crisis*, London: Macmillan.

Hamm, C. (1995) *Putting Popular Music in Its Place*, Cambridge: Cambridge University Press.

Hanke, R. (1998) '"Yo Quiero Mi MTV!": Making Music Television for Latin America' in Swiss, T., Sloop, J., and Herman, A. (eds), *Mapping the Beat: Popular Music and Contemporary Theory*, Malden, MA and Oxford: Blackwell, pp. 219–46.

Hansen, Barry (1992a) 'Doo-Wop', in DeCurtis, A. and Henke, J. (eds) *The Rolling Stone Illustrated History of Rock and Roll*, 3rd edn, New York: Random House, pp. 92–101.

——(1992b) 'Rhythm and Blues', in DeCurtis, A. and Henke, J. (eds) *The Rolling Stone Illustrated History of Rock and Roll*, 3rd edn, New York: Random House, pp. 17–20.

Hardy, P. and Laing, D. (eds) (1990) *The Faber Companion to Twentieth Century Popular Music*, London: Faber and Faber.

Harker, D. (1980) *One For The Money: Politics and Popular Song*, London: Hutchinson.

Harley, R. (1993) 'Beat in the System', in Bennett, T., Frith, S., Grossberg, L., Shepherd, J., and Turner, G. (eds) *Rock and Popular Music: Politics, Policies, Institutions*, London: Routledge.

Harris, J. (2004) *The Last Party: Britpop, Blair and the Demise of English Rock*, London: Harper Perennial.

Harron, M. (1988) 'Pop as a Commodity', in Frith, S. (ed.) *Facing the Music*, New York: Pantheon Books, pp. 173–220.

Haslam, D. (2001) *Adventures on the Wheels of Steel: The Rise of the Superstar DJ*, London: Fourth Estate.

Hatch, D. and Millward, S. (1987) *From Blues to Rock: An Analytical History of Rock Music*, Manchester: Manchester University Press.

Hawkins, S. (2002) *Settling the Pop Score: Pop Texts and Identify Politics*, Aldershot and Burlington: Ashgate.

Hayward, P. (ed.) (1992) *From Pop to Punk to Postmodernism: Popular Music and Australian Culture from the 1960s to the 1990s*, Sydney: Allen & Unwin.

——(1995) 'Enterprise on the New Frontier: Music, Industry and the Internet', *Convergence*, 1, 2.

——(ed.) (2004) *Off The Planet: Music, Sound and Science Fiction Cinema*, London: John Libbey Perfect Beat Publications.

Hayward, P., Mitchell, T., and Shuker, R. (eds) (1994) *North Meets South: Popular Music in Aotearoa/New Zealand*, Sydney: Perfect Beat Publications.

Hayward, P. and Orrock, G. (1995) 'Window of Opportunity: CD-ROMs, the International Music Industry and Early Australian Initiatives', CONVERGENCE, 1, 1: 61–79.

Hayward, S. (1996) *Key Concepts in Cinema Studies*, London and New York: Routledge.

Hebdige, D. (1979) *Subculture: The Meaning of Style*, London: Methuen.

——(1988) *Hiding in the Light: On Images and Things*, London: Comedia/Routledge.

——(1990) *Cut 'N' Mix: Culture, Identity, and Caribbean Music*, London: Comedia/Routledge.

Henderson, L. (1993) 'Justify Our Love: Madonna and the Politics of Queer Sex', in Schwichtenberg, C. (ed.) *The Madonna Connection: Representational Politics, Subcultural Identities, and Cultural Theory*, St Leonards, NSW: Allen & Unwin, pp. 107–28.

Hendy, D. (2003) *Radio in the Global Age*, London: Polity Press.

Hennion, A. (2003) 'Music and Mediation: Towards a New Sociology of Music', in Clayton, M., Herbert T., and Middleton, R. (eds) *The Cultural Study of Music: A Critical Introduction*, New York and London: Routledge, pp. 80–91.

Herbert, T. (1998) 'Victorian Brass Bands: Class, Taste, and Space', in Leyshon, A., Matless, D., and Revill, G. (eds), *The Place of Music*, New York: The Guilford Press, pp. 104–28.

Herman, E. and McChesney, R. (1997). *The Global Media: The New Missionaries of Global Capitalism*, London: Cassell.

Herman, G. and Hoare, I. (1979) 'The Struggle for Song: A Reply to Leon Rosselson', in Gardner, C. (ed.) *Media, Politics and Culture*, London: Macmillan.

Herzhaft, G. (1992) *Encyclopedia of the Blues*, Fayetteville: University of Arkansas Press.

Hesmondhalgh, D. (1996a) 'Is This What You Call Change? Post-Fordism, Flexibility and the Music Industries', *Media, Culture and Society*, 18.

——(1996b) 'Rethinking Popular Music after Rock and Soul', in Curran, J., Morley, D., and Walkerdine, V. (eds) *Cultural Studies and Communications*, London and New York: Arnold.

——(1997) 'Post-Punk's Attempt to Democratise the Music Industry: The Success and Failure of Rough Trade', *Popular Music*, 16, 3: 255–92.

——(2002) *The Cultural Industries*, London: Sage.

Heylin, C. (ed.) (1992) *The Penguin Book of Rock and Roll Writing*, London: Penguin.

——(1993) *From the Velvets to the Voidoids: A Pre-Punk History for a Post-Punk World*, London: Penguin.

——(1995) *Bootleg: The Secret History of the Other Recording History*, New York: St Martin's Press.

Hicks, M. (1999) *Sixties Rock. Garage, Psychedelic, and Other Satisfactions*, Urbana and Chicago: University of Illinois Press.

Hill, D. (1986) *Designer Boys and Material Girls: Manufacturing the 80's Pop Dream*, London: Blandford Press.

Hill, T. (1991) 'The Enemy Within: Censorship in Rock Music in the 1950s', in DeCurtis, A. (ed.) 'Rock and Roll Culture', *South Atlantic Quarterly*, 90, 4.

Hills, M. (2002) *Fan Cultures*, London and New York: Routledge.

Hirshey, G. (1985) *Nowhere to Run: The Story of Soul Music*, New York: Penguin.

Hoggart, R. (1957) *The Uses of Literacy*, Harmondsworth: Penguin.

Hollows, J. and Milestone, K. (1998) 'Welcome to Dreamsville: A History and Geography of Northern Soul', in Leyshon, A., Matless, D., and Revill, G. (eds) *The Place of Music*, New York: The Guilford Press, pp. 83–103.

Holm-Hudson, K. (ed.) (2002) *Progressive Rock Reconsidered*, New York and London: Routledge.

Holmes, T. (2002) *Electronic and Experimental Music: Pioneers in Technology and Composition*, 2nd edn, London & New York: Routledge.

Homan, S. (1998) 'After the Law: Sydney's Phonecian Club, the New South Wales Premier and the Death of Anna Wood', *Perfect Beat*, 4, 1, July: 56–83.

——(2000) 'Losing the Local: Sydney and the Oz Rock Tradition', *Popular Music*, 19, 1: 31–50.

——(2002) 'Access All Era: Careers, Creativity and the Australian Tribute Band', *Perfect Beat*, 5, 4: 45–59.

——(2003) *The Mayor's a Square: Live Music and Law and Order in Sydney*, Newtown, NSW: LCP.

Homan, S, (ed.) (2006) *Access All Eras: Tribute Bands and Global Pop*, Milton Keynes: Open University Press.

Hornby, N. (1995) *High Fidelity*, New York: Riverheads Books.

Hornby, N. and Schaffer, B. (eds) (2001) *Da Capo Best Music Writing 2001: The Year's Finest Writing on Rock, Pop, Jazz, Country & More*, Cambridge, Mass: Da Capo Press.

Horner, B. and Swiss, T. (eds) (1999) *Key Terms in Popular Music and Culture*, Malden, MA and Oxford: Blackwell.

Horowitz, D. (1993) 'The Perils of Commodity Fetishism: Tin Pan Alley's Portrait of the Romantic Marketplace, 1920–1942', *Popular Music and Society*, 17, 1: 37–53.

Hoskyns, B. (ed.) (2003) *The Sound and the Fury: 40 Years of Classic Rock Journalism – A Rock's Backpages Reader*, London: Bloomsbury.

Houghton, M. (1980) 'British Beat', in Collins, J. (ed.) *The Rock Primer*, Harmondsworth: Penguin, pp. 149–78.

Hull, G. (2004) *The Recording Industry*, 2nd edn, New York; London: Routledge.

Hutnyk, J. (1997) 'Adorno at Womad: South Asian Crossovers and the Limits of Hybridity-Talk', in Werbner, P. and Madood, T. (eds) *Debating Cultural Hybridity: Multi-Cultural Industries and the Policies of Anti-Racism*, London and New Jersey: Zed Books, pp. 106–36.

IFPI (1990) *World Record Sales 1969–1990: A Statistical History of the Recording Industry*, ed. and compiled M. Hung and E.G. Morencos, London: International Federation of the Phonographic Industry.

Inglis, I. (2001) '"Nothing You Can See That Isn't Shown": The Album Covers of the Beatles', *Popular Music*, 20, 1: 83–98.

Irvin, J. (ed.) (2000) *The Mojo Collection: The Ultimate Music Companion*, Edinburgh: Mojo Books.

Jameson, F. (1984) 'Postmodernism, or the Cultural Logic of Late Capitalism', *New Left Review*, 146 (July/August): 53–93.

Jenkins, H. (1997) 'Television Fans, Poachers, Nomads', in Gelder, K. and Thornton, S. (eds) *The Subcultures Reader*, London and New York: Routledge.

Jipson, A. (1994) 'Why Athens?' *Popular Music and Society*, 18, 3: 19–31.

Johnson, B. (2000) *The Inaudible Music: Jazz, Gender and Australian Modernity*, Sydney: Currency Press.

Johnson, P. (1996) *Straight Outa Bristol: Massive Attack, Portishead, Tricky and the Roots of Hip Hop*, London: Sceptre (Hodder & Stoughton).

Jones, A. and Kantonen, J. (1999) *Saturday Night Forever: The Story of Disco*, Edinburgh and London: Mainstream Publishing.

Jones, Simon (1988) *Black Culture, White Youth: The Reggae Tradition from JA to UK*, London: Macmillan.

Jones, Simon and Schumacher, T. (1992) 'Muzak: On Functional Music and Power', *Critical Studies in Mass Communications*, 9: 156–69.

Jones, Steve (1992) *Rock Formation: Music, Technology, and Mass Communication*, Newbury Park, CA: Sage.

——(1993) 'Music and Copyright in the USA', in Frith, S. (ed.) *Music and Copyright*, Edinburgh: Edinburgh University Press, ch. 4.

——(1995) 'Recasting Popular Music Studies' Conceptions of the Authentic and the Local in Light of Bell's Theorem', in Straw, W. *et al.* (eds) *Popular Music: Style and Identity*, Montreal: Centre for Research on Canadian Cultural Industries and Institutions.

——(2000) 'Music and the Internet', *Popular Music*, 19, 2: 217–30.

——(2002) 'Music that Moves: Popular Music, Distribution and Network Technologies', *Cultural Studies*, 16, 2: 213–32.

Jones, Steve and Lenhart, A. (2004) 'Music Downloading and Listening: Finding from the Pew Internet and American Life Project', *Popular Music*, 27, 2: 221–40.

Kahn-Harris, K. (2003) 'Death Metal and the Limits of Musical Expression', in Cloonan, M. and Garofalo, R. (eds) *Policing Pop*, Philadelphia: Temple University Press.

Kalinak, K. (1992) *Setting the Score: Music and the Classical Hollywood Film, Madison*, WI: University of Wisconsin Press.

Kaplan, E. A. (1987) *Rocking Around the Clock: Music Television, Postmodernism, and Consumer Culture*, New York: Methuen.

Kassabian, A (1999) 'Popular', in Horner, B. and Swiss, T. (eds), *Key Terms in Popular Music and Culture*, Malden, MA and Oxford: Blackwell, pp. 113–23.

Kaufman, G. (1997) 'Steering Sub Pop Into the Future', *Addicted to Noise*, 3.02.

Kay, H. (1992) *Rock'N'Roll Collectables: An Illustrated History of Rock Memorabilia*, London: Pyramid Books/Octopus Press.

Kealy, E. (1979) 'From Craft to Art: The Case of Sound Mixers and Popular Music', in Frith, S. and Goodwin, A. (eds) *On Record*, pp. 207–20.

Keightley, K. (2003) 'Album; Album Cover; Concept Album; Cover Version', in Shepherd *et al.* (eds), *The Continuum Encyclopedia of Popular Music, Volume One: Media, Industry and Society*, London and New York: Continuum, pp. 612–17.

Keil, C. (1966) *Urban Blues*, Chicago: University of Chicago Press.

Keil, C. and Feld, S. (1994) *Music Grooves*, Chicago and London: University of Chicago Press.

Kelly, K. and McDonnel, E. (1999) *Stars Don't Stand Still in the Sky*, London: Routledge.

Kempster, C. (1996) *History of House*, London: Sanctuary.

Kennedy, D. (1990) 'Frankenchrist versus the State: The New Right, Rock Music and the Case of Jello Biafra', *Journal of Popular Culture*, 24, 1: 131–48.

Kennedy, R. and McNutt, R. (1999) *Little Labels – Big Sound: Small Record Companies and the Rise of American Music*, Bloomington and Indianapolis, IN: Indiana University Press.

Kenney, W. (1993) *Chicago Jazz: A Cultural History, 1904–1930*, New York: Oxford University Press.

Kenney, W.H. (1999) *Recorded Music in American Life: The Phonograph and Popular Memory, 1890–1945*, New York and Oxford: Oxford University Press.

Kerman, K. 'A Few Canonical Variations', in Robert von Hallberg (ed.) (1984) *CANONS*, Chicago and London: University of Chicago Press, pp.177–96.

Kirschner, T. (1994) 'The Lalalooziation of American Youth', *Popular Music and Society*, 18, 1: 69–89.

——(1998) 'Studying Rock: Towards a Materialist Ethnography', in Swiss, T., Sloop, J., and Herman, A. (eds), *Mapping the Beat: Popular Music and Contemporary Theory*, Malden, MA and Oxford: Blackwell, pp. 247–68.

Klosterman, C. (2002) *Fargo Rock City: A Heavy Metal Odyssey in Rural North Dakota*, London: Simon & Schuster UK Ltd.

Kocandrle, M. (1988) *The History of Rock and Roll: A Selective Discography*, Boston: G.K. Hall.

Koizumi, K. (2002) 'Popular Music, Gender and High School Pupils in Japan: Personal Music in School and Leisure Sites', *Popular Music*, 21, 1: 107–20.

Kong, L. (1995) 'Popular Music in Singapore: Exploring Local Culture, Global Resources, and Regional Identities', *Environment and Planning: Society and Space*, 14, 3 (June): 273–92.

Kotarba, J. A. (1994) 'The Postmodernization of Rock and Roll Music: The Case of Metallica', in Epstein, J.S. (ed.) *Adolescents and their Music: If it's too Loud, You're too Old*, New York and London: Garland Publishing.

Krims, A. (2000) *Rap Music and the Poetics of Identity*, Cambridge: Cambridge University Press.

Kruse, H. (1993) 'Subcultural Identity in Alternative Music Culture', *Popular Music*, 12, 1: 33–41.

Laing, D. (1986) 'The Music Industry and the "Cultural Imperialism" Thesis', *Media, Culture and Society*, 8: 331–41.

——(1988) 'The Grain of Punk: An Analysis of the Lyrics', in McRobbie, A. (ed.) *Zoot Suits and Second Hand Dresses: An Anthology of Fashion and Music*, Boston: Unwin & Hyman, pp. 74–101.

——(1990) 'Record sales in the 1980s', *Popular Music*, 9, 2.

——(1992) '"Sadeness", Scorpions and Single Markets: National and Transnational Trends in European Popular Music', *Popular Music*, 11, 2: 127–40.

Lanza, J. (1995) *Elevator Music: A Surreal History of Muzak Easy-Listening, and Other Moodsong*, New York: Picador.

Larkin, C. (ed.) (1993) *The Guinness Encyclopedia of Popular Music*, concise edn, London: Guinness.

——(ed.) (1995) *The Guinness Who's Who of Indie New Wave*, 2nd edn, London: Guinness.

Lawrence, T. (2003) *Love Saves the Day: A History of American Dance Music Culture, 1970–1979*, Durham and London: Duke University Press.

Lealand, G. (1988) *A Foreign Egg in our Nest? American Popular Culture in New Zealand*, Wellington: Victoria University Press.

Lee, S. (1995) 'An Examination of Industrial Practice: The Case of Wax Trax! Records', in Straw, W. *et al.* (eds) *Popular Music: Style and Identity*, Montreal: Centre for Research on Canadian Cultural Industries and Institutions.

Lemish, D. (2003) 'Spice World: Constructing Femininity the Popular Way', *Popular Music and Society*, 26, 1: 17–29.

Lentini, P. (2003) 'Punk's Origins: Anglo-American Syncreticism', *Journal of Intercultural Studies*, 24, 2: 153–74.

Leonard, M. (1997) 'Rebel Girl, You are the Queen of My World: Feminism, "Subculture" and Grrrl Power', in Whiteley, S. (ed.), *Sexing the Groove: Popular Music and Gender*, London and New York: Routledge, pp. 230–56.

Leonard, M. and Strachan, R. (2003) 'Music Press', 'Music Journalism', entries in Shepherd *et al.* (eds), *The Continuum Encyclopedia of Popular Music, Volume One: Media, Industry and Society*, London and New York: Continuum.

Levine, D. (1995) *Wealth and Freedom: An Introduction to Political Economy*, Cambridge University Press.

Levy, S. (2003) *Ready, Steady, Go! Swinging London and the Invention of Cool*, London and New York: Fourth Estate.

Lewis, G.H. (ed.) (1993) *All That Glitters: Country Music in America*, Bowling Green, OH: Bowling Green State University Press.

Lewis, L. (1990) *Gender Politics and MTV: Voicing the Difference*, Philadelphia: Temple University Press.

——(ed.) (1992) *The Adoring Audience: Fan Culture and the Popular Media*, London: Routledge.

Leyser, B. (1994) *Rock Stars/Pop Stars: A Comprehensive Bibliography 1955–1994*, Westport, CT: Greenwood Press.

Leyshon, A., Matless, D., and Revill, G. (eds) (1998) *The Place of Music*, New York and London: The Guilford Press.

Ling, J. (2003) 'Is "World Music" the "Classic Music" of Our Time?', *Popular Music*, 22, 2: 235.

Lipsitz, G. (1994) *Dangerous Crossroads: Popular Music, Postmodernism and the Poetics of Place*, London and New York: Verso.

Longhurst, B. (1995) *Popular Music and Society*, Cambridge: Polity Press.

Lopes, Paul (1992) 'Aspects of Production and Consumption in the Music Industry, 1967–1990', *American Sociological Review*, 57, 1: 46–71.

Lull, J. (ed.) (1992) *Popular Music and Communication*, 2nd edn, Newbury Park, CA: Sage.

——(1995) *Media, Communications, Culture: A Global Approach*, Cambridge: Polity Press.

Lysloff, R.T.A. and Gay, Jr., L.C., (eds) (2003) *Music and Technoculture*, Connecticut: Wesleyan University Press.

Macan, E. (1997) *Rocking the Classics: English Progressive Rock and the Counterculture*, New York; Oxford: OUP.

McAleer, Dave (1994) *BEATBOOM! Pop Goes the Sixties*, London: Hamlyn.

McClary, S. (1991) *Feminine Endings: Music, Gender, and Sexuality*, Oxford, Minn.: University of Minnesota Press.

McClary, S. and Walser, R. (1990) 'Start Making Sense! Musicology Wrestles with Rock', in Frith, S. and Goodwin, A. (eds) *On Record: Rock, Pop, and the Written Word*, New York: Pantheon Books, pp. 277–92.

McDonnell, Judith (1992) 'Rap Music: Its Role as an Agent of Change', *Popular Music and Society*, 16, 3 (Fall): 89–108.

McEwen, J. (1992) 'Funk', in DeCurtis, A. and Henke, J. (eds) *The Rolling Stone Illustrated History of Rock and Roll*, 3rd edn, New York: Random House (includes discography).

McEwen, J. and Miller, J. (1992) 'Motown', in DeCurtis, A. and Henke, J. (eds) *The Rolling Stone Illustrated History of Rock and Roll*, 3rd edn, New York: Random House, pp. 277–92.

McIntyre, P. (2003) *Creativity and Cultural Reproduction: A Study of Contemporary Western Popular Music Songwriting* (Ph.D.), Department of Media and Communication, Macquarie University, Sydney.

McIver, J. (2000) *Extreme Metal*, London: Omnibus Books.

McLaughlin, N. and McLoone, M. (2000) 'Hybridity and National Musics: The Case of Irish Rock Music', *Popular Music*, 19, 2: 181–99.

McLeay, C. (1994) 'The "Dunedin Sound": New Zealand Rock and Cultural Geography', *Perfect Beat*, 2, 1 (July): 38–50.

McLeod, K. (2001) '*1/2: A Critique of Rock Criticism in North America', *Popular Music*, 20, 1: 29–46.

McNeil, L. and McCain, G. (1996) *Please Kill Me: The Uncensored Oral History of Punk*, New York: Grove Press.

McRobbie, A. (ed.) (1988) *Zoot Suits and Second Hand Dresses: An Anthology of Fashion and Music*, Boston: Unwin & Hyman.

——(1991) *Feminism and Youth Culture: From 'Jackie' to 'Just Seventeen'*, Basingstoke: Macmillan.

McRobbie, A. and Garber, J. (1976) 'Girls and Subcultures: An Exploration', in Hall, S. and Jefferson, T. (eds) *Resistance Through Rituals: Youth Subcultures in Post-War Britain*, London: Hutchinson/BCCCS.

Malbon, B. (1999) *Clubbing: Dancing, Ecstasy and Vitality*, London: Routledge.

Malone, B.C. (1985) *Country Music USA*, Austin: University of Texas Press.

Mann, B. (2000) *I Want My MP3! How to Download, Rip, and Play Digital Music*, New York: McGraw-Hill.

Marcus, G. (1989) *Lipstick Traces: A Secret History of the Twentieth Century*, Cambridge, MA: Harvard University Press.

——(1991a) *Dead Elvis: A Chronicle of a Cultural Obsession*, New York: Penguin.

——(1991b) *Mystery Train*, 4th edn, New York: Penguin (first published 1977).

——(1992) 'Anarchy in the UK', in DeCurtis, A. and Henke, J. (eds) *The Rolling Stone Illustrated History of Rock and Roll*, 3rd edn, New York: Random House, pp. 594–608.

Marsh, D. (1983) *Before I Get Old: The Story of The Who*, New York: St Martin's Press.

——(1987) *Glory Days: A Biography of Bruce Springsteen*, New York: Pantheon Books.

——(1989) *The Heart of Rock and Soul: The 1001 Greatest Singles Ever Made*, New York: Plume/Penguin.

——(1992) 'The Who', in DeCurtis, A. and Henke, J. (eds) *The Rolling Stone Illustrated History of Rock and Roll*, 3rd edn, New York: Random House, pp. 395–406.

——(1993) *Louie, Louie: The History and Mythology of the World's Most Famous Rock Song*, New York: Hyperion.

Marsh, G. and Callingham, G. (eds) (2003) *Blue Note Album Cover Art: The Ultimate Collection*, San Francisco: Chronicle Books.

Marshall, Lee (2003) 'For and Against the Record Industry: An Introduction to Bootleg Collectors and Tape Traders', *Popular Music* 22, 1: 57–72.

Marshall, L. (2004) *Music and Copyright*, London: Routledge.

Marshall, P.D. (1997) *Celebrity and Power: Fame in Contemporary Culture*, Minneapolis, NM/London: University of Minnesota Press.

Martin, C. (1993) 'Traditional Criticism of Popular Music and the Making of a Lip-synching Scandal', *Popular Music and Society*, 17, 4: 63–81.

Mellers, W. (1974) *Twilight of the Gods: The Beatles in Retrospect*, London: Faber and Faber.

——(1986) *Angels of the Night: Popular Female Singers of Our Time*, Oxford: Blackwell.

Melley, G. (1970) *Revolt Into Style*, London: Penguin.

Meyer, D. (1995) 'The Real Cooking is Done in the Studio: Toward a Context for Rock Criticism', *Popular Music and Society*, 19, 1: 1–15.

Middleton, R. (1990) *Studying Popular Music*, Milton Keynes: Open University Press.

Miguel, San, G. (2002) *Tejano Proud: Tex-Mex Music in the Twentieth Century*, College Station: Texas A&M University Press.

Miles, B. (1997) *Paul McCartney: Many Years From Now*, London: Vintage.

Millard, A.J. (1995) *America on Record: A History of Recorded Sound*, Cambridge: Cambridge University Press.

Miller, J. (1992) 'The Beach Boys', in DeCurtis, A. and Henke, J. (eds) *The Rolling Stone Illustrated History of Rock and Roll*, 3rd edn, New York: Random House, pp. 192–8.

——(1999) *Flowers in the Dustbin: The Rise of Rock and Roll, 1947–1997*, New York: Simon & Schuster.

Mitchell, T. (1996) *Popular Music and Local Identity*, London and New York: Leicester University Press.

——(1997) 'New Zealand on the Internet: A Study of the NZPOP Mailing List', *Perfect Beat*, 3, 2: 77–95.

——(ed.) (2001) *Global Noise: Rap and Hip-Hop Outside the USA*, Middletown, Connecticut: Wesleyan University Press.

Mitsui, T. and Hosokawa, S. (eds) (1998) *Karaoke Around the World: Global Technology, Local Singing*, London and New York: Routledge.

Montgomery, M. (1986) 'DJ Talk', *Media, Culture and Society*, 8, 4 (October): 421–41.

Moore, A. (2002) 'Authenticity as Authentication', *Popular Music*, 21, 2: 225–36.

Moore, A.F. (2001) *Rock: The Primary Text – Developing a Musicology of Rock*, 2nd edn, Buckingham, PA: Open University Press.

Morley, D. (1992) *Television, Audiences, and Cultural Studies*, London: Routledge.

Morley, P. (2003) *Words and Music: A History of Pop in the Shape of a City*, London: Bloomsbury.

Morthland, J. (1992a) 'The Payola Scandal', in DeCurtis, A. and Henke, J. (eds) *The Rolling Stone Illustrated History of Rock and Roll*, 3rd edn, New York: Random House, pp. 121–3.

——(1992b) 'The Rise of Top 40 AM', in DeCurtis, A. and Henke, J. (eds) *The Rolling Stone Illustrated History of Rock and Roll*, 3rd edn, New York: Random House, pp. 102–6.

——(1992c) 'Rock Festivals', in DeCurtis, A. and Henke, J. (eds) *The Rolling Stone Illustrated History of Rock and Roll*, 3rd edn, New York: Random House, pp. 174–9.

Muggleton, D. (2000) *Inside Subculture: The Postmodern Meaning of Style*, Oxford and New York: Berg.

Mundy, J. (1999) *Popular Music on Screen: From the Hollywood Musical to Music Video*, Manchester: Manchester University Press.

Murdoch, G. and Phelps, G. (1973) *Mass Media and the Secondary School*, London: Schools Council/Macmillan.

Murray, C.S. (1989) *Crosstown Traffic: Jimi Hendrix and Post-War Pop*, London: Faber and Faber.

——(1991) *Shots From the Hip*, London: Penguin.

Music Central 96, CD-ROM, Microsoft.

Myers, H. (ed.) (1992) *Ethnomusicology: An Introduction*, London: Macmillan.

Napier-Bell, S. (2002) *Black Vinyl White Powder*, London: Ebury Press.

Neal, M. (1999) *What the Music Said: Black Popular Music and Black Public Culture*, New York and London: Routledge.

Negus, K. (1992) *Producing Pop: Culture and Conflict in the Popular Music Industry*, London: Edward Arnold.

——(1996) *Popular Music in Theory*, Cambridge: Polity Press.

——(1999) *Music Genres and Corporate Cultures*, London and New York: Routledge.

Neill, K. (2000) 'Hook, Line and Singer: Maximising the Playlist Potential of Local Music in New Zealand', *Perfect Beat*, 5, 4: 60–77.

Nelson, P. (1992) 'Folk Rock', in DeCurtis, A. and Henke, J. (eds) *The Rolling Stone Illustrated History of Rock and Roll*, 3rd edn, New York: Random House, pp. 313–18.

Neuenfeldt, K. (ed.) (1997) *The Didjeridu: From Arnham Land to Internet*, London and Sydney: John Libby/Perfect Beat Publications.

Nicholson, G. (1991) *Big Noises: Rock Guitar in the 1990s*, London: Quartet.

Norman, P. (1981) *SHOUT! The Beatles in Their Generation*, New York: Simon & Schuster.

Nuttal, J. (1968) *Bomb Culture*, London: MacGibbon & Kee.

O'Brien, K. (1995) *Hymn to Her: Women Musicians Talk*, London: Virago Press.

O'Brien, L. (1995) *She Bop: The Definitive History of Women in Rock, Pop and Soul*, London: Penguin.

——(2002) *She Bop II: The Definitive History of Women in Rock, Pop, and Soul*, London and New York: Continuum.

O'Connor, A. (2002) 'Local Scenes and Dangerous Crossroads: Punk and Theories of Cultural Hybridity', *Popular Music*, 21, 2: 225–36.

O'Hara, C. (1995) *The Philosophy of Punk: More than Noise*, San Francisco, CA: AK Press.

O'Meara, C. (2003) 'The Raincoats: Breaking Down Punk Rock's Masculinities', *Popular Music*, 22, 3: 299–314.

O'Sullivan, T., Hartley, J., Saunders, D., Montgomery, M., and Fiske, J. (1994) *Key Concepts in Communications*, London: Routledge.

Ochs, M. (1996) *1000 Rock Covers*, Cologne: Taschen.

Oliver, P. (ed.) (1990) *Black Music in Britain*, Buckingham: Open University Press.

——(2001) *Yonder Come the Blues: The Evolution of a Genre*, Cambridge: Cambridge University Press.

Olson, M.J.V. (1998) '"Everybody Loves Our Town": Scenes, Spatiality, Migrancy' in Swiss, T., Sloop, J., and Herman, A. (eds), *Mapping the Beat: Popular Music and Contemporary Theory*, Malden, MA and Oxford: Blackwell, pp. 269–90.

Owens, T. (1995) *Bebop: The Music and its Players*, New York, Oxford: Oxford University Press.

Paddison, M. (1993) *Adorno's Aesthetics of Music*, Cambridge: Cambridge University Press.

Padilla, F. (1990) 'Salsa: Puerto Rican and Latin American Music', *Journal of Popular Culture*, 24: 87–104.

Palmer, Robert (1995) *Rock & Roll: An Unruly History*, New York: Harmony Books. This is a companion to the PBS/BBC ten-part television series, *Dancing in the Street* (1995).

Palmer, T. (1970) *Born Under a Bad Sign*, London: William Kimber.

Parker, M. (1991) 'Reading the Charts: Making Sense of the Hit Parade', *Popular Music*, 10, 2: 205–17.

Pearce, S.M. (1995) *On Collecting*, London: Routledge.

——(1998) *Collecting in Contemporary Practice*, London: Sage.

Pearsall, R. (1975) *Edwardian Popular Music*, Newton Abbot: David & Charles.

——(1976) *Popular Music of the Twenties*, Newton Abbot: David & Charles.

Pease, E. and Dennis, E. (eds) (1995) *Radio: The Forgotten Medium*, New Brunswick and London: Transaction Publishers.

Perry, S. (1988) 'The Politics of Crossover', in Frith, S. (ed.) *Facing the Music*, New York: Pantheon Books, pp. 51–87.

——(1992) 'The Sound of San Francisco', in DeCurtis, A. and Henke, J. (eds) *The Rolling Stone Illustrated History of Rock and Roll*, 3rd edn, New York: Random House, pp. 362–9.

Peterson, R.A. (1990) 'Why 1955? Explaining the Advent of Rock Music', *Popular Music*, 9, 1: 97–116.

Peterson, R.A. and Berger, D.G. (1975) 'Cycles in Symbolic Production: The Case of Popular Music', *American Sociological Review*, 40; republished in Frith, S. and Goodwin, A. (eds) *On Record: Rock, Pop, and the Written Word*, New York: Pantheon Books, pp. 140–59.

Pichaske, D. (1989) *A Generation in Motion: Popular Music and Culture in the Sixties*, Granite Falls, Minn.: Ellis Press (first published in 1979).

Pickering, M. (1986) 'The Dogma of Authenticity in the Experience of Popular Music', in McGregor, G., and White, R.S. (eds) *The Art of Listening*, London: Croom Helm, pp. 201–20.

Pickering, M. and Green, T. (eds) (1987) *Everyday Culture: Popular Songs and the Vernacular Milieu*, Milton Keynes: Open University Press.

Pickering, M. and Negus, K. (2004) "Rethinking creative genius", *Popular Music* 23, 2, 198–202.

Plasketes, G. (1992) 'Romancing the Record: The Vinyl De-Evolution and Subcultural Evolution', *Journal of Popular Culture*, 26, 1: 109–22.

Potter, J. and Wetherell, M. (1987) *Discourse and Social Psychology: Beyond Attitudes and Behaviour*, London: Sage.

Potter, R. (1995) *Spectacular Vernaculars: Hip-Hop and the Politics of Postmodernism*, Albany, NY: SUNY Press.

Pratt, R. (1990) *Rhythm and Resistance: Explorations in the Political Use of Popular Music*, New York: Praeger.

Prendergast, M.J. (2003) *The Ambient Century: From Mahler to Moby – The Evolution of Sound in the Electronic Age*, London: Bloomsbury.

Read, O. and Welch, W.L. (1977) *From Tin Foil to Stereo: The Evolution of the Phonograph*, Indianapolis: Howard Sams.

Redhead, S. (1990) *The End-of-the-Century Party: Youth and Pop Towards 2000*, Manchester: Manchester University Press.

——(1997) *Subculture to Club Cultures: An Introduction to Popular Cultural Studies*, Oxford: Blackwell.

Redhead, S. and Street, J. (1989) 'Have I the Right? Legitimacy, Authenticity, and Community in Folk's Politics', *Popular Music*, 8, 2: 177–84.

Regev, M. (1994) 'Producing Artistic Value: The Case of Rock Music', *Sociological Quarterly*, 35: 85–102.

Reich, C. (1972) *The Greening of America*, New York: Penguin.

Reid, J. (1993) 'The Use of Christian Rock Music by Youth Group Members', *Popular Music and Society*, 17, 2: 33–45.

Reisman, D. (1950) 'Listening to Popular Music', *American Quarterly*, 2; republished in Frith, S. and Goodwin, A. (eds) *On Record: Rock, Pop, and the Written Word*, New York: Pantheon Books.

Reynolds, Simon (1998) *Energy Flash: A Journey through Rave Music and Dance Culture*, London: Picador (published in the USA as *Generation Ecstasy: Into the World of Techno and Rave Culture*, Boston, MA: Little Brown & Company).

Reynolds, S. and Press, J. (1995) *The Sex Revolts, Gender, Rebellion and Rock'n'Roll*, London: Serpent's Tail.

Richards, C. (1995) 'Popular Music and Media Education', *Discourse: Studies in the Cultural Politics of Education*, 16, 3: 317–30.

Rietveld, H.C. (1998) *This is our House: House Music, Cultural Spaces and Technologies*, London: Ashgate.

Rimmer, D. (1985) *Like Punk Never Happened: Culture Club and the New Pop*, London: Faber and Faber.

Ritz, D. (1985) *Divided Soul: The Life of Marvin Gaye*, London: Collins/Grafton.

Roach, C. (1997) 'Cultural Imperialism and Resistance in Media Theory and Literary Theory', *Media, Culture and Society*, 19: 47–66.

Robinson, D., Buck, E., Cuthbert, M. *et al.* (1991) *Music at the Margins: Popular Music and Global Diversity*, Newbury Park, CA: Sage.

Rockwell, J. (1992) 'The Emergence of Art Rock', in DeCurtis, A. and Henke, J. (eds) *The Rolling Stone Illustrated History of Rock and Roll*, 3rd edn, New York: Random House (includes discography) pp. 492–9.

Roe, K. (1983) *Mass Media and Adolescent Schooling*, Stockholm: Almqvist and Wiksell.

Roe, K. and Carlsson, U. (eds) (1990) *Popular Music Research*, NORDICOM, University of Goteborg.

Rogan, J. (1988) *Starmakers and Svengalis*, London and Sydney: MacDonald & Co.

——(1992) *Morrissey and Marr: The Severed Alliance*, London: Omnibus Press.

Rogers, D. (1982) *Rock'n'Roll*, London: Routledge & Kegan Paul.

The Rolling Stone Interviews: 1967–1980 (1981) New York: St Martin's Press/Rolling Stone Press.

The Rolling Stone Record Guide (1984) ed. Marsh, D. with Swenson, J., New York: Random House/Rolling Stone Press.

Romanowski, W. (1993) 'Move Over Madonna: The Crossover Career of Gospel Artist Amy Grant', *Popular Music and Society*, 17, 2: 47–68.

Romanowski, W.D. and Denisoff, R.S. (1987) 'Money for Nothin' and the Charts for Free: Rock and the Movies', *Journal of Popular Culture*, 21, 3 (winter): 63–78.

Romney, J. and Wootton, A. (1995) *Celluloid Jukebox: Popular Music and the Movies Since the 50s*, London: BFI.

Rose, Tricia (1994) *Black Noise*, Hanover: Wesleyan University Press.

Ross, A. and Rose, T. (eds) (1994) *Microphone Fiends*, London and New York: Routledge.

Ross, K. and Nightingale, V. (2003) *Media and Audiences*, Buckingham and Philadelphia: Open University Press.

Rosselson, L. (1979) 'Pop Music: Mobiliser or Opiate?', in Gardner, C. (ed.) *Media, Politics and Culture*, London: Macmillan.

Rothenbuhler, E. (1985) 'Commercial Radio as Communication', *Journal of Communication*, 46, 1: 125–44.

Rothenbuhler, E. and Dimmick, J. (1982) 'Popular Music: Concentration and Diversity in the Industry, 1974–1980', *Journal of Communications*, 32 (winter): 143–9.

Rubey, D. (1991) 'Voguing at the Carnival: Desire and Pleasure on MTV', *South Atlantic Quarterly*, 90, 4.

Rutten, P. (1991) 'Local Popular Music on the National and International Markets', *Cultural Studies*, 5, 3 (October): 294–305.

Ryan, B. (1992) *Making Capital from Culture: The Corporate Form of Capitalist Production*, Berlin and New York: Walter de Gruyter.

Sabin, R. (ed.) (1999) *Punk Rock: So What? The Cultural Legacy of Punk*, London and New York: Routledge.

San Miguel, Jr., G. (2002) *Tejano Proud: Tex-Mex Music in the Twentieth Century*, College Station: Texas A&M University Press.

Sanjek, R. (1988) *American Popular Music and Its Business: The First Four Hundred Years. Volume III: From 1900 to 1984*, New York: Oxford University Press.

Santelli, R. (1993) *The Big Book of the Blues: A Biographical Encyclopedia*, New York: Penguin.

——(1999) 'The Rock and Roll Hall of Fame and Museum: Myth, Memory, and History', in Kelly, K. and McDonnell, E. (eds) *Stars Don't Stand Still in the Sky*, New York: New York University Press, pp. 237–43.

Sardiello, R. (1994) 'Secular Rituals in Popular Culture: A Case for Grateful Dead Concerts and Dead Head Identity', in Epstein, J.S. (ed.) *Adolescents and Their Music: If It's Too Loud, You're Too Old*, New York and London: Garland Publishing.

Savage, J. (1988) 'The Enemy Within: Sex, Rock and Identity', in Frith, S. (ed.) *Facing the Music*, New York: Pantheon Books.

——(1991) *England's Dreaming: Sex Pistols and Punk Rock*, London: Faber and Faber.

Sawyers, J. (2000) *The Complete Guide to Celtic Music: From the Highland Bagpipes to U2 and Enya*, London: Aurum Press.

Schaefer, J. (1987) *New Sounds: A Listener's Guide to New Music*, Cambridge, MA: Harper & Row.

Scherman, T. (ed.) (1994) *The Rock Musician*, New York: St, Martin's Press.

Schiller, D. (1999) *Digital Capitalism: Networking the Global Market System*, Cambridge, MA: MIT Press.

Schilt, K. (2003) '"A Little Too Ironic": The Appropriation and Packaging of Riot Grrrl Politics by Mainstream Female Musicians', *Popular Music*, 26, 1: 5–16.

Schloss, J.G. (2004) *Making Beats: The Art of Sample-Based Hip-Hop*, Middletown, Connecticut: Wesleyan University Press.

Schowalter, D.F. (2000) 'Remembering the Dangers of Rock and Roll: Toward a Historical Narrative of the Rock Festival', *Critical Studies in Media Communication*, 17, 1.

Schwichtenberg, C. (ed.) (1993) *The Madonna Connection: Representational Politics, Subcultural Identities, and Cultural Theory*, St Leonards, NSW: Allen & Unwin.

Scoppa, B. (1992) 'The Byrds', in DeCurtis, A. and Henke, J. (eds) *The Rolling Stone Illustrated History of Rock and Roll*, 3rd edn, New York: Random House, pp. 309–12.

Selvin, J. (1994) *Summer of Love*, New York: Plume/Penguin.

Shank, B. (1994) *Dissonant Identities: The Rock'n'Roll Scene in Austin, Texas*, Hanover and London: Wesleyan University Press.

Shapiro, B. (1991) *Rock and Roll Review: A Guide to Good Rock on CD*, Kansas City: Andrews and McMeel.

Shaw, A. (1986) *Black Popular Music in America*, New York: Macmillan.

Shaw, G. (1992) 'Brill Building Pop', in DeCurtis, A. and Henke, J. (eds) *The Rolling Stone Illustrated History of Rock and Roll*, 3rd edn, New York: Random House, pp. 143–52.

Shepherd, J. (1986) 'Music Consumption and Cultural Self-Identities', *Media, Culture and Society*, 8, 3: 305–30.

——(1991) *Music as Social Text*, Cambridge: Polity Press.

Shepherd, J., Horn, D., Laing, D., Oliver, P., and Wicke, P. (eds) (2003) *The Continuum Encyclopedia of Popular Music, Volume One: Media, Industry and Society*, London and New York: Continuum.

Shepherd, J., Horn, D., Laing, D., Oliver, P., Wicke, P., Tagg, P., and Wilson, J. (eds) (1997) *Popular Music Studies: A Select International Bibliography*, London: Mansel.

Shepherd, J., Virden, P., Vulliamy, G., and Wishart, T. (1977) *Whose Music?*, London: Latimer.

Shepherd, J. and Wicke, P. (1999) *Music and Cultural Theory*, Cambridge: Polity Press.

Shevory, T. (1995) 'Bleached Resistance: The Politics of Grunge', *Popular Music and Society*, 19, 2: 23–48.

Shore, M. (1985) *The Rolling Stone Book of Rock Video*, London: Sidgwick & Jackson.

Shuker, R. (2001) *Understanding Popular Music*, 2nd edn, London and New York: Routledge.

——(2004) 'Beyond the "High Fidelity" Stereotype: Defining the (Contemporary) Record Collector', *Popular Music*, 23/3: 311–30.

Sicko, D. (1999) *Techno Rebels: The Renegades of Electronic Funk*, New York: Billboard Books.

Sicoli, M.L. (1994) 'The Role of the Woman Songwriter in Country Music', *Popular Music and Society*, 18, 2: 35–41.

Sinclair, D. (1992) *Rock on CD: The Essential Guide*, London: Kyle Cathie.

Slobin, M. (2003) 'The Destiny of "Diaspora" in Ethnomusicology', in Clayton, M., Herbert T., and Middleton, R. (eds) (2003) *The Cultural Study of Music. A Critical Introduction*, New York and London: Routledge.

Small, C. (1987) 'Performance as Ritual', in White, A. (ed.) *Lost in Music: Culture, Style and the Musical Event*, London: Routledge.

——(1994) *Music of the Common Tongue*, London: Calder (first published 1987).

Smith, Giles (1995) *Lost in Music*, London: Picador.

Smith, P. (2001) *Cultural Theory: An Introduction*, Malden, Oxford: Blackwell

Smucker, T. (1992) 'Disco', in DeCurtis, A. and Henke, J. (eds) *The Rolling Stone Illustrated History of Rock and Roll*, 3rd edn, New York: Random House, pp. 561–72.

Spencer, J. (ed.) (1991) *The Emergence of Black and the Emergence of Rap*, a special issue of *Black Sacred Music: A Journal of Theomusicology*, 5, 1 (spring).

Stahl, G. (2004) '"It's Like Canada Reduced": Setting the Scene in Montreal', in Bennett, A. and Kahn-Harris, K. (eds) *After Subcultures*, London: Ashgate.

Stahl, M. (2002) 'Authentic Boy Bands on TV? Performers and Impresarios in *The Monkees* and *Making the Band*', *Popular Music*, 21, 3, October: 307–29.

Stambler, I. (1989) *The Encyclopedia of Pop, Rock and Soul*, revised edn, London: Macmillan.

Stanford, C. (1996) *Kurt Cobain*, New York: Random House.

Starr, L. and Waterman, C. (2003) *American Popular Music*, New York and Oxford: Oxford University Press.

Stephens, M.A. (1998) 'Babylon's "Natural Mystic": The North American Music Industry, the Legend of Bob Marley, and the Incorporation of Transnationalism', *Cultural Studies*, 139–67.

Stevenson, N. (2002) *Understanding Media Cultures: Social Theory and Mass Communication*, 2nd edn, London: Sage Publications.

Steward, S. and Garratt, S. (1984) *Signed, Sealed, and Delivered: True Life Stories of Women in Pop*, Boston: South End Press.

Stockbridge, S. (1990) 'Rock Video: Pleasure and Resistance', in Brown, M.E. (ed.) *Television and Women's Culture*, London: Sage.

——(1992) 'From Bandstand and Six o'clock Rock to MTV and Rage: Rock Music on Australian Television', in Hayward, P. (ed.) *From Pop to Punk to Postmodernism: Popular Music and Australian Culture*, Sydney: Allen & Unwin, pp. 68–88.

Storey, J. (1993) *An Introductory Guide to Cultural Theory and Popular Culture*, New York and London: Harvester Wheatsheaf.

Strachan, R. (2003) 'Music Journalism', in Shepherd *et al.* (eds), *The Continuum Encyclopedia of Popular Music, Volume One: Media, Industry and Society*, London and New York: Continuum.

Stratton, J. (1982) 'Between Two Worlds: Art and Commercialism in the Record Industry', *Sociological Review*, 30, 1: 267–85.

——(1983) 'What is Popular Music?' *Sociological Review*, 31, 2: 293–309.

——(2003) 'Whiter Rock: The "Australian Sound" and the Beat Boom', *Continuum: Journal of Media & Cultural Studies*, 17, 3 (September): 331–46.

Strausbaugh, J. (2001) *Rock Til You Drop: The Decline from Rebellion to Nostalgia*, New York: Verso.

Straw, W. (1990) 'Characterizing Rock Music Culture: The Case of Heavy Metal', in Frith, S. and Goodwin, A. (eds) *On Record: Rock, Pop, and the Written Word*, New York: Pantheon Books, pp. 97–110.

——(1992) 'Systems of Articulation, Logics of Change: Communities and Scenes in Popular Music', in Nelson, C., Grossberg, L., and Treichler, P. (eds) *Cultural Studies*, London and New York: Routledge.

——(1999) 'Authorship', in Horner, B. and Swiss, T. (eds), *Key Terms in Popular Music and Culture*, Malden, MA and Oxford: Blackwell, pp. 199–208.

——(2001) 'Dance Music', in Frith, S., Straw, W., and Street, J. (eds), *The Cambridge Companion to Pop and Rock*, Cambridge: Cambridge University Press, pp. 158–75.

Straw, W. *et al.* (eds) (1995) *Popular Music: Style and Identity*, Montreal: Centre for Research on Canadian Cultural Industries and Institutions.

Street, J. (1986) *Rebel Rock: The Politics of Popular Music*, Oxford: Blackwell.

——(1993) 'Local Differences?: Popular Music and the Local State', *Popular Music*, 12, 1: 42–56.

——(1995) '(Dis)located?: Rhetoric, Politics, Meaning and the Locality', in Straw, W. *et al.* (eds) *Popular Music: Style and Identity*, Montreal: Centre for Research on Canadian Cultural Industries and Institutions.

——(1997) *Politics and Popular Culture*, Cambridge: Polity Press.

Stringer, J. (1992) 'The Smiths: Repressed (But Remarkably Dressed)', *Popular Music*, 11, 1: 16–26.

Strong, M. C. (1998) *The Wee Rock Discography*, Edinburgh: Canongate.

Sturmer, C. (1993) 'MTV's Europe: An Imaginary Continent?', in Dowmunt, T. (ed.) *Channels of Resistance: Global Television and Local Empowerment*, London: BFI/Channel Four Television.

Sweeney, P. (1981) *The Virgin Directory of World Music*, London: Virgin Books.

Swingewood, A. (1977) *The Myth of Mass Culture*, London: Macmillan.

Swiss, T., Herman, A., and Sloop, J.M. (eds) (1998) *Mapping the Beat: Popular Music and Contemporary Theory*, Malden, MA and Oxford: Blackwell Publishers.

Szatmary, D.P. (1991) *Rockin' in Time: A Social History of Rock and Roll*, 2nd edn, Engelwood Cliffs, NJ: Prentice-Hall.

Tagg, P. (1982) 'Analysing Popular Music', *Popular Music*, 2: 37–67.

——(1989) '"Black Music", "African-American Music" and "European Music"', *Popular Music*, 8, 3: 285–98.

——(1990) 'Music in Mass Media Studies: Reading Sounds for Example', in Roe, K. and Carlsson, U. (eds) *Popular Music Research*, NORDICOM, University of Goteborg, pp. 103–14.

——(1994) 'From Refrain to Rave', *Popular Music*, 14, 3: 209–22.

Tagg, P. and Clarida, B. (2003) *Ten Little Title Tunes: Towards a Musicology of the Mass Media*, New York and Montreal: The Mass Media Musicologists' Press.

Takasugi, F. (2003) 'The Development of Underground Musicians in a Honolulu Scene, 1995–1997', *Popular Music*, 26, 1: 73–94.

Tanner, J. (1981) 'Pop Music and peer Groups: A Study of Canadian High School Student's Responses to Pop Music', *Canadian Review of Sociology and Anthropology*, 18, 1: 1–13.

Taylor, P. (1985) *Popular Music Since 1955: A Critical Guide to the Literature*, London: G.K. Hall.

Taylor, T. (2003) Review of Andreas Gebesmair and Alfred Smudits, *Global Repertoires*, in *Popular Music*, 22, 1: 109–10.

Théberge, P. (1991) 'Musicians' Magazines in the 1980s: The Creation of a Community and a Consumer Market', *Cultural Studies*, p. 270ff.

——(1993) 'Technology, Economy and Copyright Reform in Canada', in Frith, S. (ed.) *Music and Copyright*, Edinburgh: Edinburgh University Press, ch. 3.

——(1997) *Any Sound You Can Imagine: Making Music/Consuming Technology*, Hanover, NH: Wesleyan University Press.

——(1999) 'Technology' in Horner, B. and Swiss, T. (eds) *Key Terms in Popular Music and Culture*, Malden, MA and Oxford: Blackwell, pp. 209–24.

Thomas, B. (1991) *The Big Wheel*, London: Penguin.

Thomas, H. (1995) *Dance, Modernity and Culture*, London and New York: Routledge.

Thompson, D. (1994) *Space Daze: The History and Mystery of Ambient Space Rock*, Los Angeles: Cleopatra.

——(2002) *The Dark Reign of Gothic Rock: In the Reptile House With the Sisters of Mercy, Bauhaus and The Cure*, London: Helter Skelter Publishing.

Thompson, J.L. (2000) *Raised By Wolves. The Story of Christian Rock & Roll*, Toronto: ECW Press.

Thornton, S. (1994) 'Moral Panic, the Media and British Rave Culture', in Ross, A. and Rose, T. (eds) *Microphone Fiends*, London and New York: Routledge.

——(1995) *Club Cultures: Music, Media and Subcultural Capital*, London: Polity Press.

Tomlinson, J. (1991) *Cultural Imperialism*, London: Pinter.

Tong, R. (1989) *Feminist Thought: A Comprehensive Introduction*, London: Routledge.

Toop, David (1991) *Rap Attack 2*, London: Serpent's Tail.

Tosches, N. (1984) *Unsung Heroes of Rock'n'Roll*, New York: Scribners.

Toynbee, J. (2000) *Making Popular Music: Musicians, Creativity and Institutions*, London: Arnold.

Trondman, M. (1990) 'Rock Taste: On Rock as Symbolic Capital. A Study of Young People's Tastes and Music Making', in Roe, K. and Carlsson, U. (eds) *Popular Music Research*, NORDICOM, University of Goteborg, pp. 71–86.

Tsitsos, W. (1999) 'Rules of Rebellion: Slamdancing, Moshing, and the American Alternative Scene', in *Popular Music*, 18, 8: 397–414.

Tucker, K. (1992) 'Alternative Scenes: America; Britain', in DeCurtis, A. and Henke, J. (eds) *The Rolling Stone Illustrated History of Rock and Roll*, 3rd edn, New York: Random House (includes useful discographies).

Turner, G. (1994) *British Cultural Studies: An Introduction*, revised edn, Boston: Unwin Hyman.

Unterberger, R. (2002) *Turn! Turn! Turn! The '60s Folk-rock Revolution*, San Franciso: Backbeat Books.

Valentine, G. (1995) 'Creating Transgressive Space: The Music of kd lang', *Transactions: Institute of British Geographers*, 20, 4: 434–46.

Vassal, J. (1976) *Electric Children: Roots and Branches of Modern Folkrock*, New York: Taplinger.

Vermorel, F. and Vermorel, J. (1985) *Starlust: The Secret Fantasies of Fans*, London: W.H. Allen.

Vernallis, C. (1998) 'The Aesthetics of Music Video: An Analysis of Madonna's "Cherish"', *Popular Music*, 17, 2: 153–85.

——(2004) *Experiencing Music Video: Aesthetics and Cultural Context*, Columbia, OH: Columbia University Press.

Vincent, R. (1996) *Funk: The Music, the People, and the Rhythm of the One*, New York: St Martin's/Griffin.

The Virgin Encyclopedia of Rock, ed. M. Heatley (1993), London: Virgin Press.

Vogel, H.L. (1994) *Entertainment Industry Economics: A Guide to Financial Analysis*, 3rd edn, New York: Cambridge University Press.

Vulliamy, G. and Lee, E. (1982) *Popular Music: A Teacher's Guide*, London: RKP.

Waksman, S. (1996) *Instrument of Desire: The Electric Guitar and the Shaping of Musical Experience*, Cambridge, MA: Harvard UP.

——(1998) 'Kick out the Jams!: The MC5 and the Politics of Noise', in Swiss, T., Sloop, J., and Herman, A. (eds), *Mapping the Beat: Popular Music and Contemporary Theory*, Oxford: Blackwell, pp. 47–76.

——(2003) 'Reading the Instrument: An Introduction', *Popular Music and Society*, 26, 1 (October): Special Issue: Reading the Instrument.

Wald, G. (2002) 'Just a Girl? Rock Music, Feminism, and the Cultural Construction of Female Youth', in Beebe, R., Fulbrook, D., and Saunders, B. (eds) *Rock Over the Edge: Transformations in Popular Music Culture*, Durham and London: Duke University Press, pp. 191–215.

Walker, J. (1987) *Cross-Overs: Art Into Pop/Pop Into Art*, London and New York: Comedia.

Wallis, R. and Malm, K. (1984) *Big Sounds from Small Countries*, London: Constable.

——(eds) (1992) *Media Policy and Music Activity*, London: Routledge.

Walser, R. (1993) *Running With the Devil: Power, Gender and Madness in Heavy Metal Music*, Middletown, CT: Wesleyan University Press.

Ward, E. (1992a) 'The Blues Revival', in DeCurtis, A. and Henke, J. (eds) *The Rolling Stone Illustrated History of Rock and Roll*, 3rd edn, New York: Random House, pp. 343–7.

——(1992b) 'Reggae', in DeCurtis, A. and Henke, J. (eds) *The Rolling Stone Illustrated History of Rock and Roll*, 3rd edn, New York: Random House, pp. 586–93.

Ward, E., Stokes, G., and Tucker, K. (1986) *Rock of Ages: The Rolling Stone History of Rock and Roll*, New York: Rolling Stone Press/Summit Books.

Warner, T. (2003) *Pop Music – Technology and Creativity: Trevor Horn and the Digital Revolution*, Aldershot: Ashgate.

Waterman, C. A. (1991) *Juju: A Social History and Ethnography of an African Popular Music*, Chicago: Chicago University Press.

Weinstein, D. (1991a) *Heavy Metal: A Cultural Sociology*, New York: Lexington.

——(1991b) 'The Sociology of Rock: An Undisciplined Discipline', *Theory, Culture and Society*, 8: 97–109.

——(1998) 'The History of Rock's Past Through Rock Covers', in Swiss, T., Herman, A., and Sloop, J.M. (eds) *Mapping the Beat: Popular Music and Contemporary Theory*, Malden, MA and Oxford: Blackwell Publishers, pp. 137–51.

——(2000) *Heavy Metal: The Music and its Culture*, Boulder, Col.: Da Capo Press.

Weisband, E. with Marks, C. (eds) (1995) *SPIN Alternative Record Guide*, New York: Vintage/Random House.

Welsh, R. (1990) 'Rock'n'Roll and Social Change', *History Today* (February), pp. 32–9.

Whitburn, J. (1988) *Billboard Top 1000 Singles 1955–1987*, Milwaukee, MI: Hal Leonard Books.

White, A. (ed.) (1987) *Lost in Music: Culture Style and the Musical Event*, London: Routledge & Kegan Paul.

White, T. (1989) *Catch a Fire: The Life of Bob Marley*, revised edn, New York: Holt, Rinehart and Winston.

——(1994) *The Nearest Faraway Place: Brian Wilson, The Beach Boys, and the Southern California Experience*, New York: Henry Holt & Co.

Whiteley, S. (1992) *The Space Between the Notes: Rock and the Counter-Culture*, London: Routledge.

——(ed.) (1997) *Sexing the Groove: Popular Music and Gender*, London and New York: Routledge.

——(2000) *Women and Popular Music: Sexuality, Identity and Subjectivity*, London: Routledge.

Whiteley, S., Bennett, A., and Hawkins, S. (eds) (2004) *Music, Space and Place. Popular Music and Cultural Identify*, Aldershot, Burlington: Ashgate.

Widgery, D. (1986) *Beating Time: Riot'n'Race'n'Rock'n'Roll*, London: Chatto & Windus.

Williams, R. (1983) *Keywords*, London: Fontana.

Willis, P. (1978) *Profane Culture*, London: Routledge.

Willis, P. *et al.* (1990) *Common Culture: Symbolic Work at Play in the Everyday Cultures of the Young*, Milton Keynes: Open University Press.

Winfield, B.H. and Davidson, S. (eds) (1999) *Bleep! Censoring Rock and Rap Music*, Westport, CT: Greenwood Press.

Wojcik, P.R. and Knight, A. (eds) (2001) *Soundtrack Available: Essays on Film and Popular Music*, Durham and London: Duke University Press.

Wolff, K. (2000) *Country Music: The Rough Guide*, London: Rough Guides.

Woodstra, C. and Bogdanov, V. (eds) (2001) *All Music Guide to Electronica: The Definitive Guide to Electronic Music*, San Francisco: Backbeat Books.

Zak III, A.J. (2001) *The Poetics of Rock: Cutting Tracks, Making Records*, Berkeley: University of California Press.

Zappa, F. with Occhiogrosso, P. (1990) *The Real Frank Zappa Book*, London: Pan Books.

Zollo, P. (1997) *Songwriters on Songwriting*, New York: Da Capo Press.

ARTIST INDEX

('Artist' includes musicians, producers, songwriters, film/video directors, and DJs).

SUBJECT INDEX

a capella 3, 87, 184
A&R 3–4
acid jazz 149
acid rock 211–12
advertising 4, 46
aesthetics 5, 9, 15, 114
affect 6
Afro-American music 22–3
aficionados 99
albums 6–8, 161; *see also* record
    formats
album covers 7, 272
alt.country 60–1
alternative music 8–10; and dance 74;
    and fanzines 103; 231, 240;
    see also indie music
alternative music scenes 239–40, 241
ambient 10–11
Americana 60–1
amplification 26, 251
appropriation 11–12, 127, 232
art rock: *see* progressive rock
audiences 13–14, 76–7, 119
audiotape: *see* cassettte audio tape
auteur; auteurship 14–17; producers as
    209; songwriters as 247; stars as 256
authenticity 5, 17–18 76; and
    bootlegs 29; and boy bands 30;
    genres 24, 27, 38, 60, 117, 121,
    135,151, 213, 235, 249; and high
    culture 136;and indies 145; and
    voice 278.
autobiography 21–22
avant garde 18–19, 115, 215, 250

baby boom(ers) 76
back catalogue 19–20; and boxed set 29

beat (rhythm) 183
beat music 20, 32, 165
beats (beatniks) 57
bebop 149
behaviourism 92–3
bhangra 21
biography 21–2
black music 22–3, 231; and crossover
    62–3; diaspora 78; 94–5; and rap
    221
bluegrass 23
blues 23–7; lyrics 156
blues rock 26–7
boogie-woogie 27
bootlegs 28–9, 190
boxed set 29
boy bands 29–30
brass bands 251
bricolage 30–2
Brill Building (songwriters) 248
British invasion 32–3, 165
British 'new pop' 47–8, 186; fans 99
Britpop 12, 33–4
broadcasting 34
bubblegum 34–5, 207

canon 20, 35–6, 263; and biography
    22; and discography 81; and
    documentaries 87; and gender 119;
    jazz 149; and music press 177.
cassette audio tape; cassette tape
    players; cassette culture 36–7; *see
    also* record formats
cassette singles 244
CD (compact disc) 35; and back
    catalogue 19–20, 37; *see also*
    record formats

320